BRITAIN'S COLD WAR FIGHTERS

BAC Lightning F.Mk.1A XM147 with the Wattisham Target Facilities Flight, 1973. (*Tim McLelland collection*)

BRITAIN'S COLD WAR FIGHTERS

TIM McLELLAND

FONTHILL

Typhoon FGR.Mk.4 ZJ920 was delivered to No. 29 Squadron at Coningsby, and subsequently shifted to co-located No. 3 Squadron. It is pictured wearing the markings of No. 29 Squadron whilst operating over the North Sea. (*Tim McLelland*)

Fonthill Media Limited
Fonthill Media LLC
www.fonthillmedia.com

First published 2013

A CIP catalogue record for this book is available from the British Library

Typeset in 10.5pt on 12pt Sabon LT Std
Typesetting by Fonthill Media
Printed in the UK

ISBN 978-1-78155-100-4

Contents

Stunning image of the RAF's fighter-interceptor for the next thirty years or more, the Eurofighter Typhoon. Pictured here over the Dubai desert, the aircraft's wing leading edge lift devices are clearly visible in their extended position, as the aircraft manoeuvres at low speed. (*Katsuhiko Tokunaga, Eurofighter*)

Introduction

The story of Britain's Cold War fighters is as long and complicated as that of Britain's bomber force. In many respects, it was more complex as a wide range of aircraft types were developed for Britain's fighter and interceptor roles, some of which enjoyed a short service career while others failed to reach operational status at all. It is also important to understand that virtually all of the fighter types that served with the RAF and Fleet Air Arm after the Second World War were assigned to a variety of roles, only one of which was air defence. The only significant exception to this rule was the magnificent Lightning, an aircraft that deserved 'special status' in any account of Britain's post-Cold War history. Designed as a supersonic interceptor, it was employed exclusively as a fighter and despite a number of very clear flaws, it was an aircraft that performed astonishingly well. It was certainly the fastest all-British aircraft ever to enter RAF service and was undoubtedly one of the best. The irony of the Lightning's story is that it was persistently regarded as a short-term purchase that would be replaced by something better. This meant that despite a long and complicated development, its full potential was never achieved as there was a lack of serious belief that the aircraft would be around long enough to warrant the expense or effort involved.

The Lightning also marked the end of Britain's indigenous fighter design process. As the RAF and Fleet Air Arm looked to the future, it was the American Phantom that fulfilled Britain's requirements during the 1970s and beyond. Then came the multinational Tornado and more recently the international Eurofighter Typhoon. However, while the Typhoon was indeed a 'Euro' design, it was not exclusively a fighter. Unlike any aircraft that preceded it, the Typhoon was the first truly multi-role aircraft to enter RAF service designed with an equal capability to perform as a fighter and an attack platform from the very outset. Consequently, the Typhoon blurs the distinction between the conventional ground attack aircraft and the fighter-interceptor more than any other aircraft that has served Britain's forces in the past. It will be joined by the F-35 in due course, and this aircraft is also a true multi-role aircraft as reflected in its more appropriate description as the JSF – Joint Strike Fighter. Although the Typhoon began its design process in the latter years of the Cold War, the JSF is undoubtedly a project that lies far beyond the thinking of the Cold War years and is therefore outside the remit of this book.

(Further information on the Typhoon's story can be found in the companion volume to this book, *Britain's Cold War Bombers*.)

Britain's post-war fighter development and procurement story is undoubtedly complicated, often confusing and occasionally littered with tales of missed opportunities and bad decision-making. But it is also a fascinating tale of how jet engine technology enabled Britain to transition from the days of piston-engine Spitfires through to the Mach 2.2 Tornado ADV. It is a story of a half-century during which Britain's airpower changed drastically in response to the advancement of technology and the rapidly changing world in which Britain exists.

CHAPTER ONE
Meteoric Progress

Tracing the history and development of Britain's post-war fighter aircraft inevitably begins with the invention of the jet engine. Although a number of aircraft that relied upon propeller propulsion were designed after the Second World War, the key to advances in performance and capability was directly or indirectly due to the emergence of jet power. This seminal leap in technology was applicable to the design of fast and long-range, nuclear-armed bombers such as the Valiant, Vulcan and Victor. There is no doubt that once the prospect of jet power was accepted as a viable concept, it was primarily applied to the design of potential fighter aircraft. This is hardly surprising as the jet engine delivered incredible speed. However, British aircraft designers believed that although fighters should possess agility and a capability to fly as high and far as possible, the most important criterion for any new fighter was that of speed.

Jet power promised to transform fighter technology. The invention of the jet engine is a complex story and it is difficult to attribute the creation of the jet to any one person. It is certainly true that the concept of the gas turbine engine first emerged in 1791, the first patent for such a concept being credited to John Barber. It was not until 1921 that the concept to power a flying machine was raised by Frenchman Maxime Guillaume who patented the idea for the first time. Although there was no serious prospect of turning the idea into a practical system, it was a surprisingly accurate portrayal of what eventually became the axial-flow turbojet. Guillaume's vision drifted into obscurity and was forgotten until the basic concept was reinvestigated by British engineer Alan Griffith. He concluded that existing gas turbine designs were inefficient, but with redesigned compressor blades incorporated into an axial-flow motor, a system could be devised to drive a propeller, thereby creating the first 'turboprop' design.

It was Frank Whittle who abandoned the notion of using the gas turbine to drive a propulsion system and visualised the gas turbine itself as the means of creating thrust. Whittle had first turned his attention to aircraft propulsion in 1926 when he was a cadet at the Royal Air Force College in Cranwell. Cadets were required to write a thesis during each term and Whittle decided to address 'Future Developments in Aircraft Design' for his fourth term paper. His paper explored in some detail the ways in which aircraft could be designed to fly higher and faster, and how most of these developments would inevitably be hindered by the limitations of propeller performance. It was not until a year later that Whittle had his 'eureka' moment and developed his thesis further still, referring specifically to the new jet power idea. In 1929, Whittle considered his thesis complete, but after proudly presenting it to a number of RAF and industry officials, he concluded that no one believed his idea was worth developing. Pat Johnson, one of his fellow RAF officers, was a former patents agent and persuaded Whittle to register his idea.

However, after it was published in January 1930, Whittle almost forgot about his brilliant idea and it was not until five years later that it re-emerged. Rolf Dudley Williams, a former colleague from Cranwell, wrote to Whittle to state that he had met a man who was a 'big noise in an engineering concern' and that he had mentioned Whittle's 'invention of an aeroplane, sans propeller, as it were'. Whittle replied:

> Nobody would touch it on account of the enormous cost of the experimental work and I don't think they were far wrong, even though I still have every faith in the invention. However, if anybody were keen on taking it up I should think it would pay them. There is no doubt in my mind that, as things stand at present, it is the only way to high altitude flying.

The 'big noise' was James Tinling, co-partner in General Enterprises Ltd, a company specialising in the manufacture of automatic cigarette machines. Eventually, Tinling, Williams and Whittle met to discuss the jet engine. They all agreed that Tinling and Williams would act as agents for Whittle, seeking financial backing to take out new patents and to develop a jet-powered aeroplane in exchange for a quarter of shares in profits. They projected that £50,000 would be sufficient to design a working engine, but Whittle was somewhat pessimistic, possibly as a result of the complete lack of interest that his idea had received so far. He informed Williams that his proposed design was 'not a particularly efficient type of engine but there is plenty of scope for development. Its virtue lies entirely in its extremely low weight and that it will work at heights where atmospheric density is very low.'

Oddly, Whittle seems to have been disinterested in the engine's potential for delivering great speed although in his thesis from 1930, he did state that the engine would enable aircraft designs to escape from the limitations of the propeller, which effectively held top speeds at little more than 500 mph. Whittle stated that a jet engine had no such limitations and in theory a supersonic aeroplane might be possible – quite a claim when the RAF was at the time equipped with flimsy biplanes. Sadly, finding financial backing was a struggle and the most promising leads eventually failed. No one seemed sufficiently confident in the design to put money into it but in 1935, a firm of investment bankers – introduced to the team by respected aeronautical engineer M. Bramson – finally agreed to back the idea.

Whittle returned to the Thomson-Houston Company in Rugby (which he had approached without success some years previously) and proposed that they should take on the project now that it was to be financed. A suitable agreement was duly made, although Whittle was bound by an Air Ministry stipulation that he should work on the project on a part-time basis as he was a serving RAF officer. Together, the various parties formed Power Jets Ltd in early 1936. Finally, they began to create the very first jet engine as the 'WU' (Whittle Unit). With an estimated thrust of 1,300 lb, it was by modern standards almost comical, but was sufficient to demonstrate the viability of the concept if nothing more. On 12 April 1937, the first unit was bench tested and to everyone's delight worked incredibly well. Indeed, it surpassed all expectations when the turbines spun out of control, passing 8,000 rpm even when the fuel supply was cut off. As the roar of the engine grew to a crescendo and parts of the unit glowed red, the engineering team ran for cover leaving Whittle to try and bring his creation under control. The same terrifying spectacle occurred on the unit's second run, after which the team realised that pre-run tests had allowed a pool of fuel to gather in the engine's combustion chamber. In turn, this caused the unit to run out of control until the additional fuel was exhausted.

Thus, the jet engine was born and Power Jets developed the design of Whittle's creation, careful to avoid risks wherever possible as the group had scarcely any money to spend on repairs or part replacements. Thankfully, the Air Ministry gradually allocated funding to the project, but even this was hardly enough to allow Power Jets to do much. Industrial interest in the engine simply did not exist. The RAF was expanding rapidly and the aircraft industry was far too occupied with the demands of the Air Force to allocate time and money to what seemed to be a bizarre idea that would consume valuable resources. Britain's aero engine manufacturers expressed little or no interest in Whittle's project, and with hindsight it seems just as remarkable that the Air Ministry did not abandon its support for Whittle and Power Jets. Ministry funding continued to trickle through and the team were able to continue a limited amount of work on their engine, even though there seemed to be little prospect of translating the work into a more serious programme.

After the excitement of the first engine runs, the engine was dismantled, inspected, rebuilt twice and modified. Bench testing resumed in June 1939. The Air Ministry sent its Director of Scientific Research, Dr David Pye, to observe a test and to study the team's work. Pye had followed the project with interest but had not taken it seriously until now. Having seen the engine performing, Pye realised that Whittle's assertions were correct and that the WU had the potential to become the basis for a new engine that could deliver almost unimaginable power. He returned to Whitehall determined to turn the Power Jets project into something serious. At the same time, Whittle's 'special appointment' as a part-time engineer came to a close. The Treasury was reluctant to fund an RAF officer to play with his strange contraption and the Air Ministry warned Whittle that pursuing the project any further might harm his career prospects. Whittle decided to carry on regardless and requested that his appointment be extended. Just a few days later, a contract was issued for a flight-standard engine that could be tested in an aeroplane and the Air Ministry purchased the original WU, thereby ending the cash shortage that had dogged the team for so long. It had taken ten years for Whittle to translate his ambitious idea into a workable engine and although the tragedy of this long decade of indifference is clear, it is remarkable to note that even before the outbreak of the Second World War, the Air Ministry was tentatively entering the jet age.

By this stage, Whittle was considering how the engine could be tested in flight. The obvious answer was to attach the engine to an existing aircraft, preferably a larger bomber type that could operate independently when required for testing. He drew up various proposals to fix the engine to a Wellington bomber, but after experiencing a lack of interest from military and industrial officials for so long, he was mindful that such pioneering test flying might not impress those who lacked imagination and creativity. It seemed far preferable to put the WU into an aircraft that could be powered exclusively by the jet engine, thereby demonstrating not only that the engine worked but that it clearly created an aeroplane with a worthwhile performance. Consequently, Whittle designed a simple straight-wing monoplane that could be built around the engine and took this to another former colleague, Flt Lt 'Mac' Reynolds, who was an Air Ministry Overseer at the Gloster Aircraft Company where the manufacture of Hurricanes was under way on behalf of Hawker.

Whittle's plans were soon in the hands of Gloster's Chief Designer George Carter, and the Ministry of Aircraft Production awarded a contract to Gloster for two experimental aircraft built to Specification E.28/39. The Gloster design staff looked at various ways in which a small light aircraft could be built to accommodate the engine and some fairly radical proposals were considered, including tail-first designs similar in principle to the 'canard' arrangement now utilised by today's Typhoon. Consideration was also given to a twin-engine design; however, as Power Jets did not have two jet engines to test, the idea soon vaporised. By now, the country was in the darkest days of the Second World War and it was inevitable that attention shifted away from Whittle's project. Gloster became heavily committed to Hurricane production and Whittle's engineering drawings were handed to the British Thomson-Houston Company and car company Rover. Many weeks went by with little progress and when activity did resume it had caused a loss of momentum that took a long time to regain. However, during this delay the growing enthusiasm for the jet engine had not been lost and in May 1940, Gloster was given the go-ahead to design a twin-engine fighter under Specification F.9/40, even though neither of the test aircraft had been completed at this time.

It was April 1941 when the first E.28/39 test aircraft was completed. However, as the first flight-standard W.1 engine was in development, the test aircraft was fitted with the earlier W.1X for ground testing. Both aircraft were manufactured at Gloster's Brockworth factory near Gloucester, but as the first aircraft (W4041)

Rare movie stills of the very first moments of jet-borne flight as E.28/39 prototype W4041 lifts into the air for the first time at Cranwell in May 1941.

neared completion, it was quietly transported to a garage in Cheltenham. The garage had been recently occupied by Regent Motors, so that the risk of both aircraft being destroyed by enemy bombing was greatly reduced. While the residents of Cheltenham walked by in blissful ignorance, W4041 was assembled in secret, the garage guarded by armed police. It was then returned to Brockworth to begin engine runs and taxiing trials on 7 April under the control of Gloster's Chief Test Pilot Gerry Sayer. Whittle described the event as follows:

> The trials began that evening but there was little done because the light was fading by the time the aeroplane was ready. We had set the throttle stop to limit the engine speed to 13,000 rpm. The grass aerodrome was rather soggy from rain, so that it required 12,000 rpm before the aircraft would start moving and at 13,000 rpm it would only move at about 20 mph. The look of disappointment on Gerry Sayer's face was obvious. He evidently thought the engine would never develop enough urge to get the aeroplane off the ground. We were not worried because we knew how rapidly the thrust increased at the upper end of the engine speed range. I assured Gerry that with increased engine speed he would find things very different. He did not look convinced.

Testing resumed the next day, as Whittle described:

> The next morning we removed the throttle stop and adjusted the relief valve in the fuel line to give a maximum engine speed of 15,000 rpm. With this limit I made a few taxiing runs in which I reached a maximum speed of about 60 mph. It was a thrilling experience for more reasons than one. It was clear that we should not be short of thrust when we used the permissible maximum of 16,000 rpm. Also, the complete absence of vibration, the big reduction in noise as compared with conventional aircraft, the excellent view from the cockpit, and the simplicity of the controls, all added up to an impressive combination of characteristics. I felt that the engine instruments left something to be desired but otherwise, so far as one could judge from a mere taxiing run, everything seemed very satisfactory indeed. After lunch we increased the engine speed limit to 16,000 rpm. Sayer taxied off to the downwind edge of the airfield. This action caused us to suspect that he intended to do more than merely trundle over the grass, though we had warned him that the engine was thoroughly un-airworthy. It had never been intended for flight in the first place, and it had had a number of misadventures on the test bench, which had rendered it even less fit to fly than when first built. Sayer turned into the wind and increased the engine speed to the maximum permitted while holding the aeroplane back with the brakes. He then released the brakes and rapidly gained speed. We saw the elevators go up in an effort to get the tail down. He was a little too successful in this because the tail blister struck the ground and the aeroplane pitched forwards on to its nosewheel again. Nevertheless, a second or two later it left the ground and after being airborne for about 200 yards, landed. Sayer taxied back and repeated the performance twice more, the third take-off being very clean and smooth. Each time the airborne distance was 200-300 yards.

Sayer also compiled notes on these tests: 'The engine is very smooth indeed and no vibration was observed on the pilot's cockpit. The throttle control, however, is too coarse, a large increase in engine revolutions being obtained with very little forward movement of the throttle lever.' This relatively minor point was Sayer's only criticism as even the difficulty in getting the aircraft's tail down did not seem like a serious issue. He ended his report with the comment '... the engine ran very well throughout the taxiing trials'.

It was quite remarkable that the test aircraft, nicknamed 'Pioneer', had effectively flown three times with an engine that had been designed for no more than bench testing. Rather less remarkable was the astonishment of those who were within sight of Brockworth's airfield when the three test hops were made.

From any distance, W4041 appeared to be a fairly uninteresting aircraft, and it was only close inspection that revealed the absence of any obvious means of propulsion. Even this would have attracted little attention – it might have been mistaken for a glider – but when the WU power source wound up into action, there was nothing that could disguise the unique nature of the diminutive prototype. It was noisy, and emitted a sound that nobody had ever heard before – a fairly high-pitched whistle. When Sayer increased the engine's revolutions up to full power the aeroplane roared, and a number of completely bewildered spectators looked on with expressions of disbelief as it lumbered across the grass field and briefly lurched into the air. One American mechanic working on a Stirling bomber parked on the airfield almost fell off the bomber's wing as he marvelled at the bizarre event taking place before him. Whittle, however, remained calm even though he must have been delighted that his seemingly wild concept had now been translated into something tangible. The test team took the airfield back into another garage in Cheltenham and performed a series of post-test modifications to the machine, including the substitution of a longer nosewheel leg that would encourage the aircraft's nose to rise more easily on the take-off run. Like most of the aircraft's systems, the undercarriage was simple, with a straight nosewheel leg, and main gear units that incorporated a neat 'knee action' suspension designed by Dowty. The engine did not have a hydraulic pump and so a hydraulic accumulator was incorporated into the undercarriage system, and this had to be pumped up from the cockpit. The wing flaps also relied on a hydraulic hand pump.

In May 1941, the first flight-standard engine was finally ready and was fitted into W4041. The Ministry of Supply dictated (for no good reason) that it should be limited to a maximum speed of 16,500 rpm for the first flight trials, and this would deliver a meagre 860 lb of thrust compared with the more generous 1,240 lb that the engine's full 17,750 rpm would deliver. The Ministry also imposed a 10-hour limit on the engine's flight time, although like the rpm limit, these figures were purely arbitrary and the Ministry officials had no evidence on which to base their stipulations. In a less bureaucratic society it would probably have been Whittle himself who decided how to operate his own invention.

W4041 pictured at Farnborough during early flight trials. The 'P' marking on the fuselage side indicated the aircraft's status as a prototype machine.

While the new engine was being fitted to W4041, consideration was given to the choice of test site for the first flights. Brockworth was clearly unsuitable for anything more than taxi trials as the grass field was simply too small. Whittle's old haunt at RAF Cranwell seemed like a far more suitable location, as the airfield was much larger and the locality was free of hills or other obstructions. South Lincolnshire was also sparsely populated and therefore seemed like the best place to test the new aircraft in as much safety and secrecy as possible. On 12 May, the aircraft was loaded up for the journey to Cranwell and after a short visit to Power Jets' Ladywood Works (so that the staff could take a look at the machine), W4041 made its way to Cranwell and by the evening it was safely housed in a small hangar on the western edge of the airfield, guarded by Gloster security personnel. Whittle made his way back to his old home on 13 May and borrowed an Avro Tutor from the resident Central Flying School to gain a little flying practice while the E.28/39 prototype was readied for flight. Unfortunately, the weather conditions were poor and Whittle decided to return to the Ladywood Works at Lutterworth on 15 May as there seemed little prospect of getting the test aircraft into the air any time soon. As he later admitted, he was not particularly concerned about the first test flight at Cranwell and wanted to devote his time to development of a production-standard engine for the new jet fighter design that Gloster was now working on. However, he was telephoned later in the day when the weather at Cranwell started to improve, and by late afternoon he was back in Lincolnshire, ready to witness the first true flight. Shortly after 19.00 hours, test pilot Gerry Sayer climbed into W4041 and its engine was wound up to idle power. With a brisk westerly wind blowing across the airfield, he taxied to the eastern perimeter and turned the aircraft back into the wind. It was now 19.40 and in the gathering dusk Sayer brought the jet engine up to the 16,500 rpm limit and released the wheel brakes. W4041 lurched and bumped along the grass surface but slowly built up speed and after a run of just under 2,000 feet he gently eased the aircraft into the air and slowly climbed to 1,000 feet. As the aircraft roared over Cranwell's western perimeter fence he retracted the undercarriage and in a matter of seconds W4041 disappeared behind a cloud bank, leaving only traces of its smoky exhaust plume. The aircraft soon reappeared to the north near Waddington and after a short flight of only 15 minutes, Sayer was back at Cranwell with the landing gear and flaps down, ready to land. The aircraft had performed well and (perhaps more importantly) so had the engine, and Whittle was delighted that the test had been so successful:

> I was very tense, not so much because of any fears about the engine, but because this was a machine making its first flight. I think I would have felt the same if it had been an aeroplane with a conventional powerplant making its first flight.

He cannot recall the incident, but others reported that as W4041 roared into the sky, one of the test team slapped Whittle on the back and exclaimed, 'Frank, it flies!' to which he curtly replied, 'Well that was what it was bloody well designed to do, wasn't it?' Another observer who knew virtually nothing about the project was heard to claim that the aircraft was actually powered by a Merlin piston engine, driving a small propeller hidden inside the fuselage. Somebody asked how the aircraft worked, to which another officer replied, 'It just sucks itself along like a Hoover.' Over in the Officers' Mess a serving RAF officer expressed his bewilderment at what he had just seen: 'My God, chaps, I must be going round the bend. It hadn't got a propeller!'

Sadly, only a lucky few saw this historic event take place, as neither the Air Ministry nor the Ministry of Aircraft Production bothered to send along a photographer to record the first flight. One of the team did make an amateur film, but it is remarkable that official interest in what was probably the most significant British aeronautical event ever was virtually zero. Of course, W4041 was not the first jet-powered aircraft to fly (Germany's Heinkel designs had already been tested), but it is important to understand that W4041 was the final expression of a design that had been on the drawing board for a decade, and that it was already part of a process that was to lead to an operational jet-powered fighter. By any standards, the first flight was an incredibly important milestone, and yet it took place in almost complete secrecy with almost no photographic or written accounts to record it.

Sayer, as Gloster's Chief Test Pilot, did of course write up a detailed account of the first flight from his own perspective:

> The pilot's cockpit hood was in the full open position for the take-off and the elevator trimmer was set to give a slight forward load on the control column, as during the unsticks at Brockworth it was felt that the nose tended to rise rather sharply as soon as the aeroplane was in the air. The flaps were full up for the first take-off. The engine was run up to the maximum take off revolutions of 16,500 with the brakes held full on. The brakes were then released and the acceleration appeared quite rapid. The steerable nosewheel enabled the aeroplane to be held straight along the runway although there did not appear to be any tendency to swing, feet off the rudder bar. The aeroplane was taken off purely on the feel of the elevators and not on the airspeed. After a run of approximately five hundred to six hundred yards it left the ground, and although the fore and aft control was very sensitive for very small movement, the flight was continued. The rate of climb after leaving the ground and with the undercarriage still down is slow, and the aeroplane appeared to take some time to gain speed. The undercarriage was raised at 1,000 feet after which the climb rate and increase in climbing speed improved. The fore and aft change of trim when raising the undercarriage did not appear to be appreciable. The thrust available for take-off is 860 lb at 16,500 rpm and as the aircraft weight is approximately 400 lb up on estimate, the take-off run of five hundred to six hundred yards is considered to be quite reasonable. As soon as the aeroplane was on a steady climb, the engine revolutions were reduced to 16,000, which is the continuous climbing condition. The engine appeared quite smooth and the noise in the cockpit resembled a high-pitched turbine whine. The ailerons feel responsive and quite light at 240 IAS [Indicated Airspeed] at small angles. The elevators are very sensitive and on first impressions will require some adjustment. The rudder feels reasonably light at small angles and possibly slightly overbalanced. Further investigation is to be carried out during later flights. The aeroplane feels unstable fore and aft but this may be due to the over-sensitive elevators. It is very left wing low flying level at 240 IAS and carried quite a lot of right rudder. The jet pipe is slightly out of alignment, and looking up the pipe it is offset to the left, which may possibly be the cause of the turning tendency to the left. Gentle turns were carried out to the left and to the right and the aeroplane behaved normally. The engine ran well and the temperatures appeared satisfactory up to the revolutions reached during this short flight. The aeroplane was trimmed to

glide at 90 IAS with the flaps fully down and the throttle slightly open for landing. The approach was carried out in very gentle gliding turns and the controllability was very good. The aeroplane was landed on the runway slightly on the main wheels first, after which it went gently forward on to the nosewheel. The landing was straightforward and the landing run with the use of brakes was quite short.

While the testing of the engine continued, Gloster Aircraft was busy working on translating the new technology into a functional warplane. Chief Designer George Carter was very enthusiastic about the project even though he knew that the concept of jet power was barely proven. He believed that jet engines would enable great advances in performance to be made, although he had no real proof to back up his beliefs, but he had been a firm advocate of the concept ever since he first heard about Whittle's endeavours, and had already drawn up some designs that he thought were suitable for development into an operational jet fighter.

When Gloster received the E.28/39 contract he originally proposed an aircraft that featured a twin-boom tail design not dissimilar to the de Havilland Vampire that was soon to emerge, but eventually he decided to adopt a more conventional design, even though the twin-boom configuration did have some advantages as it enabled the air intakes and exhaust to remain close to the actual engine, thereby reducing any loss of flow pressure – something that was critical to these early powerplants. It is also clear that provision was made for the incorporation of machine guns in the shape of four 0.303 inch Brownings, and although structural fixings were incorporated into the aircraft for this purpose, guns were never fitted. Some reports claim that there was every intention of developing the design into a viable fighter aircraft, while other reports suggest that the aim was simply to fit guns so that the effects on engine airflow could be investigated. Carter continued to draw up designs through the summer of 1940, calculating that an aeroplane powered by two of Whittle's engines would probably be able to carry six 20 mm Hispano cannon, each with 120 rounds. Oddly, he did not propose to fit two engines side by side close to the fuselage (effectively creating a larger derivative of the E.28/39 aircraft) and instead chose to place the engines further out on the wings so that access would be far easier. The wing spar could run directly through the path of the engine air intake, as (unlike more conventional axial-flow engines that emerged later) the Whittle engine did not have a frontal compressor blade, the air being drawn in at 90 degrees via a centrifugal flow system, so there was no need to worry about blocking flow straight along the intake trunk. The rear spar incorporated a 'banjo' ring through which the engine's jet pipe could pass.

With hindsight, it may seem illogical to place engines so far away from the aircraft's centreline with all the risks of asymmetric control that this would encourage, but Carter was mindful of the unpredictability of the new engine and believed that nacelles out on the wing would be far more flexible, enabling a variety of different engine types to be fitted, regardless of their shape or size. It was a wise choice, as the early history of jet power involved a long series of very different engine designs that would have been very difficult to incorporate into a more conventional aircraft layout.

By the time that the Ministry of Aircraft Production awarded the F.9/40 contract to Gloster, Carter's design was already well established as the G.41, unofficially called the Rampage fighter. MAP specified that twelve aircraft should be manufactured but that capacity could be created to enable up to eighty aircraft per month to be constructed. Rather optimistically, MAP also called for Power Jets to produce engines at a rate of 180 units per month in order to support the fighter programme. In reality, this was never a serious possibility. Power Jets was never anything more than an experimental company, and MAP wilfully ensured that it would never be capable of producing anything on a proper industrial basis. Whittle later commented that the company, continually starved of cash, was 'bludgeoned to death' and was eventually unable even to continue experimental work. Whittle and Power Jets were compensated for their efforts, but MAP was keen to ensure that serious design and manufacture should be handled by far larger and more experienced companies. The British Thomson-Houston Company that became responsible for initial production of Whittle's engines was soon joined by Rover and Vauxhall, the famous car manufacturers. It seems that MAP quickly decided that even this arrangement was not suitable, and other work was assigned to BTH and Rover, thereby entrusting jet engine production to Rover, and it was this company that began production of Whittle's W.2 engine at the Coventry plant during August 1940, although the risk of enemy bombing meant that production soon shifted to dispersal sites at Clitheroe and Barnoldswick.

Whittle was far from confident in the W.2 engine's design and when testing began it was soon evident that, as he had feared, it was prone to failure. However, he was aware of the reasons why, and with some further work on the engine's compressor unit, it re-emerged as the W.2B late in 1941. This engine was far more reliable but it still suffered from various problems, not least the very real risk that the turbine blades might break. Thankfully, by this stage there were various engine designs under way and in December 1941, Metropolitan-Vickers ran its new F.2 axial-flow engine for the first time, while de Havilland ran its new (Halford-designed) H.1 just four months later.

In September 1941, an order was placed for 20 Gloster G.41A aircraft, these being referred to as the Thunderbolt Mk 1, although just months later the name was dropped when the American F-47 was given the same name. As an alternative, Gloster chose 'Meteor', and the first aircraft was completed by the early summer of 1942. The Meteor emerged as a relatively small aircraft with very few concessions towards advanced aerodynamics. Carter and his team deliberately made the aircraft as simple and conventional as possible so that there would be few risks of delays with testing and development. The only truly revolutionary aspect of this new fighter was, of course, the absence of any propellers. Instead, two large and bulbous nacelles sat proud of the generously proportioned wings, with the horizontal tail surfaces positioned high on the fin so that they would not be affected by the engine's exhaust flow. Some 'experts' had predicted (wrongly) that the jet engine exhaust would expand and flow uncontrollably, creating huge control problems, so the tail unit was deliberately designed to avoid this potential problem. The proposed gun armament was also changed to a more modest four 20 mm cannon, each with 150 rounds, thereby saving weight and giving the Meteor a better climb capability.

However, much to the horror of the Gloster design team, the first prototype was unable to climb at all, as it simply was not powerful enough. It was fitted with two W.2B engines that were not up to flight standard but sufficient to enable ground taxiing trials to be made. The aircraft (DG202) was taken to Newmarket Heath where a 9,000 feet grass strip was available, and Gerry Sayer completed the first run in July 1942. It soon became clear that with a limited thrust of only 1,000 lb, the W.2B would require a runway of more than 40,000 feet if the Meteor was to get safely airborne, and even then the aircraft would still be unable to climb. A bizarre situation had arisen whereby a fighter aircraft had been designed to take advantage of the new jet engine but now that it was ready to fly, the engine was incapable of powering it.

The only solution appeared to be the more powerful de Havilland engine that had been designed by Frank Halford. This engine was based on Whittle's design but greatly improved with a 'straight-through' airflow that did away with Whittle's reverse flow system that directed hot exhaust air back into the middle of the engine. It was a bigger and bulkier contraption but it delivered more thrust (potentially twice as much) and was more reliable too. The Gloster design team and the Air Ministry were disheartened and sceptical as to the true potential of the Halford engine, and rather than rely on this engine as the only practical way forward, a completely new single-engine fighter was swiftly envisaged that would be smaller and lighter, and clearly more capable of being successfully powered by either the Whittle (Rover) or Halford (de Havilland) powerplant. This new aircraft became known as the 'Emergency Jet Fighter' and Specification E.5/42 was issued. This was translated into the GA.1, an even more simple straight-winged aircraft, designed to fly with a single engine buried inside the fuselage and with a conventional tail unit (the exhaust now emerging from the tail instead of behind the wings).

Meanwhile, progress with the Meteor slowed almost to a halt, and many months passed without any signs of a first flight. Four of the prototypes were cancelled and the rest of the fleet languished at Gloster's Brockworth factory, awaiting engines that could get them into the air. It was de Havilland that finally rescued the deteriorating situation, informing Gloster that a flight-standard H.1 engine was ready for delivery, although just three days previously the Air Ministry had finally abandoned any hope of getting the Meteor and had ordered three GA.1 prototypes, cancelling the four Meteors that had yet to be completed. Gloster had also suffered the loss of its test pilot in October when Sayer was killed whilst flying a Typhoon. His replacement was Michael Daunt, and it was Daunt who finally got the Meteor (DG206) into the air on 5 March 1943. It was in fact the fifth Meteor prototype and the first to be fitted with the H.1 engine

Meteor EE397 was used by Flight Refuelling Ltd for air-to-air refuelling trials, and on 7 August 1949 the aircraft completed an endurance flight of some 12 hours, refuelling in flight ten times during the sortie.

that later became the famous 'Goblin' that powered the Vampire fighter. The H.1 engines were capable of delivering around 2,000 lb thrust each, but for the first flight they were restricted to 1,400 lb. The fifth Meteor was hardly any different from the first apart from a slightly better canopy (with a clear rear section) and an anti-spin parachute housed in a bullet fairing, attached to the trailing edge of the fin. Rather more obvious were the new engine cowlings that were enlarged to accommodate the more bulky H.1 engine. Internally, the rear spar 'banjo' holes had been enlarged and the new engines raised the aircraft's weight by more than 1,500 lb, but with a greater reserve of power this was not a significant problem.

Meteor prototype DG206 was transported to Cranwell to make the first flight, and the event took place with little fuss or fanfare. The take-off run was adequately short and it was only as speed passed 200 mph that difficulties arose when yaw instability started to become apparent and soon increased to violent proportions. Daunt slowed the aircraft and carefully eased it around the airfield circuit and back onto the runway, but after modifications to its fin the aircraft was back in the air (this time from Newmarket) and performing well, so well that the next prototype (DG207) was modified to become what was to have been the Meteor Mk II, an operational version of the Goblin-powered DG206.

Although the availability of the de Havilland H.1 engine had been critical to the Meteor's progress it became only a short-term solution, as the Ministry of

Supply expected the H.1 (Goblin) production models to be assigned to the new fighter aircraft that de Havilland was now developing (the Vampire). It was hoped that Whittle's W.2 engine would become available in quantity for the Meteor, and this finally became a possibility when Rolls-Royce struck a deal with Rover, transferring tank engine manufacture to them and enabling Rolls-Royce to take over the Clitheroe and Barnoldswick factories to produce jet engines. With their team of talented individuals such as Stanley Hooker, and useful resources such as test bed aircraft, it was not long before the W.2 engine was reliable and ready for full-scale production.

On 12 June 1943, the first production-standard W.2 engines (rated at 1,600 lb) were test flown in Meteor DG205 from Barford St John, and the first prototype finally took to the air for the first time there on 24 July, fitted with similar engines. DG204 was the next Meteor to fly, this one being equipped with Metropolitan-Vickers F.2 engines, and as these longer axial-flow powerplants would not fit into the Meteor's wing spars they were housed in separate nacelles that were attached under the wings.

This (third) engine type proved to be successful and was eventually developed into the Beryl and Sapphire, but like the H.1 Goblin, it was not needed for the Meteor programme now that Whittle's original engine was in production as the Rolls-Royce Welland I. Based on the F.9/40 prototypes, a contract was issued for an initial batch of Meteor F Mk I fighters on 8 August 1941, and the first production aircraft (EE201) made its maiden flight on 12 January 1944 from Moreton Valence, where Gloster had finally established a proper large-scale production factory adjacent to a runway-equipped airfield.

The first aircraft were immediately assigned to test flying, but as more examples emerged they were flown directly to Farnborough where sixteen examples were present by May 1944, to form the CRD (Conversion and Research Detachment) created to enable the Meteor's capabilities to be fully explored and also to establish the aircraft's performance and handling characteristics. It was soon accepted that the Meteor was a docile aircraft with no major handling problems. Its performance was unremarkable but satisfactory, and the test pilots at Farnborough could see no logical reason why the aircraft could not immediately be brought into RAF service.

No. 616 Squadron (an existing Spitfire unit) was chosen as the RAF's first operational Meteor unit, and the squadron's Flight Commanders were sent to Farnborough so that they could be introduced to the revolutionary new aircraft. Their initial apprehension was soon replaced by enthusiasm, once they flew the Meteors and learned that despite the lack of propellers, the aircraft handled well and was in many respects superior to the Spitfires that they were accustomed to flying. No dual-control Meteors existed, so each new pilot was obliged to make his first flight solo, but with some instruction and a lot of care, more and more RAF officers completed conversion onto the Meteor with no major mishaps. Pilots reported that although the Meteor's take-off performance was sluggish (especially when compared to contemporary piston fighters), once the aircraft gathered speed it was a pleasant aircraft to fly, free of propeller torque effects (that required continual trimming) and considerably quieter too.

Shortly before D-Day, No. 616 Squadron was posted to Culmhead in Devon so that the unit could fly patrols over the Channel in support of the invasion operations. Thus, it was here that the very first operational RAF Meteors entered service, with EE213 and EE214 arriving at Culmhead on 12 July. Five more arrived on 14 July and, unlike the first two, these were equipped with guns but, oddly, the Meteor's guns had yet to be tested. No test flying had been conducted to establish whether the guns would function, or if they would have any effect on the jet engines. Thankfully, the squadron soon found that despite a few teething problems, the guns worked well. The wing-mounted engine nacelles were a respectable distance from the gun ports on the Meteor's nose, so there was no risk of any significant effect on the engine's performance. However, the squadron quickly discovered that even though the guns certainly worked, achieving any success with them was a different matter.

Late in July, No. 616 squadron moved to Manston to begin interception operations against the V-1 missiles that crossed Kent every day. The Meteor pilots were delighted at how easily their fast and agile aircraft could reach the incoming missiles, but it proved to be surprisingly difficult to shoot them down successfully. A far easier means of ensuring the destruction of a V-1 was to formate abreast the missile and slowly slide the Meteor's wing under the V-1's, allowing the Meteor's wing pressure to push the V-1's wing upwards and tip the missile over. With only a rudimentary guidance system, the missile was then helpless and it could be left to crash in open countryside, long before it reached London. By the end of August, when the squadron withdrew the last of its Spitfires, some thirteen V-1 missiles had been destroyed either by gunfire or by wing tipping.

The Meteor F Mk I enjoyed only a brief period of service with the RAF, as development of the aircraft into more capable versions was achieved at a relatively rapid pace. The Meteor Mk II was to have been based on the H.1 Goblin engine, but with Rolls-Royce now producing the Welland there was no need to divert the Goblin from its planned use as the powerplant for the de Havilland Vampire. The Meteor Mk II was therefore abandoned, as was the GA.1 'Emergency Fighter' that was no longer needed. The two prototypes that were under construction were never completed, but the design did survive as the GA.2 'Ace' and although this aircraft never proceeded beyond the prototype stage, it did eventually have a major effect on the Meteor programme.

The Meteor F Mk III became the first full production-standard variant and eventually some 210 examples of this version were built. It differed very little from the F Mk I apart from the incorporation of a much improved cockpit canopy and windscreen design, and structural changes to allow the more powerful (and more reliable) Rolls-Royce Derwent to be installed in later production examples. The Derwent was a direct development of the Welland, but like the Goblin, it dispensed with Whittle's 'reverse flow' design and proved to be a much better engine. In many respects it was the first example of Rolls-Royce's unique skills and capabilities that have endured until the present day. From the sixteenth aircraft onwards, the 2,000 lb thrust Derwent was introduced and further improvements were slowly introduced, not least a ventral fuel tank that significantly improved the aircraft's range. The Meteor F Mk III soon became Fighter Command's most significant aircraft, equipping squadrons at Bentwaters, West Malling, Boxted, Duxford and Horsham St Faith.

Before the Second World War ended, No. 616 Squadron took its Meteors to Belgium and operated in the region for some time, the unit's pilots hoping that an opportunity might arise for the Meteor to clash with its German counterpart, the Messerschmitt Me 262. Sadly, the elusive Me 262 was never encountered and the unit's Meteors were mostly confined to friendly territory, painted white to ensure their identity as British fighters would not be mistaken. It might have been interesting if the RAF's Meteor had encountered the Me 262 but to compare the two aircraft was a pointless exercise. Germany's Me 262 was certainly an advanced design and it would have outperformed the Meteor, but the aircraft had been hurried into service long before it should have been. It was a dangerous aircraft to fly and was barely capable of flying at all, its engines being notoriously unreliable and temperamental, and in need of regular maintenance or replacement after only a few hours. By comparison, the Meteor was a far more modest design, but it was one that had been fully developed into a proper fighting machine, fitted with engines that worked well.

The final examples of the Meteor Mk III incorporated new engine nacelles that were designed to eradicate the buffeting problem encountered by earlier Meteors with original short-chord nacelles. By designing a longer and more streamlined housing for the engines a small weight penalty was incurred and the engine lost a little of its efficiency, but the buffeting problem was cured and drag was improved. The new nacelle was retrofitted to some earlier Mk II aircraft, and some were eventually modified to Meteor Mk IV standard, this variant being essentially a Mk III Meteor with longer nacelles, incorporating the Derwent 5 engine. This Derwent derivative was a result of Rolls-Royce's efforts to produce a scaled-down version of its 5,000 lb thrust Nene that Gloster had wanted to use as a powerplant for the Meteor. Unfortunately, its size made it incompatible with the Meteor's wing structure, and as the engine was also required for other emerging aircraft programmes, Rolls-Royce proposed to redesign the Nene specifically for the Meteor. The result was the Derwent 5, which enabled the Meteor Mk IV to almost double its thrust to a combined total of 7,000 lb. This gave the Meteor a much more sprightly performance and bestowed a much better single engine safety on the aircraft too.

When this variant entered service, the RAF had finally abandoned its practice of using Roman numerals for aircraft designations and the variant therefore became the Meteor F Mk 4. Although the new variant remained externally similar to those that had preceded it, the F Mk 4 was a great improvement on the earlier derivatives. It also introduced a revised wing design that became standard on many subsequent versions. Following the loss of one of the early-production

Three Meteor F Mk III aircraft from No. 56 Squadron, pictured during a sortie from their home base at Bentwaters in Suffolk.

Meteor F Mk 4 VT170 served with No. 205 Advanced Flying School but after only two years of use it was sadly destroyed in a crash.

F Mk 4 aircraft, Gloster focused attention on ways in which the aircraft's roll response and structural strength could be improved, and the result was a cropped wing design that drastically improved its roll rate at no great loss to performance other than at high altitude. The shorter-span wings also relieved stress on the airframe structure and marginally improved the aircraft's top speed.

The speedy and manoeuvrable Meteor Mk 4 gradually replaced most of the RAF's Mk III variants within Fighter Command and also enabled other remaining fighter types (such as the Hornet) to be withdrawn. The Mk 4 also indirectly led to the creation of a twin-seat trainer version of the Meteor, as until this stage there had been no plans to introduce a specialised conversion trainer into service. Gloster had retained one of its Mk 4 production fleet as a company demonstrator, but when it was destroyed in a crash landing (whilst being flown by an inexperienced Belgian pilot) Gloster concluded that the accident might have been avoided had the aircraft been equipped with a second seat for an experienced company test pilot. It was decided that in future the company would only allow its demonstrator aircraft to be flown under the supervision of a Gloster test pilot, so the demonstrator (G-AIDC) was rebuilt with a longer fuselage that incorporated a second cockpit, complete with dual controls. The longer fuselage also improved the Meteor's directional stability and freed the aircraft from the need for ballast in the nose or intake rings.

The RAF showed some interest in the new variant, not least because there was a growing feeling that the Meteor's accident rate was unacceptably high, now that post-war tolerance of mishaps was far less than it had been in 1945. Although the RAF had never felt any need for a dual-control Spitfire, it was finally accepted that in a post-war era there would be a greater need for safer and more reliable conversion training, and so some sort of jet trainer would be required to fill the increasingly evident gap between the capabilities of the Harvard piston trainer and the operational Meteor jet. Thus, the RAF ordered what became the Meteor T Mk 7, essentially a standard Mk 4 airframe with a lengthened nose, incorporating the second cockpit (the Mk 5 and Mk 6 were design derivatives of the F Mk 4 that were not pursued).

Eventually, a staggering 640 Mk 7 aircraft were built for the RAF, Fleet Air Arm and test establishments, and by any standards the T Mk 7 was a remarkably useful and valuable aircraft. Unfortunately, the aircraft was possibly too successful in some respects, in that its availability suddenly led to huge demand not only from Britain's Ministry of Supply but also from the many overseas export customers that had purchased the Meteor. Consequently, its development was hurried and resulted in an aircraft that suffered from some shortfalls. It had no cannon armament, nor any provision for any other armament; therefore it could not be used for operational training. The instructor's cockpit did not contain any fuel gauge, engine temperature indicator or even an engine relight button, nor did the aircraft have cockpit pressurisation, even though it was capable of reaching 50,000 feet. Ejection seats were still in their infancy, so the crew were obliged to sit on fixed seats, and in an emergency their escape would be hindered by

A line-up of factory-fresh Meteor F Mk 4 aircraft, probably with No. 245 Squadron. The application of 'High Speed Silver' paint became standard on most Fighter Command Meteors for many years.

Meteor F Mk 4 VT340 pictured during a stay with Fairey Aviation at Ringway (now Manchester International Airport). A Gannet is just visible in the background.

the huge, one-piece metal canopy that had to be bodily lifted aside. On a more practical level, the solid canopy was also far from ideal, as even with its numerous windows, visibility was hardly perfect.

However, the Meteor T Mk 7's most significant deficit was a lack of increased tail area to compensate for the longer forward fuselage. It could hardly have been surprising that flying accidents occurred all too frequently, especially when students were flying around the airfield circuit. A phenomenon began to emerge that was referred to as the 'phantom dive' in which T Mk 7s suddenly plummeted to the ground during final approach to the airfield, almost inevitably with fatal results. It was discovered that with the aircraft at slow speed, and with the landing gear extended and wing air brakes deployed, it had only marginal directional stability. If the aircraft was allowed to yaw even only slightly, a lethal situation arose in which the forward fuselage's lateral position could no longer be held by the relatively small tail fin and rudder, and the result was an uncontrollable yaw that immediately developed into a roll from which there was insufficient height to recover. There was no cure for this problem other than strict rules on how the aircraft should be handled in the low-speed configuration, but even after decades of service, the notorious phantom dive was still a danger and the RAF's very last Meteor (WF791) was destroyed in May 1988 when a CFS pilot encountered the very same problem during an air display at Coventry Airport.

Gloster was aware of the T Mk 7's limitations from the outset and the company quickly developed a solution, in the shape of the tail unit that had been fitted to its GA.2 Ace prototype. Following the termination of the Ministry of Supply order for the GA.1 'Emergency Fighter', Gloster continued with the aircraft's design and produced the GA.2, largely in response to a Ministry of Supply requirement for an experimental aircraft with which to test the new Rolls-Royce Nene engine. Based on the GA.1 design, the improved GA.2 prototype performed only adequately, and Gloster redesigned the tail section to incorporate a much larger fin and rudder, with the tailplane mounted in 'T' fashion towards the top. The GA.2 Ace programme was eventually terminated but Gloster reused the aircraft's tail unit design as an ideal solution to the Meteor T Mk 7's stability problems, substituting the standard Meteor tail for the Ace's bigger (and far better) design. But despite this seemingly simple solution, the improved Mk 7 was never adopted for large-scale production and apart from a few export examples (and a few aircraft assigned to experimental duties in the UK) almost all of the Mk 7 aircraft manufactured retained the standard Meteor Mk I tail section. The reasons why the larger tail unit never became standard are unclear, although it seems likely that cost and time delays were the main factors, and of course many T Mk 7s were already delivered or in production before the extent of the stability problem was entirely clear. But despite this problem which dogged the dual-control variant, the T Mk 7 was in most respects a stable, docile and reliable aeroplane that most pilots were delighted to fly.

The Ace's larger tail unit did play a very significant part in the Meteor's history, as the next variant to emerge after the T Mk 7 trainer was the Meteor

Mk 8, another fighter version destined primarily for the RAF, but this derivative ultimately became the 'standard' Meteor fighter and was built in much larger numbers than any other version. It was the creation of the T Mk 7 that eventually led to the F Mk 8, after Gloster realised that with the twin-seater's longer fuselage and clipped wings much better performance could be wrung out of the original Meteor airframe. A Mk 4 aircraft (RA382) was modified to incorporate a 30 inch fuselage plug between the ammunition bay and main fuel tank, stretching the fuselage and creating space for more fuel, raising capacity to 420 imperial gallons (instead of the standard 325).

It was initially proposed to retain the Mk 7's old-style tail unit, but flight testing demonstrated that with a repositioned ammunition bay and more fuel the aircraft became unstable in pitch when ammunition was expended, the empty ammunition bay now being countered by the additional fuel tankage, and so the Ace's large tail section was adopted as standard for the new variant. RA382 was suitably modified to accept the tail unit taken from one of the Ace prototypes that had now been withdrawn from use. An ejection seat was introduced in the shape of the Martin-Baker Mk 1 or Mk 1E (the 'E' version automatically separating the pilot from his seat after ejection) and a new retractable gyro gunsight was adopted, together with a new one-piece cockpit canopy that afforded much better all-round visibility. Most importantly, the Mk 8 was equipped with the Derwent 8 engine, delivering 3,500 lb thrust, and structural modifications required to accommodate this engine, together with the other improvements, raised the aircraft's weight quite significantly (requiring a strengthened undercarriage that raised weight still further) but despite this, the Mk 8 promised to deliver a top speed of 592 mph and possibly more with further refinements.

This was not much more than the F Mk 4 could achieve, but the new variant was certainly faster, could fly further, and had the advantage of an ejection seat. The only disadvantage of the new design was that the Mk 8 could not climb as quickly as the early long-span Mk 4 aircraft, but this was a minor issue and pilots were far more impressed by the greatly improved take-off performance, which almost halved the usual take-off run to around 480 yards. Armament remained unchanged with the 20 mm Hispano cannon fitted as standard, although some consideration was given to the introduction of the 30 mm ADEN cannon, but the costs and time delays associated with this proposal were enough to dissuade Gloster from pursuing the idea very far. As it was, the 20 mm cannon was more than adequate, especially when compared with the 0.50 calibre machine guns fitted to most comparable US aircraft at that time. RAF Fighter Command was keen to get the new F Mk 8 as swiftly as possible, and there was no enthusiasm for the pursuance of design improvements that were not strictly necessary. It was no surprise, therefore, that other proposals were also dropped, such as Gloster's plan to give the aircraft ventral gun packs and assisted take-off rockets.

Meteor VT150 was the first true F Mk 8 prototype and made its first flight on 12 October 1948 in the hands of Gloster's Jan Zurakowski, a test pilot who soon earned a reputation as a very skilled and flamboyant character, becoming

Pictured on the ramp at RAF Waterbeach in October 1953, Meteor F Mk 8 from No. 63 Squadron proudly displays the unit's markings on its fuselage and wing tips. (*Tony Clarke collection*)

Meteor F Mk 8 VZ517 was assigned to Armstrong Siddeley in 1955 as a test bed for the company's Screamer rocket engine, visible in its streamlined pod under the aircraft's fuselage.

Meteor F Mk 8 WK784 from No. 604 (County of Middlesex) Squadron, North Weald, pictured at Heathrow on 7 June 1965. (*Tony Clarke collection*)

something of a star within the aviation industry. Production deliveries commenced with VZ440, delivered to No. 43 Squadron in August 1949, the first production F Mk 8 (VZ438) going to No. 1 Squadron in December of that year. With the Korean War approaching and the Cold War climate growing ever worse, the RAF was desperately keen to adopt the Meteor F Mk 8 as its standard fighter, and export interest was also very high. Gloster eventually built more than 1,200 examples, many being subcontracted to Armstrong Whitworth's Baginton factory. All of the RAF's front-line fighter squadrons re-equipped with the Mk 8 and many more examples eventually went to second-line units, and although the aircraft was slowly replaced by either the F-86 Sabre or Hunter over the next decade, it remained in RAF service with Royal Auxiliary Air Force units until the RAuxAF disbanded, and also continued to serve with second-line units into the 1960s, the last examples acting as target facilities aircraft with No. 229 Operational Conversion Unit at Chivenor. When this unit disbanded, the very last of the RAF's Meteors went to No. 1 TWU at Brawdy and it was here that the very last Mk 8 (VZ467) was retired in 1991, more than forty years after the first examples had been delivered to the RAF.

The Meteor Mk 8 became one of the RAF's most familiar post-war aircraft, and although primarily assigned to the role of fighter-interceptor, it also assumed many other tasks and performed them well. The Mk 8 was the first RAF fighter to incorporate an aerial refuelling capability and after trials had been conducted

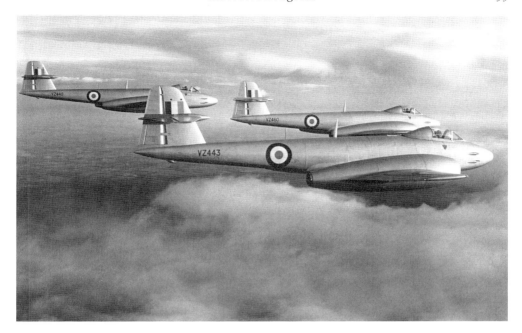

A trio of Meteor F Mk 8 aircraft from the RAF's Central Fighter Establishment. As can be seen, the aircraft are early-production F Mk 8s with partially framed metal canopy hoods. These were later replaced by one-piece clear hoods.

Two Meteor F(TT) Mk 8 aircraft from No. 85 Squadron, pictured during a sortie from RAF Binbrook. The aircraft in the foreground wears an overall Light Aircraft Grey paint scheme, which was progressively applied to Meteors towards the end of the 1960s.

by Flight Refuelling Ltd the concept was extended to service trials, No. 245 Squadron at Horsham St Faith receiving sixteen F Mk 8 aircraft suitably modified with fixed refuelling probes and associated fuel piping. Trials were flown with USAF KB-29 tankers, and the unit succeeded in making numerous long-endurance flights with the Meteor, some lasting for up to 4 hours. The Mk 8 also introduced a larger air intake design, developed as a result of trials conducted by Rolls-Royce. Widening the intake created greater mass flow and improved engine thrust by 240 lb, and these new 'deep breather' intakes were gradually introduced into the Mk 8 production lines.

The Mk 8 was followed by the FR Mk 9, which was a reconnaissance derivative featuring a new nose section incorporating camera gear. The Mk 10 was also a photo-reconnaissance variant, but fighter development resumed with the Mk 11, based on the RAF's requirement for a jet-powered night fighter. Now that the Meteor's performance had improved markedly, and with the more powerful Derwent 8 now becoming available, the Gloster design team turned their attention to ways in which the Meteor airframe could be modified to carry radar, and when the Air Ministry issued Specification F.24/48 for a jet night fighter, Gloster was already working on a suitable design. Because the company was heavily committed to existing Meteor production, design of the night fighter was transferred to Armstrong Whitworth at Coventry, a company within the same Hawker Siddeley Group as Gloster.

Some trials work had already been conducted with Meteors and radar, the Central Radar Establishment and Telecommunications Research Establishment having flown a number of Mk III and Mk 4 aircraft suitably modified with rudimentary radar gear. The fourth production T Mk 7 trainer (VW413) was allocated for modification into the NF Mk 11 prototype and it duly emerged from Armstrong Whitworth's at Baginton with longer-span wings, four 20 mm Hispano cannon relocated to the wing leading edges, a long nose cone designed to incorporate interception radar, and the Mk 8's large tail surfaces. Although still very much a Meteor, the aircraft seemingly bore little resemblance to the wartime jet that had flown four years previously, but as the prototype Mk 11, VW413 made its first flight from Baginton during October 1949.

Three prototypes were produced, fitted with American AI Mk 10 interception radar, and much to the RAF's delight, the aircraft performed well, easily achieving the required 2-hour mission requirement stipulated by Fighter Command and demonstrating a good altitude interception capability at 30,000 feet. Although heavier than previous Meteor variants, the longer wings afforded good manoeuvrability, and pilots reported that the Mk 11 could out-turn the Mk 8 in the right circumstances. The only significant developmental problem was the introduction of underwing fuel tanks that had to be modified when it was found that they collapsed in high-speed flight at low level. The Mk 11 was slower than its day fighter counterpart, but it was a great improvement over the RAF's existing fleet of night fighter Mosquitos that could barely achieve 380 mph. Production aircraft duly went to UK-based squadrons and also to units based in Germany, and some 338 aircraft were eventually delivered.

Meteor F Mk 8 VT460 pictured during its stay with the Central Fighter Establishment. As can be seen, the aircraft flew trials with various weapons fits including rocket projectile racks.

The short-lived Gloster GA.2 TX148 never entered production as a fighter but its tail design was eventually used as part of later Meteor variants, starting with the F Mk 8.

Meteor NF Mk 11 WD597 enjoyed only a relatively short service life, as did most RAF Meteor NF Mk 11 aircraft. After being delivered to the RAF in August 1951, it was withdrawn late in 1957.

Development of the night fighter design then led to the NF Mk 12, an improved version which incorporated American AI Mk 21 radar requiring an even longer nose cone, stretching the Meteor's fuselage length to 49 feet 11 inches. Even the existing tail fin derived from the stillborn Ace was barely capable of compensating for this almost ridiculous stretch of the Meteor's structure, and additional area was added to the leading edge of the fin, above and below the tailplane intersection bullet. Even heavier than the Mk 11, the NF Mk 12 was equipped with Derwent 9 engines, delivering a respectable 3,800 lb. Only ninety-seven production NF Mk 12s were built, financed by America under MDAP (Mutual Defense Assistance Program) arrangements, the first aircraft being allocated to No. 238 OCU at North Luffenham late in 1953. However, the night fighter variant was also produced as the NF Mk 13, a minimum-change derivative of the Mk 11, designed for operation in the Middle East. A fleet of forty aircraft was manufactured, the first of these pre-dating the earlier Mk 12 by many weeks.

With the RAF's Mosquito night fighters proving themselves to be ill-suited to 'tropical' climates (bonded wood construction being far from ideal in a hot and humid environment), the RAF swiftly assigned Meteor night fighters to the Canal Zone, and after withdrawal the aircraft were shifted to Malta where they served with No. 39 Squadron. Although essentially similar to the Mk 11, the NF Mk 13 featured cold air ram air intakes under the fuselage to supply cooling for the cockpit and equipment bays, and improved navigation equipment was installed to enable the aircraft to operate over featureless desert terrain. A few late production examples were modified still further with larger wing flaps outboard of the engine nacelles, but in most respects this particular night fighter version was merely a specialised derivative of the existing design, and it was not until the NF Mk 14 emerged that the Meteor's seemingly endless development story moved still further.

The Meteor NF Mk 14 was not the last Meteor variant to be produced, but it was effectively the ultimate expression of the Meteor's development potential. Sadly, it was perhaps a step too far, as by the time that it had been created it was already beginning to lag behind the standards of performance that the RAF might have expected from it. Worse still, improvements that could have been made were not made, and the result was an aircraft that gave the appearance of modernity whilst delivering little more than was already available. In order to incorporate the more advanced AI Mk 21 radar that was now available, the aircraft's nose cone had to be stretched yet again, bestowing a total fuselage length of a

A quartet of Meteor NF Mk 14 night fighters from No. 85 Squadron. The aircraft in the foreground (WS782) was destroyed in an accident at Church Fenton on 4 March 1958 when it collided with Meteor WS700.

Meteor NF Mk 14 WS775 from No. 85 Squadron, pictured on a sortie from its base at West Malling in Kent. The Mk 14's huge clear canopy is clearly visible, as is the greatly extended nose section.

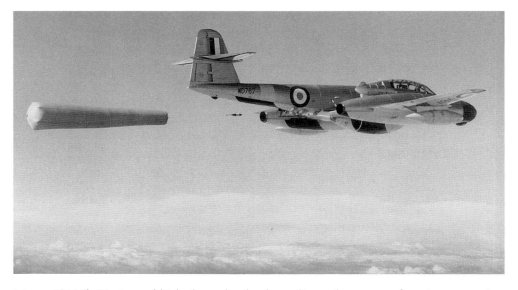

Meteor TT Mk 20 pictured high above the clouds, trailing a sleeve target from its target wing. The TT Mk 20 was a conversion of the standard Mk 11 night fighter airframe, designed for the target tug role.

staggering 51 feet 4 inches on the Meteor, which, when combined with the same longer-span wings and enlarged tail unit, produced an aircraft of almost ludicrous proportions. It was also the heaviest Meteor variant, weighing in at 21,200 lb when fully fuelled, and it was hardly surprising that even with Derwent 9 engines it was hardly a great performer.

To add to the Mk 14's difficulties, the RAF was now introducing the remarkable Canberra bomber, and it soon became evident that the Meteor Mk 14 was incapable of intercepting it. This might have been a reason for pride within Bomber Command, but when their crews were asked to limit their altitudes during exercises to 'give the fighter boys a chance' it was not a situation that Fighter Command relished at all. Modifications to the Mk 14 design included spring-tab ailerons and an auto-stabiliser system, both intended to improve high-speed handling. Unfortunately, the Mk 14 could barely reach 575 mph; therefore it seemed pointless to have devoted effort and expense to improvements that served no obvious purpose. Just as absurd was the Mk 14's new cockpit canopy design, which featured a one-piece blown Perspex hood that could be retracted courtesy of an electric motor. It afforded excellent visibility (although quite why visibility was needed for a night fighter is unclear) and it would have enabled the crew to eject directly through it, had they been equipped with ejection seats – but they were not.

However, the Meteor NF Mk 14 duly entered service in 1954, and most of the existing Meteor night fighter fleet was eventually replaced by this type. In addition to service with UK-based units, the Mk 14 was also operated by No. 60 Squadron from its base at Tengah in Singapore, flying the last operational Meteor NF Mk 14 sortie in August 1961. It was perhaps sad that the Meteor's development story reached the end of its potential with a derivative that was, by any standards, a disappointment.

The Meteor was a truly revolutionary aircraft that ushered in a completely new era for the RAF (and, indeed, many other air arms too). By modern standards it was unremarkable, but when it was first delivered to the RAF it was undoubtedly a first class fighter that served Fighter Command with distinction for many years. The Meteor's versatility and adaptability enabled it to be used for a huge variety of roles other than interception, and even after it had been withdrawn from use as a fighter it stayed with the RAF for many years, operating in the photo-reconnaissance role and as a navigation trainer, advanced trainer, target tug, radio-controlled drone, and as a trials aircraft for new equipment and systems. Tragically, the RAF's very last Meteor (WF791) was lost in a crash during 1988, as described previously. It was a tragic way to mark the end of the Meteor's long and distinguished RAF service career, but it is perhaps indicative of its significance that this particular aircraft had long since been withdrawn from operational use and had been retained by the RAF to fly only at air shows, celebrating the Meteor's importance to the RAF and the affection with which it was regarded by the pilots that flew it and the ground crews who looked after it.

CHAPTER TWO
Single Engine Success

Although the Meteor was Britain's first jet-powered fighter, it did not appear in complete isolation, at least not for long. It was swiftly joined by another aeroplane that was designed to undertake the same role, and although it might be imagined that both aircraft types might therefore have been very similar, they were in fact completely different. Frank Whittle's engine had suffered from a troubled start, but when more industrial and military figures finally grasped the potential of jet power, Whittle's creation gradually attracted more and more attention. By the time that the E.28/39 trials aircraft made its first flight at Cranwell in 1941, the Air Ministry and the Ministry of Supply were obviously well aware of the jet engine's emergence, and they deliberately encouraged interest in the concept within the aviation industry, passing developmental and design details to engine and aircraft manufacturers as they emerged. De Havilland was one of many companies that were following developments and in May 1941, Geoffrey de Havilland and his Chief Engineer, Frank Halford, travelled to Cranwell to see the E.28/39 aircraft perform. Of course, Halford was already connected with jet engine development, as his position as an adviser to Vauxhall Motors meant that he had been directly involved in the original plans to set up production of Whittle's engine at Vauxhall, before the plans were subsequently changed. Their visit to Cranwell was probably the seminal moment when de Havilland decided to pursue jet engine development, as the company design team had already looked at the concept and needed little more persuasion to conclude that jet propulsion was the way forward for aircraft design.

It was Sir Henry Tizard (Air Member for Development and Production) who set things in motion, and following detailed negotiations between Ministry officials and de Havilland, Specification E.6/41 was issued during 1941. Initially, the Specification called for a purely experimental aircraft, although it was refined to embrace the production of two prototypes of a jet fighter, jet propelled and capable of reaching an altitude of at least 48,000 feet. (It would therefore have to be pressurised.) It would also include armament in the shape of four 20 mm Hispano cannon and incorporate a degree of armour protection, including a bullet-proof windscreen. Maximum speed was specified as being at least 490 mph at 35,000 feet, and internal fuel capacity was to be at least 250 gallons.

In some respects the Ministry of Supply was unclear as to precisely what kind of fighter might be needed, as developmental progress gave no reliable clues as to what kind of capabilities any potential adversary might have. It was assumed that if Britain was developing jet fighters, the Soviet Union (and others) would be doing the same, and therefore that jet bombers would also follow. It was already understood that jet aircraft performed best at low level. But with no clues as to what might emerge, the Air Ministry had to assume that new jet bombers might be capable of achieving both high speed and high altitudes; therefore it made perfect sense to design a fighter that was capable of countering this kind of threat.

Of course, the key reason for the issuing of the new Specification was simply to create an aircraft that could accommodate the new jet engine that Halford was developing, now that de Havilland had agreed to take on further design and production of a developed version of the engine. In many respects the new aeroplane was to be created simply because there was a new engine available to power it – a rather odd situation but one that was very similar to the circumstances in which the Meteor had also been designed.

It is important to understand, however, that Halford's engine was somewhat different to the one that had been created by Whittle. For example, Whittle's engine featured double-entry centrifugal compressors (that fed air into the engine), whereas Halford opted for a more simple single-sided compressor with an inlet at the front, that required fewer bearings and therefore made the powerplant lighter and more reliable. Halford also dispensed with Whittle's reverse flow system that directed hot air back into the middle of the engine in order to reduce overall length. Instead, he opted for a straight-through flow via sixteen combustion chambers, and his new design (codenamed 'Supercharger') was assembled during the summer of 1941 at the Car Mart factory at Hendon. It was bench tested for the first time at de Havilland's facilities at Hatfield on 13 April 1942 and performed well, although another run on 5 May resulted in the collapse of the test bed intakes, causing the engine to stall. It was dismantled and investigated but there were no signs of damage, illustrating that the new engine was certainly rugged. With further improvements the engine was soon run up to full speed, and it was decided to put the engine (named 'Goblin') into production during September 1942.

Development of the Goblin engine moved rather more swiftly than the creation of the aeroplane it was to power, de Havilland being heavily committed to manufacture of Mosquito bombers and fighters at that time. Meanwhile, other delays had affected Gloster's Meteor programme and as a solution it was agreed that the Goblin be test flown in a Meteor so that both projects could continue to make progress. Meteor DG206 had therefore become the first Goblin-powered aircraft to fly, on 5 March 1943, in the capable hands of Michael Daunt. This had enabled the Meteor's flight testing to continue without delay, but as problems with the Welland were soon resolved, attention quickly shifted back to de Havilland's fighter design.

One of the main reasons why the project had been delayed (other than the distractions of Mosquito manufacture) was that the Ministry of Supply decided to bring Hawker aircraft into the story, after Sir Sydney Camm had expressed his interest in jet propulsion. This led to the Ministry of Aircraft Production stating:

> It is suggested that the design of the E.6/41 should be put in the hands of Camm of Hawkers, one of our most experienced designers of fighter types. Although there is a business connection between de Havilland and Halford, it would be unwise to press this to the extent of a construction of aircraft building which might fall down because of the lack of experience of one of the aircraft partners on the specialized design techniques associated with this type. This class of design calls for the best design capability we have on both the engine and the airframe. Hence, the right thing to do is to ask Camm of Hawkers to take it on, shelving his fighter/bomber for it.

In short, this communication to Sir Henry Tizard meant that there was a very clear preference for assigning the project to a company that had plenty of experience in fighter design, although this attitude seems to be almost an insult towards de Havilland, a company that was hardly inexperienced itself, and of course Hawker had no more knowledge of jet propulsion than anyone else. It was perhaps fortuitous that Camm saw no reason to abandon his P.1105 bomber project (although it was subsequently terminated) and he expressed no further interest in taking on the jet fighter. This finally persuaded the Ministry of Aircraft Production to sanction the go-ahead for de Havilland's DH.99, to be created by a design team at Hatfield consisting of Chief Designer R. E. Bishop, Chief Aerodynamicist R. M. Clarkson, and Chief Engineer C. C. Walker, under the leadership of Company Chairman Sir Geoffrey de Havilland.

The DH.99 was designed with some important factors in mind. Firstly, it was agreed that the aircraft should be as small and light as possible, to ensure both agility and good altitude performance with the limited thrust that the single Goblin engine would deliver. The option of creating a twin-engine design was considered but de Havilland favoured something smaller so that the aircraft would be simple to operate and maintain, and also ease demand for the number of engines that would have to be produced. The pressurised fuselage was made as small as possible, and this permitted a corresponding engine diameter of 50 inches. The engine's voracious appetite for air was calculated to equate to around 100 tons per hour, and it was understood that good air intake airflow would be vital, but while the Meteor enjoyed good flow characteristics through the use of wing-mounted nacelles, the situation was rather different for an aircraft with the engine buried inside the fuselage. This meant that the intake trunks would have to be as short as possible, and the design was deliberately set out to ensure that the engine was not dogged by long intakes that would ruin efficiency, and eventually the intakes (fixed into the wing leading edges at their roots) were designed to accept up to 95 per cent of available ram air effect. Likewise, the exhaust pipe would also have to be as short as possible to avoid losing efficiency within the exhaust flow. The simplest solution to this requirement was to make the fuselage extremely short, effectively wrapped snugly around the engine and ending abruptly at the engine's exhaust point. In order to equip the aircraft with tail surfaces and the necessary balance it would require, the fuselage would then be split into two tail booms (attached to the wing trailing edge) that would run either side of the jet exhaust flow, with a tailplane and twin rudders fixed to their extremities. It was not an ideal arrangement, as twin tail booms inevitably add weight and lessen the tail's structural stiffness, but with some careful design work the de Havilland team created a neat design configuration which, in very basic terms, was essentially a jet engine with wings attached to it, and very little else.

The tiny cockpit was positioned ahead of the engine intake and although it was a cramped fit by any standards, the pilot's forward view was undoubtedly a drastic improvement over that which had been endured by pilots of propeller-driven fighters. Without a huge propeller and a long piston-engine cowling to incorporate, the DH.99's windscreen would be virtually on the nose. Forward view would be improved further by the incorporation of a tricycle undercarriage, now that there was no need to employ the usual tail-sitting configuration that was necessary for piston fighters. This also meant that the landing gear could be much shorter and therefore much lighter. Indeed, the aircraft's heaviest equipment (apart from the engine) would be the cannon armament, and this would be incorporated in the nose section, under the tiny fuselage, providing an ideal firing position and creating good centre of gravity for the aeroplane as a whole.

During April 1942, an order was placed for two prototypes – LZ548 and LZ551 – at a cost of £40,000, although a third aircraft was subsequently added (MP838) that would be fitted with the proposed operational armament, the other two prototypes being assigned purely to aerodynamic and engine performance testing. Manufacture of the aircraft (now referred to as the DH.100) began immediately, although progress was slow because de Havilland was required to devote most of its energy to continuing Mosquito production, and design work on a new piston-engine bomber. However, by the end of 1942, an airframe mock-up had been constructed and agreement had been reached to abandon the bomber project so that the company's efforts could be concentrated on the Hornet fighter and the DH.100 jet.

Construction of the prototypes began in November and continued through the winter, and with so much experience derived from the magnificent Mosquito, de Havilland opted to employ some of the same construction techniques in the DH.100. Although most of the airframe was manufactured from metal alloy, the fuselage was mainly constructed in precisely the same way as the Mosquito had been, with a birch and spruce layered skin formed in two moulds, one for each half of the fuselage. Balsa and Quipo wood was used for filling, and the whole structure was glued into a huge one-piece shell with resin adhesive. The external surface of the fuselage was then covered in Madapollam fabric and dope applied, so that the wooden structure was completely sealed from the outside environment. It might be imagined that building a jet fighter out of wood was a pretty archaic practice, and indeed it was, but the technique made a great deal of sense in that the construction material weighed very little, and the way in which it was used

DH.100 prototype LZ548, pictured shortly before its first flight at Hatfield in September 1943.

enabled the aircraft structure to be as simple and light as possible. It had worked well for the Mosquito and de Havilland saw no reason why it would not work well for the DH.100 too.

By August 1943, the first prototype of the DH.100 was completed. A memo from the Director of Technical Development, N. E. Rowe, on 21 August included a reference to one of the Government's technical team and stated that they had given the project 'the code word "Spider Crab" which will be used henceforth with work referring to the E.6/41'. The odd name has often been referred to in history books as being the original name of the DH.100, but Spider Crab was merely a codename for the project as a whole, and when the aircraft emerged for taxiing trials on 24 August, it had yet to be officially named. Geoffrey de Havilland Junior piloted LZ548 on five high-speed runs during which the aircraft made short hops of up to 100 yards each time. The design team were pleased with the tests, although the aircraft did display a tendency to scrape its tail boom tips on the ground if over-rotated, and the tail section was raised slightly as a result in order to create slightly better ground clearance.

On 20 September, the DH.100 made its first flight and LZ548 performed well, observed from Hatfield by a number of VIPs including Frank Whittle. Only slight modifications were required as a result of the first flight, the ailerons being slightly out of balance at speeds above 400 mph, and a slight wing-down attitude was also evident, while directional stability was poor when the aircraft was yawed. However, in overall terms the aircraft was judged to be a success, and even with a modest 2,700 lb thrust from its H.1 Goblin engine it looked more than capable of being turned into a viable fighter jet. The second and third prototypes joined the test programme during 1944, although the first prototype (LZ548) had its test career cut short when it crashed in July 1945 after a fuel pump failed shortly after take-off from Hatfield. However, the other prototypes remained active and by September 1945, LZ551 had gone to Farnborough, equipped with a tail arrestor hook to act as the prototype for a proposed naval variant, while MP838 also went to Farnborough, complete with its Hispano cannon armament. It was used to conduct tactical trials and to allow more test pilots to familiarise themselves with the diminutive aircraft and its novel means of propulsion.

The DH.100 was finally given a proper name in April 1944 – it became the Vampire F Mk 1 – and at the conclusion of the trials the Tactical Flight CO of the Royal Aircraft Establishment (RAE) commented:

> The stall characteristics of the aircraft are now considered completely satisfactory. The directional stability characteristics are considered acceptable, but not ideal. The view from the cockpit and the freedom from noise and vibration inspire the pilot with great confidence and, personally, I have never flown a nicer aircraft.

It is perhaps interesting that there was no great praise for the Vampire's altitude or speed capabilities, but then it was hardly better than the piston-engine fighters that had preceded it. Its true value lay in the potential that it demonstrated, and its prospective ability to allow the RAF to begin embracing jet power. MP838 moved on to Boscombe Down where it was assessed by the Aeroplane & Armament Experimental Establishment (A&AEE) test pilots. They concluded that the Vampire compared well to existing piston-engine aircraft with good manoeuvrability, crisp aileron response, and docile handling qualities. However, they also criticised the relatively poor climb rate and the sluggish acceleration that compared badly with the rapid response provided by most propeller-driven fighters. They also commented that despite the cockpit's snug but comfortable conditions, the canopy framework was thick and made all-round visibility difficult, even though the forward view was undoubtedly superior to almost any other aeroplane. The directional stability issues were not fully cured for some time, but it was a problem which had to be solved, otherwise there was little hope of operating the Vampire as a useful gun platform. Tests with a bolt-on fin placed ahead of the windscreen served to highlight the cause, and wind tunnel tests enabled the design team to establish precisely how to modify the fin and rudder surfaces, reducing their overall area and thereby reducing the 'snaking' tendency to an acceptable level. All three prototypes were subsequently modified to incorporate flat-topped tails. The ailerons were also modified to render them less sensitive, and the Vampire's tendency to enter a stall without any physical warning was also overcome by modifying the air intake lips.

These relatively minor alterations were soon incorporated into the DH.100 design and the way was then clear to begin series production. Hatfield was still heavily involved with the Mosquito, so English Electric was chosen as subcontractor for the programme. On 14 May 1944, a contract was issued for 120 aircraft and manufacturing began at English Electric's Strand Road factory in Preston just a couple of weeks later. As was often the case during this era, urgency was a key issue and in order to speed up production it was agreed that the first fifty aircraft could be completed without cockpit pressurisation, and that the first forty machines would be equipped with the Goblin Mk 1 engine, after which the Goblin Mk 2 would be introduced with a better thrust of 3,100 lb. One other significant modification introduced from the eighty-seventh aircraft onwards was a new single-piece 'teardrop' canopy, designed to be safer than the original design (which was prone to failure) and better for pilot visibility, in response to the A&AEE reports. It was a minor but important modification that proved to be so successful that it was retrofitted to almost all of the earlier production examples.

The first production Vampire F Mk 1 (TG274) made its first flight from English Electric's Samlesbury airfield on 20 April 1945, before transferring to Hatfield just three days later to commence flight trials. It then moved to Boscombe Down for evaluation and, like the Vampire prototype, was found to be a very satisfactory aeroplane, despite suffering from a few small but important faults. The aileron over-balance that had been present on the prototype recurred but more noticeably, and the test pilots reported that control column force required during high-g looping manoeuvres was unacceptably low. Surprisingly, the troublesome snaking tendency reappeared and the A&AEE pilots believed that rudder authority was not good enough to ensure the aircraft's usefulness as a gun platform. The revised cockpit canopy was reported as being considerably better but still far from perfect, and the positioning of flap and undercarriage levers was reported as being confusing, but in most respects the Vampire was regarded as being an aircraft with plenty of potential as a jet fighter, especially when it was learned that speed trials had shown the aircraft to be capable of a very respectable 526 mph at 25,000 feet.

Sadly, the A&AEE trials were ended abruptly when TG274 crashed on 3 December 1945. Jan Zurakowski (of Meteor test pilot fame) was on a low-speed demonstration flight when the aircraft stalled and was destroyed. It was a setback, but as the crash had not been due to any technical flaw it did not affect the Vampire programme as a whole, and a second order for another 120 Vampire Mk 1 aircraft had been placed seven months previously, although the order books were subject to a great deal of change. The second batch of 120 aircraft was subsequently reduced to 34 so that the rest could be completed as Vampire F Mk 3 derivatives, and a final batch of F Mk 1 aircraft was placed in August 1945 before being cancelled again a month later.

It was inevitable that the Vampire would be directly compared to the Meteor, and trials were conducted during 1945 and again in 1946, the latter trials also involving a Griffon-engined Spitfire. The results were somewhat disappointing for de Havilland, as the trials pilots concluded that the Meteor was undoubtedly the better fighter aircraft, as it could achieve a higher Mach number (i.e. speed at altitude) and had a better rate of climb. Perhaps most significantly, it was clear that the Meteor was a steadier gun platform as it did not suffer from the Vampire's stability problems. The Vampire was certainly capable of flying further than the Meteor and was undoubtedly manoeuvrable, but the Meteor's twin, wing-mounted engine layout obviously offered the prospect of development potential and also conferred greater safety on the aircraft. However, the most important conclusion was that the CFE (Central Fighter Establishment) had proved the Vampire capable of intercepting piston-engine aircraft such as the Mosquito, but

Seven Vampire F Mk 3 aircraft, pictured shortly after delivery to the RAF. Visible is the modified all-clear canopy hood and the external fuel tanks, their attachment pylons standing proud of the wing leading edges.

would be incapable of intercepting jet bombers. On the other hand, the Vampire was superior to the Meteor in 'tactical combat manoeuvres' and this effectively meant that the Vampire was best suited to short-range and low-level interception. Of course, it also meant that the Vampire was therefore better suited to the tactical fighter role, and the trials were influential in establishing its main role within the RAF.

While the Vampire's longer-term future was being decided, the first Mk 1 aircraft were delivered to the RAF, starting with No. 247 Squadron at Chilbolton in March 1946. This unit then moved to Odiham and was joined by two more Vampire squadrons. The Vampire F Mk 1 also entered service with the RAuxAF from 1948 when the F Mk 1 began to be withdrawn from the front-line RAF squadrons. The diminutive Vampire fighter was a source of huge interest when it entered service, attracting media attention from around the world and a great deal of enthusiasm from those who were lucky enough to fly it. Despite its problems, it was undoubtedly an improvement over the aircraft that it replaced (such as the Tempest), and the Vampire's agility and speed, plus the impressive forward view from the cockpit, made the Vampire squadrons very popular postings.

The development of the Vampire continued as the F Mk 1 entered service, and de Havilland shifted attention to the F Mk 2, based on a design proposal that had been drawn up early in 1945. This was based around the Rolls-Royce Nene engine, a derivative of the Derwent engine that promised to deliver around 4,000 lb thrust. In fact, it produced a very impressive 5,000 lb and the Directorate of Aircraft Research suggested that a version of a Nene-powered Vampire could be developed for the ground attack role. Of course, de Havilland had already examined the Vampire's potential as a ground attack aircraft, and the more powerful Nene engine did seem to be an ideal powerplant for an aircraft dedicated to the attack role. Work began on both concepts and required some changes to the Vampire's structure in order to accommodate the bigger and heavier engine. The existing intakes were unsuitable for the Nene's double-sided compressor impeller and tests proved that the air intakes simply did not deliver enough air for the increased flow that was required. The solution was the installation of two large scoop intakes on top of the fuselage, these 'elephant ears' modifications enabling intake efficiency to increase by some 50 per cent. Unfortunately, they also created aerodynamic handling difficulties that were never satisfactorily resolved.

A better remedy was the complete redesign of the existing wing root air intakes, and the first Vampire F Mk 2 (TG276) was duly sent to Boulton Paul's factory at Wolverhampton to have new intakes fitted. This required some fairly significant engineering work, including the splitting of the main wing spar, and the internal structure of the wing root also had to be changed, eventually raising the aircraft's weight by some 1,000 lb. The results were satisfactory and the modified aircraft was free of the handling difficulties experienced by the 'elephant ears' fit.

The Air Ministry, however, had by now begun to develop a greater interest in the development potential of the Goblin engine, and a combination of progress with the Goblin and the technical difficulties that dogged the Nene meant that an

A number of Vampire F Mk 1 aircraft were delivered in an unusual (and short-lived) paint scheme comprising two shades of grey and low-visibility insignia.

Close-up view of the 'elephant ears' intakes on Vampire F Mk 11 TG276. This aircraft was subsequently sold to France and became the test bed aircraft for the French Vampire Mk 51.

order for F Mk 2 and a batch of Mk 4 ground attack derivatives was placed but subsequently cancelled as the RAF turned its attention to the Vampire F Mk 3, a direct development of the existing Mk 1 aircraft that was in RAF service. The Vampire F Mk 2 did survive, however, most notably with the Royal Australian Air Force, but for the RAF the Nene-powered Vampires were soon forgotten and it was the Royal Navy that eventually embraced the Nene as a powerplant for its new fighters.

Although the Vampire F Mk 1 was the RAF's first production model of the DH.100 design, it represented only one step towards a more developed design that would deliver better range, even if it did not get any faster. The Vampire F Mk 3 was derived from experiments conducted with TG275 (a Mk 1) that de Havilland's engineers fitted with a new wing, designed to contain more fuel. Additional outer tanks were incorporated into the wing, and the modification increased the Vampire's total fuel capacity to 330 gallons. The metal fuselage fuel tanks (together with those in the wing) were exchanged for Marston bag tanks, and provision was made for even more fuel in externally mounted tanks, one of which could be attached under each wing. However, no matter how the designers changed the shape of these tanks, they had a major effect on the aircraft's longitudinal stability, and the only way to cure this problem was to modify the tail, increasing the chord of the tailplane and reducing the chord of the elevator. The entire tailplane structure was also lowered and the twin fins were modified again, back to a more curved outline that de Havilland had used on many of its earlier designs.

The Goblin engine had continued to develop, and the opportunity was taken to adopt the more powerful 3,100 lb thrust Goblin Mk 2. Although these (and other minor) modifications raised the aircraft's weight, the result was deemed to be a much better aircraft than the F Mk 1. TG275 flew on 4 November 1946 as the prototype Vampire F Mk 3 and was sent to Boscombe Down the following April for evaluation and clearance. It was accompanied by VF343, a production-standard aircraft that, unlike the prototype, possessed a pressurised cabin. The A&AEE pilots were distinctly unimpressed with the new variant, reporting that even without external tanks the aircraft was only marginally stable longitudinally, at high speeds or high altitude. General control authority was judged to be poor, and with external tanks fitted the aircraft was, if anything, even less satisfactory. De Havilland addressed the stability issues by adding ballast in the aircraft's nose section and by adding weight to the control column system to give a heavier feel as more g-force was applied. But even with this problem resolved, the A&AEE was not entirely happy with the tendency of the Vampire Mk 3 to enter a spin when it was stalled with undercarriage and flaps down. The test pilots were also concerned that an inexperienced pilot would be hard-pressed to maintain control of the aircraft in cloud or at night, but despite these misgivings they agreed to clear the aircraft for RAF use provided that the longitudinal stability modifications were made and that the Pilot's Notes clearly warned of the spinning risk in certain configurations.

The existing production order for Vampire F Mk 1 aircraft was revised to allow later production examples to be completed as F Mk 3 versions, and the first delivery to the RAF was made in May 1947, the Odiham Wing beginning its transition from the earlier variant in 1948. In order to demonstrate the potential of the new longer-range Vampire (and because rumours were circulating that the USAF was planning something similar) the RAF decided to stage a crossing of the Atlantic with Vampire aircraft, something that no jet-powered aircraft had yet achieved. The 2,000 mile journey from Stornoway to Goose Bay in Canada was beyond the capabilities of the Vampire, even though attempts to stretch its endurance this far were made, the main problem being that the escorting Mosquito fighters needed to make slower climbs than the Vampires, and as a result the Vampire's range was effectively shortened. Consequently, the only way to cross the Atlantic would be to stage via Iceland and Greenland, and on 1 July 1948, a flight of six Vampires departed Odiham for this long and tiring journey. Despite delays caused by bad weather, the aircraft did reach Canada on 14 July, although the necessity to make the flight in stages did take the shine off what would otherwise have been a very exciting achievement. But while the aircraft were in Canada they performed air displays for a greatly impressed public and then moved-on to Andrews Field in Washington, Langley Field in Virginia, and Greenville in South Carolina. Finally, they appeared at Mitchel Field and displayed at an air show at Idlewild Airport (now better known as JFK International). The return trip was uneventful and the whole exercise was judged to have been a great success not only for the RAF and British Government, which naturally wanted to parade its capabilities across the Atlantic, but also for de Havilland, which seized the opportunity to promote its diminutive aircraft whenever and wherever possible. While the Vampires were in the US, trials were conducted with the USAF, and interception missions mounted against the F-51 and F-80 demonstrated that despite its shortcomings, the Vampire was still an excellent fighter, one USAF F-80 pilot commenting (after flying the Vampire) that it was the best aeroplane he had ever flown.

The Vampire Mk 3 went on to enjoy a satisfactory period of service with the RAF. It was a popular aircraft to fly, even though the RAF undoubtedly regarded it as inferior to the Meteor, but it was an agile and (fairly) fast jet, and one that was certainly an improvement over the earlier Vampire F Mk 1. However, the Mk 3 was not the end of the Vampire's development, and ultimately the F Mk 3 proved to be only an intermediate 'stepping stone' between the rather austere Mk 1 and what effectively became the definitive Vampire variant, the Mk 5/9.

The origins of the Vampire F Mk 5 are chiefly associated with a 1947 project, created by the RAF and de Havilland, to investigate the suitability of the Vampire for operations in tropical climates and, in particular, the Vampire's ability to operate as part of Britain's commitments in the Far East. Experience with the Mosquito had revealed that airframes largely manufactured from wood were far from ideal in the humidity and high temperatures of the tropics, and it seemed likely that the Vampire would be no more suitable than its predecessor, and might even be worse, because of its fairly poor cockpit ventilation and potentially troublesome jet engine. But the trials were also designed to assess its abilities as a ground attack aircraft in the Far East theatre and it was this key issue that formed the basis of the Vampire Mk 5's development.

The RAF had concluded that even though the Vampire was a good aircraft, the Meteor was a better fighter jet, and this judgement inevitably implied that the Vampire would be better suited to the ground attack role. In fact, it was no better suited to ground attack operations than the Meteor, but with the Meteor having been adopted as the RAF's standard jet fighter type, the Vampire would be reassigned to ground attack operations almost by default. Two Vampire F Mk 3 aircraft (VG702 and VG703) were shipped to Singapore, arriving in January 1948. VG702 was reassembled at Seletar and after air testing it was placed in long-term storage so that the effects of the local climate on the airframe could be assessed. VG703 was brought back up to flight standard and transferred to Tengah, from where it was operated on a tour of airfields in the region so that a variety of operational conditions could be assessed. The aircraft ventured quite some way during the following months, including stays in Saigon, Bangkok and even Hong Kong, although the Vampire's arrival here was something of a disaster as the local area was shrouded in thick cloud and as VG703 was at the very limits of its fuel endurance when it arrived, its pilot (Flt Lt George Francis) was obliged to glide the aircraft onto a beach after the aircraft ran out of fuel. The beach was in Bias Bay, an area frequented by Chinese pirates, and an RAF Sunderland flying boat was brought in to protect the aircraft and crew until it could be hoisted onto HMS *Belfast* to complete its journey.

From February 1949, the aircraft and its crews moved on to the Philippines and Borneo, before heading to the Middle East for further trials. After stays at such exotic locations as Calcutta, Delhi and Rangoon, the aircraft slowly made its way back to the UK via Aden, Malta, Sardinia and Istres in France before arriving at Manston, and finally Hatfield on 14 October. The exercise had been a particularly long and complicated one, but it demonstrated that the Vampire would be suitable for operations in both the Far East and Middle East, subject to some minor modifications, most notably an improvement of cooling for the cockpit. Investigations of both trials aircraft showed that there had been no significant effect on the airframe's condition, and the RAF concluded that the Vampire would therefore be suitable for use in the ground attack role overseas, with fighter or reconnaissance purely as a secondary role. In July 1948, No. 32 Squadron at Nicosia and No. 73 Squadron at Ta' Qali (Malta) re-equipped with the Vampire Mk 3 and became the first operational jet fighter squadrons outside continental Europe.

By the time that the RAF adopted the Meteor as its preferred jet fighter type, de Havilland was already developing the Vampire's abilities in the ground attack role, as both the manufacturer and the RAF had already identified this role as one that the aircraft would be suited to. Indeed, the first signs of official interest in this role had been expressed in 1946 when the Air Ministry stated that the Vampire 'might not meet all our requirements as a Ground Attack type [but that] it is a useful step in the transition to the use of jet aircraft in the role'.

Eventually, this interest culminated in the issuing of Air Staff Requirement OR.237 for a derivative of the Vampire, designed to replace the Hawker Tempest in RAF service. This effectively changed the Vampire's role from one of a fighter to that of a 'fighter-bomber', which effectively meant that although the aircraft would retain the capabilities of an interceptor, it would be assigned almost exclusively to the ground attack role. Furthermore, the new Requirement also specified that the aircraft would be capable of deployment worldwide, using cannon or rocket projectiles for low-level and dive bombing. De Havilland calculated that the Vampire could carry a single 1,000 lb HE bomb under each wing or a combination of two 500 lb bombs and eight 60 lb rocket projectiles, together with the internally housed four 20 mm cannon. The switch to attack operations required some redesign of the wing structure so that external stores could be carried. Some wing stringers were doubled, while the upper wing skin was thickened. The wing tips were also reshaped to a more squared-off style, reducing overall span by one foot at each tip, so that low-level manoeuvrability could be improved slightly, albeit at the expense of altitude performance (which was no longer deemed to be as important).

The new ground attack derivative was to have been based on the Vampire F Mk 4, a design already under development. It was to have been powered by the Rolls-Royce Nene engine, but the 3,000 lb Goblin was eventually chosen for the new Vampire derivative in preference to the Nene, chiefly because the latter engine was 300 lb heavier and would therefore require additional ballast in the aircraft's nose in order to retain pitch stability. However, the Mk 4 development programme did not proceed smoothly, and the troubled project was affected still further when the interest of potential export customers in Canada and France also evaporated. Eventually the RAF also opted to abandon its order for the Mk 4. This left the issue of a ground attack Vampire to be addressed. The RAF proposed that the existing Vampire F Mk 3 could be modified to incorporate many of the proposed changes that had been planned for the Mk 4, and this plan was eventually adopted as Specification F.3/47 for a 'Ground Attack Version of the Vampire Mk III', which was duly designated as the Vampire FB Mk 5.

As part of the plan to re-role the Vampire as a ground attack aircraft, ejection seats were to have been fitted to the Mk 5, but the Vampire's cockpit was small by any standards and with a lateral clearance of only 22 inches it simply was not possible to accommodate an ejection seat safely. The only practical solution was to create a new metal fuselage and this was tested on Vampire Mk 1 TG338, but the cost and delays associated with such a major redesign programme did not thrill the RAF so the concept was dropped. De Havilland did not abandon the idea entirely, however, and after a great deal of work with Martin-Baker, an ejection seat system was successfully introduced on the Vampire Mk 6, destined for export to Switzerland. VT818 (an F Mk 3 derivative) was eventually re-manufactured to FB Mk 5 standard and flew as the prototype of this new version

FB Mk 5 VV217 is one of very few single-seat Vampires to have survived almost intact to the present day. It currently resides with the North East Aviation Museum in Sunderland.

on 23 June 1948. Deliveries to RAF squadrons began in December 1948, the new variant eventually becoming the standard equipment of no fewer than nineteen operational squadrons both in the UK and Germany.

The FB Mk 5 proved to be a useful and reliable ground attack aircraft, but in Germany the aircraft was still required to perform fighter operations as well and it did not take too long before the RAF was eagerly looking for another aircraft that could successfully counter the new breed of MiG fighters emerging on the other side of the Iron Curtain. Fighter Command re-equipped with Meteors by September 1952, but the RAuxAF continued to fly the aircraft until it disbanded in March 1957.

Meanwhile, the Vampire FB Mk 5 reached the Middle East and Far East squadrons and they had completely re-equipped with the Mk 5 by the summer of 1951. Despite the tropical trials that had been conducted, the Vampire was (as had been feared) less than ideal for operations in the hot conditions of the Middle East, or the humid conditions found in Hong Kong. Almost as if the trials had achieved nothing, the Vampires soon exhibited problems climbing to altitude, thanks to the effect of high temperatures on the Goblin engine. Cracked canopies and windscreens also appeared, usually caused by the rapid shift from the baking heat of the airfield to the ice cold of high-altitude flight. Worse still, conditions inside the tiny cockpit were almost unbearable for Vampire pilots. Temperatures could reach 165 degrees Fahrenheit inside the cockpit if a pilot was obliged to

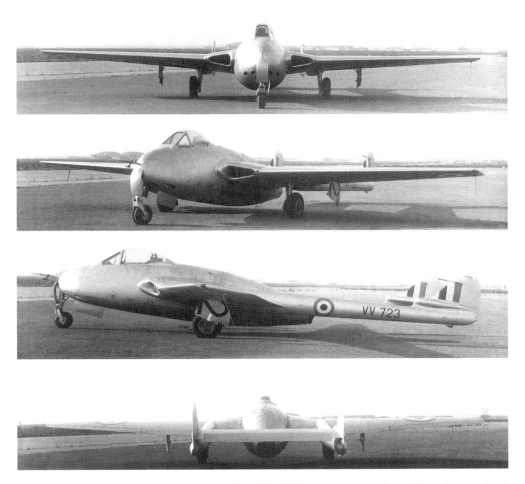

A series of images showing Vampire FB Mk 5 VV723 from various angles. Although completed with RAF insignia and serials, this aircraft was subsequently exported to France.

stay on the ground with a closed canopy. Flying conditions were little better, and as part of the 1948 trials, Flt Lt John Wilson reported:

> Below 5,000 feet at high speed, the cockpit temperature became excessive, rising to 135 degrees Fahrenheit at 500 mph (435 knots) IAS. This heat was the cause of much discomfort to the pilot and must adversely affect his flying ability. It is thought that nothing can be done to cure this high temperature trouble, which is primarily caused by skin friction heating, until refrigeration equipment is carried.

By October 1949, de Havilland (working with Sir George Godfrey & Partners) had found a means of installing a refrigeration system that promised to cool the cockpit to an acceptable level. Vampire VV675 was taken from short-term storage at Kemble and modified to incorporate a cold air unit within the starboard wing root (necessitating the alteration of the intake and the extension of the intake fillet by some 8 inches). The equipment was duly tested and appeared to work well but it had to demonstrate its capability in the conditions found overseas, so the aircraft was flown to Khartoum, from where trials were conducted in September 1950. The results were satisfactory but not perfect. Cockpit temperature came down to an acceptable level but the noise of the cold air system operating at pressure was so high that pilots could barely hear radio transmissions. The best comment that one evaluation pilot could offer was that the system was 'a step in the right direction' but it was duly recommended that the system should be retrofitted to the Vampire Mk 5.

Although the cockpit cooling problem was at least partially solved, the persistent appearance of cracked windscreens and canopy hoods was another issued that needed to be addressed, together with the inevitable misting that occurred at altitudes of 15,000 feet or more. The Perspex sandwich construction allowed condensation to form between the two layers and of course the pilot was often unable to remove it, and a great deal of time and effort was wasted simply trying to achieve a decent view, which could usually only be achieved by constant fiddling with the cockpit heating controls. Landings were often made with one hand on the control column and the other on the windscreen, wiping away condensation. Clearly, something had to be done and a new single-skin design was developed and tested on VV675. This, together with a new air system and cold air unit, became the basis for the Vampire FB Mk 9, this variant being introduced into Vampire production late in 1951, with WG848 becoming the first production example.

This – the final derivative of the basic Vampire airframe – eventually replaced many, but not all, of the RAF's Vampire FB Mk 5 aircraft in front-line service. However, its operational life was fairly short, as plans were soon under way for the introduction of more capable aircraft in the shape of the Venom and the F-86, and by 1959 the very last Mk 9 had been withdrawn, marking the end of the RAF's association with the single-seat Vampire. It had been a relatively short and often troubled relationship, but the Vampire had been a useful step along a path towards more capable jet fighters, and had also afforded the RAF a very useful opportunity to introduce jet power into an equally important role for which the Vampire had certainly not been envisaged when it first appeared. But even the withdrawal of the last FB Mk 9 was not the end of the Vampire's operational history; in fact, it was only the end of just one facet of a much wider story.

Although most of de Havilland's resources were devoted to production of aircraft for the RAF, the company naturally had a commercial interest in potential export orders for its products too. Various potential export models of the Vampire were proposed and some were of course manufactured and sold, although most were essentially minor variations of the basic single-seat fighter design. However, de Havilland also developed a potential night fighter version of the Vampire, largely in response to interest from Egypt. The aircraft was designed to employ the AI Mk 10 radar as fitted to the RAF's fleet of Mosquito night fighters, and as

Vampire FB Mk 5 VV217 banks to port, illustrating the nose-mounted gun ports and the clean, uncluttered undersurfaces, broken only by small bulged fairings over the main landing gear wheels.

Vampire FB Mk 9 WL562 joined the RAF in 1952. It is pictured here with WX207, WL615 and WX218 over the Egyptian desert whilst operating with No. 213 Squadron, based at RAF Deversoir in the Suez Canal Zone. WL562 was withdrawn during 1957 and sold for scrap at Shawbury.

Vampire FB Mk 9s from No. 8 Squadron over the British Protectorate of Aden in 1955. No. 8
Squadron operated Vampires from December 1952 until 1955, when they were exchanged for
Venoms.

the Vampire's fuselage nacelle was almost identical in diameter to the Mosquito,
the de Havilland design team naturally simplified the design process by adopting
the same cockpit layout as the Mosquito, complete with a navigator and radar
operator position placed slightly behind the pilot. The Vampire's fuselage nacelle
was lengthened by 3 feet 10 inches so that the Mosquito radar unit could be
comfortably housed ahead of the cockpit in a glass fibre nose cone. Unusually, the
nose section was not detachable and access to the radar unit was to be achieved
via two access panels located either side of the nose. In all other respects the
night fighter Vampire was essentially unchanged from the existing single-seat
design. The same wing structure was used and the aircraft retained the same
internal armament fit of four Hispano 20 mm cannon. The bulky radar equipment
increased the aircraft's weight, and in order to compensate for this, the engine fit
was changed to the Goblin Mk 3, designed to develop 3,350 lb of thrust. Two
prototypes were manufactured and the first of these (G-5-2) made its first flight on
28 August 1959 at Hatfield, with test pilot Geoffrey Pike at the controls. The night
fighter's rather portly appearance earned it the nickname 'Pike's Pig', although the
aircraft performed rather more adequately than this name might imply. Even with
radar gear and an additional pilot, the aircraft was still manoeuvrable, and thanks

to the longer fuselage and more powerful engine, it was in fact slightly faster than its predecessors.

Egypt placed an order for the type (the DH.113), but with relations between Egypt and Israel deteriorating rapidly, the British Government stepped in and placed an embargo on sales of military hardware to Middle East countries. However, the Ministry of Aircraft Production had maintained an interest in the night fighter Vampire project from the start, and it was proposed that the aircraft being manufactured for Egypt should be transferred directly to the RAF. In typical British fashion, a Specification was duly written around the aircraft (even though it had already been designed and was under construction), outlining an 'Interim Night Fighter' with an endurance at 30,000 feet of at least 2 hours, a crew of two, four 20 mm cannon and provision for the carriage of bombs. Ejection seats were not specified, even though the redesigned cockpit was obviously capable of accommodating them. This was probably because the Vampire NF Mk 10 was regarded as only a short-term purchase, plugging a gap between the withdrawal of the ageing Mosquito night fighters and the new Meteor night fighters that were being manufactured. It could be argued that the Vampire NF Mk 10 was hardly worth purchasing at all, and it seems clear that the order was essentially a political move to negate the commercial damage caused by the imposition of the arms embargo.

The first aircraft reached RAF units in the summer of 1951, with No. 25 Squadron at West Malling becoming the first operational unit with this type. The aircraft was liked by its pilots although there was some concern that the Vampire's single engine was hardly ideal for interception sorties that often took the crews far out over the North Sea. Likewise, the lack of ejection seats was a concern, but the Vampire was an agile and relatively fast machine, and one that could be more than a match for most bomber types that it intercepted. It could even compete with other fighter aircraft in the right circumstances, sometimes out-turning USAF F-86 Sabres at low level. But it could not match the capabilities of the new Canberra bomber (but then, neither could the Meteor) and its radar equipment was undoubtedly obsolescent (being little changed from the wartime equivalent).

With Meteor NF Mk 11 aircraft slowly emerging from the production line, the Vampire NF Mk 10 was soon redundant and it was replaced in RAF service from 1953. However, the aircraft were not abandoned, as the RAF had a growing requirement for navigation training that could be conducted at more realistic high speeds and include manoeuvring that would be more representative of operational conditions. The relatively 'new' Vampires were ideal candidates for the job and Airwork was contracted to convert thirty-six aircraft to NF(T) Mk 10 standard, the work being undertaken at Speke Airport. The radar equipment was removed and replaced by concrete ballast, but the cannon armament was retained in order to maintain the aircraft's centre of gravity. Navigation and radio equipment was improved and the heavy framed cockpit canopy was replaced by a new clear-view design that afforded much better visibility and could be opened far more easily. These Vampires re-entered RAF service during the summer of 1955, remaining

Prototype Vampire NF Mk 10 G-5-2 pictured in flight during September 1950. Clearly visible is the original metal-framed canopy, featuring an upper 'lid' which hinged upwards to enable crew access.

Vampire NF Mk 10 WM659 enjoyed only a brief service life with the RAF before being sold back to de Havilland prior to being exported to India.

active for some four years with No. 2 Air Navigation School at Thorney Island, after which they were replaced by converted Meteors. The NF(T) Mk 10 was also operated by the Central Navigation and Control School at Shawbury, and No. 1 Air Navigation School at Topcliffe.

By the end of 1959, the last of these aircraft had been withdrawn, and this effectively marked the end of the Vampire fighter's service history with the RAF. Beyond this date, the Vampire was far from forgotten, however, as the aircraft remained in use with many RAF units as an advanced trainer and as a versatile 'general duties' type. De Havilland developed a twin-seat trainer version of the Vampire as a private venture (work on which began in 1950), using the night fighter fuselage as the basis for the new design. By lowering the canopy side rails the cockpit width was extended to 44 inches, enabling proper side-by-side seating to be installed. A new nose fairing was devised to replace the radar nose, and this incorporated a hinged section so that radio sets, a camera, oxygen bottles and batteries could be housed inside. The cannon armament was retained not only in order to retain the aircraft's centre of gravity but so that the aircraft could be used as an operational trainer, suitable for weapons training. This was a wise move that made the aircraft a much more useful export model.

The dual-control variant, Vampire T Mk 11, performed satisfactorily but suffered from a few deficits that de Havilland swiftly rectified. The twin rudders were prone to over-balancing and often required full travel at low speeds. Spin recovery was poor too, and it was clear that (once again) the tail unit needed to be redesigned. Vampire WZ466 was used as a trials aircraft for modified fins that had the familiar bullet fairings removed and the tailplane structure extended outboard either side of the fins. The fin area was increased slightly and extended forwards onto the tail boom. This modification was only partially successful and although some aircraft entered RAF service in this partially modified form, most were subject to a more satisfactory modification that saw the fin leading edge extended still further, resulting in a smooth and rather elegant leading edge that slowly blended into the tail boom. The clumsy framed canopy was also changed in favour of the clear-view canopy adopted for the NF Mk 10, and ejection seats were fitted – a vital asset for an aircraft dedicated to training.

Eventually, a staggering 526 Vampire T Mk 11 aircraft were built for the RAF, most being built at Hawarden, with further examples being completed at Christchurch, Hatfield and even Ringway and Cambridge. The versatility and reliability of the T Mk 11 can be illustrated by the fact that it was not withdrawn from RAF service until January 1972, when the very last examples departed from No. 3 CAACU at Exeter. Even this was not the complete end of the Vampire's association with the RAF, as XH304 was retained by the Central Flying School and eventually became part of the 'Vintage Pair' display team, with Meteors WA669 and WF791. Tragically, the aircraft was destroyed on 26 May 1986, when it was involved in a collision with WA669 at Mildenhall.

Of course, the Royal Navy was also a major air arm in its own right, and the Admiralty watched the development of jet power with great interest. During

Prototype Vampire T Mk 11 G-5-7, pictured shortly after its maiden flight from Christchurch on 15 November 1950, in the hands of test pilot John Wilson.

1944, a feasibility study was conducted, looking at the suitability of jet-powered aircraft for carrier operations. Although it might seem logical to assume that jet aircraft would be perfectly suited to this kind of environment, the Admiralty was not so sure. For example, jet fighters were unlikely to accelerate as quickly as their piston counterparts and this would obviously be a risk during catapult launches or go-around take-off procedures. Likewise, the limited endurance of jet aircraft would be an issue when carrier operations often required aircraft to stay aloft for long periods without any means of recovery. There were other potential problems too, but it was decided to perform some dummy deck trials at Hatfield, using Vampire LZ551 for the tests. The aircraft was modified for deck operations and the aircraft's flap area was increased by 40 per cent, by extending the flaps under the engine nacelle. The dive brakes were also extended chord-wise, by 8 inches. This enabled the Vampire to achieve a lower stalling speed and helped to eliminate the aircraft's tendency to 'float' in ground effect shortly before touchdown.

The RAE's Aerodynamics Flight, based at Farnborough, was commanded by the legendary test pilot Lt-Cdr Eric 'Winkle' Brown. He was tasked with making these first deck landings, and he reported that the aircraft handled well and would be suitable for further trials, if the Vampire was modified to incorporate a tail arrestor hook. A suitable hook modification was fitted at de Havilland's Christchurch factory and LZ551 returned to Farnborough in October 1945 to undertake more thorough dummy deck landing trials. The initial tests were delayed after hook testing on Farnborough's runway resulted in the hook assembly separating from the Vampire's wing root, necessitating a return to Christchurch for repairs and strengthening. This delay also enabled the aircraft's Goblin engine to be replaced by a more powerful Goblin Mk 2 delivering 3,000 lb of thrust, and afforded an opportunity to replace the cockpit canopy with a later 'teardrop' component. The fin-mounted pitot head was also moved to the port wing to avoid position errors when flying at large angles of attack. Once the aircraft was returned to the RAE it was quickly transferred to RNAS Ford to conduct yet more dummy deck tests on the Fleet Air Arm facilities that were already in use at that airfield. There was a certain sense of urgency, as rumours were circulating that the Lockheed P-80 was being modified for possible naval use, and the Royal Navy was keen to try and ensure that the world's first aircraft carrier landing by a jet aircraft should be a British achievement.

It was 3 December when the first aircraft carrier landing was attempted. HMS *Ocean* was cruising off the Isle of Wight and at 11.05 Eric Brown got airborne from RNAS Ford in LZ551, arriving overhead HMS *Ocean* just a matter of minutes later. He performed a low pass over the aircraft carrier and then settled onto an approach at a speed of 100 knots. Seconds later the diminutive Vampire gently touched down on HMS *Ocean* and the aircraft's tail hook picked up the No. 1 arrestor wire. The arrival was uneventful and Brown proceeded to repeat the procedure twice more. The fourth attempt was less successful, however, and as the aircraft touched down the port wing was slightly low, causing the trailing edge of the wing flap to hit the deck and shear its hinge brackets. The flap structure was modified as a result, cutting away part of the flap to increase wing-down clearance. Further tests proved satisfactory and the Vampire went on to make more landings on board HMS *Triumph* in June 1946.

Eric Brown had reported that the Vampire might not be suitable for regular service use as deck landings required a certain degree of skill and experience that might not be possessed by regular squadron pilots. However, handling trials conducted by the A&AEE were more positive, and the test pilots concluded that despite the relatively low power of the Vampire's engine, the tricycle undercarriage and excellent forward view from the cockpit more than compensated for this. The Vampire also enabled the test pilots to introduce the concept of landing with full power (or almost full power) applied – something that would have been almost suicidal for a piston-engine aircraft. Making arrested landings with a good reserve of power still applied ensured that if the arrestor wires were missed by the hook, the aircraft could continue ahead and climb away without any risk of 'wallowing' at low speed until power wound up. This clearly would make deck landings a far safer proposition than they ever had been in piston-engine machines.

However, despite the Vampire's qualified success as a carrier-capable aircraft, the Admiralty concluded that it would never be suitable for operational use, chiefly because its engine did not deliver an acceptable amount of acceleration and because the aircraft had insufficient range. But it was agreed that the Vampire

Historical movie stills of the first deck
landing of a jet aircraft. Vampire LZ551
touches down on HMS *Ocean* on 3
December 1945.

could be acquired to act as a training aircraft, used for the task of introducing naval pilots to jet-powered aviation. Specifications 45/46P and 46/46P were issued on 14 January 1947 for what became the Sea Vampire F Mk 20. Some eighteen aircraft were eventually produced, converted from standard Vampire FB Mk 5 airframes but with the addition of tail hooks, redesigned dive brakes and wing flaps, an improved undercarriage and a revised radio fit. Delivery of the first aircraft was achieved in October 1948, and the Sea Vampire went on to become a familiar part of Fleet Air Arm operations, although, as had been agreed, the aircraft was never embraced as an operational type. It enabled the Royal Navy to introduce its pilots to jet operations both on land (where many standard 'non-navalised' Vampires were also used) and on aircraft carriers, where the skills peculiar to jet operations could be practised.

Despite the misgivings of Eric Brown and others, the Sea Vampire was operated from carriers without any major difficulties, although without the assistance of catapults, take-offs were always something of a struggle for an aircraft with relatively little available thrust. It was this deficiency that persuaded the Admiralty to pursue a particularly bizarre concept of operating the Vampire without undercarriage, enabling the aircraft to become substantially lighter, with better range and acceleration. Three Vampire F Mk 1 aircraft were modified for trials at Farnborough, and numerous landings were duly made on the rubber 'mattress' deck set up on the airfield. The first landings were certainly exciting, but approach techniques were soon adopted that enabled the Vampire to be recovered onto the 'flexible deck' without any difficulties, and further trials were conducted on HMS *Warrior*. Although the landings were made without the use of undercarriage, the take-offs were all performed normally with the landing gear extended, and although the concept clearly worked, it did not address the issues of how the aircraft could be launched, or handled on deck, without the use of complicated trolley and crane systems. Eventually, the cost of the projected concept encouraged the Admiralty to lose interest in it, especially when engine development soon offered far more reserves of power that rendered such wild ideas unnecessary.

The Sea Vampire was certainly a very important aircraft in the history of the Fleet Air Arm, not only because it introduced the concept of jet power but because it also introduced countless pilots to a whole new era of high-performance operations. The aircraft also enabled the Fleet Air Arm to develop a mirror landing system that became standard for carrier operations, and it was no surprise that the Royal Navy also embraced the Vampire T Mk 11 dual-control aircraft for advanced and tactical training. The naval version of this aircraft was designated as the Sea Vampire T Mk 22.

The final expression of the Vampire's development potential created an aircraft that was so different from the original design that it eventually earned itself a new name. Its origins lay within the 1947 trials with Vampire TG278 that was fitted with a Ghost engine used to achieve a record altitude of 59,446 feet. De Havilland concluded that with a new Ghost 103 engine (delivering 4,850 lb thrust) the Vampire could be developed into a much better aircraft, particularly if the existing

Sea Vampire VV419 about to disappear into the carrier hangar, courtesy of the deck lift. As can be seen, the Vampire could comfortably be accommodated on the lift without any need for wing, tail or nose folding mechanisms.

Sea Vampire F Mk 21 VT802 conducted Flexible deck trials on board HMS *Warrior* in February 1949. It is pictured after having made a standard recovery with landing gear extended.

Pictured in 1945 before being delivered to the RAF, TG278 illustrates the Vampire's compact design, built around the Goblin engine, and the (relatively) excellent view afforded to the pilot.

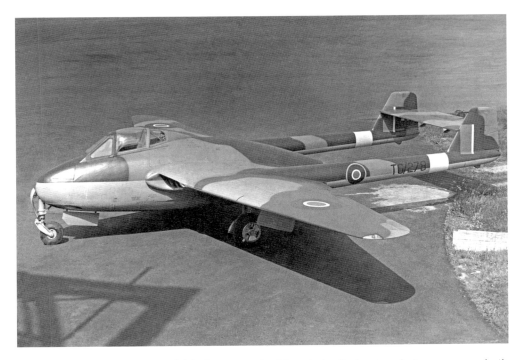

This view of TG278 at Hatfield illustrates the Vampire's diminutive design concept, built around the Goblin engine. Just visible is a gun port, above the nosewheel bay door.

wing design was abandoned in favour of a thinner and reshaped layout. This resulted in Operational Requirement No. 277 for a 'Thin Wing Vampire' powered by a Ghost engine. The existing Vampire single-seat fuselage was capable of accommodating the slightly larger Ghost engine; therefore the key change to the new design was the adoption of a completely different wing that incorporated a swept leading edge, a reduced thickness/chord ratio, and other refinements such as small fences. Perhaps most noticeable was the incorporation of external fuel tanks, mounted in detachable wingtip pods. It was estimated that the aircraft would be capable of achieving better altitude and a faster speed of around 650 mph, and the aircraft's tail structure was strengthened in order to handle this projected capability. Two aircraft were produced as prototypes of what was the Vampire FB Mk 8, but VV612 and VV613 (DH.112 models) were so different from their predecessors that de Havilland opted to bestow a new name on the aircraft, and as such they became the first examples of the Venom FB Mk 1.

Test pilot John Derry took VV612 into the air for the first time on 2 September 1949, and after initial evaluation at Boscombe Down the aircraft was modified to incorporate lighter ailerons and elevators, and minor alterations were made to the air brake and flaps. The Venom entered service in August 1952, by which stage the aircraft had been largely assigned to the ground attack role, after Fighter Command had opted to use the Meteor as its standard fighter type. Venoms duly went to RAF squadrons in Germany, the Middle East and Far East and the aircraft were eagerly accepted by the RAF crews, who were keen to get their hands on a Vampire derivative with a measurably better performance. The Venom performed well, although problems with the integrity of the wing structure resulted in limitations being placed on the aircraft's use until modifications could be made. A number of accidents arose as a direct result of the wing problems, including the loss of WE368 when its starboard wing ripped off during a pull-out manoeuvre. Thankfully, the Venom was equipped with an ejection seat and its pilot parachuted to safety. Despite this period of difficulty, the Venom was regarded as a success and it was developed into the FB Mk 4, with power-operated ailerons, redesigned rudders, provision for underwing fuel tanks and other minor modifications. This variant gradually replaced the earlier Mk 1 and the type remained in use until the early 1960s, by which time the RAF was moving on to more advanced aircraft such as the Hunter. But just as the basic Vampire airframe had been developed into a larger twin-seat night fighter, the Venom was also subjected to the same process, resulting in an aircraft that incorporated the same modifications that had been applied to the 'interim' night fighter Vampire NF Mk 10.

The result was the Venom NF Mk 2, and the prototype aircraft (G-5-3) was flown for the first time by Derry on 22 August 1950. As with the night fighter Vampire, the new Venom derivative incorporated the same larger cockpit structure and the Mosquito-type radome. The prototype was given the serial WP227 and it went to Boscombe Down for handling trials in 1951. It flew fairly well and produced no unpleasant surprises, although the A&AEE test pilots were critical of the lack of ejection seats, especially when Venom FB Mk 1 was fitted with this

The second Venom prototype was VV613, pictured here in overall silver finish. Completed in February 1949, it was assigned to test duties until 1953 when it was relegated to ground training duties at Arbroath.

The first production Venom, WE255, pictured whilst assigned to A&AEE Boscombe Down, on weapons release trials.

form of escape system. Various handling criticisms were swiftly addressed by de Havilland, not least the trim change problems experienced as speed increased. The cause was the canopy structure, as the radar operator's canopy side panel was bulged, while the pilot's was not, and it was hardly surprising that this asymmetric design affected handling. A new symmetrical canopy was introduced and the first production Venom NF Mk 2 took to the air in March 1952, with No. 23 Squadron at Coltishall becoming the first (and indeed only) Venom NF Mk 2 operational squadron. The aircraft had a troubled service life, marred by an initial period of restrictions after further wing structural weaknesses were discovered, and the air crew's perception that the canopy was unsuitable to rapid emergency egress. (In fact, they wanted ejection seats.) De Havilland introduced modifications to both the wing and tail structure and the canopy design was changed, resulting in the Venom NF Mk 2A, and this variant entered service in April 1955 with No. 253 squadron at Waterbeach. Two more squadrons adopted the aircraft, but within two years they had relinquished the NF Mk 2A, as by this stage the Venom had been refined still further into the NF Mk 3.

This variant had a more powerful (4,950 lb) Ghost engine, a reshaped radome, improved AI Mk 21 radar, a clear canopy, revised tailplane design, and power ailerons. It entered RAF service with No. 141 Squadron at Coltishall in June 1955, but like all of the Venom night fighter variants, it remained in use for a remarkably short period of time. With more capable Meteor night fighters becoming available and the Javelin on the way, the Venoms were regarded only as a short-term solution to the RAF's needs, and by the end of 1961 they had all been withdrawn.

It could be argued that they were an expensive and unnecessary purchase, but it is important to remember that at this stage in Britain's post-war history, the RAF was facing a huge burden of commitments across the globe, and as the Cold War grew ever colder, even short-term equipment programmes were deemed essential. The Venom was a small part of the Vampire's story, but it was certainly an important one.

However, even if the Venom was not a particularly significant part of the RAF's history, the aircraft did play a very important part in the post-war history of the Royal Navy's Fleet Air Arm. The Senior Service maintained a keen interest in the development of jet engine power, and the carrier trials with Vampire fighters had served to illustrate that even if the Vampire was not really suited to the maritime environment, the concept of carrier-borne jet operations was valid if more suitable aeroplanes could be designed for the roles than had hitherto been handled by piston-engine aircraft.

The Royal Navy eventually opted to re-equip its carriers with Sea Vixen fighters, but until this mighty machine could be properly designed and developed there was a shorter-term need for an 'interim' jet fighter that would enable the Fleet Air Arm to relinquish the Hornet. In truth, the Hornet was an excellent machine and the Navy's enthusiasm for adopting first-generation jet aircraft to replace it was possibly premature, but no matter how good the Hornet was, it was inevitably

Venom NF Mk 3 WX787 was assigned to A&AEE at Boscombe Down for manufacturer's trials. Visible on this photograph is the modified tail section with the outer tailplane extensions removed. Also visible is the modified clear canopy hood.

An unusual nose-on view of Venom WE255, illustrating clearly the wing root air intakes and the aerodynamic bullet fairings under the fin structure. Also visible is the gun port under the port nose area.

regarded as being obsolescent simply because it had propellers and was of course a direct descendant of the wartime Mosquito. The Navy gathered a great deal of experience with the Vampire and also evaluated the Venom NF Mk 2 (WP227) during February 1951.

The Admiralty concluded that a navalised version of the Venom could be adopted as a twin-seat, all-weather fighter capable of operating from carriers. Specification N.107 was issued and in response to this de Havilland swiftly redesigned the Venom NF Mk 2 into the NF Mk 20, complete with arrestor hook, folding wings, catapult pick-up lugs, an improved undercarriage and enlarged tail bumpers. Other less obvious alterations included fixed wingtip fuel tanks (with a slightly revised shape) and, once again, a redesigned vertical tail. The Ghost 103 was selected as the engine for the new variant and three prototypes were duly manufactured, the first of these (WK376) taking to the air on 19 April 1951 as the first Sea Venom NF Mk 20 (later changed to FAW Mk 20, as a more accurate description of its all-weather role).

By July 1951, this aircraft was performing deck landing trials both at Boscombe Down and on board HMS *Illustrious*. The aircraft demonstrated various potential problems, not least inadequate elevator authority and a possible need for aileron trimmers. The test pilots also regarded the metal-framed cockpit canopy as being unsuitable for rapid emergency egress, and of course they also deplored the lack of ejection seats fitted to the twin-seat Venom series. After modifications, further trials were undertaken, the aircraft performed almost flawlessly, and an initial order for fifty Sea Venoms was placed. These aircraft were built to an initial standard that varied from other aircraft, most noticeably in the provision of the same metal-framed canopy used on the RAF's Venom NF Mk 2A and without ejection seats. M.L. Aviation devised an underwater canopy jettison system that would blow off the canopy if the aircraft ditched. It was hardly a substitute for the safety of ejection seats, but it did at least offer some chance of escape if a carrier landing or launch went wrong.

By the summer of 1954, the first Sea Venoms had entered Fleet Air Arm service (with No. 890 Naval Air Squadron at Yeovilton) and this unit embarked on HMS *Albion* the following year. Sadly, the Navy's early experience with the Sea Venom was plagued by problems, partly caused by undercarriage weakness but most notably by continual arrestor hook failures that resulted in many aircraft ditching into the sea. Despite modifications, the problem persisted and eventually the Navy was forced to withdraw the aircraft from carrier operations. The hapless Sea Venoms were relegated to land-based training duties and work began on addressing the aircraft's potentially lethal deficiencies.

The result was the Sea Venom FAW Mk 21, powered by a 4,950 lb Goblin 104, with a longer-stroke (and stronger) undercarriage, a strengthened arrestor hook, non-skid brakes, a raised pilot's seat affording a better forward view, a new, clear canopy bulged to accommodate the raised pilot's seat and, perhaps most significantly, two Martin-Baker Mk 4 ejection seats. A batch of 99 aircraft was built at Christchurch, with the first production example (WM568) flying before

Prototype Sea Venom was WK376. Pictured here without the wing tip tanks that were standard to all Sea Venoms, it also featured Vampire-type fin structures that were subsequently modified for production-standard aircraft.

The first Sea Venom NF Mk 20 was destroyed during a high-speed run over Farnborough on 27 August 1952. The accident was caused by a detached elevator trim tab.

No. 890 NAS Sea Venom NF Mk 21 WW223 proudly displays the unit's emblem. This unit briefly operated a three-aircraft Venom aerobatic display team which appeared at venues across the UK.

Sea Venom prototype WK376 pictured during early carrier trials. The large wing fences are clearly visible together with the small leading edge modifications adjacent to the wingtip fuel tanks. Also visible is the tail hook fairing extending from the rear fuselage.

the prototype (XA539), on 22 April 1954. The reintroduction of the Sea Venom was successful this time, and three aircraft were soon allocated to Blue Jay missile trials, this weapon eventually becoming the Firestreak. The Sea Venom was not designed to use air-to-air missiles but as a trials aircraft it performed well, and live launches were made against Fireflies off Malta, with the three Venoms operating from HMS *Albion*. The exercise proved the capabilities of the missile and validated the concept of operating AAMs as part of the carrier force, therefore paving the way for the development of Firestreak for the Sea Vixen fighter that was to follow.

The Sea Venom FAW Mk 21 was introduced into front-line Fleet Air Arm service during May 1955, and although there were some initial problems with the troublesome tail hook, the aircraft soon settled into service. Of course, it was only a year later that the Sea Venom was to be used 'in anger' as part of Operation Musketeer (the Suez Campaign). Five Royal Navy carriers sailed to the Middle East where aircraft from HMS *Albion* (No. 809 NAS) and HMS *Eagle* (Nos 892 and 893 NAS) conducted a series of ground attack missions on Egyptian targets, starting on 30 October. Using rockets and 20 mm cannon, it was perhaps ironic that the Sea Venom fighter was actually used as a ground attack aircraft when it was called into action. The Sea Venom fleet, comprising the surviving Mk 20 aircraft and the main force of 167 FAW Mk 21 aircraft, was eventually augmented by the delivery of a further 39 Sea Venom FAW Mk 22 aircraft, these being improved versions with 5,300 lb thrust Ghost 105 engines.

As part of Operation Musketeer, Sea Venoms were deployed to the Suez region with no fewer than five Navy carriers assigned to the operation. Sea Venoms were employed on attack missions in co-operation with RAF and French units.

No. 808 NAS was a Royal Australian Navy unit, formed to operate the Sea Venom. Initially, the unit operated Fleet Air Arm aircraft for training, based at Culdrose. The unit eventually acquired its own aircraft and embarked upon HMAS *Melbourne* before sailing to Australia.

Sea Venom returns from a mission during the 1956 Suez Crisis, recovering successfully despite a malfunctioning landing gear. The in-theatre black and yellow stripes applied to all 'Allied' aircraft involved in the operation can clearly be seen.

This unusual image of a Fleet Air Arm Sea Venom on board a US Navy carrier illustrates the aircraft's asymmetric canopy hood, with a larger, bulged section to accommodate the pilot.

The Air Directors School (based at St Davids, Brawdy and finally Yeovilton) was the last British operator of the Sea Venom, its last aircraft being retired in October 1970.

A handful of Sea Venoms were also converted to ECM Mk 21 and ECM Mk 22 standard for No. 831 NAS, assigned to the Electronic Countermeasures role. Externally similar to standard Sea Venom aircraft, the cannon armament was removed and replaced by ECM equipment, together with associated controls in the cockpit. Purchased as an 'interim' aircraft, the Sea Venom enjoyed only a brief period of front-line service with the Fleet Air Arm, and by the end of 1960 the fighter had been replaced by the far more powerful and capable Sea Vixen. However, the Sea Venom continued to fly with the Royal Navy for another ten years, operated as part of the Air Directors School (the forerunner of the Fleet Requirements and Direction Unit, FRADU) under the management of Airwork Services. It was not until 1970 that the very last Royal Navy Sea Venom (XG683) was retired, making its way to Culdrose on 6 October to embark upon many more years as a ground-based training airframe.

Despite a very troubled entry into service, the Sea Venom proved to be a useful aircraft that plugged a perceived gap between the piston era and the arrival of the second-generation jet fighters. It was also the final design derived from the diminutive Vampire, a very small aeroplane that left a very big mark on aviation history.

CHAPTER THREE
All at Sea

The design and development of the Meteor and Vampire required huge resources and eventually became projects so large that both Gloster and de Havilland were obliged to transfer partial or even whole production of both aircraft types to other companies. Design and production capacity was a major issue and was the key reason why another major British manufacturer remained surprisingly detached from the early story of jet aircraft development. Hawker Aircraft Ltd was perhaps the most famous of all British aircraft manufacturers, responsible for the immortal Hurricane and many other classic types, almost all of which were fighters. It was this legacy that kept Hawker very busy, and ultimately dissuaded the company from pursuing the potential of jet power too keenly. While the Meteor and Vampire slowly emerged, Hawker Aircraft was busy developing its Tempest and Fury designs, and there simply was not capacity to devote too much attention towards anything else. However, developments taking place elsewhere were to have a direct effect upon Hawker's future.

Stanley Hooker and his team at Rolls-Royce were busy creating what eventually became the Nene engine, capable of delivering a very respectable 4,200 lb thrust that was swiftly developed to an even more impressive 5,000 lb. It was an achievement that even Hawker's Design Director Sydney Camm could not ignore, and when full details of the engine became available late in 1944, he began to investigate ways in which the engine could be used to power a fighter aircraft. The first study was Project P.1035, and this was based on a very straightforward concept of fitting the engine to the existing Fury/Sea Fury by removing the piston engine and placing the jet engine inside the fuselage. Air intakes were incorporated into the wing root and the engine exhausted through a jet pipe under the tail and rudder. With the engine placed fairly centrally, the cockpit was moved forward to the nose, but the relatively long jet exhaust pipe was judged to be potentially inefficient and a new design was drawn up, with the exhaust directed through bifurcated jet pipes, to emerge either side of the fuselage. Hawker patented this new design concept, but the Air Staff and Ministry of Aircraft Production were far from enthusiastic about the proposed design (the P.1040, submitted in February 1945). They believed that the whole idea was too advanced to pursue and showed little interest in encouraging Hawker to take it any further. But at the same time, orders for Furies and Tempests were being cancelled, and Camm opted to maintain his interest in the P.1040, even if he had to continue without official support.

By the end of 1945, Camm and his team had enough design data to begin work on a prototype aircraft, but the Air Staff still showed no interest in the idea. Their reluctance to pursue the radical bifurcated jet pipe design was only part of the reason for their indifference; the key reason was undoubtedly the existence of the Meteor, and its demonstrated ability to achieve speeds of over 600 mph. No matter how innovative Hawker's design might have been, there was little reason to embark upon a completely new programme that would create a fighter that was little better than the Meteor. Camm was disappointed but he was also determined, and Hawker Aircraft duly resolved to build a prototype with company money, as a private venture.

Luckily for Hawker, its 'go-it-alone' attitude was not necessary for too long, as the Admiralty had also been following progress with the P.1040, and it had become increasingly obvious that the aircraft ought to make a good jet fighter for the Fleet Air Arm. Hawker refined the proposed design to incorporate folding wings and a tail hook, and the Admiralty liked what it saw. The proposal was accepted and Specification N.7/46 was issued, followed by an Instruction to Proceed with three prototypes and a structural test specimen. Camm's response was perhaps predictable – 'Thank God for the Navy!'

Work on the prototype began at Hawker's famous Kingston upon Thames headquarters, with sub-assemblies being manufactured here before being transported to Langley in Buckinghamshire for final assembly. The first aircraft (VP401) was completed during 1947, and by August it was out on the airfield at Langley, making taxi runs in the hands of Hawker's Chief Test Pilot Bill Humble. There was no reason why the aircraft could not have been flown from Langley, but as the site was small and equipped only with a grass surface it was decided that the prototype should be transported to Boscombe Down, and it was from here that VP401 flew for the first time on 2 September. It was then transferred to Farnborough, chiefly because more hangar space was available there but also because Humble had reported unusual airframe vibrations, and Hawker thought a second opinion would be useful.

The ideal man to investigate was the legendary Captain Eric 'Winkle' Brown, the RAE's chief naval test pilot. After flying VP401 for some 75 minutes, Brown reported that the vibrations were probably caused by the engine exhaust fairings on the fuselage sides. By changing their shape to a streamlined 'pen nib' style, the vibrations went away. Some vibration was also due to airflow around the vertical and horizontal tail intersection, and a bullet-shaped fairing installed here cured the problem. The beautiful one-piece curved windscreen certainly looked impressive but it was not optically clear, so Hawker substituted a more conventional flat armoured windscreen that gave the test pilots a clear forward view without degrading performance. An aileron trimmer was also needed, and the control column stick force had to be adjusted so that less force was needed at high speed and more force required at low speeds. Take-off performance was also

Hawker P.1040 VP401 was completed at the company's Kingston factory and first flown from Hawker's test site at Boscombe Down.

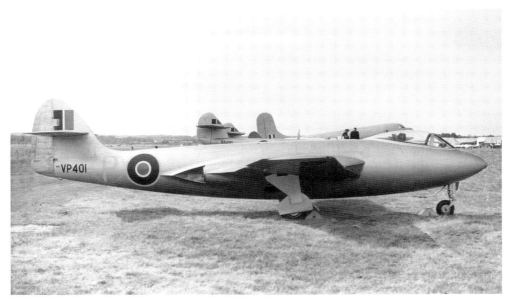

Hawker P.1040 prototype VP401 at the 1947 SBAC show at Radlett. Various Meteors are visible in the background, together with the tail of an Avro Tudor.

judged to be rather poor, but as the prototype's engine had been limited to 4,500 lb thrust it was accepted that performance would increase substantially when a production-standard 5,000 lb engine was installed. A year later, the first of the two prototypes completed to the Specification standard took to the air. VP413 flew to Farnborough just days after its first flight (which took place on 3 September 1948), but without the mandatory ten hours of flying, it was displayed only on the ground at that year's SBAC show. After the show week it went to Boscombe Down to undertake dummy deck landing trials, after which a series of real deck landings were made on board HMS *Illustrious*.

Brown subsequently commented on his initial experience with the aircraft:

I got down to the general handling and deck landing assessment of the N.7/46 prototype VP413, and what a delightful task that proved to be. VP413 had the full rated Nene of 5,000 lb static thrust and was at an all-up weight of 10,500 lb. The all-round view was excellent, although the curved windscreen side panels gave a distorted effect to anything seen through them. This was cured in production aircraft by a modified windscreen shape. The cockpit layout was first class and the seating very comfortable. For taxying, the hydraulic brakes were not so powerful as the pneumatic type on the P.1040 but were adequate to control the weathercock tendency in a crosswind. On lining up for take-off the brakes would hold the aircraft up to 11,500 rpm before they started to slip, but from that point the engine could be instantly opened up to the full 12,350 rpm without any adverse effects on the jet pipe temperature. The take-off run, even with the use of 'Take Off' flap setting of 27.5 degrees, was surprisingly long. Using two divisions of nose-up elevator trim and with the stick held fully back the nosewheel would not come off the ground until a speed of 110 mph was reached, and the unstick occurred at 120-125 mph. After unstick there was no appreciable change of trim with retraction of the undercarriage, although raising the flaps gave a strong nose-up pitch which could be quite comfortably held while re-trimming. Undercarriage retraction was rather slow. In cruising flight the ailerons were light and effective, although not so good as on the P.1040. The elevators and rudder were light and effective; stability was neutral both laterally and longitudinally, and positive directionally. The aircraft did snake in rough air, and damping was somewhat sluggish but as good as I had met on a jet to date. The all-up stall occurred at around 125 mph and was preceded by a gentle buffet at 130 mph. At the stall itself there was a gentle port wing drop of some 10-15 degrees. The all-down stall with the engine set at 10,000 rpm as for a deck landing approach displayed similar characteristics except that there was slightly less stall warning with buffeting at 110 mph before the stall occurred at 107 mph. With the flaps thus lowered to the full drag position of 86.5 there was a continuous tremor to be felt all the time before it developed into a pre-stall buffet. With the flaps in the maximum lift position of 53 degrees, the only difference in stalling characteristics was a reduction in the buffet speed to 109 mph and increase in the stalling speed to 107.5 mph and the absence of continuous tremor. Opening the hood raised the stalling speed by one knot but gave an unpleasant updraught of dirt from the cockpit floor, as well as an oppressive thrumming noise emanating from an airflow bubble around the open cockpit. This was cured in production aircraft by a modified hood shape. A reduction of 60 gallons of fuel gave a corresponding reduction of 3 mph in the stalling speed. The landing characteristics of the N.7/46 were really superb, with perfect view, good control characteristics and a soft tricycle undercarriage. In the circuit it was difficult to reduce speed as this prototype had no dive brakes, because the type to be fitted had not been decided. For this reason no dive tests were conducted on the N.7/46 although I had dived the P.1040 up to Mach 0.84 without dive brakes. It showed a progressive nose-up trim change from Mach 0.79. For deck landing the optimum approach speed was 118 mph at 10,500 lb and 115 mph at 10,000 lb and the use of full drag flap kept the engine rpm well above the Nene's 'flat spot'. In the event of a baulked landing the maximum lift flap setting could be selected instantaneously on opening the throttle by use of the flap trigger switch located on the throttle. This retraction action gave a nose-down pitch, which cancelled out the first-stage trim change. After touchdown the landing run necessitated full use of brakes, for the nosewheel could not be held off the ground by use of the elevator. At the conclusion of these tests my assessment was that the N.7/46 was undoubtedly an outstanding aircraft and certainly fit to undertake its deck landing trials even in prototype condition.

The sea trials were satisfactory, but a number of attempted landings had to be aborted when the tail hook failed to engage the carrier's arrestor wire, although the resulting 'bolters' (go-around take-offs) did at least demonstrate that the aircraft was perfectly suited to carrier operations. VP422 (the second prototype to N.7/46 standard) was duly equipped with a longer tail hook, as were all subsequent aircraft, and the wing tips were extended by 15 inches on each wing to improve take-off and landing performance with full operational gear fitted (which added substantially to the aircraft's weight).

Progress was satisfactory and during January 1949, Specification 25/48P was issued, referring to the production of an operational version of the aircraft, now named Sea Hawk. The Specification covered most of the improvements that had already been made to the design, but also outlined performance aspirations and clarified the aircraft's intended role as a day interceptor, operating from sea level to 15,000 feet, or at high level of around 35,000 feet with a combat endurance of 15 minutes. It was also necessary to have loiter capability of up to 20 minutes before landing, so that an allowance could be made for bad weather or a busy recovery period on the carrier. External (jettisonable) fuel tanks would also be included, enabling the aircraft to achieve a range of up to 560 miles. Armament would comprise four 20 mm Hispano cannon mounted in the nose under the cockpit, and rocket projectiles would be carried under the wings on the external fuel tank attachment points. The Specification also called for cartridge starting for the Nene engine, an ejection seat for the pilot, and a 'day and night' carrier landing capability, although the aircraft's potential use in anything other than daylight conditions would obviously be very limited.

The second production Hawker Sea Hawk, WF144, pictured on a test flight shortly after completion at Armstrong Whitworth's Baginton facility.

Also contained in the Specification was a limit on the aircraft's dimensions, as it would obviously have to fit inside the existing carrier hangars and deck lifts, although by this stage the proportions of the Sea Hawk were well established; therefore any stipulation of overall size was rather pointless. Meanwhile, work on the aircraft continued, although there was a delay during the summer of 1949, thanks to the National Air Races held at Elmdon (now Birmingham International Airport), an event that Britain's manufacturers keenly supported, chiefly in order to promote their products. VP401 was modified with a more powerful Nene engine for the event and test pilot Trevor Wade duly won the SBAC Challenge Cup Race, achieving a speed of 562 mph on one lap. This event marked the end of VP401's contribution to the Sea Hawk programme and after returning to Hawker it was allocated to a completely separate project.

Rocket propulsion had first been demonstrated during the Second World War (most notably in the Me 163 Komet) and the concept had been pursued with varying degrees of interest in the early post-war years. Because the early jet engines did not deliver particularly high levels of thrust, the advantages of using rocket power to augment or even replace the jet seemed clear, even though rockets required huge quantities of often very volatile fuel. Someone within the Hawker team suggested that the P.1040 could be fitted with a rocket motor relatively easily, but there simply was no suitable rocket motor available. The situation changed when the Armstrong Siddeley Snarler rocket motor emerged during 1950. Delivering 2,000 lb of thrust, the motor promised to give the 5,000 lb Nene engine a considerable boost and a motor was installed into VP401 during the summer of 1950, located in the extreme rear fuselage and emerging through an exhaust pipe situated directly under the modified rudder (much like the original plan for the Nene engine in the P.1035, in fact). A spherical fuel tank containing liquid oxygen was installed in the forward fuselage behind the cockpit, and a tank containing water and methanol was installed behind the existing jet fuel tank. The engine functioned well, and produced a long plume of flame, speckled with shock cones and accompanied by an incredibly loud roar. Thankfully, the crescendo lasted for only 3 minutes before all of the fuel was used up, but this was enough to give the aircraft a huge boost of thrust at any altitude and without any slow build-up. Thrust of 2,000 lb might not seem much, but when combined with the Nene's 5,000 lb it could have improved the aircraft's performance considerably. VP401 was redesignated as the P.1072 and made its first flight in modified form on 20 November 1950, from Bitteswell. The rocket motor was demonstrated on a series of test flights, but during one flight with test pilot Neville Duke at the controls, the engine exploded, causing major damage to the airframe. The aircraft was repaired but the test programme never resumed, chiefly because a great deal of progress was being made in engine performance and now that reheat (afterburning) concepts were also being studied, the advantages of rocket power no longer seemed quite so significant.

XE339 pictured whilst assigned to the Fleet Requirements Unit at Hurn. Visible under the wing is a Harley light pod, a modified external fuel tank incorporating a powerful light, used to enable the aircraft to be easily identified during training sorties.

The Sea Hawk made its proper public debut as a flying exhibit during the 1949 SBAC show at Farnborough, in Duke's very capable hands. By this stage, however, Hawker had also constructed the P.1052, a faster and more manoeuvrable aircraft that was in effect a Sea Hawk fuselage and tail unit fitted with 35 degree swept wings. This project had been started in 1948 in response to a Specification for a potential day fighter design, based on the 'swept-wing Sea Hawk' configuration, and as knowledge of swept-wing performance began to emerge (mostly from America), Hawker had embraced the new concept with great enthusiasm. By the time that the 1949 SBAC show approached, two examples of the P.1052 were flying, and the crowds assembled at Farnborough were treated to the sight of two new Hawker fighter designs in the air, even though it was the rather less sophisticated example that was destined for operational service.

The P.1052 demonstrated some potential but also suffered from various handling deficiencies, so the RAF was not particularly keen to pursue it. It is perhaps surprising that the Navy did not take more interest in it, but with the Sea Hawk already on its way to delivery status, the experimental nature of the P.1052 meant that translating the project into a viable fighter was likely to take some time, and the Navy had no interest in delaying the Sea Hawk's progress, especially when there was a growing perception within the Admiralty that the RAF was somehow sneaking ahead of the Navy with its new Meteors and Vampires. The P.1052 was eventually assigned to deck landing trials, but by the time that the aircraft reached this stage, the Sea Hawk was in production and it was the RAF that maintained more interest in the P.1052 and the P.1081 that was developed from it, with a new rear fuselage and tail structure, and a single engine exhaust, designed in anticipation of new engines with reheat. This eventually led to the creation of the P.1067, which became the legendary Hunter. The Navy, meanwhile, stuck with the straight-wing and relatively unremarkable Sea Hawk, presumably secure in the knowledge that a far more sophisticated fighter (with all-weather capability) would be available soon, in the shape of the de Havilland DH.100 (the Sea Vixen).

It seems clear that even before the Sea Hawk entered service it was already regarded as something of an 'interim' aircraft, destined to provide the Navy with a simple day fighter that would maintain the Fleet Air Arm's capabilities, or at least its credibility, until something rather more ambitious came along.

An order for thirty-five Sea Hawk F Mk 1 aircraft was placed late in 1949, and with the Government's 'Super Priority Programme' in progress – an overt political attempt to expedite progress on various significant aircraft programmes – Hawker was obliged to get the Sea Hawk into production as swiftly as possible. The company was in a rather odd situation: committed to the completion of Sea Fury orders and refurbishments whilst preparing to begin production of the RAF's Hunter. The Sea Hawk was somewhere in the middle of this strange spread, and with the Langley factory closing (Hawker considered the grass airfield inadequate and the development of Heathrow Airport nearby made operations there increasingly difficult) a new facility was opened at Dunsfold in Surrey. However,

Proudly wearing Lossiemouth's 'LM' tail code, WM975 is pictured with wings folded, illustrating to advantage the two-piece landing gear door arrangement.

With wings folded, XE30 heads a line-up of Sea Hawks on board HMS *Centaur*. The underwing rocket projectile rails are empty.

production capacity was still a problem, but as part of the Hawker Siddeley Group, Hawker had the option of outsourcing the Sea Hawk to Armstrong Whitworth, another Hawker Siddeley Group company that had good facilities at Coventry and Bitteswell and was in the process of completing Meteor subcontractor production. Completion of the Sea Hawk's design and production of the F Mk 1 was therefore transferred to Armstrong Whitworth's Baginton factory at Coventry, with final assembly taking place at Bitteswell. However, the initial batch of Sea Hawks was completed at Dunsfold and it was from there that the first F Mk 1 (WF413) made its maiden flight on 14 November 1951. Numerous examples of the initial batch of F Mk 1 aircraft were retained by Hawker for testing and acceptance trials, and although the aircraft exhibited no significant problems, the introduction of power-assisted ailerons was felt necessary. A suitable system was introduced on WF147, the fifth production aircraft, and as such it effectively became the prototype of what was to be the Sea Hawk F Mk 2.

A further contract for sixty Sea Hawk F Mk 1 aircraft was placed directly with Armstrong Whitworth, and the first of these aircraft made its maiden flight in December 1952. The first of the Hawker-built aircraft entered Fleet Air Arm service during March 1953, with No. 806 NAS at Brawdy, with further aircraft going to No. 898 NAS at the same base. Lossiemouth also became a Sea Hawk base, No. 804 NAS re-forming there during November under the command of Lt-Cdr Eric 'Winkle' Brown. Meanwhile, construction of Armstrong Whitworth-built machines continued, and development of the Sea Hawk progressed. The F Mk 2 reflected the need for power-boosted ailerons with spring feel to counter lateral control problems encountered under some conditions in the F Mk 1. A batch of 20 aircraft was ordered, and the first of these (WF240) took to the air on 24 February 1954, from Bitteswell. They duly entered service with Nos 802 and 807 NAS and proved to be successful, although they were in effect only a step towards what became the definitive Sea Hawk variant, the FB Mk 3.

In much the same way that the Sea Venom was acquired as a fighter and subsequently re-roled to undertake ground attack duties, the Sea Hawk followed the same path. This was not a reflection of the Sea Hawk's capabilities; in fact, the aircraft was regarded as an agile and fairly fast machine, liked by all the pilots who flew it. But the Navy needed much more than fighters, especially when the larger proportion of its operational commitments inevitably required aircraft with an attack capability rather than merely the capacity to intercept other aircraft. Although it was unlikely that a ground attack aircraft could be adopted for the fighter role, the reverse situation was far more practical, so it was inevitable that the Sea Hawk's abilities would be developed to embrace a wider capacity for undertaking attack missions. Some 116 Sea Hawk FB Mk 3 aircraft were ordered, these being essentially similar to the Mk 2 but with strengthened wings that could carry external fuel tanks, sea mines and 1,000 lb bombs or rocket projectiles in addition to the standard internal cannon armament. WF280 was the first of these 'dual-role' Sea Hawks, making its maiden flight on 13 March 1954.

Sea Hawk FB Mk 6 WM968 wearing the markings of No. 898 NAS on board HMS *Ark Royal* in 1957.

A Sea Hawk of No. 898 NAS about to take the arrestor cable on board HMS *Ark Royal*. In addition to external fuel tanks, the aircraft is carrying rocket projectile launcher racks.

Not surprisingly, the new variant proved to be even more popular than its predecessors, and various equipment fits were proposed for the aircraft to increase its capabilities still further, although few if any reached operational status. The type was almost provided with a reconnaissance capability and camera positions were incorporated into the aircraft's structure from the outset, but a more flexible system of accommodating cameras in converted external fuel tank pods was also tested and achieved some success. But the Fleet Air Arm did not pursue the idea, and although the Sea Hawk remained in service ostensibly as a fighter, it effectively became a ground attack machine with a secondary interceptor capability. The Navy never quite came to terms with the notion of operating the relatively unsophisticated Sea Hawk, while the RAF was proudly boasting its new swept-wing Hunters, and as if to demonstrate that the Sea Hawk was not to be regarded as inferior to the Hunter, a Fleet Air Arm pilot made a timed flight from Bovingdon to Schipol Airport on 29 July 1954, achieving an impressive time of 23 minutes and 39 seconds. The significance (if indeed there really was any) of this point-to-point flight was that it represented the same distance as between London and Amsterdam. It demonstrated an average speed of 571.5 mph and the Navy believed that it served to illustrate the Sea Hawk's capabilities. Of course, it could be argued that it merely demonstrated the Sea Hawk's inferiority, as a Hunter (albeit a heavily modified one) had achieved 727.63 mph during the previous year.

Unusual underside view of the Sea Hawk, illustrating the position of the nose gun ports, the arrestor hook and the undercarriage bay doors.

The importance of the Sea Hawk's ground attack capability led to the creation of the FGA Mk 4, the designation having been changed from 'FB' to 'FGA' to describe more accurately the aircraft's ground attack role, which embraced far more than just bombing. The Mk 4 featured an even stronger wing that could carry four 500 lb bombs and rocket projectiles spread between four underwing pylons. The heavier aircraft, laden with stores, was obviously a more sluggish performer than the 'clean' interceptor, but it was regarded as an important asset and some 97 aircraft were ordered, the first (WV792) flying for the first time on 26 August 1954. Deliveries began just a couple of months later and continued through 1955 until four Naval Air Squadrons were equipped with the new variant.

The aircraft's reduced performance prompted Hawker and Armstrong Whitworth to look at ways in which aerial refuelling could be incorporated into the Sea Hawk (a trial with RAF Meteors inevitably encouraged the Navy to follow suit). With the Sea Hawk's nose section already crammed with equipment, the only suitable place to attach a refuelling probe was onto an external drop tank, and trials were conducted with WV840, some 'dry prods' being made with a Canberra tanker. Unfortunately, the concept was less than successful as the Sea Hawk pilot could not see the probe without turning his head to the rear, and even then it was difficult to judge lateral spacing; therefore lining up the probe with a trailing drogue basket was judged to be too much of a challenge to consider using such a system operationally.

The idea was dropped, but a great deal of effort was made to improve the aircraft's performance, including trials with powered elevators and even vortex generators attached to the tailplane surfaces in an effort to improve handling at high speed and allow the aircraft to achieve a speed of Mach 0.87. But aerodynamic modifications yielded little improvement and it was engine power that needed to be improved. Rolls-Royce eventually succeeded in modifying the Nene engine to deliver an additional 200 lb of thrust and the new Nene Mk 103 was introduced to the Sea Hawk fleet, some fifty FB Mk 3 aircraft being refitted with the new engine and re-emerging as the Sea Hawk FB Mk 5. The same process was also applied to the Mk 4, and the re-engined aircraft emerged as the Sea Hawk FGA Mk 6, these later aircraft (the last of the Sea Hawk's derivatives) supplementing and replacing earlier Sea Hawks in Fleet Air Arm service.

In 1955, an order was placed for 86 new-build FGA Mk 6 aircraft and these were delivered to the Fleet Air Arm during 1956, but only two years later the Sea Hawk's withdrawal was under way, with the new Scimitar and Sea Vixen now ready to enter service. The last front-line Sea Hawk unit disbanded in December 1960, although the aircraft remained in use with second-line units for some years to come, and it was not until 1969 that the last Sea Hawks were retired, these being with the Fleet Requirements Unit at Hurn. However, this was not the very end of the Sea Hawk's association with the Royal Navy, as FGA Mk 4 WV908 was returned to the Fleet Air Arm in 1978 and restored to flying condition at Culdrose. It became a popular performer at air shows around the country and

Sea Hawk FB Mk 3 aircraft from No. 897 NAS on board HMS *Eagle* during 1956, wings folded, preparing to launch a five-aircraft sortie.

Undoubtedly the most unusual Sea Hawks were the all-black aircraft operated by the Fleet Requirements Unit based at Hurn airfield, near Bournemouth.

today forms part of the Royal Navy's Historic Flight at Yeovilton, still active nearly sixty years after it first flew.

The Sea Hawk was a versatile and successful first-generation fighter but one that quickly became adapted for ground attack operations rather than the interceptor role for which it had first been designed. It was inevitably overshadowed by the sleek Hunter that was manufactured and delivered to the RAF during the same time period, but it was rugged and reliable, and by no means a slouch when it came to speed and agility.

The 'flexible deck' trials conducted at Farnborough were performed mostly with Vampire fighters, as described in the previous chapter, but the concept of operating aircraft without conventional landing gear had to be applied as a general principle, so the Sea Hawk was also brought into the programme. VP413 made a number of landings on the rubber matting deck at Farnborough and also made the only complete wheels-up launch and recovery, as part of a concurrent project to develop a launch system for aircraft without undercarriage. The slotted-tube catapult system certainly worked but the concept required a great deal of development, VP413 being the only aircraft to complete a launch with this system, before landing again at Farnborough, all performed without ever extending the landing gear.

The concept of operating carrier aircraft without undercarriage made good sense while jet engines were capable of producing relatively low amounts of thrust, as the weight of the aircraft's landing gear was a significant handicap that, at least in theory, could be completely removed. But as engine development continued, it became clear that engines would soon be available that would deliver enough thrust to overcome any worries about undercarriage weight. Therefore the whole concept soon became redundant. However, before the whole idea was abandoned by the Admiralty in 1947, some fairly major steps towards embracing the concept had been taken, most notably in the shape of the Supermarine Type 505, an aircraft designed specifically for flexible deck operations. This potential fighter design featured a twin-engine configuration, using two of Rolls-Royce's new Avon engines positioned abreast with the fuselage, creating a broad and flattened lower fuselage that would be ideal for landing on a flexible deck. Unusually, a twin-finned 'butterfly' tail was adopted, although the rest of the aeroplane was conventional, with straight wings and engine air intakes located either side of the fuselage, ahead of the wing root.

When the Admiralty finally lost interest in the flexible deck concept during 1957, the Type 505 was also abandoned, but Supermarine opted to continue developing the basic design, but with normal retractable landing gear. The redesigned aircraft was largely based on Supermarine's Attacker aircraft that was about to join the Navy's ranks as another first-generation jet fighter (and, indeed, another jet fighter that soon became a ground attack aircraft). Using the Attacker's fuselage structure as the basis for the new design, the overall dimensions of the aircraft were increased, not only to enable more of the Attacker structure to be used but also to enable the aircraft to fly at slightly lower carrier approach speeds.

Sea Hawks start their engines in unison at the beginning of an air defence sortie during the 1956 Suez Crisis. The smoky cartridge start system was a familiar feature of the Sea Hawk.

Sea Hawks on board HMS *Ark Royal*, passing the Forth Bridge en route to the North Sea, in 1957. Also on deck are Wyvern strike aircraft and a Skyraider AEW aircraft.

WV917 is pictured being recovered onto the deck after suffering a minor landing accident. The same aircraft was ditched off Malta in March 1959 following a catapult launch accident on board HMS *Centaur*.

The new design (the Type 508) looked similar to its predecessor but was in fact quite different, not least in terms of overall size and predicted weight which would be substantially higher thanks to the incorporation of 30 mm cannon and newly developed radar in its nose, together with camera gear to equip the aircraft for the fighter-reconnaissance role. The proposed aircraft was certainly ambitious and in many respects represented a transitional step between the Sea Hawk and the far more advanced Sea Vixen that replaced it in the interceptor role. The prototype of what became the Supermarine Type 508 was VX133, and it took to the air for the first time on 31 August 1951 from Boscombe Down.

The Type 508 was rushed into the air so that it could perform at the 1951 SBAC show at Farnborough, but after this event the aircraft was assigned to flight testing. Initial experience with the type was far from satisfactory and on 5 December test pilot Mike Lithgow was almost forced to abandon the aircraft when it departed from controlled flight. After pitching upwards whilst flying at low level, Lithgow disengaged elevator power in an attempt to regain control, but this simple act made the aircraft misbehave even more and as the g-force become intolerable, Lithgow blacked out and only regained consciousness some time later, by which time the aircraft was at 11,000 feet in an upward vertical rolling attitude. Lithgow

Supermarine Type 508 VX133 on board HMS *Eagle* during carrier trials. The huge 'butterfly' tail assembly was abandoned in favour of a more conventional arrangement as the design progressed towards what eventually became the Scimitar.

Type 508 VX133 about to take the cable on board HMS *Eagle*. The 508 was a fairly large aircraft, but one that displayed great elegance. It was, however, little more than a development of the rather unsophisticated Attacker.

managed to bring the aircraft back under control and land at Supermarine's airfield at Chilbolton. The design staff concluded that the undercarriage must have accidentally extended during flight at high speed, and modifications were made to ensure that this could not happen again. However, after returning to test flying, VX133 suffered precisely the same potentially lethal loss of control, demonstrating that the undercarriage was not the cause. This time, the incident had been observed from the ground and it was established that aileron flutter was the cause, and providing the aircraft with power controls soon cured this problem.

After this unsettling period, the Type 508 continued to fly with few problems. Supermarine proceeded to complete the second aircraft (VX136), which was fitted with cannon armament, together with a variety of design improvements. In fact, the aircraft was so different from its earlier counterpart that it was redesignated as the Type 529. This aircraft and the Type 508 provided the manufacturer with a huge amount of test flight data and a great deal of experience in jet fighter design, and both aircraft were deployed to aircraft carriers for deck landing and launch trials. The Navy thought the aircraft suitable for development into an operational fighter and Supermarine continued to develop the design still further, resulting in a third test aircraft, this time designated as the Type 525. Even the most cursory examination of the 525 revealed just how different it was from the earlier aircraft. Gone were the straight wings and in their place was a new swept-wing design, combined with swept tailpanes and swept fin, arranged in a more conventional cruciform style. It was in effect a completely different aircraft even though it retained the Type 529's landing gear, fuselage and cockpit.

On 27 April 1954, the test pilot flew this aircraft for the first time and the design team was naturally eager to establish the extent to which the aircraft's performance had been improved by introducing swept wings. Much to their disappointment, it was soon discovered that the aircraft performed only marginally better than the previous prototype, even with more powerful Avon engines rated at 7,500 lb thrust. The reason for this became clear when American research data was studied, revealing that substantial increases in performance could only be achieved if 'area rule' principles were observed, requiring the aircraft's fuselage to be recontoured to present a constant frontal cross-section to the airflow. Supermarine set to work on reshaping the Type 529 and the result was yet another aircraft that by now bore absolutely no resemblance to the Type 505 first proposed. The new aircraft (the Type 525) retained the same swept wings, tailplane and fin, but now incorporated a shaped 'Coke bottle' fuselage with a 'pinched' centre fuselage to counter the frontal area of the wings. Just as significantly, the Type 525 and the new aircraft also incorporated a BLC (Boundary Layer Control) system comprising high-pressure air drawn from the engines and vented through narrow slots ahead of the wing trailing edge flaps. The high-pressure air smoothed airflow over the flap where it would otherwise have been turbulent and caused drag. The BLC system effectively allowed the aircraft to be flown some 18 mph slower on approach and also provided the pilot with a better forward view (with a lower angle of attack), and these were useful assets for a new carrier aircraft.

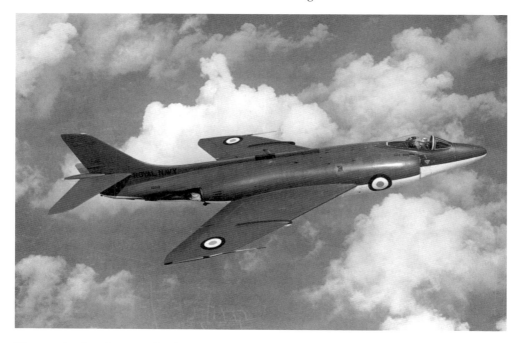

First production Supermarine Scimitar XD212, illustrating the type's sleek, swept-back wings and tail surfaces.

Scimitar F Mk 1 XD248 pictured whilst serving with No. 807 NAS, complete with the very appropriate unit marking on its tail, and HMS *Ark Royal*'s code letter. Rocket projectiles can be seen under the wings.

The new Type 544 completed its maiden flight on 19 January 1956, and this design was the basis of an aircraft fully suited to the Navy's requirements. As such, it was in effect the prototype of what became the Scimitar, the first production example of this type (XD212) flying in January 1957. Designated as the Scimitar F Mk 1, the aircraft's description was somewhat misleading, as by the time that the Scimitar was ready to enter service with the Fleet Air Arm, the Navy was already looking towards the Sea Vixen as the basis for its new all-weather interceptor. Although the Scimitar would enter service with a capability to operate as a fighter, armed both with ADEN cannon and Sidewinder air-to-air missiles, the Navy had already decided to adopt the aircraft as an attack aircraft, armed with AGM-12 Bullpup air-to-surface missiles, conventional high-explosive bombs, and rocket projectiles. But the Scimitar's primary role would be as a nuclear strike aircraft, each aircraft armed with a single Red Beard tactical nuclear weapon carried on a wing pylon. The Scimitar would be operated as a low-level bomber, capable of launching its lethal nuclear weapon against naval targets or land-based tactical targets as a secondary capability.

Although designed as a fighter, the Scimitar was fast, rugged and manoeuvrable, and well suited to the strike role, but even as it entered service the Navy regarded it as only a short-term acquisition that would eventually make way for a more capable maritime strike aircraft in the shape of the NA.39 Buccaneer. Consequently the Scimitar's service life was short and after becoming operational in 1960, the type was withdrawn from the front line just six years later.

Two Scimitars prepare to launch from *Ark Royal*'s catapults, both aircraft clearly fitted with bolt-on refuelling probes, fixed ahead of the cockpit windscreen.

The Scimitar suffered more than its fair share of carrier landing accidents, although most were due to pilot inexperience and not a result of any technical difficulties associated with the aircraft. *Terry Goulding*

A Scimitar pictured in typical naval conditions, sharing HMS *Centaur*'s carrier deck with two Sea Vixens.

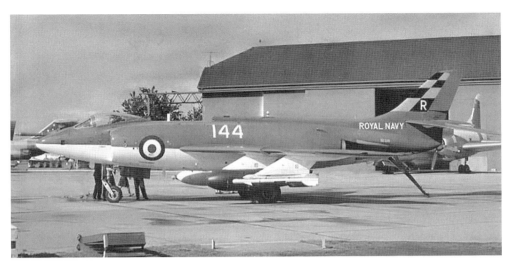

An extremely rare photograph showing a Scimitar carrying its primary weapon – the Red Beard atomic bomb. The weapon can be seen attached to the port inner pylon, with an external fuel tank attached to the starboard pylon as an aerodynamic balance.

The arrival of the Buccaneer was the key reason for the Scimitar's hasty retirement, but the Navy's experience with the Scimitar had been less than happy and the Fleet Air Arm was probably glad to be rid of the aircraft. This was perhaps unfair, as although the Scimitar suffered from a large number of accidents (some thirty-nine of the entire fleet of seventy-six aircraft eventually being written off), the accidents were mostly caused by the Navy's inadequate training system and poor maintenance procedures that required greater logistical support. The Scimitar pilots flew carrier launches and recoveries all too infrequently, and it was this factor that ultimately gave the Scimitar a reputation that it really did not deserve. But with the Admiralty firmly committed to the new Buccaneer strike aircraft and the Sea Vixen established as a very capable all-weather fighter, the Scimitar was soon redundant. The very last examples were retired late in 1970 from the Fleet Requirements Unit at Hurn.

The Scimitar was an interesting story of how a 'flexible deck' fighter eventually became the carrier of the Navy's first atomic bombs, and although the aircraft enjoyed only a brief time with the Navy, it introduced many pilots to heavier and more powerful jet fighter operations and inaugurated the revolutionary BLC system that became a vital part of the aircraft that succeeded it in Fleet Air Arm service. It was perhaps ironic that after the first Buccaneer S.1 aircraft entered service, the Gyron Junior engines were soon found to be barely capable of getting the machine safely into the air in 'hot and high' conditions. The only useful way that the Buccaneer could be operated was for the Scimitar to be used as a refuelling tanker, allowing the Buccaneer to be launched at lighter weight before being 'topped up' with fuel by the Scimitar once airborne. Considering the way in which the Scimitar had started out as a small undercarriage-less fighter and had eventually matured into a nuclear bomber and refuelling tanker, nobody could deny that it was a versatile machine.

CHAPTER FOUR
Swept Wing Saga

Supermarine's 'flexible deck' project ultimately led to the creation of the Scimitar fighter-bomber, even though the production-standard machine was very different (completely different, in fact) from the aeroplane that was first envisaged when the project began. Supermarine's proposal was for a relatively small fighter aircraft, but what emerged many years later was a much bigger and heavier design that was eventually assigned to a role very different from that of a fighter-interceptor. But the Scimitar was not the only jet fighter that Supermarine developed. As the creator of the immortal Spitfire, the company continued to develop the basic Spitfire design over many years, until it reached the very end of its development potential.

By this stage, the Spitfire had become the Spiteful (and Seafang in Royal Navy service). Ostensibly developments of the Spitfire, these aircraft were effectively completely different aircraft, sharing virtually nothing with the RAF fighter from the Battle of Britain era. The Spitfire's basic layout remained, but with a reshaped fuselage, different tail and much more powerful engine the Spiteful and Seafang were hardly relatives of the Spitfire at all. Most importantly, these aircraft did not even have the Spitfire's classic elliptical wing; in fact, they were equipped with completely different wings of different structural construction, profile shape and plan form layout. The wing design was a result of Supermarine's investigations into ways in which the performance of a fighter aircraft could be improved by increasing the speed at which compressibility became an issue, and to reduce overall drag. The original Spitfire's wing obviously had a limit beyond which no refinements could be made to improve performance, but Supermarine's design team understood that even the basic wing design could deliver more speed if surface irregularities were removed, roughness of external finish smoothed out, and foreign bodies (even insects) were removed. Creating a smooth 'laminar flow' of air over the wing reduced the creation of turbulence and airflow break-away near to the wing's surface, thereby reducing drag and increasing speed. Supermarine's Specification 470 covered the design of a new laminar flow wing and this designation was eventually widened to describe what became the Type 371 Spiteful fighter. The new wing was designed, with assistance from the National Physical Laboratory, to create a laminar flow of air as far back along the wing chord as possible, creating a maximum thickness at 42 per cent of the chord. The standard Spitfire wing shape was abandoned in favour of a simple straight leading and trailing edge, as the design team accepted that the plan form of the wing would be far less important than its profile, and a simple straight wing could be produced more easily with conventional two-spar construction. The result was a wing some 38.5 square feet smaller than that of the Spitfire in overall area and one that was 200 lb lighter than the Spitfire Mk 21. Supermarine estimated that the new design would enable at least an additional 50 mph to be attained.

Flight testing of the Spiteful did indeed demonstrate that the new wing would enable faster speeds to be achieved. However, the aircraft also exhibited a number of deficiencies, not least aileron 'snatching' and some serious stall characteristics such as wing drop just prior to a stall and a tendency to flick into a potential spin. Although a level speed of 494 mph was achieved, it was reluctantly accepted that the Spiteful was no great improvement over the last of the Spitfires, even if the wing design did show some potential. The Air Ministry lost interest in the aircraft and Supermarine looked towards the Navy, creating a navalised version of the aircraft with folding wings and arrestor gear, but even in its nautical guise as the Spiteful, the aircraft was still no great performer. Despite performing well during carrier landing trials, the Navy also decided not to pursue the Seafang, and an order for 150 aircraft was cancelled. Only ten production aircraft were completed, together with the two prototypes, while the fourteen Spiteful aircraft produced were retained by the manufacturer and various test establishments so that the properties and potential of the new wing design could be properly explored.

The Supermarine Spiteful was the final expression of the Spitfire series. Its new laminar flow wing design became the basis for Supermarine's jet-powered Attacker.

With jet engine development becoming an important and greatly publicised issue among Britain's aircraft manufacturers, it was not surprising that Supermarine quickly adopted the new wing design for a jet-powered design, and even before the first Spiteful took to the air, on 30 June 1944, the company was drawing up design concepts for a jet fighter design, related to Specification E.10/44. Within two weeks, Supermarine had submitted a basic proposal to the Air Ministry (company Specification 477). Some weeks previously, Rolls-Royce had been given the go-ahead to produce its new RB.40 engine, promising to deliver at least 40,000 lb thrust, and it was this powerplant that the Ministry of Supply expected Supermarine to adopt as the basis for the new fighter based on E.10/44. However, and rather unusually, Supermarine's Chief Designer Joe Smith favoured a slightly smaller engine that would deliver less thrust but would also be smaller and lighter, and this stipulation led to a significant amount of redesign work at Rolls-Royce, resulting in the RB.41 Nene. The new aircraft was therefore built around the laminar flow wing and the dimensions and requirements of the Nene engine. The cockpit was brought forward towards the nose (affording the pilot a much better view than the Spiteful ever could) and the same fit of four Hispano Mk 5 20 mm cannon was retained, two buried in the leading edge of each wing. Designated as the Type 392, this became the Attacker, although the Ministry of Aircraft Production initially referred to the aircraft as 'Jet machines of the Spiteful type' when an order for three prototypes was placed on 5 August 1944. The Ministry of Supply indicated at this stage that although there was still a possibility of ordering the Spiteful, the order would be shifted to the Attacker if its test programme proved to be successful. Unfortunately, this created a difficult situation for Supermarine, as both the Spiteful and Attacker had to be pursued in parallel, with no real indication as to which type would be adopted for production. This inevitably wasted resources and time, but in some respects it made the Attacker programme rather less complicated, as much of the flight testing revolved around the wing design, and this was shared by both the Attacker and Spiteful, and a lot of test data was therefore applicable to both aircraft. Of course, tooling was also already in place for production of the Spiteful and so this was an economic advantage that more than outweighed the disadvantages of pursuing two projects simultaneously.

In July 1945, approval was given for an order for twenty-four aircraft. Six of these would be essentially trials aircraft in accordance with E.10/44, while the rest would be built in accordance with Specification E.1/45, a naval requirement written around the aircraft. Unfortunately, progress slowed because of the Spiteful's troubled programme, marred by the loss of the first aircraft in a crash and a variety of aerodynamic problems that manifested themselves. The Air Ministry became even less enthusiastic but the Navy persisted, although it requested that work on the production-standard aircraft should be suspended while development of the initial three prototypes should be pursued. A batch of eighteen de Havilland Vampires was ordered as a substitute for the shelved Attacker order and Supermarine redirected its efforts towards the Spiteful's flight trials, while the first Attacker prototype was completed. Aileron control problems dogged the Spiteful programme and at speeds of more than 400 mph, the test pilots reported that the complicated slotted aileron was too heavy.

Supermarine decided that the second Attacker prototype would be allocated to resolving this issue, but first of all the maiden flight of the first Attacker (TS409) had to take place, and this occurred on 27 July 1946 at Boscombe Down, with Supermarine's famous Chief Test Pilot Jeffrey Quill at the controls. The flight was a success and while Supermarine's design team congratulated themselves for this achievement, Rolls-Royce was equally happy to have finally got its new Nene engine into the air for the first time. By this stage the Nene engine had already comfortably exceeded expectations and could deliver 4,300 lb thrust, and this figure rose still higher within a matter of months to 5,000 lb.

By any standards, the Nene was a remarkably successful engine for its time, and the only difficulty that it presented was the risk of damage to runways, taxiways and (perhaps most importantly) carrier decks, if the hot engine exhaust was to emerge directly from the Attacker's rear fuselage. The initial taxi trials with TS409 had illustrated that considerable damage would be caused by a tail-sitter fitted with a jet engine, and rather than redesign the aircraft to incorporate a tricycle undercarriage, attempts were made to lengthen the tailwheel assembly. However, with no more space available in the rear fuselage, the only simple alternative was to extend the jet pipe slightly and angle it upwards, deflecting most of the hot efflux away from the ground without affecting the aircraft's performance too significantly.

More than satisfied with the first flight, Supermarine quickly prepared TS409 for an appearance at the first post-war SBAC show, which was then held at Radlett. But before the show week in September, the second aircraft made its first flight, in the hands of Mike Lithgow, on 17 June. This aircraft (TS413) was more representative of the proposed production aircraft and as such it was designated as an Attacker F Mk 1. The vertical tail (already small in comparison to many contemporary aircraft) was reduced in size still further, although the tailplane surfaces were enlarged. The aircraft's wing flaps were modified and wing spoilers were incorporated into the upper surfaces. The aileron tabs were improved, air intakes modified and the landing gear strengthened in anticipation of the first deck landing trials. Although a tail hook was fitted, the wing folding mechanism was not, as it was deemed unnecessary for initial trials. Perhaps most importantly, a Martin-Baker ejection seat was also installed.

The first flight of TS413 revealed that the aircraft suffered from the same directional 'snaking' that had affected the first prototype, but the effect seemed even more pronounced on the second aircraft and appeared at speeds right across the aircraft's range. As a short-term fix the rudder trailing edge was modified with beading, and the aircraft resumed flying, first with some dummy deck landings before deploying to HMS *Illustrious* to perform real tests. The Attacker was found to be quite well suited to carrier landing, although it did have a tendency to 'float' at the point of touchdown, without the usual braking effect of a large

Prototype Supermarine Type 398 TS413 completed its maiden flight on 17 June 1947, in the hands of test pilot Mike Lithgow.

A magnificent image of the Attacker prototype TS413, racing across Chilbolton airfield at low level for the benefit of Supermarine's photographer.

propeller. The spoilers on top of the wing were judged to be adequate, but for production aircraft it was decided to introduce air brakes, created as extensions of the wing flaps. The Attacker's tailwheel undercarriage arrangement, potentially so troublesome for land-based operations, was ideal for carriers, as the nose-high attitude enabled the aircraft to approach and launch at higher angles of attack. Rather like the Sea Venom, the Attacker's tail hook was found to be inadequately attached to the aircraft's fuselage structure and on the initial deck landing tests it detached itself from the aircraft. After repairs and modifications there were further problems with the hook, but eventually the difficulties were resolved and the Attacker was judged to be a satisfactory aircraft for carrier operations, even if it was not regarded as outstanding. Sadly, TS413 was destroyed in a fatal crash whilst operating from Boscombe Down on 22 June 1948, but the accident was not attributed to any design deficiency so work continued on modifying TS409 to a more representative Navy standard. In September, an order for sixty aircraft was finally placed, much to Supermarine's relief.

The Attacker had been a long and difficult project, particularly when Supermarine was obliged to develop the Spiteful, Seafang and Seagull amphibian at the same time. The Attacker's laminar flow wing had been taken directly from the Spiteful in order to make the design of a jet fighter both easier and swifter, but the aircraft still struggled to reach production standard when so many seemingly minor issues combined to delay development. The resulting aircraft was hardly a spectacular leap of capability, but the Navy anticipated receipt of a simple, docile and relatively speedy jet fighter that would at least fill an important perceived gap between the last of the Fleet Air Arm's piston-engine aircraft and more capable jet fighters. Without any major armament fit and no interception radar, the Attacker was never envisaged as anything other than a very basic day interceptor, but if it could be manufactured and delivered quickly the Royal Navy believed it was worth having.

The third of the three Attacker prototypes was TS416 and this aircraft made its first flight on 24 January 1950. With a pressurised cockpit, larger air intakes and slightly repositioned wings (some 13 inches further aft but still non-folding), the aircraft was essentially a refinement of the earlier prototypes, and it was TS409 that was used to win the SBAC Challenge Cup at Sherburn-in-Elmet during July 1950. Mike Lithgow achieved an average speed of 533 mph and Supermarine hoped to exceed this during the 1951 event, but bad weather caused the event to be cancelled and TS409 never got a chance to fly still faster. However, Lithgow did accept a rare opportunity to fly along the Champs Élysées in Paris at low altitude (precisely how low has not been established) at a speed of almost 600 mph, and after displaying the aircraft to French officials he returned to Hurn in just 25 minutes.

The first production Attacker (of some 181 that were eventually built) was WA469, the first Attacker to have folding wings, so necessary for Fleet Air Arm operations. It flew for the first time on 5 April 1950, in Lithgow's capable hands. This aircraft had a fully modified fin with a new dorsal extension, elegantly faired

Rear view of TS413, illustrating the dihedral angle applied to the aircraft's tailplane surfaces, and the low-slung engine exhaust pipe.

An early production Attacker, emphasising the surprisingly small vertical tail and the up-turned engine exhaust, behind the tail wheel.

A rare image of the Attacker's early carrier trials. The aircraft was well suited to carrier operations even though its tailwheel arrangement was distinctly old-fashioned and far from ideal.

Attacker prototype TS413 pictured as the aircraft's tail hook is about to engage the carrier's arrestor cable. Although the Attacker was an unremarkable aircraft, it performed well and proved to be well suited to carrier operations.

into the upper fuselage, together with redesigned elevators and lighter aileron controls. Supermarine believed that the unmodified fin fitted to the other aircraft may have contributed to the loss of TS413 as well as production-standard aircraft WA477, and the revised design with the additional dorsal fillet was fitted as standard on all aircraft thereafter, curing a tendency for the rudder to lock during some side-slip conditions, especially when the large ventral bolt-on fuel tank was attached under the fuselage.

Production of the Attacker then proceeded fairly uneventfully, although on 23 May, test pilot Les Colquhoun was flying WA409 on high-speed trials, involving dives at 400 knots or more, before deploying the air brakes that had been introduced into the production aircraft. During one dive over the manufacturer's airfield at South Marston the aircraft was diving at 430 knots when the air brakes were deployed. The aircraft pitched up slightly before pitching downwards, after which a load bang was heard and the starboard outer wing folded upwards on its hinge. The wing immediately dropped, but with judicious use of the port rudder Colquhoun was able to control the aircraft, carefully reducing speed to 270 knots and bringing the aircraft back to the airfield. The ailerons were locked solid but the flaps extended successfully and a landing was made at 200 knots, the hapless Attacker coming to rest less than 50 feet from the end of the runway. Apart from a burst tyre (and a very distressed pilot), the aircraft was undamaged and after modifications to the wing fold mechanism the production programme continued, Colquhoun receiving the George Medal in recognition of his efforts to recover the stricken aircraft safely.

From the fifty-fifth aircraft onwards the Attacker's designation was changed from F Mk 1 to FB Mk 1, in response to a change in the aircraft's operational role. By this stage, the Navy had an increasing requirement for ground attack aircraft rather than fighters, but Supermarine had wisely anticipated this during the Attacker's development, so the airframe structure was already suitably designed to enable the aircraft to carry external ordnance with few additional modifications. However, only six aircraft were fully completed to FB Mk 1 standard and it was the Attacker FB Mk 2 that fully embraced the ground attack role, with an improved Nene engine, an electric starter unit, a metal-framed cockpit canopy and provision for the carriage of two 1,000 lb bombs or six 12 inch rocket projectiles under each wing, arranged in two tiers. The first of these Mk 2 aircraft was WK319, which made its maiden flight on 25 April 1952, as the first of eighty-four production machines.

On 5 February 1951, tragedy had struck the Attacker programme when Sqn Ldr Peter Roberts was killed in WA477 during its third test flight. This particular aircraft was almost ready for delivery and on its third flight the cockpit pressurisation system was to be checked and handling was to be examined, now that the aircraft had had its ventral fuel tank fitted. Roberts got airborne in WA477 at 12.41, the second test flight having taken place some hours previously, and after an uneventful departure a further 12 minutes elapsed before observers saw what appeared to be a trail of smoke coming from the aircraft, followed by the muffled

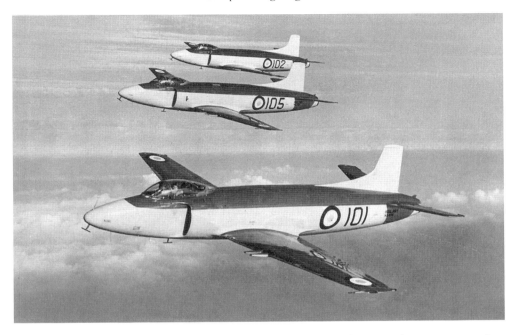

A trio of Attackers in flight, emphasising that despite the aircraft's ungainly appearance when seen on the ground, it was cleanly designed and simple in overall configuration.

Although the Attacker was designed as a fighter, it possessed a very impressive ground attack capability. In addition to twelve rocket projectiles, this aircraft is also fitted with RATOG and a large ventral fuel tank.

sound of an explosion, after which the aircraft went into a dive, became inverted and then descended at approximately 80 degrees until it impacted with the ground just a couple of miles from Marlborough. Roberts was killed and everyone at Supermarine was both astonished and bewildered. Although the Attacker had exhibited more than a few faults, it was essentially a simple and reliable aircraft that had never offered any hints of potentially fatal flaws.

The Accident Investigation Board recovered the aircraft's wreckage, all of which was found within a 30 yard-diameter crater some 15 feet deep, although the engine and parts of the undercarriage had buried themselves rather deeper. The nature of the crash had crushed most of the aircraft's structure and components but the accident investigators were able to establish that the airframe was intact at the point of impact and that the flying controls were functional. The undercarriage was retracted and when the airspeed indicator was recovered it showed 525 knots, and this was accepted as the speed at the point of impact. The engine appeared to have been functioning normally, so there was no obvious cause for the catastrophic accident. However, when the port wing structure was slowly lifted from the impact crater, a section containing the port inner flap and wing spoiler mechanism was raised in one piece, and as it was removed a 5 inch-long spanner fell from the wreckage. Examination of the spanner indicated that it had been lodged between the spoiler operating rod and a steel spar reinforcing plate, and this would have severely restricted movement of the wing spoiler. At the moment of impact the port inner and outer spoilers were extended by 0.25 inches, while the starboard spoilers were extended by 2 inches. The flap mechanism was unaffected as this operated independently of the spoilers, but with the spoilers extended in this asymmetric fashion it was calculated that the ailerons would have been unable to control the rolling effect that this created, and the stick force would have been beyond the pilot's strength. The AIB team concluded that on the basis of eyewitness reports, the smoke trail and the sound of dull explosions were probably caused by an engine flame-out that had been followed by an intermittent relight. The Attacker was prone to this problem because of a troublesome relight button solenoid that could jam in some circumstances, and special instructions had been issued on this issue as part of the Pilot's Notes. It seemed likely that the pilot may have thought that the aircraft was suffering a 'wet start' (surplus fuel igniting in the engine) and in order to cure this problem he would have put the aircraft into dive to 'dry out' the engine before attempting a restart. With the aircraft in a dive at high speed, the engine probably started up again, as indicated by the wreckage results, but in order to slow the aircraft the airbrakes (spoilers) would have been deployed, and with a spanner jamming their mechanism, the asymmetric deployment would have put the aircraft into a roll of some 30 degrees per second. With little altitude to recover, the aircraft hit the ground before it could be saved, and did not afford Roberts enough time to attempt an ejection.

As mentioned previously, the second prototype (TS413) had also been destroyed in a crash on 22 June 1948, killing its Royal Navy test pilot Lt-Cdr King-Joyce. The AIB team immediately raised the issue of whether the two crashes might have had any common causes, and on the basis of the subsequent investigations it seems that they may well have had. TS413 had been flying for some time, having amassed more than 100 flying hours, and at the time of the accident it was with the A&AEE for flight trials with the large (270 gallon) ventral tank fitted under its fuselage. Test flights were made with the tank both empty and full, and despite its size, the tank demonstrated no significant effect on the Attacker's handling, other than a very slight degradation in performance and an increase in the stalling speed. On 22 June, TS413 got airborne for another flight with the ventral tank full, the aim being to test the aircraft's stick forces at 30,000 feet. The pilot had lots of experience, including nearly 4 hours on the Attacker, and nobody expected any problems to be encountered on the flight, but after almost an hour in the air, radio contact was lost with the aircraft and it was reported as having crashed 2 miles north of Boscombe Down. The crash site was similar to that found after WA477's crash, with a deep crater containing badly compressed and fragmented wreckage, and attempts to determine any possible causes for the crash proved to be particularly difficult with so little evidence to work with. All that could be established was that the aircraft appeared to have been intact with the landing gear retracted and that the engine was probably running. However, further investigation revealed that the ventral tank had somehow been released whilst in flight and that the cockpit canopy had also been torn off. The pilot's helmet was found with the hood's broken remains and it was believed that the canopy had therefore failed because it had been struck violently by the pilot's helmet, probably as a result of a violent 'bunt' caused by the unexpected release of the ventral tank. Rather ominously, a spanner was found in the wreckage, but nobody could establish where it had come from or whether it might have had any influence on the accident. The AIB team concluded that no definite cause for the crash could be established at the time.

Some time later, during the early months of 1950, a slightly different 250 gallon ventral tank was tested on the Attacker and although it too had little effect on the aircraft's handling, it did produce a noticeable destabilising force on its directional stability, and at airspeeds below 250 knots it could cause the rudder to lock in certain circumstances. Various 'fixes' were tried but the problem persisted and actually became more severe, but it was finally solved when the fin was redesigned to incorporate the dorsal fillet extension that was fitted to production aircraft.

The experience suggested that the loss of TS413 might have been caused by rudder over-balance, caused by the ventral tank's destabilising effect, but with so much favourable feedback on the tank's behaviour nobody was willing to accept this as a conclusive explanation. But, of course, the spanner's presence in both accidents did seem like too much of a coincidence. It may well have been that when King-Joyce entered a dive from 30,000 feet as part of the test flight he would have deployed the spoilers (which had yet to be modified to work as part of the flap system) to slow the aircraft down, and the errant spanner might well have become lodged in the spoiler mechanism as it did in WA477. The aircraft would have started to roll in much the same way and although the pilot may well have retracted the spoilers in order to attempt a recovery, the damaged mechanism would have fixed the spoilers in an asymmetric configuration that the pilot was unable to control by aileron force alone. With the aircraft descending at speed with no means of control, the ventral tank would have been torn away and this would have forced the aircraft into a negative-g 'bunt' that threw the pilot upwards into the canopy before he and his aircraft hit the ground.

Tragically, it eventually seemed more than likely that the loss of both Attackers (and two very able pilots) was literally caused by a spanner in the works, and Supermarine was tasked by the Ministry of Supply to ensure that maintenance and manufacturing procedures were radically improved to ensure that the seemingly innocent loss of a simple spanner would never again lead to such catastrophic accidents. Not only were the crashes both tragic and entirely avoidable, they also had a hugely negative effect on the Attacker programme, slowing progress of both the test programme and aircraft production, whilst sowing the seeds of uncertainty in the minds of both Supermarine and the Fleet Air Arm as to whether the Attacker was harbouring some undiscovered fatal flaw. In fact, the Attacker was a well-behaved aeroplane that certainly did not deserve a reputation for being potentially lethal.

Attacker WA497 posing for a publicity photograph in the Solent, with the *Queen Elizabeth* cruise ship in the background. This aircraft flew for just six years before being withdrawn and scrapped at Abbotsinch.

Service entry began in August 1951, when No. 800 NAS at Brawdy re-formed with Attacker F Mk 1 aircraft at RNAS Ford in Sussex. After training, the unit deployed on HMS *Eagle*. No. 803 NAS followed, both units eventually receiving additional aircraft from the second-line unit No. 890 NAS. All three units made regular deployments on board carriers, and Attackers operated from *Eagle*, *Albion* and *Centaur* during the type's brief front-line service with the Royal Navy. The Attacker's protracted developmental programme effectively curtailed its potential before it even entered service, and by the time that it joined the Fleet Air Arm's front line it was already outclassed by other contemporary designs. Designed as a fighter, it was assigned largely to surface attack duties, although it retained its dual-role capability throughout its brief career. The Navy regarded the aircraft as a useful short-term acquisition, and even after it was withdrawn from operational duties it soon became a valued part of the Fleet Air Arm's reserve and training fleet. Trials units were formed at West Raynham and at Ford, enabling the Attacker to be employed on a wide variety of trials and evaluation tasks, all of which contributed to the Navy's knowledge and experience of jet operations. Attackers also went to Culdrose where they were assigned to advanced training duties with No. 702 NAS, and these aircraft eventually went to Lossiemouth where they became part of the Naval Air Fighter School. No. 767 NAS at Stretton also received the Attacker, and the aircraft was used there to train deck landing control officers.

When the Hawker Sea Hawk began to reach operational status, Attackers were slowly withdrawn and many were placed in open storage pending a decision on their future. Others went to Royal Navy Volunteer Reserve units such as No. 1831 Squadron at Stretton, followed by Nos 1832 and 1833 Squadrons. The RNVR units were all disbanded in March 1957, along with the Royal Auxiliary Air Force, as part of wide-ranging defence cuts and it was this political act that effectively signalled the end for the Attacker. The very last examples flew with the Fleet Requirements Unit at Hurn until February 1957, when the last of the Attackers was withdrawn. Countless examples remained in open storage for some time at various sites, but most notably at RNAS Abbotsinch, where numerous Attackers languished on the airfield until they were all eventually cut up as scrap metal. Only one Attacker survived this process. After spending some time as a gate guard at Abbotsinch, it was transferred to the Fleet Air Arm Museum at Yeovilton, where it still resides, on show to the public, as a reminder of the Royal Navy's first steps into the world of jet power.

Supermarine's Attacker proved itself to be a useful aircraft, even if it was not around for long and was never regarded as particularly outstanding. The Royal Navy was satisfied with the aeroplane, but it was clear even from the early days of the Attacker programme that it was a product of the time and would soon be outclassed by more advanced fighter designs. Supermarine was undoubtedly disappointed that the RAF had shown so little interest in the Attacker, and when the Air Ministry issued Specification F.3/48 the company was eager to ensure that this time the RAF would be interested in whatever Supermarine had to offer.

Specification F.4/48 was in fact a refinement of an earlier Specification (F.43/46) for a new day interceptor that had been floundering for some time. With developments in aerodynamics and jet engine technology moving at a rapid rate, there was some difficulty in establishing precisely what type of aeroplane would be best suited to the Specification if it was not to become obsolete before it was even manufactured. When Hawker created its swept-wing designs that eventually led to the P.1067 (which became the Hunter), the Air Ministry effectively rewrote Specification F.3/48 around it, but Supermarine immediately came up with its own design (the Type 526). However, once again, the RAF did not exhibit much interest in it. By now, Supermarine had plenty of experience with jet aircraft design, thanks to the Attacker, and like Hawker (from where the Sea Hawk had emerged), the company had now embraced the concept of swept wings, largely as a result of data that came from America and which was demonstrated quite vividly in the shape of the new North American F-86 Sabre.

The notion of using swept wings had of course originated in Nazi Germany, but it was not until the wartime hardware and data had been examined that anyone in the USA or the UK could establish whether the concept really had any great merit. American designers soon understood the potential of swept wings and in Britain many aerodynamicists reached similar conclusions, but in the stuffy corridors of power, Britain's service chiefs had no interest in such seemingly wild ideas. However, Supermarine's design team, under the leadership of Joe Smith, did persuade the Ministry of Supply to issue a contract for the creation of an aeroplane (two prototypes in fact) that would be built and flown purely for research. This was the Type 510, a jet aircraft based on the existing Attacker aircraft, retaining the same fuselage and landing gear but fitted with completely new swept wings and – unlike Hawker's equivalent aircraft being built as part of its P.1067 programme – a swept tail. By using the Attacker as a starting point, the new aircraft was designed and built quickly, and in December 1948, the completed aircraft (VV106) made its first flight.

Although similar in appearance to the Attacker whilst on the ground (retaining the same tail-sitting undercarriage arrangement), the Type 510 certainly looked very different once airborne, with its sleek swept wings. It performed rather differently too, exhibiting a marked improvement in overall speed whilst demonstrating none of the horrific handling vices that many 'experts' had predicted (almost in complete ignorance of the F-86 that was demonstrating the validity of such designs). Having been manufactured at Hursley Park, the aircraft would have gone to the manufacturer's airfield just a few miles away at Chilbolton to make its first flight, but Ministry of Supply officials were reluctant to allow what they regarded as a radical new aircraft to attempt a take-off from the confines of Chilbolton's tree-lined site. Consequently, VV106 was transported to Boscombe Down, although most of the aircraft's test flying was subsequently conducted from Chilbolton and in a matter of weeks the aircraft was achieving speeds of around Mach 0.9 on some flights. Handling was found to be satisfactory, although there were problems, not least a tendency to pitch up at low speed as a

Supermarine Type 510 VV106 pictured shortly after completion in 1948. It was in effect an Attacker aircraft with new swept wings and tail surfaces.

result of wingtip stalling. Leading edge slats had been built into the design, but they were regarded as unnecessary and after being locked up for early flights were subsequently removed. Lateral trim change was required as the aircraft reached higher speeds until Mach 0.93 when control was lost completely, and despite the addition of partially powered controls, this was effectively the 510's limiting speed without the introduction of aerodynamic improvements and full power controls. Engine problems were also a headache, and engine vibration also became a concern especially at lower rpm when directional stability could also be affected. The cause was an interaction between engine and air speed, causing turbulence inside the intakes. The intake area was modified as a result, and the blunt Attacker-type nose was replaced by a pointed cone that improved speed still further until more than 635 mph was attained.

The Type 510 made its public debut at Farnborough in September 1949, after which it went to Boscombe Down for evaluation. The A&AEE pilots concluded that the aircraft was capable of being turned into a good fighter aircraft if some of its deficiencies were addressed. Most of these were fairly minor, but it was recommended that the tailwheel undercarriage be dropped and that greater elevator control should be incorporated. The Type 510 was an unqualified success, although it was something of a short-lived triumph, as once the concept of swept flying surfaces had been so ably demonstrated, there was little else that could

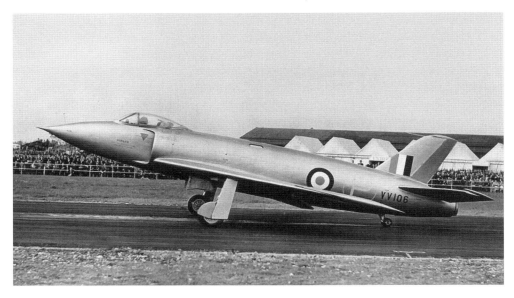

Supermarine Type 510 during its public debut at Farnborough. Surprisingly, the aircraft has survived intact and is now part of the Fleet Air Arm Museum collection at Yeovilton.

be done with the aircraft and the project slowed almost to a standstill for some time while Supermarine turned its limited resources towards production of the Attacker and the Seagull amphibian.

By the summer of 1950, however, Supermarine had produced a second Type 510 and although this aircraft (VV119) was outwardly similar to its predecessor, it had a modified Nene engine fitted with a rudimentary afterburner unit that exhausted through a twin-eyelid nozzle. In much the same way as Britain's interest in swept wings had been somewhat half-hearted, the relatively new concept of adding reheat to jet engines (spraying additional fuel into the hot exhaust where it was ignited to produce a major increase in thrust) was another potentially important new idea that was developing at some pace over in the USA. The Type 510 soon demonstrated that this concept also worked well and could make a major contribution to future jet aircraft designs. Supermarine also decided – especially after the A&AEE's recommendation – finally to abandon the distinctly old-fashioned tailwheel undercarriage layout that had been necessary for propeller-driven aircraft but was hardly ideal for jets. The Type 510 was rebuilt with an additional nosewheel assembly and a revised nose section that brought the aircraft's centre of gravity forward. Redesignated as the Type 535, it flew in this new form for the first time on 23 August 1950.

Meanwhile, the first Type 510 had gone to Farnborough where comparative tests were made with the F-86 Sabre. Although it was accepted that the 510 was a relatively unsophisticated research airframe, it still compared well to the Sabre, and at heights of around 25,000 feet the performance characteristics of the two aircraft were quite similar. Supermarine's engineers and test pilot Dave Morgan

VV119 was the second of two prototypes, and designated by Supermarine as the Type 528. This view emphasises the revised undercarriage arrangement, with a nosewheel structure introduced, together with a longer (balancing) nose section.

actually went to RAF North Luffenham to examine RCAF Sabres in some detail, although the visit did little more than demonstrate just how much work would have to be done if Supermarine was to catch up with the dazzling F-86. The RAE at Farnborough were quite impressed with the 510, though, and felt that the only major shortfall when compared to the Sabre was the 510's relatively poor surface finish that was a symptom of the aircraft's 'one-off' nature, although given Supermarine's recognition of the value of smooth surface finishes (which led to the Attacker's laminar flow wing) it is surprising that more attention was not given to this seemingly minor matter. After its stay at the RAE, VV106 returned to Supermarine for modification to a standard compatible with Royal Navy operations, and in addition to a tail hook, the undercarriage was strengthened for carrier trials. Lt Jock Elliot duly performed the first carrier landing by a swept-wing jet on 8 November 1950. For take-off the aircraft was fitted with RATOG (Rocket Assisted Take-Off Gear) packs attached to the fuselage above and below the wing trailing edges. With only two rockets fitted, the 510 required just 500 feet to get airborne, although on one test launch a rocket failed and the aircraft slewed to the left, hitting a gun turret. Thankfully the pilot, Lt-Cdr Parker, maintained control and managed to fly the aircraft back to shore safely and the sea trials were judged to be successful, although the Royal Navy subsequently expressed no great interest in ordering a production version of the aircraft.

The Type 535 in its much-modified form continued into 1951, and by July the aircraft was being subjected to level flight speed recordings, demonstrating an impressive 622 mph at 15,000 feet, 609 mph at 26,000 feet, and 583 mph at 35,000 feet. It suffered some damage during a landing in January 1952, but by March it was airborne again, although by this stage progress was being made by another developmental aircraft in the shape of the Type 541, which was in effect the last aircraft in the process that would lead towards a production-standard fighter. Two 541 aircraft were ordered under Specification F.105P2, outlining an aircraft that was essentially the same as that which Hawker was developing (the Hunter).

The Type 541 looked outwardly similar to the 535 but was in fact markedly different, especially in terms of the engine that powered it. Gone was the bulky Nene and in its place was a considerably smaller (but more powerful) axial-flow Rolls-Royce RA.7 Avon, delivering 7,500 lb of thrust. Oddly, a reheat system was not fitted, although for the purposes of flight testing it was probably regarded as unnecessary. The additional space created internally by the removal of the Nene engine was not used either, and the fuel capacity remained the same. However, the notion of gun armament being fitted into the wings was dropped and this enabled the aileron span to be increased. The wing tips were reshaped as was the leading edge of the fin, and in place of the unusual tailplane incidence system adopted by the 535 (in which the entire tail cone section was hinged to move with the tailplane) a new variable-incidence tailplane design was introduced. Preparations were made for an appearance at the 1951 SBAC show, but the new Avon engine was unreliable and on 3 August it failed in flight. Test pilot Mike Lithgow was flying the aircraft in formation with a Supermarine Spitfire (for publicity photographs) but when the rendezvous was completed, the 541 began to develop airframe vibration. As engine power was increased, vibrations quickly grew to an uncontrollable level and the engine failed, after which Lithgow slowed the aircraft until the vibrations ceased. He then made a controlled glide back to Chilbolton and recovered the aircraft to the airfield without any further difficulties. The cause – which was found to be aileron flutter – was easily rectified, but just two days before the SBAC show on 8 September, David Morgan was flying the Type 541 (WJ960) again, when the engine suddenly failed at 800 feet on approach to Chilbolton. Morgan was presented with a very difficult situation as he had little speed and height from which to rescue the aircraft, and ahead of him was a river, with hills to each side. He elected to raise the aircraft's undercarriage and turn downwind, allowing the aircraft to land on open ground, where it skidded under high-tension cables and finally collided with an apple tree and a brick building (allegedly a toilet). Remarkably, WJ960 (and Morgan) survived the incident without any major damage and just three months later the aircraft was flying again, only to encounter yet another engine failure on 8 April 1952, this time with rather less catastrophic results.

The engine problems were finally resolved by Rolls-Royce over the following weeks and by July, Supermarine had enough confidence in the aircraft to send it

Type 541 prototype WJ965 made its first flight on 18 July 1952. It went supersonic for the first time on 26 February of the following year over Chilbolton airfield.

Pre-production Swift WJ960 first flew on 1 August 1951. As can be seen, it retained much of the Supermarine Type 510's design, despite having a longer nose and a new tricycle undercarriage arrangement.

to the Brussels Exhibition. A recorded flight time from London to Brussels was made, the average speed being 665.9 mph and the journey taking just 18 minutes. In August, the aircraft was transferred to Boscombe Down and by this time the second Type 541 was flying. WJ965 made its first flight, from Boscombe Down, on 18 July in the hands of David Morgan.

This aircraft, which was in fact the first on which the name 'Swift' was bestowed, was far more representative of a production-standard aircraft, with additional internal fuel capacity (raising the total to 778 gallons – much more than Hawker's rival design), modified air intakes (better suited to the Avon engine), repositioned wings, a modified fin, a shorter nose (giving the pilot a better view) and provision for operational equipment. Flight testing revealed a repetition of the aileron flutter that had affected the first prototype (this time it was caused by weight-saving changes to the wing skin) and in order to cure the problem, full power-operated ailerons were fitted, although the initial 'fix' was to remove the aileron spring tabs. In September, the Swift made its public debut at Farnborough and the gleaming silver jet attracted a great deal of attention, especially when it thundered past the assembled crowds at high speed. It was perhaps a good thing that the crowds could not see the effect that the display was having on the aircraft's wings. Morgan later admitted that at speeds of around 550 knots the aircraft 'practically dissolved' with vibration. However, the aileron flutter issue was finally resolved over subsequent weeks and, on 24 February, Morgan recorded a speed of just over Mach 1, thanks to the attachment of a pitot/static test boom, although he had encountered similar conditions on the previous flight, suggesting that he may well have already gone supersonic. But to confirm that the Swift could now achieve supersonic flight, a carefully aimed dive was made over Chilbolton on 26 February, planting a very impressive sonic boom over the airfield, much to the delight of the Supermarine personnel who were there to hear it.

A production order for 100 aircraft was placed by the Ministry of Supply in November 1950, and from an initial development batch of twenty aircraft the first two were completed at the company's Hursley Park facility. Subsequent aircraft were manufactured at Supermarine's South Marston factory and the first production Swift F Mk 1 took to the air for the first time on 25 August 1952.

At this stage, the RAF was unable to judge whether the Swift or Hawker's Hunter would be more suitable for production in larger numbers, and both designs were pursued with equal enthusiasm. It was believed that the Swift was initially the favoured aircraft because of its greater fuel capacity, created by the internal space that was previously occupied by the bulky Nene engine. However, it is also true that the Swift Mk 1 was not exactly over-endowed with armament. Unlike the Hunter, it boasted only two ADEN 30 mm cannon located under the cockpit, and although Supermarine eventually decided that the cannon fit should be doubled, the Swift was already too advanced to introduce a better armament fit from the outset.

The Swift F Mk 2 was therefore introduced into the production schedule as rapidly as possible, this variant representing the modified aircraft, incorporating

WJ965 in fight, its polished metal surfaces glistening in winter sunlight. The small vertical tail surface compares to the even smaller tail fitted to the Type 510, which did not include the substantial dorsal spine extension seen here.

WJ965 during a Farnborough performance in 1952. Sadly, the aircraft was destroyed in a fatal crash late in 1953.

Swift F Mk 1 WK194 enjoyed a service life of little more than three years. It was eventually used for fire and rescue practice at Farnborough until the early 1960s.

four ADEN cannon. Ammunition was now stored in a space created by extending the inboard wing root leading edge and although this seemingly minor aerodynamic modification was barely noticeable to a casual observer, it had a profound effect upon the aircraft's performance. If it was flying at speeds of Mach 0.85 or more, the application of any backwards pressure on the control column caused the Swift's nose to immediately pull upwards and the Swift flipped over onto its back. This was not the kind of behaviour expected from a front-line fighter jet and although it was not sufficiently severe as to be a danger to either the aircraft or pilot, it clearly had to be cured. Various wing modifications were explored, including fences, 'dog-tooth' leading edges and vortex generators, but the eventual cure was found by shifting the aircraft's centre of gravity forwards. This 'fix' worked well, but as it required the installation of concrete ballast in the nose it came at a price and the aircraft's altitude capability was compromised.

To add to Supermarine's problems, further difficulties were encountered with the early Avon engines and many gleaming new Swifts made dead-stick glides back to South Marston after experiencing engine failures during their pre-delivery flights. Rolls-Royce had encountered no such difficulties with the same engine when it was installed in the Hunter, Canberra and other types, and concluded that the cause was the Swift's inlet ducts that contributed to the risk of the engine's compressor disc failing. Consequently, Supermarine's designers were obliged to

Swift F Mk 2 WK214 was delivered to the RAF in December 1954. After being assigned to trials at Boscombe Down it was withdrawn early in 1957 and scrapped at RAF Kirkham in 1958.

devote time to improving this part of the airframe, whilst still trying to fix the aircraft's troublesome wing.

The seemingly endless difficulties were compounded by the 1953 Coronation Review of the RAF – an event that the Air Ministry clearly regarded as a huge showcase, and one that had to include the latest of the RAF's acquisitions. It was decided that a Hunter and five Swifts would end the huge flypast, and Supermarine worked hard to ensure that five aircraft were fit to take part in this major event. In fact, the participation of the Swifts was a huge gamble and nobody was entirely confident that they would successfully fly over Her Majesty and RAF Odiham before suffering engine failures. Brand-new engines were installed in each aircraft for the flypast and on the day they did of course make their appearance over Odiham, but just minutes later Mike Lithgow's aircraft lost its engine and Lithgow was obliged to glide back to Chilbolton. Rather ironically, Rolls-Royce then discovered that the cause of the engine failures had nothing to do with the Swift's engine inlet ducts and had in fact been due to a minor alteration to the engine's compressor attachments made by one of the companies to which Avon manufacture had been outsourced. All of the modifications and testing performed by Supermarine had been entirely pointless.

The Swift entered service with the RAF on 20 February 1954, when F Mk 1 WK209 was delivered to No. 56 Squadron at Waterbeach, and was followed by the first F Mk 2 on 30 August. Eight of the early F Mk 1 aircraft had been delivered by May, but WK209's stay was short and on the 7th of that month it was destroyed after entering a spin near West Raynham. WK208 was also destroyed, on 13 May, when it crashed shortly after take-off, killing its pilot who was making only his second flight in the Swift. The entire fleet was immediately grounded while modifications were made to the aileron controls and various other minor modifications were introduced. The first modified aircraft was flown by a Supermarine test pilot on 23 July, but various problems still persisted within the F Mk 1 fleet and on 25 August only one F Mk 1 (WK213) was deemed serviceable. During a flight from Waterbeach that day, the aircraft suffered an undercarriage failure (the nosewheel refused to extend); the pilot (Flg Off. Hobbs) ejected near Newmarket and the aircraft was abandoned. The F Mk 1 fleet was immediately grounded.

Deliveries of the F Mk 2 continued, however, but serviceability was still poor and various in-flight handling difficulties persisted. A great deal of No. 56 Squadron's flying was therefore conducted on Meteors, so that the unit's pilots could retain flying proficiency while the Swift's problems were sorted out. The F Mk 1 had gone to Boscombe Down for evaluation from January until April 1954, and although most of the aircraft's faults were known (and Supermarine believed that they could all be rectified easily), the A&AEE pilots reported that the Swift displayed 'major deficiencies' that rendered it unfit for full service use. The nose pitch-up problem that affected the F Mk 2 had also been encountered in different circumstances on the F Mk 1 and this had a marked effect on the aircraft's safe turning performance. Elevator control was poor at high Mach numbers, the extension of the airbrakes caused a severe nose-down trim change above Mach 0.96, and the turning performance at altitude was often curtailed by the onset of buffeting. Even the engine was regarded as unsatisfactory and prone to surging either when the guns were fired or even in normal flight conditions. Stall and spin tests revealed that dangerous rates of descent and pro-spin tendencies were present too, and the combined effect of all these problems (plus others) made the aircraft far from suitable for routine operations. It was probably only the RAF's sense of urgency that allowed the aircraft to enter service so soon, when it was clearly not ready for operational use.

The RAF did impose restrictions on the aircraft when it first entered service, and a 633 mph limit was applicable up to 5,000 feet, and Mach 0.9 thereafter, with an altitude limit of 25,000 feet. But while the A&AEE were quite scathing with their comments, the AFDS (Air Fighting Development Squadron) at West Raynham were rather more positive. They established that in a dive from 40,000 feet the Swift accelerated rapidly, and at an angle of 30 degrees it quickly attained Mach 0.96 IAS, equating to a true Mach number of 1.0. In fact, the aircraft could do even better and on one flight the Swift was rolled onto its back at 40,000 feet at Mach 0.8 and pulled down into a vertical dive, at which stage Mach 1 was immediately achieved, and acceleration continued to Mach 1.13. Even if the Swift had its faults, nobody could deny that it was fast. The AFDS also reported that the Swift's aerobatic qualities were good, with a high rate of roll and good control. However, when it came to the more serious issue of fighting ability, the outlook was not so good, thanks to the imposition of an altitude limit and the demonstrably poor turning performance. In trials against other fighter types it was established that the Swift could prevail only if its superior speed was exploited, but when contemporary fighters had a better turning ability and a much better altitude performance, the Swift was clearly at a disadvantage.

When the F Mk 2 was evaluated at Boscombe Down it was soon discovered that the aircraft suffered from the same deficiencies, plus some new ones of its own, the A&AEE reporting that the aircraft was 'far below the standard of an operational interceptor fighter', although with modifications and more flying restrictions it was judged suitable for limited use. The RAF's unhappy experience with the first Swifts led to a decision in March 1955 to withdraw the type from RAF service, and No. 56 Squadron's aircraft were flown out of Waterbeach over the following weeks to No. 33 Maintenance Unit at Lyneham for storage and eventual reuse as instructional airframes. Much to the disappointment of Supermarine, No. 56 Squadron was allocated a new batch of Hawker Hunter fighters.

The Swift F Mk 3 was an improvement over the earlier variants, not least because it boasted a new Avon engine equipped with reheat, together with an improved wing design, tailplane vortex generators and other improvements. The CFE evaluated the new variant in January 1955, and it demonstrated a much better altitude performance, plus a better time-to-height capability thanks to its reheated engine, but the afterburner needed to be ignited continually to achieve this performance and this obviously had a major effect on the aircraft's endurance. It was also heavier and this reduced its manoeuvrability, as exemplified by dive tests that showed how the Hunter required 4,000 feet in which to recover from a 45 degree dive, while the Swift needed 8,600 feet. In its favour, the pitch-up problem had finally gone, longitudinal control was better and the approach and landing qualities were improved, but despite these positive points the RAF decided not to adopt the Mk 3 for operational use and it never entered RAF service. Two were used for evaluation and testing, while the remaining twenty-three aircraft were completed at South Marston and immediately relegated to ground instructional duties.

The story of the F Mk 4 was rather more positive, but for reasons that were not evident when the new variant first emerged. The prototype of this version (WK198) introduced a revised wing shape incorporating a saw-tooth leading edge (although this was not present when the aircraft was first completed), together with a variable-incidence tailplane, engine reheat and only two guns instead of four. These changes were intended to resolve all of the Swift's outstanding deficiencies and demonstrate to the RAF that the aircraft could be adopted as an operational fighter. The Mk 4's fin was also subsequently enlarged in order to provide better control when a new 220 gallon ventral tank was attached under the fuselage. The gun fit was restored to four and with an all-flying tail (eventually modified to a 'slab' tailplane) the F Mk 4 became the full expression of the long design process that had begun with the Type 510 and effectively ended with this, the Type 546, which was the first truly viable Swift fighter variant. But by this stage, the RAF had lost almost all of its confidence and interest in the Swift, whilst far more enthusiasm was being directed towards Hawker's Hunter. Apart from the growing feeling that the RAF had ordered more new fighters than it actually now needed (and certainly more than the Treasury felt it could afford), the Hunter was demonstrating that it was more than capable of becoming the RAF's second-generation jet fighter, even though it did not have the Swift's range and could not fly as fast. As if to press home this point, WK198 established a new world air speed record on 25 September 1953, achieving 735.7 mph over Libya, in the hands of Mike Lithgow, just weeks after he had flown the aircraft from London to Paris at a record speed of 669.3 mph.

However, the Swift's speed and endurance could not compensate for the many problems that had dogged its development and early production. The Hunter's success sealed the Swift's fate and like the F Mk 3, the Swift F Mk 4 was not ordered into full-scale production. Nine Mk 4 aircraft were eventually built, but the RAF no longer wanted the Swift as a fighter. Supermarine hoped that the aircraft might be suitable as a ground attack aircraft, but this concept did not seem to interest the RAF any more than the prospect of reintroducing the Swift as a fighter.

The RAF did, however, recognise that the Swift's speed and endurance would potentially make the aircraft more than suitable for the reconnaissance role, and the Mk 4 was therefore developed into the Swift FR Mk 5, complete with a longer nose designed to accommodate cameras, together with a reduced armament of two cannon and provision for external wing fuel tanks (plus a new clear canopy hood). In this new guise, the FR Mk 5 flew for the first time on 27 May 1955. It was judged to be a very satisfactory reconnaissance platform and eighty-nine aircraft were produced for the RAF, No. 2 Squadron in Germany taking delivery of the first reconnaissance Swift in January 1956. No. 79 Squadron also received the Swift, and the two units found their experience with the Swift to be more than satisfactory. At low level the Swift performed well, with plenty of fuel to embark upon long missions, and a reheated engine to provide a burst of speed whenever it was needed. The airframe was rugged and ideal for high-speed and low-level sorties across Germany and although the RAF soon acquired Hunters for the reconnaissance role, the Swift squadrons were reluctant to part with their aircraft, and the Swift continued to fly with both units for quite some time after they had ostensibly re-equipped with Hunters.

The Swift's connections with fighter operations effectively came to and end when No. 56 Squadron disposed of its aircraft, but the Swift made a brief reappearance in 1956 in the shape of the F Mk 7, a variant first proposed during August 1952, based around the carriage of four Blue Sky air-to-air missiles in addition to the Swift's usual armament of four cannon. With an Avon 116 engine rated at 7,550 lb thrust and a new nose section containing radar, the Swift Mk 7 promised to be a potent fighter, but after so many difficulties with the Swift's earlier development, the RAF was not exactly over-enthusiastic, and the Ministry

An unusual view of the Swift FR Mk 5, illustrating the nose camera installation and the huge belly tank that provided the Swift with a very respectable endurance capability.

of Supply ordered just twelve aircraft, all of which would be assigned to trials work.

The first production aircraft (XF113) made its maiden flight in August 1956 and subsequent aircraft were delivered to Boscombe Down for testing, while two aircraft eventually went to RAF Valley to conduct live missile firing trials within the Aberporth range. Ten aircraft eventually were assigned to No. 1 Guided Weapons Development Squadron at Valley and as such they were the first British aircraft in military service to be equipped with missiles. The Blue Sky missile became the Fairey Fireflash and although a great deal of trials work was undertaken at Valley (some 300 missiles were eventually fired), the testing was devoted largely to development of the missile rather than the aircraft that was launching it, and when the Fireflash test programme was complete, the Swifts were withdrawn from use. One of these aircraft was XF114 and after being assigned to Bristol Siddeley Engines at Filton, it became a trials aircraft with the Cranfield Institute of Technology, repainted in an overall black paint scheme. As such, it was the very last active Swift, and remained in use until 1967.

The Swift programme had been troubled from the start, and the way in which so many were ordered and subsequently abandoned became a public scandal. Both the media and politicians took up the issue and a great deal of governmental investigation was conducted in order to try and establish how so much expenditure had produced so little. The Swift was dogged by developmental problems, but in reality these deficiencies were no more than would be expected with any new combat aircraft. The problem was that with the Cold War developing and the Korean War suddenly emerging, the British Government suddenly needed fighters fast, and the adoption of the Swift was undoubtedly premature. The Swift's design and development was hurried, and its introduction into RAF service was implemented much sooner than it should have been. The decision to order the Swift made sense, but to cancel it when so many aircraft had been ordered was costly and wasteful. Many observers suggested that the Swift's faults were often exaggerated by those would sought to justify the abandonment of the aircraft (particularly the F Mk 4) and many people who were involved with No. 56 Squadron's brief association with the type believed that the Swift was a good aircraft that simply needed further refinements. Others felt that the Swift was a costly mistake, and that it should have been abandoned at a much earlier stage. What is undeniably true is that even though the Swift never became the fighter that it could have been, it did become a first-class reconnaissance aircraft and like many other British combat aircraft, it was more a victim of politics than technical failure.

CHAPTER FIVE
Sabre Rattling

During the years that immediately followed the Second World War, Britain possessed a huge aviation industry that was the envy of the world. Of course, Britain's capacity for designing and manufacturing aircraft was born of necessity, and the dark years of the war had pushed British scientists and designers to their limits. When the conflict ended, things changed quite dramatically and, at least for a short while, Britain no longer had the same eagerness for advancement or the appetite for production. While the wartime fighters and bombers were largely dumped and cut up as scrap metal, the RAF and Fleet Air Arm moved into the jet age, although this process was slow and laborious now that there was no longer any obvious enemy to fight, or even prepare to fight. Of course, the prospect of long-term peace did not last for long, and when the Korean War suddenly developed and the first steps towards what became the Cold War were taken, Britain's politicians quickly shifted their positions. Suddenly there was a need for rearmament and although the RAF was already embarking on a programme of re-equipment with new jet bombers and fighters, it needed them sooner rather than later. Britain's aviation industry soon stepped up its design and production capacity when it needed to, but the early post-war years were a time when the country had almost imperceptibly lost its leading flair for innovative design, the leading technological progress coming almost inevitably from across the Atlantic. America's aviation industry had kept pace with Britain's throughout the war, and when Nazi Germany was defeated, many of its leading scientists (particularly those specialising in aviation) were taken to the USA, while a great deal of captured data was recovered by the US as its troops progressed through Germany. It was not surprising, therefore, that America soon acquired a great deal of technological know-how, and of course there was already plenty of scientific, industrial, commercial and political will to do something useful with it.

One of the most significant concepts that came directly from German research was the swept wing. America acquired a lot of knowledge on this subject, as did Britain, but it was in the USA that the concept was first translated into a truly practical application. The story began with the NA-134, an aircraft proposed by North American Aviation (NAA), to operate from the US Navy's carriers in support of an expected invasion of Japan sometime in 1946. Work on the project began in 1944 and created a simple fighter design that incorporated a jet engine, a nose intake and a straight, thin-wing set low down on a fairly short fuselage. The US Navy duly ordered three prototypes in January 1945 and by May an order had been placed for 100 of what was to become the FJ-1 fighter.

While this process was taking place, the US Army Air Force issued a design request for a day fighter capable of undertaking both an escort fighter role and that of a ground attack aircraft (a 'fighter-bomber'). A rather ambitious 600 mph was stipulated as a desired top speed, and NAA developed its FJ-1 design into the RD-1265 in order to meet this new request. Just days before the Navy placed its initial order, the USAAF ordered three of what had by now become the XP-86. The two requirements were brought together into one design, but it soon became clear that two distinctly different aircraft would be needed to meet what were very different requirements. Despite this, both designs shared the same basic configuration and also shared the same armament (0.5 calibre machine guns) and the same engine, a General Electric J35. It was estimated that the XP-86 would be capable of reaching 574 mph at sea level and 582 mph at 10,000 feet. This was good, but not as good as the 600 mph that the USAAF had hoped for, and in order to accommodate the Air Force's ambitions, NAA decided to adopt an improved design, based on data that had emerged on swept wings. Approval was given by the Head of Air Force Research and Development to refit the existing design with swept wings, a swept fin and tailplanes, and although it was accepted that changing the design so radically would incur delivery delays, the Air Force believed that these delays would be worthwhile if a much faster aeroplane was the result. In fact, the redesigned XFJ-1 flew almost a year later, on 27 November 1946.

An order for thirty-three production P-86A aircraft was issued on 20 December 1946, the 'P' prefix (for 'Pursuit' aircraft) being changed to a more modern 'F' for 'Fighter' in June 1948. The prototype XP-86 was powered by a J35 engine as planned, but production aircraft (the F-86A) were equipped with General Electric's J47 engine. The prototype made its maiden flight on 1 October 1947, and the aircraft was immediately hailed as a great success. NAA proceeded to produce developments of the aircraft in the shape of the F-86E, F-86F, F-86H, and the more advanced F-86D and F-86L, equipped with reheated engines and radar. The aircraft was also developed for the Navy, but naval interest in the aircraft was markedly less than the enthusiasm expressed by the Air Force.

Not surprisingly, the F-86 also quickly became a potential export product, and by the beginning of 1949 the Canadian Government was negotiating with NAA, with the new Sabre on the table. However, the USAF was keen to acquire as many examples of the F-86 as swiftly as possible, and NAA was simply unable to find any capacity to manufacture any aircraft for any other customer. The solution was to extend a licence to Canada (obtained for $1 million) to manufacture the aircraft in Canada under the management of the Canadair company in Montreal. In March 1949, the F-86 was named 'Sabre' and in August a contract was signed for Canadair to produce 100 aircraft. The first of Canadair's aircraft emerged

RAF Sabres pictured in Canada at the beginning of their long delivery flight to the UK as part of Operation Bechers Brook.

from the factory early in August 1950. Essentially an F-86A, it was redesignated as the CL-13 Mk 1, although all subsequent aircraft manufactured were Mk 2 aircraft, based on the F-86E with its more advanced all-flying tailplane design. The prototype's maiden flight was on 8 August, and the first production-standard Sabre Mk 2 flew for the first time on 31 January 1951, the first of some 350 aircraft delivered to the RCAF during April of that year. The introduction of a Canadian-built Orenda 3 engine, rated at 6,000 lb, enabled many of the RCAF aircraft to be powered by an indigenous powerplant, and various Mk 3, 5 and 6 aircraft were developed as part of the overall production batch. The Mk 4, however, was to see service far from Canadian shores.

The British Government (and particularly the Air Ministry) had followed the development of the Sabre with great interest from the very beginning of the project. English Electric's test pilot Roland Beamont test flew the aircraft during a visit to the USA in May 1948, and even with a 4,000 lb engine the second prototype XP-86 certainly impressed him. He reported that the aircraft handled remarkably well, achieved excellent speeds and altitudes, and even had a well laid out cockpit that was a joy to fly in. A serving RAF pilot, Flt Lt Paddy Harbison, subsequently became the next 'Brit' to fly the Sabre, after becoming an exchange pilot with the 1st Fighter Group at March AFB in California. He too was greatly impressed by the aircraft and on his return to the UK during the summer of 1950, he shared his enthusiasm with his RAF colleagues and more than a few Air Force chiefs. However, few people in the UK were convinced that either he or Beaumont were being entirely honest about the Sabre's capabilities. After all, the RAF had the Meteor and the Vampire and both aircraft were regarded as being

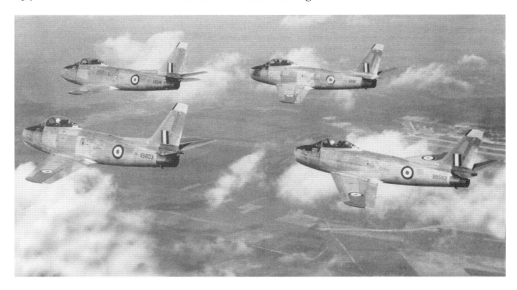

Four Sabres from the newly formed Sabre Conversion Flight. These aircraft still retain high-visibility red patches that were applied to some aircraft for their delivery flight. Home base (RAF Wildenrath) is just visible in the distance.

at the very forefront of jet fighter design, and it seemed likely that the American experience must have been a triumph of presentation over capability. However, this view quickly changed when the Korean War began. The Meteor saw service in the theatre with the Royal Australian Air Force, and the Meteor pilots soon discovered that the jet was no match for the MiGs that marauded in the skies over Korea. The hapless Meteor was quickly shifted from the role of a fighter to that of a ground attack aircraft, and the USAF was left to take on the MiGs with the fast and agile F-86 Sabre.

The RAF reluctantly learned the lessons of Korea, realising that a new swept-wing fighter was needed – and needed fast. Supermarine's Swift was on the proverbial horizon as was Hawker's Hunter, but in the shorter term there was no prospect of a new swept-wing fighter being produced in Britain. The only means of getting one would be to buy from overseas. Indeed, the only aircraft that could possibly give the RAF what it needed was the F-86 Sabre. However, on 13 September 1950, the Chief of the Air Staff (CAS) Sir John Slessor obtained a briefing on Canada's Avro CF-100 all-weather fighter as a potential candidate to meet the RAF's Specification F.4/48. In response, the Ministry of Defence outlined to Slessor all of Canada's aircraft projects, including the licence production of F-86 Sabres. Slessor was not particularly interested in the Sabre, believing that an off-the-shelf purchase of an existing aircraft was unnecessary when the Swift and Hunter would be available to the RAF in due course. The problem with this view was that the development of British fighters would take time, and of course there was no guarantee that any of the projects would create a viable combat aircraft. By comparison, the Sabre already existed and it was demonstrably capable of providing the performance that the RAF required. Slessor remained unimpressed, but in October 1950 he flew to Canada to tour aircraft production facilities and to see precisely what was on offer. Canada's extensive, high-quality facilities were sufficient to change his view and he quickly accepted that the F-86 was perhaps not such a crazy idea. It was clear that Canada had the capability and capacity to manufacture the Sabre quickly, and to provide the RAF with a very capable jet fighter far faster than any British manufacturer ever could. His conclusion was that the 'F-86 looks like being far the earliest answer to our most unpleasant problem'.

Meanwhile, the Air Standardisation Co-ordination Committee Combined Test Project Agreement had been signed on 14 September. This rather unwieldy title outlined an arrangement that would enable Britain to evaluate the F-86 Sabre more extensively without any interference from commercial and industrial interests (indeed, Britain's aircraft manufacturers were specifically excluded from any access to the aircraft). Two F-86A aircraft were delivered to RAF West Raynham on 14 October 1950 and temporarily assigned to the CFE.

During their stay at West Raynham the Sabres were investigated thoroughly. Key areas explored in detail included general handling and performance, engine handling and performance, and tactical operations. As part of this latter phase the Sabres were flown against Meteor fighters and B-29 bombers in low-, medium- and high-level combat exercises. The Sabre's direct comparison with the Meteor was something of a revelation as although the Meteor performed well, the Sabre had a better rate of climb, a better rate of roll, a faster level speed and a faster dive speed. In fact, the Sabre was judged to be far superior to the Meteor in every practical aspect and was therefore a much better fighter aircraft than any other available at that time. The only possible shortfall was the Sabre's machine gun

The CFE conducted trials to establish the effect of camouflage paint on the Sabre's performance. The trials proved that paint had no significant effect and as a result the RAF's Sabre fleet was progressively camouflaged.

armament, which was undoubtedly inferior to the cannon armament fitted to the Meteor.

By March 1951, the evaluation flying at West Raynham was complete and the Sabres went to Boscombe Down where the A&AEE test pilots conducted further handling tests and also performed some weapon suitability exercises together with some instrument error calibration and engine thrust research. The pilots agreed with the CFE's findings that the Sabre was an excellent aircraft, although they believed that the aileron surfaces did not profile sufficient 'feel' through the pilot's controls and that at low speed they were unnecessarily sensitive. Rather oddly, they also commented that the Sabre's cockpit layout was poor, and was somewhat confusing when compared to British aircraft. This was totally at odds with the view expressed by Roland Beamont.

One of the Sabres then went to Farnborough where the aircraft's lateral stability was investigated, followed by a closer look at the aircraft's rudder trim tab and its effectiveness. The aircraft was also examined as part of a profile-drag analysis, to compare with the Supermarine and Hawker fighter designs that were being developed. But the Sabre's stay at Farnborough came to a premature end on 14 August 1952, when the aircraft crashed following an elevator 'runaway' incident. The pilot ejected safely, and the second Sabre was duly sent to Farnborough to continue testing. It was grounded on arrival for rectification of an aileron trim problem and stayed in an RAE hangar until January, but after repair a number of other minor faults had arisen requiring another lengthy stay on the ground. When spare parts were finally obtained, they were found to be the wrong type for this particular variant, so it was not until early March 1953 that the aircraft flew again. After just three days the aircraft suffered hydraulic failure and flying was not resumed until June, some thirteen hours being completed before the aircraft was grounded again for inspection. It returned to flying in February 1954 when a series of flights were conducted to investigate ways in which the aircraft's high-speed performance could be improved. As part of these tests the wing leading edge slats were fixed in a retracted position and sealed smooth, after which vortex generators were tested followed by wing fences, of various sizes and at various positions on the wings. The vortex generators reduced wing drop above Mach 0.92 and increased longitudinal stability, whereas the wing fences delayed the aircraft's tendency to pitch up, at the expense of a slight reduction in overall performance. Finally, a leading edge extension was fitted to each wing, created by fixing the outer two-thirds of the leading edge slats in the two-thirds extended position. This improved the nose-up pitching tendency at Mach 0.8, but had no great effect by the time the aircraft reached Mach 0.92. Much of this testing was a repetition of work that was being conducted by the manufacturer (NAA), but it provided useful independent data for the RAE and served to confirm every detail of the Sabre's performance. Because the second loaned aircraft had spent so much time grounded, two extensions to the load agreement were made and it was not until November 1954 that the aircraft was finally flown back to Burtonwood and handed back to the USAF.

An excellent in-flight image of XB891, wearing the distinctive markings of No. 4 Squadron, together with a white code letter.

Slessor's agreement to procure Sabres for the RAF did not immediately result in a purchase, not least because there was some concern that Britain could barely afford them. Initially, it was expected that US Military Aid would finance the project, but any hopes that the USA would buy the aircraft for Britain were thwarted in October 1950 when the British Joint Services Mission learned from US officials that Military Aid was to be provided for the acquisition of ground attack aircraft only, and that the design and manufacture of fighter aircraft should be undertaken by European NATO members themselves. Although the Sabre was ostensibly a fighter-interceptor, it was accepted that like many other contemporary fighter designs it also had a good ground attack capability, but the US Government regarded the aircraft as a fighter, so there seemed to be no prospect of procuring the aircraft unless it was paid for by the British taxpayer. Slessor continued to plan for a purchase, and outlined a requirement for 380 aircraft to equip six squadrons, each with twenty-two aircraft and a three-month war reserve fleet. He stated that it would be at least two years before so much as one squadron in the RAF would be equipped 'with a type that is not outclassed by the MiG-15'. He advised the Canadian and American governments that the RAF would require 300 Sabres (rather less than he had originally proposed) and the Air Ministry sought clarification from Washington as to precisely what their definition of 'tactical aircraft' was. The response was that it effectively meant fighter-bombers, light bombers and tactical reconnaissance aircraft; therefore the RAF would not be able to use the aircraft as a fighter if it was purchased through MDAP (Mutual Defense Assistance Program) funding. Canada confirmed that Sabres could be manufactured and delivered quickly within MDAP funding arrangements, but if the RAF accepted an order it would have to agree not to use them in the fighter role.

Despite these setbacks, the British Government supported an application from the Air Staff for Slessor's 300 aircraft (and a larger plan for up to 402 aircraft), but when this was submitted on 30 October 1950, it was refused on the grounds that it contravened US policy. Slessor was expecting this response and stated that if the Treasury purchased the aircraft, the RAF could obviously use the Sabres in whatever way British policy required. He added that NAA could supply Sabres at $200,000 per aircraft, whereas Canadair could offer a price tag of $323,000, so an outright purchase from NAA of the F-86E would be the best option for Britain. Washington subsequently informed Britain that NAA simply did not have the production capacity to build Sabres for the RAF quickly and any purchase would therefore have to be placed with Canadair, but many components could be supplied directly from US companies and these could be financed by MDAP funding, thereby making the purchase less expensive without contravening US Government policy. The US Government wanted to help Britain as best it could, but Slessor remained unmoved, stating: 'It hardly seems wise that the US should confine themselves under MDAP to supply of fighter-bombers which we and even France can produce, and withhold high-performance interceptors which at present we cannot.' He subsequently suggested that if the Sabres were assigned to overseas tactical squadrons within the RAF, it might be possible to justify MDAP funding, even if the aircraft were used as fighters once they were acquired. Eventually an agreement was made on this basis, and the US accepted that MDAP funding could cover the purchase of Sabres to equip RAF overseas squadrons, and that they would be used to provide 'top cover' for the RAF's existing Vampire and Venom ground attack aircraft. Of course, this effectively meant that the Sabres would be used as fighters, but the incorporation of the Sabres into a tactical role was enough to cloud the issue sufficiently and enable funding to be made available. On 2 October 1951, the Canadian Government approved the proposed deal, and funding for 395 Sabres was approved by the US Government in February 1952.

After negotiation, it was agreed that 370 Sabres would be produced for the RAF and all of the aircraft would be Mk 4 variants, apart from three which would be F-86E variants with J47 engines. By November 1952, the American attitude on the supply of fighter aircraft had also changed slightly, and the Air Ministry was advised that MDAP would now fund the supply of a further batch of sixty aircraft, these being Canadair Sabre Mk 4 variants that were now surplus to requirements. Crucially, it was agreed that they could be supplied directly to Fighter Command and that some additional aircraft could be transferred from the tactical squadrons in Germany to form three fighter squadrons, each with twenty-two aircraft. By the middle of the following year the RAF's plans had changed and proposals were made for just two Sabre squadrons to be formed in the UK, beginning in September of that year and remaining active until March 1955, when it was estimated that Hunter fighters would be coming into RAF service. However, the RAF's procurement plans were affected by a growing shortage of Sabres

Possibly the most well-known photograph of a British Sabre: XD727 gets airborne from Linton-on-Ouse, proudly wearing the markings of No. 92 Squadron.

within the RCAF squadrons in Germany. The RCAF asked if Sabres destined for the RAF could be loaned to them so that their re-equipment plans could continue at full strength. Despite the obvious fact that the RAF needed the Sabres just as quickly as Canada, it was agreed that sixty aircraft would be diverted to the RCAF until Canadair's production schedule could catch up, at which stage these aircraft would be transferred back to the RAF. The loan was very short-term and, as agreed, the aircraft were withdrawn from Canadian service by December 1953 and ferried to the UK where they were inspected by Airwork before being placed in storage at Kemble, pending delivery to operational units.

Meanwhile, plans had been made to receive the main fleet of Sabres, and rather than take the risky and laborious step of having each aircraft shipped across the Atlantic, the RAF decided to fly them from Canada. The RCAF had flown its aircraft across to Germany (via the UK) and had encountered no significant problems; therefore it seemed logical to follow the same procedure. A final decision was made on 10 July 1952, and with sixty aircraft being allocated to the RCAF loan, some 370 Sabres would require ferrying across the Atlantic under Operation Bechers Brook.

The first task was to train three RAF pilots to fly the Sabres, and the RCAF agreed to provide the training at No. 1 Operational Training Unit based at

A rare image of a Sabre from No. 112 Squadron, in formation with its replacement aircraft in the shape of a Hunter. Both aircraft wear the unit's famous shark's mouth marking.

Chatham, New Brunswick. The three pilots (from No. 1 Overseas Ferry Unit) left for Canada during August and after converting onto the aircraft they were tasked with the ferrying of three aircraft that would be used for initial familiarisation in the UK. While the pilots were training, RAF ground crews were instructed on the Sabre at RAF North Luffenham in Rutland – already an active RCAF Sabre base. The three Sabre F Mk 2 aircraft departed from St Hubert in Canada on 28 September 1952, arriving at Prestwick on 4 October, after which they made the short hop to North Luffenham on the 10th. Although they arrived with RCAF serials, they were soon repainted as XB530, XB531 and XB532 and were immediately allocated to RAF ferry pilot training with No. 1 OFU. Training each pilot took approximately two weeks and with a ground school and 10 flying hours, each ferry pilot was then ready to head for Canada to conduct additional training (including another 15 hours of flying) as well as some very important survival training. Some sixty pilots (all with at least 400 hours of jet flying experience) were also temporarily transferred from 2 TAF in Germany to take part in the ferry exercise, so that sufficient crews would be available for the major task that was at hand.

When each Sabre was completed by Canadair, it was test flown and transferred to Bagotville, Quebec, by RAF pilots. Final maintenance was conducted here and then each aircraft was handed to No. 1 OFU for a few hours of preparatory flying to ensure that the aircraft was free of any potential problems. Airborne servicing teams were gathered in the UK and flown to Canada so that they could accompany the Sabres on their long journey in a Hastings transport, one team flying ahead of each ferry 'package' while the other followed behind, with some additional crew assigned to the care of the Hastings transport itself. The first of the Bechers Brook ferry flights began on 9 December 1952, consisting of nine Sabres rather than the proposed full 'package' of thirty aircraft. A full-sized servicing crew was assigned to the exercise so that as many personnel as possible could gain experience. After leaving Bagotville, the aircraft routed via Goose Bay, Bluie West One, Keflavik and finally Prestwick in Scotland.

Bechers Brook One proceeded without any significant problems until the every end of the exercise, when XB534 crashed whilst on final approach to Prestwick, the pilot being killed in the accident. The remaining eight aircraft finally arrived at RAF Abingdon on 2 January 1953, and the Sabres were officially handed over by the Canadian High Commissioner, who read a message from the Canadian Minister of Defence:

> This ceremony marks the arrival and delivery of the first of the F-86E Sabres provided to the Royal Air Force by Canada. The RAF has already received three aircraft from us, which were flown over in October by RAF pilots, but these were advanced out of our own supply. A little more than a year ago, Mr Arthur Henderson, at that time the Secretary of State for Air, and Marshal of the RAF Sir John Slessor, then Chief of the Staff of the RAF, discussed with Air Marshal Curtis, CAS of the RCAF, and myself the possibility of obtaining Sabre fighters to supplement the air defences in Britain. At about the same time, approaches were made to the United States. The result was an arrangement whereby the United States at their expense provided the engines and other components to be put into aircraft produced by Canadair Ltd, and paid for by Canada, to be delivered for use by the RAF. This was a three-way partnership for our common defence. Production has proceeded so satisfactorily that it has been possible to advance the delivery dates originally proposed so that they are some six months in advance of the original target date. We are now beginning the regular delivery of so many each week and month until the total is completed. The exact number of aircraft has not been announced, but it is between 300 and 400 and I can tell you that it is closer to 400 than to 300. This arrangement represents by far the largest single act of military assistance given by Canada to the United Kingdom since the war. It represents, in the part contributed by Canada alone, a total of about $100 million. We are glad to do this because it is part of our common defence.

Despite the tragic end to Bechers Brook One (the crash being unrelated to the ferry process), the RAF proceeded with Bechers Brook Two and Three. Encouraged by the success of these flights, Bechers Brook Four, which began in March 1953, became a 'double' exercise and when the first gaggle of thirty-two Sabres arrived at each staging post the support crews were flown back to the previous point to support a second wave of another thirty-two aircraft. Some serviceability issues arose but despite minor problems, sixty Sabres were delivered to Abingdon in just four days through this process. The ferry flights continued and a total of 372 aircraft had crossed the Atlantic by May 1954, and Operation Bechers Brook was over.

With the Sabres delivered, the RAF now had to begin converting fighter pilots onto the type, planning for this process having been under way for some time. Pilots assigned to the Sabre were initially sent to the USA where they underwent standard USAF flight training on the F-84 Thunderjet and the F-86. Although this arrangement ensured that the pilots gained a very thorough training, it was an expensive and inconvenient procedure, so from late March 1953, No. 147 Squadron at Abingdon began to undertake Sabre training, and from June the task transferred to Wildenrath in Germany. The plan was for the Germany-based squadrons to be trained at Wildenrath, after which Sabres would be assigned to No. 229 OCU at Chivenor so that the UK fighter pilots could convert onto the Sabre there. The Sabre Conversion Flight was duly formed at Wildenrath, and from June 1954 the training task was undertaken by the OCU at Chivenor.

The first operational RAF squadron to receive the Sabre was No. 67, based at Wildenrath. After receiving aircraft directly from the Bechers Brook ferry flights, the unit began flying operational sorties in May 1953. No. 3 Squadron then began to re-equip with Sabres, and No. 93 Squadron began to receive Sabres in March 1954. Fighter Command took delivery of the second batch of Sabres towards the end of 1953, and in December No. 66 Squadron re-equipped with the type, followed by No. 92 Squadron in February 1954. Both units were based at Linton-on-Ouse in Yorkshire and had previously operated the Meteor.

As expected, the Sabre proved to be an excellent aircraft and one that was liked by all those who flew it. A variety of aerobatic teams appeared, all prompted by the sheer enthusiasm of the squadrons that were lucky enough to fly the sleek and manoeuvrable fighter. It was a major progression from the rather pedestrian Vampire and Meteor, and one that finally enabled the RAF to realise the potential of the jet engine. The Sabre's time with the RAF was short but intentionally so, as the aircraft had never been regarded as anything other than a stopgap until the Hunter entered service. But when the Hunter F Mk 1 first joined the ranks of the RAF, it was less than perfect and it was not until the Hunter F Mk 4 began to appear that the Sabre finally had a successor. During the spring of 1956, the Sabres based at Linton-on-Ouse were replaced by Hunters and by the summer the type had also been withdrawn from Germany, the last aircraft to leave being XB670 of No. 3 Squadron.

Plans to withdraw the Sabre actually began in July 1953, when the Air Staff first discussed how the Sabre would eventually be replaced by the Hunter. It was proposed that the Sabres should be replaced on a one-for-one basis and funded in the same way by the Military Assistance Program (MAP). In August, it was agreed that 220 Sabres could be made available for return to the USA, all overhauled and returned in airworthy condition. In exchange for these, Britain could receive Hunters. Of course, the ownership of the Sabres was split between the USA and Canada, and there was a great deal of discussion as to how the Sabres should be disposed of. Britain favoured the transfer of the aircraft to European nations, particularly Denmark, the Netherlands, Belgium or Norway, but Italy and Yugoslavia were also identified as secondary choices. Agreement was eventually made with Canada to transfer complete ownership of the Sabres to the USA, and despite a lot of discussion, it was effectively the US that finally dictated that the Sabres would be transferred to Italy and Yugoslavia when the RAF disposed of them. In exchange for the return of what the US estimated would be at least 370 Sabres, the RAF hoped for 350 Hunters, although the US Government had to be advised that their estimations on 'returnable' aircraft were wrong. The US assumed that ninety Sabres remained unused in storage, but the RAF estimated that by the end of 1954, there would be only twenty-five aircraft left in storage.

Conversion onto the Hunter began late in 1955, and as each Sabre was withdrawn it was sent to a Maintenance Unit for overhaul. By the time of withdrawal, many of the Sabres had been modified whilst in service, and the original wing with a leading edge 'slat' device had been progressively replaced by a fixed wing of slightly greater span and chord, complete with a small wing fence. The aircraft that had yet to receive this modification were duly brought up to this standard after withdrawal and slowly they were redistributed to Italy and Yugoslavia. The final batch of aircraft delivered to Yugoslavia were not supplied as part of the original agreement, however, as relations between the US and Yugoslavia had deteriorated and MAP aid for that country was cancelled by the end of 1957. However, the aircraft that had yet to be delivered were paid for as an outright purchase from the US, and seventy-eight machines were delivered at a price of between $5,000 and $15,000 per aircraft. Some 302 aircraft were eventually refurbished and transferred to new operators and a further fifty-two Sabres were broken up as scrap. Despite having been overhauled at considerable expense, there was no further interest in them from Italy or Yugoslavia, and the US no longer had any need for them, so the simplest means of disposing of them was simply to write them off. Some were scrapped immediately although a few airframes were still abandoned awaiting destruction even as late as 1973.

The RAF's Sabres were certainly short-lived, but the decision to obtain them was undoubtedly a wise move, especially when the RAF effectively received them for free. A former Sabre pilot is perhaps the best person to sum up the RAF's experience of this fighter:

Compared to the Vampire and the Venom, and even the Meteor, the new Sabre was a real thrill. It seemed like a much more sophisticated aeroplane and even looked the part, whether you looked at it from the ground or sat in its cockpit. With its swept wings it looked like it was meant to be fast and it was. The cockpit was busy with lots of gauges and lights, and it just seemed to fit the part totally, but it wasn't an aeroplane that relied on just appearances as it flew as well as you expected it to fly. Up at altitude of 35,000 feet or more you could easily go supersonic by simply tipping over into a gentle dive and letting the speed shoot upwards. I don't think anyone got tired of the novelty of exceeding Mach One, and in those days there were no major restrictions on noise of the type of flying that you did, so making sonic bangs was something that everyone did all the time and nobody complained; in fact, I think most people were proud and happy to hear them. As the Sabres settled into service we often flew them with external fuel tanks under the wings and these kept the top speed just under supersonic, so the bangs tended to decrease. We were able to put the Sabre into a spin as it was cleared for intentional spinning, unlike many other aircraft. To get into a spin one needed a heavy application of rudder but once into a spin the whole thing was fairly gentle and to recover one simply had to let go of the controls and let the aircraft sort itself out. It could be stalled without any problem too and with external tanks attached it was a predictable aeroplane and it usually stalled straight ahead, and then it tended to vary in pitch as it lost height, but that was all there was to it. Normal handling was excellent with a good rate of roll and responsive controls. It's true that aileron reversal could occur at very high speed but this wasn't a great problem as long as one was aware of it, as it simply reduced the rate of roll. It was caused by the wing flexing, and this says a lot about the strength and integrity of the airframe. I don't think anyone was in any hurry to say goodbye to the Sabre and even though the Hunter that replaced it was a fine machine, I don't think there's much that can be said to criticize the Sabre, apart from its machine gun armament, which was poor when compared to the cannon that would have been so much better. But in terms of performance, especially for the time when it came into service, the Sabre was a great aeroplane.

CHAPTER SIX
Camm's Classic

Like other British designers, Hawker followed the progression of jet engine development with great interest. When work began on the development of a new high-speed bomber design ordered under Specification B.11/41 (a project that was subsequently cancelled), the Hawker team considered the possibility of substituting a pair of Whittle's Power Jets engines to replace the Napier Sabre pistons that had originally been specified. The idea did not progress far, but the idea of using jet power was already beginning to infiltrate the minds of Hawker's design team.

Various projects emerged at the company's Kingston headquarters that seemed suitable for jet power, including the concept of fitting a Power Jets engine to an existing Hawker piston-engine design such as the Sea Fury and Tempest. Fascinating though these proposals may have been, little serious progress was made until Hawker began to learn more about the gas-turbine engines being developed by Rolls-Royce, particularly the new B.41 engine (which eventually became the Nene). The P.1031 essentially consisted of a Sea Fury airframe fitted with a B.40 jet engine in the nose section, replacing the Centaurus piston engine and exhausting under the forward fuselage. The result was an aircraft with an unusual outline but a performance scarcely better than the standard piston-engine Sea Fury. Rather more advanced was the P.1035, which was also based on the Fury airframe but with a B.41 jet engine mounted amidships and with the exhaust in the tail section of the fuselage. The engine's air intakes were positioned in the wing roots (the B.41's double-sided centrifugal compressor enabled air to be fed easily into it from both sides of the fuselage). As the design was refined, the exhaust was also similarly modified so that it fed through bifurcated (split) pipes emerging on either side of the fuselage behind the wing trailing edge, thereby avoiding the predicted loss of valuable thrust caused by a long jet pipe to the tail. This development was given the designation P.1040, and in 1945 Hawker's Project Office continued to develop the design until it reached a stage where it demonstrated a clear potential for significant improvements in performance over earlier designs, and a decision was made to manufacture an unarmed prototype, funded entirely by the company.

The Air Ministry remained sceptical, believing that the design would offer little improvement over the existing Meteors that were still being produced. However, a much more favourable response was received from the Admiralty, which concluded that Hawker's design would certainly perform better than the Supermarine Attacker that was entering Fleet Air Arm service. The Admiralty quickly issued Specification N.7/46 around the new design, and this eventually led to the production of the elegant (and remarkably successful) Sea Hawk. Although the Sea Hawk did not make its first flight until September 1947, Hawker's design team, headed by Sydney Camm, was by this stage looking at more advanced developments of the P.1040 design. Studies that might meet the requirements of the Air Ministry Specification E.38/46 (to undertake studies into the aerodynamic properties of swept wings) prompted Camm to approve the concept of mating the P.1040 fuselage with a new swept wing under the designation P.1052 (which also initially anticipated the use of a rocket engine as a means of propulsion, although this project was ultimately allocated to part of the continuing P.1040 programme), and research on this proposal captured the interest of the RAE at Farnborough. Hawker and the RAE exchanged a great deal of information on the proposed wing layout before settling on a pressure-plotted span of 31 feet 6 inches and a sweep of some 35 degrees, but with an unswept tail unit. The powerplant was to be a 5,000 lb Nene 2, and Hawker expected the aircraft to be capable of reaching a speed of 560 mph at 36,000 feet. The first prototype of the new P.1052 flew on 13 April 1949 and quickly demonstrated that it was more than capable of achieving its predicted performance figures, and ought to be capable of forming the basis of a new jet fighter.

Rolls-Royce was also making further progress with its Nene engine, and with the increased use of magnesium alloy (to reduce weight) and the installation of an afterburner (reheat) unit a further 25 per cent increase in thrust was predicted. This development – which became the Tay engine – together with a suitably modified P.1052 airframe, captured the attention of the Australian Government, where a requirement was emerging for a new fighter aircraft to replace the existing force of Meteors. The second P.1052 prototype was selected for modification, and following trials with the first prototype, which had been conducted from Boscombe Down (including combat exercises flown against Meteors), the opportunity was also taken to introduce swept tail surfaces, as these early P.1052 flight trials had revealed a lack of adequate elevator control. In all other respects, the aircraft had performed remarkably well, apart from a tendency to 'Dutch roll' (an out-of-sequence yawing and rolling movement). The Tay engine's reheat system was not suitable for a bifurcated exhaust layout, so the rear fuselage was also modified to incorporate a straight-through jet pipe emerging under the tail.

However, the development of the Tay engine suffered numerous delays and Hawker was forced to continue work on the new aircraft (designated P.1081) based around the earlier (less powerful) Nene. Not surprisingly, Australia eventually began to lose interest in the project as the delays mounted, and after an NAA mission visited the country to look at the possibility of selling Australia

Hawker P.1052 VX279 over southern England during an early test flight. As can be seen, the aircraft was in effect a Sea Hawk with new swept wings.

the F-86 Sabre, the choice was finally made to abandon the P.1081 in favour of the Sabre (albeit one that was fitted with a Rolls-Royce engine). The prototype P.1081 was eventually completed and showed considerable potential, but without any prospect of a production order it was transferred to the RAE at Farnborough to conduct high-speed research flights. Sadly, the aircraft crashed on 3 April 1951, and Hawker's Chief Test Pilot Trevor Wade was killed. The cause of the accident is unclear, but the aircraft may well have inadvertently gone supersonic and, without adequate elevators, control may have simply been lost. Possibly slowed by the drag of an open cockpit, the aircraft survived the crash almost intact (which says a great deal about the rugged nature of Hawker's construction), but the P.1081 story ended with this tragic incident.

Hawker's interest turned towards even more powerful engines, particularly the new AJ.65 axial-flow turbojet that was being developed by Rolls-Royce. With an anticipated thrust of some 6,500 lb, the new engine would enable Hawker to produce a fighter design that would meet the requirements of the existing F.43/46 requirement, using just a single engine instead of the twin powerplants envisaged in the original specification. Unfortunately, the development of the AJ.65 (which became the Avon) was a difficult and protracted process that extended to some seven years, but at the time of Hawker's initial interest there was no reason to imagine that the engine would not be available within a much shorter timescale,

VX279, modified with swept tail surfaces as the Hawker Type P.1081, created in response to a short-lived requirement expressed by the Australian Government. Its similarity to the later Hunter is evident in this unusual plan-view image.

even though many people felt that the Air Ministry's (and Hawker's) interest in the engine was premature. The Armstrong Siddeley Sapphire was more reliable, less expensive and a more mature design, but Camm's enthusiasm for Rolls-Royce and its Avon was undiminished, so his design team embarked upon a new fighter design based around the new engine. In fact, Hawker produced no fewer than twelve different design studies before settling on a definitive choice.

The long-standing Specification F.43/46 had effectively been abandoned by default, so a new Specification was issued, based on Hawker's plans. F.3/48 called for a single-seat land-based day-interceptor and fighter, able to achieve Mach 0.94 (620 mph at 36,000 feet or 724 mph at sea level), armed with either four 20 mm Hispano cannon or two of the new 30 mm ADEN guns. A radar gunsight would be incorporated together with an ejection seat system for the pilot, and fuel endurance would be some 60 minutes (plus climb-to-height and 10 minutes of combat power). Operational Requirement OR.228/3 (drawn up around the design) specified that the powerplant would be either the Rolls-Royce Avon or the Armstrong Siddeley Sapphire (both types wisely being specified in case further development or production difficulties were encountered with either powerplant). A time-to-height (45,000 feet) of less than 6 minutes from engine start would be necessary, and at a higher altitude of 50,000 feet the aircraft was expected to be able to achieve a climb rate of 1,000 feet per minute and be capable of reaching 547 knots at more than 45,000 feet. The specification also covered the aircraft's airfield performance, and a take-off distance of 1,200 yards was required to clear a 50-foot obstacle. For armament, the P.1067 was initially studied for compatibility with a single 4.5 inch recoilless gun, but when development of this weapon was abandoned Hawker concentrated on the 30 mm ADEN cannon, studying the use of two such weapons with 10 seconds of firing time (200 rpg) or four guns with 7.5 seconds of firing time (150 rpg). As another option, the older Hispano 20 mm cannon was still incorporated into the design as an alternative weapons fit, and the provision for air-to-air rocket batteries or beam-riding air-to-air missiles was also specified, even though such concepts were new and largely unproven.

The new design featured a T-tail structure, twin intakes under the wing roots, and a fattened elliptical fuselage. This unrefined layout was gradually developed so that the intake was repositioned to the nose and the fuselage was reshaped to a more conventional circular cross-section. The four cannon in the nose were repositioned so that two were now fixed in the wing roots, but concern was expressed by avionics experts that the revised intake had resulted in a centrally mounted shock cone that would be too small to accommodate the projected ranging radar that was to be fitted inside it. Likewise, Rolls-Royce expressed its own concern that the long intake ducting would reduce the engine's efficiency, suggesting that Hawker look at shifting the intakes to the wing roots. Camm resisted the pressure to reposition the intake again (a move that would effectively lose the two wing root-mounted guns), but having also been concerned at the increasing lack of space in an already cramped cockpit (where the Air Ministry gradually specified the addition of more and more equipment) it eventually seemed clear to Camm that wing-root intakes would be the only practical option, especially when it became obvious that the revision of the intakes would free up more vital fuselage space for fuel capacity. Consequently, a pair of P.1081-style intakes was incorporated and 50 per cent additional space was created in the cockpit at a stroke, albeit at the expense of losing two of the aircraft's cannon armament.

Camm remained confident that two cannon would be more than sufficient for the new fighter; indeed, it was also the chosen option for the new Swift fighter, which was being designed by Supermarine at the same time. However, one of the Hawker installation design staff suggested that no fewer than four guns, together with their magazines, could be incorporated into a removable pack if it was positioned directly behind the cockpit. Camm had always wanted the P.1067 to be an adaptable and simple design incorporating easily removable components that would be capable of interchangeability wherever possible, so the concept of a removable gun pack (which could be rapidly replaced by a pre-loaded pack, thus improving aircraft turn-round times significantly) appealed to him immensely. The cannon would have only a 7 second firing time (at 135 rpg) in order to give a more reliable ammunition feed, but the pilot would be able to select only one of the two pairs if necessary, to extend the firing time. Together, the four guns gave the new Hawker design a blistering destructive power that was, at the time, unsurpassed by any other operational fighter. Even the F-86's armament was less impressive, comprising just six 0.5 inch machine guns, which were completely outclassed by Hawker's new concept. On the other hand, the F-86E was to be fitted with an all-flying tail, and it is perhaps surprising that more attention was not given to this deficiency in the P.1067.

As the aircraft approached what would be its finalised form, it proceeded to a mock-up stage within the experimental shop at the Kingston factory. Considerable attention was then given to the tail area of the design, after wind tunnel tests suggested the possibility of control problems associated with the high-set tailplane (something that was eventually to cause Gloster plenty of difficulties with its Javelin design). Ultimately, the wing sweep of the tailplane was increased and its position shifted to a location further down the fin, leaving Camm's team to redesign the upper portion of the fin with a graceful sweeping curve that would become a famous characteristic of the completed design.

By April 1949, the basic design of the P.1067 had been fixed, and assembly of the construction jigs for the prototype airframes got under way towards the end of the same year. Of the three planned prototypes, Hawker proceeded to complete one of the aircraft with an Armstrong Siddeley Sapphire engine, largely as part of the 'insurance' policy against possible delays or deficiencies with the continuing Avon programme, although it was agreed that if both engines lived up to their potential, aircraft powered by both types would be ordered into production. The construction jigs were 'hand-built', based on the design staff's figures and practical experience with the full-scale mock-up. Although by modern standards this sort of practice might seem expensive, outdated and impractical, at the time of the new fighter's development, Hawker (like every other British aviation manufacturer) was still very much set in the ways of wartime production procedures. Conforming to Second World War practice, Hawker had decided that the P.1067 should be divided into major units that could be completed individually and would be available as fully equipped spares if needed. It was broken down into six fully interchangeable major components: front fuselage, which carried the cockpit, armament pack, nosewheel and the cowling for the radar-ranging sight and camera gun; centre fuselage, with integral wing roots, engine supports and air intake ducts; detachable rear fuselage, with integral fin base and removable jet pipe/tail cone unit; tail unit assembly; and main planes, complete with the main undercarriage legs. For final assembly it was necessary only to connect together the structural members and to plug the pipes and leads together, and one reason for this method was the difficulty inherent in building a relatively complex aircraft in a number of factories some distance apart.

Hawker's facilities were not conveniently housed under one roof. Construction and flight testing of the P.1067 would have taken place at Hawker's Langley airfield (famous as the home of the wartime Hurricane), but as mentioned earlier, although the airfield had been perfectly suitable for piston-engine designs, it

WB188, the Hunter F Mk 1 prototype, is high above the clouds, resplendent in its unusual Duck Egg Green paint scheme, complete with distinctly oversized national insignia.

was considered unsuitable to accommodate jet operations safely, especially with the ever-growing Heathrow Airport not too far away. While the company's new airfield at Dunsfold was being prepared for test flying, the completed P.1067 prototype (WB188) was dismantled at Kingston and transported by road to Boscombe Down, from where it emerged from its hangar in June 1951.

The first engine run was conducted on 1 July and although taxi trials were then conducted without any major difficulties, the prototype's differential braking system developed a fault on 8 July during a high-speed taxi run, causing the brakes to burn out and WB188 to veer off the runway. Dunlop rectified the problem in just ten days and the programme continued without any further delay. Satisfied that the prototype was ready for flight, after a series of high-speed runs along the runway the P.1067 was topped up with 220 gallons of fuel and test pilot Neville Duke took WB188 into the air for the first time on the afternoon of 20 July for a 47 minute flight over Wiltshire, Hampshire and Dorset. Duke later commented:

> The Hunter seemed a pilot's aeroplane all the way from drawing board to roll-out; it looked right both on paper and in its finished form. The cockpit felt right and was just small enough to make one feel entirely a part of the aeroplane. It was slightly narrow at the shoulders, giving the snug effect common to British fighters, and the

position of the seat gave a commanding view and a feeling that the aeroplane was an extension of oneself.

This first test flight included a climb to 32,000 feet where a series of fairly gentle handling manoeuvres was conducted, before Duke descended to 10,000 feet to complete a series of stall tests at various flap settings, with the undercarriage both raised and lowered. Overall, speed was kept subsonic, not exceeding Mach 0.88. After completing the flight, and removing his American-style 'bone dome' helmet (possibly the first time such gear had been worn by a British pilot), Duke reported that the aircraft had handled extremely well, although there was some post-flight concern that it had consumed rather more fuel than Rolls-Royce had predicted. This matter was not resolved until further test flights had been completed, at which stage it was discovered that the rear fuselage fuel tank had a small leak and had been losing fuel during each flight. For the first flight, the elevator hydraulic boost had been disconnected, although the aileron's system was active (caution was exercised because so little practical knowledge of such systems was available at the time), but the result of this configuration was that the elevator forces were unreasonably heavy, while in comparison the ailerons were extremely light. Another minor problem was that the tailplane trimmer (electrically actuated) was set within an unacceptable range, and Duke had to exercise a considerable amount of brute force to keep the aircraft set up for the first landing:

> The UK was particularly backward in powered flying controls. This is why the Hunter first flew as the P.1067 with the elevators in manual mode. Any Hunter pilot will tell you that manual really does mean manual and it is the emergency means of control should the normal system be lost. This manual control, plus the all-moving trimming tailplane, which had inadequate trim range for landing, resulted in a very considerable two-handed heave-to round-out for the first landing. These were the days of the 'super-priority' production programme, which was a mixed blessing under which development was expedited, while the incorporation of improvements and modifications found necessary during flight testing was affected by the need to freeze production drawings. The Hunter was one of the few aircraft ordered in large quantities from the drawing board. The flight-test programme proceeded with few snags or delays, and the aircraft was being flown at speeds of more than 700 mph within a month of the first flight. At first we were not entirely sure of achieving supersonic flight. Mach number indicator (MNI) readings were unreliable and grossly in error at extreme high speed. But the supersonic boom soon provided confirmation and heralded the era of the phenomenon at Farnborough-type public displays (until people got fed up with it). Needless to say, among the recipients of our early bangs were our friends and rivals Supermarine and de Havilland at South Marston and Hatfield. We wasted no time in letting them know of our progress by means of a couple of sharp detonations. They were struggling with the Swift and the DH.110 and weren't yet supersonic. After five sorties from Boscombe Down the P.1067 was flown on August 10th to Farnborough, where company testing was carried out until

A stunning plan view of WB188 en route to Farnborough for its public debut. The prototype exhibited remarkably sleek and clean lines, indicative of its very impressive performance.

WB188, modified with revised windscreen, nose and rear fuselage, ready for Neville Duke's record-breaking world speed record flight on 7 September 1953.

we moved our test facility from Langley to Dunsfold in Surrey on September 7th, 1951. After only 11 hours' total flight test time the aircraft was being demonstrated at the Farnborough Air Show at speeds of up to 700 mph, so development had progressed at a fairly satisfactory pace.

It was April 1952 when the P.1067 officially broke the sound barrier, and after the initial test flights from Farnborough, WB188 was grounded while a production-standard version of the Rolls-Royce Avon RA.7 was installed. When the aircraft re-emerged, it had officially been named 'Hunter' and testing began from Hawker's new base at Dunsfold. The aircraft's flight envelope was gradually expanded, but the Hunter did not seem to handle particularly well as it approached supersonic speed. Severe rudder vibration and airframe buffeting became pronounced as the speed approached Mach 0.97, and although Duke took WB188 to Mach 1.3 in a test dive during April, the instrument readings could not be relied upon, thanks to the effect of shock waves on the pitot head. A simple 'fix' was finally found, as Duke explained:

Many fixes were tried but the remaining buffet precluded pushing beyond 0.97 M. In an endeavour to cure these troubles various modifications were tried: spoilers on the fin, a combination of fin and tail turbulators, a short rudder, an additional dorsal fin, and modified rear-end shapes around the jet pipe area. Our efforts finally bore fruit on June 6th, when we were rewarded with a first vibration-free flight after fitting a bullet fairing to the fin and tailplane trailing-edge junction. Having researched photographs of certain Russian and American aircraft, I noted some fitted with a rear-facing bullet fairing. Shortly after submitting these pictures to Kingston, a similar bullet was incorporated (I believe on the basis of trying anything) and we went supersonic immediately – not, as sometimes stated, after encouragement by Ministry of Supply test pilots.

On 5 May 1952, the second prototype Hunter (WB195) made its first flight from Dunsfold in the hands of Duke, complete with both a production-standard Avon engine and a working ADEN gun pack. Much of the aircraft's early work was centred on development of a suitable air brake. The Hunter's powerful engine gave the aircraft an outstanding high-speed performance, but slowing the aircraft was a far from simple task. Originally, the P.1067 design employed the use of small brake flaps fitted into the upper surfaces of the wing, similar in nature to those fitted on earlier Hawker jet designs. However, these were intended to work in company with strengthened landing flaps, but on the Hunter this system quickly proved to be inadequate. Various modified versions of the air brake layout were tested, but none proved satisfactory, and generally caused the aircraft to pitch down quite seriously when they were deployed, as Duke recalls:

> The P.1067 was designed with an air brake system. It consisted of landing flaps coupled with small dive-recovery flaps on the upper inboard wing surfaces, and had been tested satisfactorily on the P.1052 and P.1081. But the P.1067 dive-recovery flaps did nothing and the anticipated nose-down effect from the very powerful landing flap/air brake was quite unacceptable. During tests we nearly got the answer with third-span landing flaps, which were extremely successful and powerful up to a maximum speed of 610 kt (or Mach number in excess of 1.0). Only in a small speed range around 550 kt/0.94 M were there unacceptable trim changes.

The air brake saga proved to be a persistent difficulty and ultimately resulted in an airframe modification that inevitably had all the appearance of an afterthought and marred the elegant lines of the fighter. The third of the Hunter prototypes was WB202, first flown on 30 November 1952, again in Duke's hands. Unlike the two earlier prototypes, which had the 6,500 lb Avon 103 and 7,550 lb Avon 107 respectively, the third prototype was powered by an Armstrong Siddeley Sa.6 Sapphire engine rated at 8,000 lb, and was in effect the prototype Hunter Mk 2. Unusually, production Hunters had already been effectively ordered 'off the drawing board' with the first Instruction to Proceed having been issued on 20 October 1950, leading to a contract for the production of 198 aircraft at a unit cost (including powerplant) of some £172,000. By the time of WB202's first flight, it had become clear that a significant number of early-production Hunters from this initial batch would need to be assigned to various trials programmes before the Hunter could be cleared for entry into RAF service. Hawker did a great deal to hasten the production effort, and while trials with the prototypes continued, the company's newly acquired factory at Blackpool was prepared to begin production of twenty-six aircraft, while the Armstrong Whitworth factory at Coventry (Baginton) was prepared to commence construction of forty-five Sapphire-powered Mk 2 aircraft. In many respects, the production facilities at the AW factory were actually superior to those at Kingston, where subsections had to be fabricated and transported to Langley for assembly before being moved to Dunsfold for flight testing (and sometimes transported back to Kingston again for modifications). At Coventry the assembly and flight testing could all be conducted at the one site, and even the Hunter Mk 2's powerplant was also part of the same Armstrong Whitworth set-up.

As the Hunter test programme continued, the Air Ministry's Operational Requirements Branch was already looking at future developments of the aircraft, particularly the possibility of squeezing more speed, range and endurance from the airframe. Hawker addressed this future requirement by studying a truly supersonic version of the Hunter (the P.1083) that featured a 50 degree swept wing and a Rolls-Royce RA.14 Avon with an afterburner unit. Manufacture of the new wings for this project was commenced at Kingston in October 1952 while the early Hunter prototypes were busy conducting their pre-service tests

B202, seen here high over Hampshire, was the third Hunter prototype and the first to be equipped with an Armstrong Siddeley Sapphire engine.

from Dunsfold. In anticipation of the new design, WB188 was withdrawn from the test flight programme, and while WB195 transferred to Boscombe Down to begin initial operational trials, WB188 was fitted with an afterburning Avon and internal wing fuel tanks. The difficulties surrounding the design of a suitable air brake prompted Hawker to completely abandon its attempts to refine the various wing brake configurations, and instead the company opted for a completely new air brake fixed within the rear fuselage. Consequently, WB188 reappeared with twin clamshell brakes, one on each side of the rear fuselage, powered by tough hydraulic rams.

The Air Ministry threw Hawker's plans into chaos when senior staff visited Kingston and announced that, with the end of the Korean War now a reality, future policy appeared to be drifting back towards an almost traditional obsession with short-term economy. It had been decided that work on the increased swept wing would no longer be necessary, and while the Directorate of Military Aircraft Research was keen to explore the potential of larger 'dry' Avon engine developments, and the Directorate of Operational Requirements wanted to continue exploring the reheated Avon, there was no longer any real requirement for the P.1083 as a stand-alone programme. Consequently, construction of the prototype (WN470) was halted on 13 July 1953, when the project was officially terminated. Of course, this decision also left Hawker with WB188, which had been extensively modified and was now effectively redundant.

Despite this major setback, the Hawker design team opted to use the aircraft to study reheat developments still further, and with a surprisingly modern instinct for good publicity they also seized the opportunity to make an attempt on the world air speed record, which was currently held by an American F-86D, at 715.15 mph. Rolls-Royce prepared a 'racing' version of the Avon (the RA.7R) which delivered a thrust of 6,750 lb, rising to 9,500 lb with reheat (complete with a two-stage nozzle), and with this engine installed WB188 became the sole Hunter Mk 3. The nose section of the aircraft was modified to incorporate a sharper cone, while the canopy windscreen was redesigned to create a more aerodynamically smooth contour (and a better view for the pilot). Strangely, however, Hawker opted to remove the clamshell air brakes (restoring them after the record attempt), and the doors were skinned over (this was done because of the recognised potential for unnecessary drag created by the brake actuating fairings that emerged on the fuselage sides). Painted in an eye-catching red colour scheme, WB188 was ferried to Tangmere in Sussex, and Neville Duke flew his first practice run on 31 August. It was on 7 September 1953 that he successfully achieved a speed of 727.6 mph during three runs over the course, and even to this day this figure stands as a British record for speed at low altitude.

The Hunter Mk 3 was a one-off and, with a valuable prototype lost from the trials fleet, the remaining aircraft were worked even harder. The third prototype (WB202, the first Hunter to be fitted with an 8,000 lb thrust Sa.6 Sapphire engine) was assigned to gun-firing trials, and the aircraft began ground firing tests in February 1953. From the outset, the trials looked encouraging, although there

A movie still taken from Neville Duke's world absolute speed record flight as WB188 streaks past the calibration camera.

had been some initial concern based on experience with a series of test flights that had been made with an ADEN gun installed in a Beaufighter, which suggested that there was potential for damage to the Hunter's undersides from spent cartridge cases and links. However, no significant problems were encountered with the ADEN, and WB202 was eventually re-tasked with Hawker's seemingly insurmountable problem of how to fit the aircraft with a suitable air brake.

Experience with the now abandoned Mk 3 indicated that fuselage clamshell brakes were not an ideal solution as they also created a significant change in pitch when they were operated. Having explored all the options (using WT566, the twelfth production Hunter F.1 and WB202), it became clear that the only practical location for an air brake that would be satisfactory for the Air Ministry's performance requirements would be under the rear fuselage. This meant that a neat (and aerodynamically clean) built-in air brake would not be possible; it would have to be literally added on to the outer skin. In accordance with this decision, WB202 was equipped with a vernier-mounted ventral air brake, which was flown on eight test flights, each with a different brake deflection angle set on the adjustment rails. Even at this stage, the problem was still not solved and it was not until further flights were conducted with WT566 that a production-standard air brake was tested and eventually fixed at an optimum deflection angle of 60 degrees, with further refinements being made to the aerodynamic fairing fixed ahead of the air brake mechanism on WT573, enabling the brake deflection to be set at a maximum of 67 degrees. Only in June 1954 was the air brake saga finally resolved, but it had ultimately proved impossible to perfect an ideal system for the Hunter in this retrospective post-production manner. The finalised air brake looked like (and was) an afterthought, and was far from ideal. Most inconveniently, its ventral position meant that it could not be used on a landing approach and it was automatically locked up when the landing gear was extended. Hawker's frustration at the rather 'fudged' nature of the air brake outcome was compounded by the fact that early-production Hunters were now already emerging from the production lines only to be rendered unfit for service acceptance until an air brake was fitted. Consequently, early Hunters left the three production lines only to be stored at Dunsfold and Kemble until air brakes could be fitted – hardly an ideal situation for a 'super-priority' programme.

On 16 May 1953, the first production Hunter F.1 (WT555) made its maiden flight from Dunsfold, illustrating how the flight test programme lagged behind the completion of what were meant to be production-standard airframes. The first few production aircraft (including the first sixteen) were used for the necessary trials work, which would have been performed by additional prototypes or pre-production aircraft had they been ordered. Gun firing, spinning and other expansions of the aircraft's envelope were conducted while other aircraft were flown on more specific test and evaluation tasks, including preparation of the Pilot's Notes, which would be vital before service entry could commence. WT558 flew trials with a wing fence design (subsequently dropped), WT559 flew canopy-jettisoning trials, WT562 was fitted with one-third-span landing flaps, and WT570 was equipped with full-power ailerons. A limited Certificate of Release was finally issued on 1 July, enabling the first aircraft to be transferred from No. 5 MU at Kemble (where aircraft were held after being ferried from Dunsfold) to the CFE at West Raynham, and during the same month a dozen aircraft (starting with WT577 and WT578) were delivered to the RAF, immediately embarking on evaluation flights with the unit's experienced pilots. Indeed, Hunters participated in Exercise 'Dividend' during their first month with the CFE and performed well despite their limitations. Successful intercepts on USAF B-45 and B-47 bombers were made, and for Fighter Command it was refreshing to hear of RAF Canberra pilots expressing some surprise at suddenly finding themselves vulnerable to interception from a brace of Hunters that were actually above their hitherto unattainable altitude.

Although Hawker had identified the Hunter's glaring range deficiency (internal fuel capacity was just 80 imperial gallons), no provision for additional internal fuel had been attempted and external fuel tanks were only just being investigated at this stage; only WB202 had been fitted with dummy drop tanks to begin an exploration of their aerodynamic qualities. The air brake problem had been all too evident (and was not rectified until the nineteenth production Hunter finally entered service with a ventral air brake), and the original requirement that combat damage from a single bullet would not lead to the loss of more than 20 per cent of remaining fuel had simply been overlooked, as had another requirement for gas purging of the fuel tanks and even the sun blinds for the pilot, although the early experiences of CFE pilots demonstrated that it was actually high-altitude misting and icing that was the main (and most dangerous) visibility deficiency within the cockpit. The 'all-flying tail' had yet to be incorporated, despite being a standard fit on all emerging American designs, but perhaps most importantly, the Avon-powered Hunter proved to be far from compatible with the ADEN guns with which most production aircraft would be equipped.

Trials with the ADEN gun had progressed relatively smoothly with the first Sapphire-powered prototype, but nobody had predicted that the situation would be very different when pilots of the Avon-powered F Mk 1 began to operate their weapons. To the dismay of service pilots, the Avon suffered violent engine surging when the guns were fired, due to the ingestion of the ADEN's exhaust gases. Although the Sapphire engine had coped almost faultlessly, the Avon engine's compressor was rather more temperamental, and it was quickly established that gun-firing engine surges could happen in a variety of situations, sometimes without any obvious warning or reason. At altitudes above 25,000 feet and speeds in excess of 400 mph, engine surging seemed almost inevitable, and with the Hunter's airframe and powerplant effectively 'fixed' by this stage, Hawker had a potential disaster on its hands. As a short-term measure, a system was developed that automatically reduced fuel flow to the engine whenever the guns were fired, and this provided a solution to the problem, although it was a less than ideal 'fix' when one considers that the ADEN guns produced a hefty recoil force when they were fired, and reducing fuel to the engine at the same instant was hardly a good idea. Likewise, firing the guns produced a very significant nose-down pitch, which did nothing to enhance the Hunter's ability as a stable weapons platform. As Neville Duke recalled:

> The gun-firing trials with the Sapphire Hunter went extremely well, and things looked good when the first production Hunter Mk. 1 flew on May 16th. The modified WB188 made its first flight as the reheat-equipped Hunter F.3 on July 7th. All seemed well with the Hunter programme until we ran into the gun-firing results achieved at Boscombe Down with an early production Avon-powered Hunter Mk. 1. At first engine surging occurred at altitude, but later (and after we had practised setting up the right combination of flight factors) this undesirable phenomenon could be obtained under a variety of conditions. Surge had not shown up at all during the gun-firing trials with the Sapphire Hunter, the difference lying in the variable swirl-vane system on the Avon engine. Fuel dipping (briefly reducing fuel flow as the guns were fired) eliminated the problem in due course, but the cure was a long and trying process coming at a politically awkward time, just when the Hunter was going into service with No. 43 Squadron.

In fact, the gun problems were never completely solved until later developments of the Avon engine were made available, which were able to handle the gun gas ingestion without undue difficulty, and the Hunter Mk. 1 was doomed to remain

The twin-seat and dual-control Hunter T Mk 7 became a familiar sight throughout Fighter Command, with at least one aircraft assigned to every Hunter squadron. A number of twin-seat Hunters have survived intact and continue to fly as civilian-owned warbirds.

The only surviving example of the Supermarine Attacker is WA473, now proudly displayed as part of the Fleet Air Arm Museum's collection at Yeovilton.

A rare colour image of Hunter XF386 from No. 229 OCU, based at Chivenor. It is pictured during a visit to St Mawgan in 1965, sporting a white spine and tail. *Tony Clark collection*

Hunter FGA Mk 9 and Meteor F(TT) Mk 8 from No. 79 Squadron, both aircraft part of No. 229 OCU during the early 1970s. The Meteor was used to provide target facilities for Hunter pilots, the two classic types operating together from Chivenor for many years.

Hunter FGA Mk 9 streaks over home base at RAF Brawdy in Pembrokeshire. Brawdy's No. 1 TWU was the last major RAF operator of the Hunter, and more than twenty examples are visible in this photograph, together with numerous Hawks.

As part of No. 1 TWU's high-visibility paint trials (designed to enable pilots to distinguish between Hunters and Hawks) three Hunters were painted in high-visibility colours. One aircraft received red trim, another yellow trim, and a third sported fluorescent orange trim, as illustrated.

An unusual angle on the Sea Vixen, showing the observer's escape hatch. Burying the observer inside the aircraft's interior enabled the radar screen to be seen easily, but the conditions were of course claustrophobic and unpleasant for the occupant.

An unidentified Sea Vixen FAW Mk 1 pictured whilst assigned to trials work at Hatfield, sporting high-visibility orange external fuel tanks, dummy Firestreak missiles and refuelling probe.

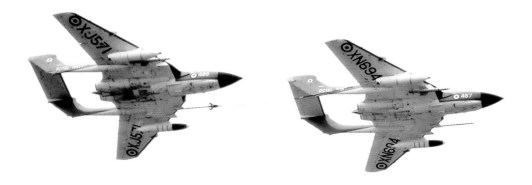

XJ571 and XN694 demonstrating the Sea Vixen's 'buddy buddy' refuelling capability. Both aircraft, fitted with flight refuelling pods on their starboard wings and a balancing external fuel tank on the port wing, are carrying a dummy Firestreak missile.

XP924 is the sole surviving airworthy Sea Vixen. Registered as C-CVIX as a civilian-owned warbird, it was sponsored for some time by a drinks company and suffered the indignity of being painted in the company's ghastly colours.

Following the termination of a sponsorship deal, XP924 was repainted in authentic Fleet Air Arm colours and is now a much-treasured performer on the air show circuit.

A rare image of No. 56 Squadron's Lightning F Mk 3s at Wattisham in 1965. The red and white tail markings survived for less than a year before officials demanded that more sober colours should be applied.

A well-known image of four Lightnings taken in 1965. In the foreground is an F Mk 2 from No. 19 Squadron with an F Mk 3 from No. 56 Squadron next to it. Third in line is an F Mk 1A from No. 111 Squadron, and in the background is an F Mk 2 from No. 92 Squadron. Less than a year later the colourful markings had all been removed.

Lightning F Mk 3 XP737 operated with No. 29 Squadron before joining No. 226 OCU (as illustrated) where it was used as a solo display aircraft for show appearances around the country. It later served with No. 11 Squadron at Binbrook before being abandoned near RAF Valley in August 1979, following undercarriage failure. *Mike Freer*

Lightning F Mk 6 aircraft from No 5 Squadron pictured over Spurn Point during the early 1970s. The aircraft were based at nearby Binbrook with No. 11 Squadron, less than 5 minutes' flying time away, across the Humber estuary.

Pictured shortly after delivery to No. 56 Squadron, XR718 soon lost its flamboyant markings and subsequently served with the Lightning OCU as well as Nos 5 and 11 Squadrons at Binbrook. After flying with the Lightning Training Flight it was withdrawn from use in January 1987.

The first F-4K Phantom was XT595, pictured here after completing its first flight from McDonnell's facility at St Louis. Sadly, the aircraft was not preserved, being scrapped in 1999.

Phantom FG Mk 1 XT861 at Yeovilton after being delivered to No. 767 NAS. After service with the Fleet Air Arm it was transferred to the RAF and served with No. 43 Squadron until September 1987, when it crashed in the North Sea.

The last British Phantom to fly was XT597, an aircraft that was assigned to test duties with the A&AEE, used for both trials work and as a high-speed calibration 'pacer' aircraft. It could be fitted with two types of radome, one incorporating an instrumentation boom while the other incorporated Tacan equipment, as illustrated.

A striking publicity photograph of two Phantoms from No. 56 Squadron, racing over the North Yorkshire Moors at low level. Both aircraft are carrying external fuel tanks and a full missile fit comprising four Sparrows under the fuselages and four Sidewinders on wing pylons.

Above: XV394 ended its RAF career with No. 92 Squadron at Wildenrath in Germany. After suffering a heavy landing in October 1990, it was decided that repairing the aircraft would be uneconomical due to the type's impending retirement. It was therefore scrapped at Wildenrath.

Below: The Sea Harrier was the Fleet Air Arm's last fixed-wing fighter (at least for the time being), and although the aircraft was by no means as capable as the Phantom that preceded it, the Sea Harrier did give the Navy a very effective attack and defence capability, courtesy of its fleet of through-deck cruiser carriers.

Above: ZA283 made its first flight on 18 November 1980 and was fitted with an improved 'B Model' version of the much-troubled Foxhunter AI Mk 24 radar.

Below: A brace of Sea Harrier FRS Mk 2 fighters leaping into the air during the final few months before their premature retirement from Fleet Air Arm service. Clearly visible are the air intake auxiliary doors designed to spring open when the engine required additional airflow during low speed or hovering manoeuvres.

Movie stills showing the launch of a Skyflash AAM from a Tornado F Mk 3 over the Aberporth test range.

ZG753 proudly wears the markings of No. 111 Squadron, together with the name *Bandeirante 3* in commemoration of a similarly marked Spitfire operated by the squadron during the Second World War and funded by the people of Brazil.

Above: ZE964 descends over North Yorkshire, returning to Leeming after a supersonic flight over the North Sea. The huge fuselage-mounted airbrake is fully extended.

Oppopsite above: Tornado F Mk 3 interceptors from Nos 111 and 43 Squadrons, the final two Tornado F3 units, both based at Leuchars. The aircraft in the foreground shows signs of some recent cannon firing, with streaks of exhaust soot visible along its fuselage.

Opposite below: A colourful line-up of the RAF's final four Tornado F Mk 3 units, shortly before the type's withdrawal from service. An aircraft from No. 11 Squadron is in the foreground, followed by Nos 43, 56 and 25 Squadrons.

Above: Sixty years after Spitfires sat on the very same spot, a Tornado F.Mk.3 from No. 56 Squadron prepares for take off at RAF Biggin Hill. Devoid of any external stores, the aircraft is configured for a high speed flying display. *Tim McLelland*

Opposite above: Two generations of RAF fighters together in the air. A Spitfire from the RAF's Battle of Britain Memorial Flight is accompanied by a Typhoon from RAF Coningsby, representing today's high-tech equivalent of the Second World War-era Spitfire. *BAE Systems*

Opposite below: A Eurofighter Typhoon pictured en route to the Dubai Air Show, showing the aircraft's distinctive square-shaped air intakes and the canard foreplanes either side of the cockpit. *Eurofighter*

Above: An atmospheric night image of a Typhoon from No. 3 Squadron returning to RAF Coningsby's runway after completing a training mission over the North Sea.

Opposite: The venerable Gloster Meteor was still wowing the air show crowds in 2012, as privately owned WA591 zooms into a misty sky. *Mark Holt*

Meteor TT.Mk.20 WD647 pictured at Exeter during July 1970 whilst serving with the resident No. CAACU (Civilian Anti Aircraft Co-operation Unit). *David Whitworth collection*

Lightning T.Mk.5 XS422 was one of the last Lightnings to fly in the United Kingdom. Operated by A&AEE Boscombe Down (primarily with the Empire Test Pilots School), the aircraft was ultimately purchased by a civilian buyer and is currently being restored to flyable condition in the USA. *Tim McLelland collection*

Tornado F.Mk.3 ZG755 proudly wearing the markings of No. 43 Squadron, pictured high over the North Sea, carrying practice missile rounds, external fuel tanks and chaff/flare dispensers. *Tim McLelland*

A nostalgic view of the flight line at RAF Akrotiri during 1975. The resident Lightnings of No. 56 Squadron are accompanied by Phantoms from No. 17 Squadron, visiting from RAF Germany. *Tim McLelland collection*

A very unusual close-up view of a Phantom FGR.Mk.2 from No. 74 Squadron, pictured high over Suffolk shortly before retirement from RAF service. Of particular interest is the 'reverse view' of the Phantom pilot, illustrating his surprisingly restricted view through the forward wind screen. *Tim McLelland*

permanently saddled with an engine that was incompatible with the weapons system of the aircraft it powered.

It was also at this stage that the feared problems with ejected gun cartridges and links began to come true. It had been assumed that the ADEN's heavy cartridges would simply fall away from the aircraft, but as service experience began to grow and more firing exercises were conducted, aircraft were suffering damage and it was clear that something had to be done about it. The simple solution (and the one that was adopted) was to create a blister housing that caught the links as they were ejected, leaving the heavier cartridges to fall clear. This system worked well, but resulted in a pair of rather ungainly bulges appearing under the Hunter's fuselage, which quickly became known by service pilots as 'Sabrinas' in honour of an appropriately well-endowed television star of that era. Like the air brake saga, the ammunition link collectors also gave the impression of being a hasty 'add-on', but like the air brake they became a familiar part of many subsequent Hunter airframes.

In addition to the link collection 'fix', a great deal of attention was also devoted to the vibration caused by the ADEN's operation. The ADEN gun pack was an impressive piece of kit and it was hardly surprising that the airframe suffered a great deal of localised punishment when it was fired, and the simultaneous operation of all four guns quickly led to the development of structural cracks in the forward fuselage. Stainless steel reinforcement plates were added in the appropriate areas and aircraft were restricted to operating individual pairs of guns (rather than all four) until the reinforcements were embodied into the production line schedule. Further modifications included the fitting of an air scoop under the gun pack, which opened when the guns were fired, ventilating the nose section and enabling gun gases to be vented. However, despite these problems, the ADEN gun pack was an excellent system that worked very well and was only troubled by relatively minor teething problems that could only be expected from what was something of a quantum leap in aircraft firepower.

It is fair to say that despite the Hunter quickly demonstrating plenty of potential, the Mk 1 was by no means an ideal aircraft for the day fighter role. Although its deficiencies could be corrected, the production of F.1s was already too advanced to make any fundamental changes to the aircraft, and it was accepted that with the air brake problem having been solved, the aircraft would enter regular RAF service without any further significant changes.

The first operational squadron to re-equip with the Hunter was No. 43 at Leuchars, and four aircraft were delivered during July 1954, with more deliveries continuing until October, when the squadron began operational flying. Although aware of the Hunter F.1's faults, the squadron's initial experience with the aircraft was encouraging, even though a number of serious gun-related flame-out incidents occurred. With some 150 Hunter F Mk 1s having been completed by the end of 1954, more units were able to take delivery of the new aircraft, and No. 222 Squadron (another Leuchars unit) re-equipped in December of that year. No. 54 Squadron at Odiham followed in February 1955, to be joined by collocated 247

The Hunter F Mk 1 entered RAF service in July 1954, beginning a short RAF career that was dogged by problems, some of which were aerodynamic but which were mostly caused by the unreliability of the early Avon engine.

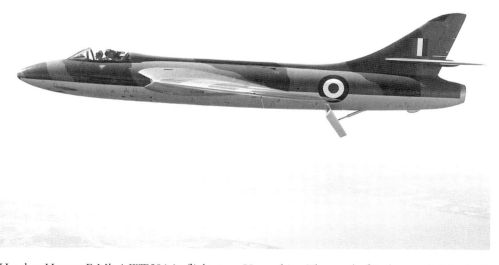

Hawker Hunter F Mk 1 WT591 in flight over Hampshire. The newly fitted ventral airbrake is extended, illustrating the distinctly 'add-on' nature of this modification that was subsequently fitted to all Hunters.

Squadron in July. Because of the Hunter F.1's various problems, it was decided that Germany-based squadrons would not receive the aircraft, as there was good reason to keep the F.1s within economical range of UK Maintenance Units and the various manufacturer sites.

The Hunter F Mk 2 enjoyed a slightly smoother transition into operational status. Having been produced with a Sapphire engine, it did not suffer from the same gun-firing problems that dogged the F.1, and with the air brake difficulties having been largely solved, the Hunter F.2 was certainly a more successful machine, even though it still had the same serious lack of range and endurance. The F Mk 2 was slightly faster (698 mph at sea level as compared with the F.1's 693 mph) and it also had a slightly better rate of climb. With hindsight, it is clear that the Sapphire engine should have been selected as the primary powerplant choice for the Hunter, as it was a reliable and less expensive engine than the Avon and did not suffer from gun-induced engine surges. In total, just forty-five Hunter F Mk 2s were produced at Coventry (the first being WN888, which took to the air on 14 October), and the first deliveries were made to No. 257 Squadron at Wattisham in September 1954, the collocated No. 263 re-equipping in February 1955.

Both the F.1 and F.2 were effectively regarded as being the same 'basic' early-production Hunter, which, although far from perfect, was a suitable aircraft with which Fighter Command could begin to build experience with a modern, transonic high-performance interceptor. In January 1956, No. 43 Squadron embarked upon firing trials with the Hunter's ADEN cannon, and although their pilots were restricted to gun firing in a narrow band between 20,000 and 25,000 feet, the restriction was later relaxed so that firings could take place from sea level up to 25,000 feet at speeds up to 550 knots. The intensive trials were temporarily suspended while modifications to the guns were made (the fuel-dipping system as previously described), but eventually the flights resumed and continued until Fighter Command terminated the trials because of the heavy toll on aircraft serviceability; many Hunters had been flown so hard that they required plenty of attention from the Leuchars engineers.

The Hunter was a beneficiary of the Offshore Procurement Bill, which enabled American funds to be allocated to European defence programmes, and a total of 367 Hunter F Mk 4 aircraft were ordered for the RAF, paid for by American tax dollars. Production of the aircraft, split between Kingston and Blackpool, commenced with the 114th F Mk 1 (WT.MK.701), which was the first to be completed to F Mk 4 standard. The first flew on 20 October 1954.

Rather perversely, most of the early-production F Mk 4s did not go directly to operational squadrons but were immediately placed in storage (many such aircraft being ferried to Kemble and other RAF stations following completion), as they had emerged from the production lines with F.1-standard Avon 113 engines, and in order to simplify the F Mk 4's introduction into RAF service it was decided that it would be more practical to retain these early versions in storage until they could be fitted with the later Avon 115 engine (later production F Mk 4s were fitted with the Avon 121). Likewise, even though the Hunter now had provision for the carriage of drop tanks, these were virtually never carried on the F Mk 4 in RAF service, the improved internal fuel capacity being sufficient for typical training sorties.

Such was the pace of Hunter production that the first Mk 4 took to the air before the production of F Mk 1 airframes had even been completed, and the first F Mk 5 (WN954) took to the air the day before the first flight of the F Mk 4. In the same way that the F Mk 4 was a direct development of the F Mk 1, the F Mk 5 was an equivalent Sapphire 101-engined derivative of the F Mk 2 with the same improvements in fuel capacity. Evaluation and pre-service trials with the F Mk 4 and F Mk 5 went well, although they were marred by the tragic loss of WT707 on 25 January 1955. Test pilot Frank Murphy was flying the aircraft over the South Coast when he was forced to make an emergency wheels-up landing at RNAS Ford. Although the initial landing was successful (Murphy emerging from the incident unscathed), the aircraft skidded on wet grass and careered through a nearby caravan park, killing three people in the process.

On a more positive note, the first Hunter F Mk 4s entered RAF service three months later, when Nos 98 and 118 Squadrons, both located at Jever in Germany, each received twelve aircraft. Many service personnel thought that the re-equipment of RAF Germany squadrons was long overdue, but the decision not to introduce the still unproven Hunter at an earlier stage was probably a sensible one. Even so, the later F Mk 4 aircraft suffered their own minor problems and were delivered in varying states of modification, so much so that aircraft often had hastily scribbled notes applied to their instrument panels to remind pilots of the particular modification state of particular aircraft. Over the next five months the flow of completed Hunter F Mk 4s continued and more squadrons received the new aircraft. In much the same way that RAF Germany had been omitted from initial Hunter re-equipment plans, it was decided that the Sapphire-powered Hunter F Mk 5 would also be confined to UK-based units, so that the additional logistics and expense of supporting a different powerplant could be avoided. Consequently it was No. 263 Squadron at Wattisham that received the first Mk 5 aircraft in March 1955, followed by No. 56 Squadron at Waterbeach in May, this squadron having finally abandoned its short and very unhappy association with the Supermarine Swift. Production of the 105 Hunter Mk 5s (all built at Coventry) ended in August 1955 and by the end of 1956, RAF Fighter Command was successfully integrating the Hunter into its Order of Battle; indeed, two Hunter squadrons had been deployed to Cyprus in support of Operation Musketeer, but with their limited endurance (and lack of opposition from Egyptian forces) they were mostly confined to maintaining an alert posture from their temporary bases in Cyprus, and were not called upon to fire any shots in anger.

The infamous 1957 Defence Review had a far-reaching and permanent effect on the RAF's future. The Hunter force was one of many casualties of the Government's new policy. By 1957, it had been accepted that the early marks of Hunter would eventually be passed on to RAuxAF units to replace their ageing Meteors and Vampires; indeed, many RAuxAF pilots had already

Hunter GA Mk 11 XF297 was operated for many months as the lead aircraft for the 'Rough Diamonds' aerobatic team of No. 738 NAS at Brawdy, from 1965 until 1969. As lead aircraft, the Hunter wore fluorescent orange markings on its nose and spine.

Some forty former Hunter F Mk 4 aircraft were converted to GA Mk 11 standard for the Royal Navy. Although fitted with arrestor hooks, the aircraft were not carrier-capable and were used exclusively for training.

been making familiarisation flights with collocated Hunter squadrons in anticipation of this event. The decision to disband all of the RAuxAF fighter units was a bitter blow that nobody had expected. Fighter Command was obliged to dispose of many Hunter squadrons that had barely declared themselves operational, and over in Europe RAFG had to do likewise with nine of the thirteen Hunter squadrons, and these were gone within a year of the Review.

Once the Hunter F Mk 4 began to arrive in Germany, the aircraft settled into service with relative ease, quickly earning the respect and enthusiasm of the former Sabre and Venom pilots who were assigned to it. However, by this stage, plans to introduce an even more capable variant of the Hunter were already under way as the F Mk 4 settled into service, and there was certainly never any intention of retaining the Hunter F Mk 4 and F Mk 5 for any longer than was strictly necessary. Indeed, as mentioned previously, the aircraft would ultimately have been transferred to the RAuxAF had the 1957 Defence Review not intervened. The fact that the RAuxAF fighter squadrons suddenly no longer existed effectively meant that the F Mk 4 and F Mk 5 would quickly be redundant. The savage cuts that took place from 1957 onwards meant that having peaked at a strength of eighteen operational squadrons, Fighter Command would now be left with just eight, while in Germany nine of the thirteen squadrons would go. A smaller force would remain in Germany, tasked primarily with policing duties, while in the UK the Hunter force would be largely responsible for defending the new V-Force nuclear bombers, even though it was already accepted that the bombers would possess performance figures that were somewhat greater than those of the fighters that would be protecting them. However, a much more advanced interceptor was already being developed (the Lightning) and, unlike many other programmes, this fighter had survived the 1957 Review and was still expected to enter RAF service. But in the meantime, until the Lightning became available, it would be the Hunter that remained at the forefront of the RAF's fighting capability. The F Mk 4 and F Mk 5, good though they were, still suffered from deficiencies that rendered them less than ideal for the front line, but at long last the Hunter was about to mature into a much more capable version.

When the truly supersonic P.1083 was cancelled, work on the prototype aircraft (WN470) was already well advanced, and although the redesigned wings were no longer applicable to any other development programme, the basic fuselage was new and unused, and Hawker opted to use it as the basis of a new Hunter variant that could be fitted with the latest version of the Avon engine that Rolls-Royce was still doggedly developing. The Avon had persistently remained inferior to the Sapphire engine, which, as even Rolls-Royce admitted, had 'a greatly superior flow/pressure characteristic' and delivered more thrust. It was fortunate for Rolls-Royce that information on engine developments was exchanged fairly freely between itself and Armstrong Siddeley, which provided detailed information on the design of the Sapphire's compressor stage. This enabled Rolls-Royce to develop the Avon so that it took advantage of the Sapphire's first four compressor stages, while incorporating a further eleven stages that were redesigned, maintaining a straight-through flow into the combustion chamber. The result was the first of the 200-series engines, first tested in November 1951, which quickly demonstrated that an output of 10,500 lb thrust would be possible. Hawker assembled a new Hunter based on WN470's redundant fuselage and, with a new RA.14 engine installed, the new aircraft (XF833) became the prototype P.1099 – the Hunter F Mk 6.

The new Hunter variant also had a greater fuel capacity, with the small centre fuselage tanks having been replaced by a pair of bag tanks adjacent to the jet pipe, containing 25 imperial gallons, together with a 200 gallon fuselage tank and 14 gallon bag tanks in the wings. Additionally, with 'Mod 228' wings the aircraft could carry a total of four 100 gallon drop tanks on the inboard and outboard pylons, and could also be fitted with a pair of huge 230 gallon drop tanks on the inboard pylons, although the use of these tanks would foul the operation of the landing flaps, and could only be carried for long-distance ferry flights. Even so, the new tanks certainly gave the Hunter a much-needed boost in range capability, as demonstrated in October 1958 when a Hawker test pilot made a non-stop flight from Dunsfold to El Adem in Libya – a distance of 1,588 miles.

Another very significant improvement over earlier Hunter variants was the fleet-wide introduction of a fully functional powered elevator system, which linked tailplane and elevator controls to produce much better longitudinal handling.

An excellent Hawker photograph of Hunter F Mk 6 XE592 at Dunsfold before being delivered to the RAF. Just visible below the cockpit are the ADEN cannon gun muzzle gas deflectors.

This was arranged so that, after 2 degrees of elevator movement, micro-switches were contacted to change the tailplane incidence at the rate of 0.7 degrees per second. This had the effect of an 'all-flying' tail, but small adjustments remained free from tailplane follow-up, making fine control during formation flying very much easier.

The Hunter Mk 6 also disposed of the unreliable cartridge starter system and employed an Avpin (isopropyl nitrate) starter system (later used on the Lightning). This new system worked well, but with hindsight it is clear that it also had its fair share of disadvantages, not least the unavailability of replenishment at airfields that simply did not handle the relatively unusual Avpin. Consequently, if a Hunter was forced to land at an ill-equipped airfield, it was likely to remain there for some time. Avpin was also very unstable and prone to explosions, many of which caused catastrophic damage to airframe components, and many Hunter pilots (and more than a few members of the hardworking ground crews) claimed that it might have been wise to have persisted with the older cartridge system, troublesome as it sometimes was.

The prototype F Mk 6 first flew on 23 January 1954, some time before the airbrake-dogged Hunter F.1 had even been accepted for RAF service, and some nine months before the first production F Mk 4 flew. XF833 was transferred to Boscombe Down to conduct flight observation trials and it was at this stage that, with much disappointment, the new Avon was found to be no less troublesome than its predecessors. In under two weeks the aircraft was force-landed following engine failure and was transported by road back to Dunsfold where it was fitted with a new engine. Five days after the aircraft resumed flying, the new engine also failed and Rolls-Royce was left with the embarrassing headache of establishing what the latest in a long line of problems was. Investigations revealed that fatigue fractures were causing compressor blade failures and this resulted in more modifications, including a new steel stator and rear rotor blades, as well as a revised fuel system, de-rating the thrust from 10,500 lb to 10,000 lb.

Flight trials resumed at Boscombe Down in July 1954, and at long last things began to run smoothly and the handling trials were completed successfully. Having learned the lessons of the F.1's protracted development, Hawker set aside seven Mk 1 airframes to be used as 'interim Mk 6' pre-production aircraft, and the first of these (WW592) took to the air on 25 March 1955. Flight trials revealed that in certain conditions, particularly at speed and altitude when 'g' was applied, the aircraft had a tendency to pitch up, and investigations by A&AEE pilots resulted in various modifications such as wing fences, all of which proved ineffective. The final solution was to extend the wing's outer leading edge in order to reduce its thickness/chord ratio and move forward the aerodynamic centre of pressure. The result was a 'dog-tooth' extension of 9 square feet, which became a standard fit on all Hunter Mk 6s and subsequent variants, although the first aircraft to emerge from the production line were completed before the modification had been finalised and had to be refitted retrospectively. (A few late-production Hunter F Mk 4s were also retrofitted.)

The ever-present engine surging problem was still far from being completely resolved at this stage, and the aircraft still suffered from a pitch-down tendency when the guns were fired. Hawker was now determined to eradicate these deficiencies once and for all. A series of intense firing trials was commenced, and more than 20,000 rounds were fired off at high speed, the complete ammunition load being exhausted each time. The aircraft was then returned to Dunsfold, rearmed and immediately sent off to repeat the process. The gun pack was then removed and inspected, and after a few small 'fixes' was reinstalled and the whole firing process repeated. The key to solving both the surge and pitch problems completely was to design a suitable gun blast deflector around the gun muzzle, and after a variety of designs had been fitted and flown, a final modification was found that successfully diverted blast away from the aircraft at 90 degrees and in the process provided 150 lb of upward thrust from each gun as it fired. The result was the familiar small protuberances that subsequently appeared on many (but not all) single-seat Hunters' gun muzzles, which finally put to rest the seemingly endless saga of problems surrounding the use of the mighty ADEN cannon.

Flight testing of the F Mk 6 then continued without any major difficulties and proved to be a much smoother process than had been experienced with the F Mk 1. The first production F Mk 6 aircraft were XE526 and XE527, which were delivered to Nos 5 and 19 Maintenance Units respectively on 11 January 1956. Their arrival was at a time when both MUs were already stretched to capacity with the delivery of F Mk 4s, so the F Mk 6s languished in storage until October of that year, when No. 19 Squadron at Church Fenton took delivery of them as the first squadron to operate what was often referred to as the 'definitive' Hunter variant.

The introduction of the F Mk 6 into RAF service enabled squadrons to dispose of virtually all of the preceding Hunter variants, together with their various vices and restrictions. It marked the end of the Sapphire-engined Hunter completely, even though in performance terms the F Mk 5 was not greatly inferior to the F Mk 6 and could outperform it in some situations, such as a flat-out climb to 45,000 feet, in which it would beat the F Mk 6 by nearly half a minute. Certainly there was no obvious performance deficiency that hastened the F Mk 5's withdrawal – it was the logistical aspect of operating aircraft with completely different engines that ultimately sealed the Sapphire's fate, even though the engine had been proved to be just as good as the Avon.

As with deliveries of the F Mk 2, the first F Mk 6s to reach Germany arrived in various states of modification and inevitably had to be routed through the MU for completion to a common standard. Most aircraft arrived without the 'dog-tooth' wing leading edge extension and also lacked the gun blast deflectors and extended cartridge ejector chutes. Unlike the earlier F Mk 4, the increased thrust of the F Mk 6, combined with a slight reduction in internal fuel capacity, meant that the aircraft had somewhat shorter 'legs' than its predecessor. This meant that external tanks would now be a necessity rather than an option. Unfortunately, production of 100 gallon tanks lagged behind production and delivery of the F Mk 6, and many months passed before significant numbers of tanks became available. In the meantime, the Hunter pilots took advantage of the 'clean' F Mk 6's outstanding performance and regularly enjoyed some distinctly one-sided combat exercises with other RAF and NATO units, but always with a very careful eye on the Hunter's fuel gauge.

The 1957 Defence White Paper had a drastic effect on Hunter F Mk 6 production, which was terminated with immediate effect. Cancelled aircraft were spread between the Blackpool factory (where fifty were to have been built) and Kingston, where 100 aircraft would have been built. This left a total of 119 manufactured by Armstrong Whitworth at Baginton and some 296 aircraft from Kingston, although twenty-three of these aircraft were not delivered to the RAF and were sold to India. Further new-build batches comprised 128 aircraft for India and 100 for Switzerland. This might have been a devastating time for Hawker had it not been for two key developments: first, interest in the Hunter from potential overseas customers was growing (and would eventually result in orders that surpassed even the most optimistic predictions); and second, Hawker was already making strenuous efforts to expand the Hunter's capabilities in terms of the weaponry it could carry. These factors ultimately served to save the Hunter (and Hawker) from disaster. Rather than being a major setback, the 1957 Review became a seminal moment in the Hunter's history, which prompted Hawker to intensify its efforts to develop the Hunter's versatility. For the RAF, the drastic cuts in F Mk 6 production were certainly unexpected and unwelcome, but the embryonic Lightning had survived the Government's axe and, with the promise of a supersonic interceptor now a reality, the Hunter (at least as a fighter) was rapidly becoming regarded as yet another 'interim' aircraft that would soon be replaced by the Lightning and Javelin. Of course, as is often the case with optimistic predictions, the arrival of the Lightning was delayed quite significantly and the Hunter remained active at the forefront of Fighter Command well into the early 1960s. Thankfully, the trouble-free, fast and manoeuvrable Hunter F Mk 6 was more than adequate for the task.

It was overseas interest in the Hunter that first drew Hawker's attention to the possible need for a trainer version, and as this concept began to emerge it was only then that the RAF showed some interest in the idea. However, even at this stage, the RAF only regarded the Hunter trainer as being a potential useful addition to single-seat operations and had no interest in the aircraft as an advanced trainer in its own right. Eventually, however, it was accepted that if a twin-seat variant of the Hunter could be developed, it would improve the RAF's ability to train new pilots, especially when the early Hunter F.1 was demonstrating that conversion onto the Hunter from the Meteor and Vampire was not as simple as had been envisaged.

The most fundamental issue that occupied the minds of both the Air Ministry and Hawker was the choice between producing a tandem-seat layout (the instructor sitting behind the student) or a side-by-side arrangement. There was no clear indication which would be the better option and the final choice was essentially one of personal preferences. Sydney Camm undoubtedly advocated the tandem layout, believing that it would enable the clean lines of the Hunter to be largely retained (and Camm always believed that if a design looked right, then it would fly right), but some service chiefs were convinced that side-by-side seating would be better, especially for applied flying training such as weapon delivery and instrument flying. Likewise, experience with the Meteor and Vampire had encouraged the belief that although the Meteor's tandem seating encouraged students to develop a single-seat 'go-it-alone' mentality, the rather more cosy seating in the Vampire allowed instructors to be much more 'hands on' in terms of demonstrating and explaining techniques to students. Consequently, the side-by-side arrangement won the day and in 1954 Specification T.157D was issued for the manufacture of two prototype P.1101 trainers.

Initial progress on the design of the aircraft was slow, as both attention and resources were directed largely towards production of the Hunter F Mk 1, which was suffering from delays in achieving CA (Controller Aircraft) Release status. The basic design concept was built around a standard Hunter airframe but with a redesigned twin-seat cockpit section that would simply be attached forward of the Hunter's transport joint (where the rear and centre fuselage section was divided from the forward section), just behind the air intakes. This new nose section precluded the installation of the ADEN gun pack, but it was assumed that the trainer would not require such armament; however, provision was made in the design process for potential single and twin ADEN arrangements. As the design progressed towards the mock-up stage, the new trainer exhibited some rather quirky features. The side-by-side seating concept had been adopted quite literally to such an extent that even the single-seater's canopy layout had been retained, with two single-seat sections simply being joined together in the new design to create an unusual 'double bubble' effect. Even more bizarre was the initial proposal (subsequently changed) to locate the instructor's throttle quadrant on the right-hand side of the cockpit. Wind tunnel tests quickly demonstrated that the canopy arrangement was unsatisfactory and it was swiftly redesigned to produce a more conventional smooth contour.

When XJ615 (the prototype T Mk 7) began flight trials (after first flying on 8 July 1955) it was quickly established that even the redesigned hood arrangement was still far from perfect and was responsible for creating severe buffeting, directional snaking and a considerable amount of noise inside the cockpit as airflow broke away behind the widened cockpit section, the contours of which contracted rapidly before rejoining the standard Hunter fuselage at the transport joint. A variety of trials were embarked upon using different types of vortex generators fitted in different positions around the windscreen arch, all designed to solve the buffet problem. Further changes to the canopy shape were also attempted and, in order to save on both time and cost, the prototype's canopy was replaced by a temporary metal substitute that could be reconfigured as necessary until a satisfactory design shape was fixed. After a great deal of experimentation, it was eventually accepted that the whole area would have to be redesigned again from scratch, and it was Cliff Bore (a Hawker project engineer) who applied the principles of 'area rule' to the fuselage, resulting in the Hunter T Mk 7's distinctive bulged fairing aft of the cockpit, which extends beyond the transport joint before smoothly rejoining the standard fuselage contours ahead of the fin leading edge. The redesigned fuselage might have been expected to create all manner of drag difficulties, but thanks to the application of the 'area rule' principle the twin-seat Hunters proved to be capable of virtually matching the single-seater's performance. Many people also firmly believed that the redesigned fuselage created a Hunter with an even more elegant outline than its single-seat predecessor. It was also considered prudent to address the twin-seat Hunter's airfield performance (particularly with export customers in mind) and a drag parachute was designed to improve the aircraft's landing distance. The parachute installation was a fairly simple process thanks to the layout of the Hunter's fuselage and tail, which provided a very handy space to accommodate the packed tail chute in a fairing built above the tail exhaust pipe, under the fin trailing edge.

Rather perversely, the Air Ministry decided that the new twin-seat Hunter should be based on the conversion of the standard Hunter F Mk 4 airframe. It was accepted that by the time the first trainers entered RAF service, the Hunter F Mk 4 would have been almost completely replaced by the Hunter F Mk 6; therefore it would have been logical to design the trainer around the more powerful F Mk 6 in order to match handling performance and to avoid the complication (and cost) of maintaining Hunters with different engines. However, the Air Ministry took the view that as so many Hunter F Mk 4s would become surplus to the RAF's requirements, it made sense to use them as the basis for the trainer conversion; indeed, the ability to convert the Hunter F Mk 4 easily into a trainer had been written in to the production specification from the outset. Of course, the decision to convert F Mk 4s made good sense in the short term, but the complications and cost of operating two very different versions of the Hunter for so many years suggest that the choice was rather short-sighted. The irony of the decision was that only six Hunters were converted from F Mk 4 airframes for the RAF, the rest being new-build aircraft that could have been based on the F Mk 6.

Hawker – being rather less short-sighted than the Air Ministry – proceeded with the production of a second P.1101 trainer that was based on the later F Mk 6, complete with a 10,000 lb thrust engine, and the aircraft (XJ627) first flew on 17 November 1956. Unlike the RAF's trainers, XJ627 was also equipped with a pair of ADEN cannon, whereas the Air Ministry opted to arm the T Mk 7 with just one. (As a trainer variant, it was assumed that the aircraft did not need to carry the 'punch' of the Mk 6's four cannon.) XJ627 performed well during flight trials (apart from a high-speed rudder 'buzz' that was rectified by the installation of a small spoiler unit on the rudder), but despite considerable efforts being made by Hawker, Air Ministry interest in a 'large Avon' trainer was not forthcoming, especially when the Hunter's future was effectively sealed by the infamous 1957 Defence Review. However, the creation of a more powerful trainer variant was undoubtedly a wise decision for Hawker and provided the know-how for the production of many export versions. XJ627 was transferred to Martin-Baker, where it flew many high-speed and low-level ejection seat firing flights before being handed back to Hawker for refurbishment and resale to Chile.

The first Hunter T Mk 7s entered RAF service in May 1958 with No. 229 OCU at Chivenor, while further examples (usually just one aircraft but sometimes two) were assigned to operational squadrons to act as continuation trainers. Despite the Hunter T Mk 7's less powerful engine, the aircraft was just as manoeuvrable as its single-seat counterpart, and in terms of overall flying performance it was not significantly different, and could never be described as being deficient in any way. Instructors liked the aircraft's rugged construction and vice-free performance, and also appreciated the excellent forward view and the ability to closely monitor their students. Naturally (for much the same reason) students were less enthusiastic and preferred the better visibility and the 'go-it-alone' feeling of the single-seater. When the RAF's Vampire advanced trainers were replaced by the Gnat, many commentators were surprised that the Hunter was not chosen, as almost everyone believed that the Hunter would have been a much better aircraft for the job. Ultimately, Hunter trainers did join No. 4 FTS at Valley, but only to supplement the Gnats rather than replace them – students were often assigned to Hunters if they were physically just too big to fit inside the diminutive Gnat's cramped cockpit. Certainly, when given the choice between the Hunter and the Gnat, the advanced flying training students invariably wanted to fly the Hunter.

Although the Hunter F Mk 6 was regarded as being the definitive version of the breed, it was the development of the FGA Mk 9 that ensured the Hunter would remain active as a significant part of the RAF's armoury for many years. Hawker had been aware of the Hunter's potential as a ground attack aircraft from the very beginning of its design and development and had already devoted a significant amount of time and resources to an exploration of the F Mk 6's capabilities in this role. However, it was the decision to replace the Venom in 1958 that finally kick-started the creation of the FGA Mk 9. The CFE embarked upon a series of trials in Aden to select the most suitable aircraft to replace the Venom, and Hawker sent a pair of F Mk 6s (XK150 and XK151, both standard F Mk 6s fitted with tail chutes) to take part in the trials. The competition was almost a foregone conclusion, with only the Jet Provost and Gnat being selected as alternative candidates for the role. It was hardly surprising that the Hunter was quickly recognised as being the ideal aircraft, and Hawker was instructed to begin work on the new Hunter variant, designed for the ground-attack role.

With Mk 6s already in production, the new FGA Mk 9 airframes were created from the existing Mk 6 design by simply incorporating the new modification standards into the production line. An initial order for forty aircraft was placed in 1958, followed by a further order for thirty-six 'interim' aircraft (sometimes referred to as F Mk 6As), which would be delivered with the F Mk 6's Avon 203 engine before being brought up to full FGA Mk 9 standard complete with a new Avon 207. Other modifications introduced on the FGA Mk 9 included full 'tropicalisation' (cockpit ventilation and refrigeration, necessary for operations in the Middle East), and the introduction of 230 imperial gallon underwing tanks as standard fit, necessitating the fitment of a bracing strut between the wing and the tank's outboard surface, to enable them to withstand the rigours of combat manoeuvres. In order to enable the aircraft's flaps to be operated when the tanks were carried, a small section of flap surface was removed to allow the flaps to drop inboard of the tank's tail. The heavier landing weight of the two huge external tanks (and the 'hot and high' conditions in which the aircraft would probably be operating) prompted Hawker to introduce a braking parachute that was fitted over the tail cone in a similar fashion to the T Mk 7, although the parachute diameter was slightly larger. Perversely, having spent so much time developing gun blast deflectors for the F Mk 6 (and yet more time on a similar arrangement for the T Mk 7), the muzzle modifications were judged to be unnecessary for the FGA Mk 9's low-level role and were omitted. The resulting aircraft was a sturdy, manoeuvrable, fast and versatile machine, and it became the 'standard' model from which many of the Hunter's expert versions were created. It could have been even more versatile had further development been pursued by Hawker.

If the FGA Mk 9 had any flaw, it was the arrangement of its underwing hard points, which, had they been relocated, could have given the aircraft a better offensive capability. A centreline pylon under the fuselage would have enabled the aircraft to carry at least a couple of 1,000 lb bombs, whereas the FGA Mk 9's inboard pylons were too close to the undercarriage to allow twin stores carriers to be fitted (although a single bomb could be carried). Likewise, the outer pylons were too far outboard and aft to allow bombs to be carried safely (they would create a dangerous pitch change on release, as was demonstrated during Hawker's trials). Fuel capacity could also have been improved, but as is often the case with RAF combat aircraft, there was never any appetite to allocate more resources to the Hunter than was strictly necessary. At many stages of the Hunter's career it was inevitably regarded as yet another 'interim' aircraft that would be superseded by more capable machines – an attitude that prevented many British aircraft from realising their full potential.

In RAF service the Hunter was gradually withdrawn from operational squadrons to take up second-line duties, and although this move might have appeared to mark the beginning of the end for the Hunter's RAF career, it was in fact the beginning of what was effectively a 'third life', which took the aircraft from the late 1960s through into the 1980s. No. 4 FTS at Valley received a fleet of Hunters, which were assigned to the advanced flying training role, augmenting the diminutive Gnat (indeed, many RAF personnel felt that the Hunter should have been used to equip the entire FTS in preference to the Gnat), but always operating as a distinctly separate unit, situated on the far side of the airfield. Officially, the 4 FTS Hunters were assigned to the training of overseas students, but a considerable number of RAF pilots physically unable to fit into the Gnat's cramped cockpit were automatically posted onto Hunters, together with a few other individuals who, by luck or by design, managed to get a much-sought-after seat on the Hunter course. The twin-seat Hunter T Mk 7 was used for basic handling and conversion training onto the type, but much of the 4 FTS course was conducted in the single-

Although No. 111 Squadron's Hunters became famous as the RAF's 'Black Arrows' aerobatic team, the squadron also continued to operate as a regular fighter squadron. XG200 is pictured during a routine training flight, complete with rocket rails and external fuel tanks. (*Tony Clarke collection*)

Five Hunters from No. 111 Squadron's legendary 'Black Arrows' aerobatic team in perfect line-abreast formation. At the time this picture was taken, the aircraft's serial numbers were applied in red on the rear fuselage, although they were also applied in white for some months.

seat Hunter F Mk 6. In stripped-down form, minus various items of equipment (and the removal of the ADEN cannon), this was a hugely popular machine, being both fast and manoeuvrable, often referred to locally as the 'GT6'.

Meanwhile, in 1974, Hunter FGA Mk 9s (and some T Mk 7s) were delivered to Wittering to form two new squadrons (Nos 45 and 58) assigned to the ground-attack role, acting as temporary units for newly qualified students who would ultimately be assigned to the new Jaguar. Until a substantial number of Jaguars could be brought into squadron service, the Wittering squadrons provided a means of maintaining pilot skills and qualification while also providing the RAF with an additional ground-attack capability. When the Jaguar started to settle into squadron service, Nos 45 and 58 Squadrons were scheduled to disband and their Hunters reassigned to tactical training. However, in order to effectively keep the tactical training concept in business, these two squadrons were disbanded rather sooner than originally planned. Wittering had also played host to a small number of Hunter T Mk 7s and FGA Mk 9s, which formed the basis of what would become the Harrier Operational Conversion Unit, providing the unit with additional aircraft while deliveries of the new Harrier slowly trickled through. Hunters also remained active with the RAF's Buccaneer squadrons, with a handful of twin-seat aircraft being assigned to the conversion of new Buccaneer pilots. As the Buccaneer was never produced in a dual-control version, a small number of Hunters were equipped with an Integrated Flight Instrument System (IFIS) to enable instructors to train new Buccaneer pilots in the Hunter, prior to making

A nostalgic image of the legendary Hunter, captured during a low-level aerobatic display performed by Neville Duke.

their first flight in the RAF's new bomber, and it was ultimately in this role that the Hunter finally ended its RAF career many years later.

Ever since the Hunter had entered RAF service, RAF Chivenor had been regarded as its home, responsible for the training of huge numbers of British and overseas students. When the Hunter was withdrawn from front-line service, the role of No. 229 OCU began to change, and instead of converting students onto the Hunter prior to being assigned to a front-line Hunter squadron, it began to widen its scope by preparing students for the Harrier, Phantom, Lightning, Buccaneer and Jaguar. The OCU wound down during the early 1970s, and its training role was taken over by No. 1 Tactical Weapons Unit, based at Brawdy, eventually supplemented by No. 2 TWU based at Lossiemouth. In April 1981, when new-build Hawks aircraft began to be delivered to the RAF, No. 2 TWU was relocated back to Chivenor and the Lossiemouth-based Hunters were returned to Brawdy, although no Hunters returned to Chivenor to renew their long association with the base

The all-new Hawk trainer (effectively the very last Hawker creation) entered service with No. 234 Squadron at Brawdy in May 1978, followed by No. 63 Squadron, where the last Hunter course ended in May 1979. This left only No. 79 Squadron operating the Hunter, operations continuing into 1984, when the unit finally began to dispose of its ageing aircraft in order to make way for more new Hawks. A formation of nine Hunters was flown to St Athan in July (the aircraft being placed into storage there), but a handful remained at Brawdy, used for general 'hack' flying, chase and 'bounce' flying, and for towing targets, until the end of 1984, when, at long last, the final Hunters left Brawdy for good.

The new Hawk was certainly a welcome development for both the hard-worked ground crews and the TWU's syllabus planners, but from a pilot's viewpoint it was received with mixed emotions. It was undoubtedly easier to fly, but that was not necessarily an asset for a unit that needed to test its students thoroughly. The Hawk was unable to compete with the Hunter's range and speed, and even the tandem seating arrangement was not always regarded as being an improvement over the Hunter T Mk 7's side-by-side arrangement, which many instructors preferred. On a more subjective level, many pilots (both instructors and students) regarded the Hawk as an excellent aircraft, but the Hunter was in a class of its own – a special aircraft with all the characteristics, quirks and demands of a 'real' aircraft from the 1950s. More than a few TWU instructors often remarked that if a student expressed a preference for the Hunter, he was likely to be the sort of student who truly relished a challenge and would therefore be ideally suited to the demands of an operational squadron.

The withdrawal of the last TWU Hunters marked the end of a very significant chapter in the aircraft's history, but it was by no means the end of the Hunter's military activity in the UK. The Buccaneer operational squadrons and the Buccaneer OCU still employed twin-seat Hunters as lead-in trainers, equipped with Buccaneer navigation equipment and instrumentation (including the Buccaneer's Airstream Direction Detector). They remained an essential part of the Buccaneer force and were destined to continue in service until the final withdrawal of the remaining Buccaneer fleet at Lossiemouth. However, it was also the Buccaneer that indirectly led to the reintroduction of the 'standard' twin- and single-seat Hunter back into front-line squadrons during 1980-81, a quarter of a century after having first entered RAF service. Following two fatal accidents involving the Buccaneer, the bomber fleet was grounded after serious metal fatigue problems were found in large numbers of the aircraft. Some were relatively undamaged but, when investigated, others were already beyond economical repair. The majority of the remaining Buccaneer force was repairable, but a significant amount of time would pass while the aircraft were modified and strengthened, and this would leave five operational squadrons (and an OCU) without any aircraft in which to maintain flying proficiency. The solution to the problem was the Hunter, with a variety of airframes in storage and a relatively large number of aircraft still actively flying the Navy's FRADU at Yeovilton. Twin-seat T Mk 7s and single-seat F Mk 6As and FGA Mk 9s were quickly brought back up to flying condition and delivered to Honington, Lossiemouth and Laarbruch, while additional T.8 aircraft were 'borrowed' from the FRADU, enabling the Buccaneer squadrons to maintain a flying programme while the Buccaneers were slowly brought back up to a serviceable standard. It was quite a remarkable sight to witness a line of 'front-line' Hunters (albeit assigned to training duties) back in business, particularly at Honington, where a number of aircraft could be seen wearing the markings of No. 208 Squadron – a unit that had relinquished the Hunter some ten years previously.

After the Buccaneer's problems had been resolved and the aircraft settled back into squadron service, most of the Hunters were again withdrawn to storage or flown back to Yeovilton as appropriate, although some of the 'temporary' Hunters lingered with the squadrons for quite some time after the Buccaneers had returned. Ultimately, only the specially modified trainers remained, and the last operational single-seat Hunter in RAF service (No. 12 Squadron's F Mk 6 XF383) was withdrawn from flying duties at Lossiemouth in 1984. The remaining RAF Hunters soldiered on with the Buccaneer OCU before being passed on directly to the remaining Buccaneer squadrons (Nos 12 and 208) when the OCU was disbanded. They remained active until the final Buccaneer squadron (No. 208) disbanded on 31 March 1994, when both the Buccaneer and Hunter were simultaneously retired from RAF service.

CHAPTER SEVEN

The Big Delta

The Meteor and Vampire ushered in a new era of fighter operations for the RAF. They freed it from the seemingly decrepit propeller-driven aeroplanes that lingered in front-line service long after the Second World War had ended, and promised a bright future of hitherto unimaginable capabilities. The shiny, sleek jet fighters represented a bold leap in technology, even though in reality these early jet aircraft offered few advantages over the aircraft that they replaced, in terms of actual performance. However, even as these aircraft settled into service, the Air Staff were obliged to look towards the future and examine the kind of capabilities that would be needed in maybe a decade's time. It seemed likely that advances in jet engine design would enable future fighter aircraft to fly faster and higher, but improved performance was not an end in itself. Most importantly, the RAF needed all-weather capability, as it was unrealistic to imagine that any future conflict would be conducted only in daylight and in perfect conditions. The experience of the Second World War had demonstrated that bomber operations were rarely curtailed completely because of poor weather; therefore it was important to have a fighter force that could counter an enemy that might attack at any time, in any conditions.

In December 1946, the Air Staff issued two Operational Requirements: OR.228 was for a single-seat interceptor designed for daytime operations, while OR.227 was for a twin-seat night fighter (the second seat being necessary for a radar operator). The Operational Requirements were duly translated into Specifications F.43/46 and F.44/46, and while F.43/46 eventually translated into the Hawker Hunter, F.44/46 became the Gloster Javelin.

It was not surprising that Gloster Aircraft quickly submitted a proposal to meet this Specification, as the Meteor fighter project was hugely successful and the prospect of developing another equally important fighter was too great to resist. George Carter (Gloster's Chief Designer) put forward a development of the Meteor, featuring a larger airframe accommodating two crew members, and a fairly conventional gull wing with a moderately swept leading edge. The Air Staff stipulated that the fighter would have to be capable of achieving a rapid 5 second engine start and be able to reach 45,000 feet in 10 minutes, where it would be expected to have a top speed of at least 605 mph. Carter's design included the necessary four 30mm cannon and also allowed for the installation of a 4.5 inch recoilless gun that was being developed by the Royal Armament Research and Development Establishment. This weapon was essentially a tube through which a shell could be fired, connected to a counterweight that would shift backwards as the shell fired, thereby ensuring that the recoil load was not absorbed by the aircraft structure. It was an interesting proposal but one that ultimately did not result in a practical weapon for fighter operations. Carter also designed the proposed fighter (the P.228) so that the engine nacelles (mounted on the wing in the same fashion as on the Meteor) could house either the Rolls-Royce AJ.65 Avon (delivering 6,500 lb thrust) or the Metropolitan-Vickers (which became Armstrong Siddeley) Sapphire, with its slightly better 7,000 lb thrust.

After proposing the P.228, Gloster also produced another design that was intended to represent a more linear development of the Meteor. The P.234 was a single-seat fighter created in response to Specification F.43/46, with an unusual 'butterfly' tail and a delta wing layout, plus a single 40mm cannon for armament. The Air Ministry liked the proposal and Gloster continued to refine the design. In April 1947, the developed project (now known as the P.234) was accepted for go-

Javelins in production at Hucclecote. More than thirty aircraft can be seen, in various stages of construction.

ahead as the RAF's next day fighter. However, no order was forthcoming, chiefly because the Air Staff were now unsure as to precisely what they wanted. Their thinking had been influenced by the development of air-to-air missile technology that promised to replace the machine gun and cannon as armament for fighter aircraft. Although missiles were relatively new, the Air Staff were impressed by their potential and it was inevitable that they would want the next generation of fighters to be capable of carrying this type of weapon. This meant some fairly significant design changes to Gloster's proposal, not least the incorporation of a large radome to house interception radar, and a change from single-seat to twin-seat configuration. A variety of design configurations emerged in order to meet the evolving requirements that were being expressed by the Air Ministry. Gloster's design team endeavoured to combine their day and night fighter designs into one generic configuration, but their efforts were ultimately unsuccessful. Eventually, the Air Staff began to lose interest in the Gloster proposal (which had now become the P.259), even though they had already effectively agreed to adopt it for production.

Developments at Hawker Aircraft had shown great promise in a new single-seat fighter design that its team had been working on in response to the RAF's day fighter requirement. This eventually became the Hunter, and the Air Staff concluded that instead of pursuing Hawker's less than promising night fighter proposal, its single-seat fighter should be chosen as the basis for the RAF's next day fighter, while Gloster's P.259 should be selected as the basis for a new night fighter, this well-worn term slowly being replaced by a more appropriate 'all-weather fighter' description. From January 1948, the Gloster proposal was regarded purely as an all-weather fighter design, while Hawker was encouraged to continue development of its P.1067 day fighter.

George Carter became Gloster's Technical Director and Richard Walker became Chief Designer, tasked with the design of the new all-weather fighter. By April 1948, the design had become a delta with a slab delta tailplane on top of a substantial fin structure. As the P.272, the aircraft was to be powered by two Sapphire ASSa.2 engines delivering a combined thrust of 18,000 lb, and the armament proposal had been fixed as four 30mm cannon, in preference to a short-lived proposal to use four of the recoilless guns that had been considered previously. The weight of these weapons effectively ruled them out, as even with a respectable amount of thrust, the aircraft was still extremely heavy at some 25,500 lb, which was 25 per cent more than any of the previous projected designs. The engines were now to be fixed in the aircraft's wing roots, with intakes emerging ahead of the wings, either side of the fuselage, and while the T-tail design was unusual (but not entirely revolutionary), the aileron controls were to be abandoned in favour of rotating wing tips, as these were believed to be a better insurance against the risks of lateral control problems associated with the delta wing layout.

In 1948, there was very little practical experience of delta wings on which any design could be based, and most of Gloster's work relied on data that had come from German research captured at the end of the Second World War. The work of Alexander Lippisch was well known and the RAE had analysed a great deal of his work, but very little data had been translated into demonstrable aerodynamics. Boulton Paul was working on some experimental delta designs and Avro was to create its 707 delta research aircraft (as part of the 698 Vulcan project), but all of these designs emerged in parallel with Gloster's work and were completed too late to have a significant effect on Gloster's fighter design, other than sometimes confirming the validity of design choices as the project progressed. In effect, the Gloster team were working with a proverbial blank piece of paper, with only data from which a design could be created. The delta wing appeared to make sense, as it guaranteed a rugged and stiff structure that was still comparatively light, and also provided a suitable low aspect ratio and generous wing area. It was, of course, a form of swept wing too, and the inner portions of the wing would provide plenty of internal space for fuel and undercarriage assemblies. The wings were designed to blend partially into the flat fuselage that would itself provide some 20 per cent of the overall lift, and the high-mounted tailplane ensured that its control effectiveness would not be affected by airflow from the wings – it would also enable the aircraft to approach and land at a relatively modest attitude.

The project looked very promising, but progress was not entirely smooth because the Air Staff also had their sights on another design being proposed to meet Specification F.4/48 (the final expression of F.43/46). De Havilland had

A low-angle view of the prototype Javelin, illustrating the nose-mounted air data probe and the simple geometry of the delta wing leading edges.

continued to develop its diminutive twin-boom Vampire and Venom family and had drawn up a much larger twin-engine aircraft to meet the emerging night/all-weather fighter requirements of both the RAF and Fleet Air Arm. The result of de Havilland's efforts was the DH.110, and the RAF considered the aircraft to be a serious contender for its all-weather fighter requirement. In March 1948, the Ministry of Supply opted to order four examples of the Gloster design (now referred to as the GA.5) together with a static structural test specimen. It also placed a similar order for the DH.110. Gloster immediately began refining its design, adopting an all-moving tailplane with elevators, and conventional ailerons instead of rotating wing tips. But after having received an Instruction to Proceed on 13 April 1949, the order for the four prototypes was reduced to just two in November, as part of Government economy measures and also because the GA.5 was regarded as an 'insurance' against the potential failure of the DH.110, which the RAF preferred on account of its proven heritage and simplicity.

The decision to reduce Gloster's order was a bad idea as it would require the manufacturer to conduct all of the GA.5's testing and trials with just two aircraft. Even for a simple aircraft this would be quite a challenge, but for a complex, high-speed, all-weather fighter it would be almost impossible. The test fleet was to be assigned to a variety of trials, including engine performance, handling, aerodynamics, weapons, radar and much more, and it was only when the Director of Military Aircraft Research intervened that the Ministry of Supply had a rethink. He stated that with only two aircraft, the GA.5 would probably not be cleared for service use until 1954 at the earliest, and at long last the Ministry of Supply accepted the absurdity of its decision and a revised order was placed for three additional aircraft, but by then more than a year of progress had been wasted unnecessarily.

By this stage, the Air Ministry had also begun to accept the limitations of the DH.110's developmental potential, as despite the aircraft's predicted performance, it was becoming increasingly clear that the design was not going to be capable of any major improvements. This effectively improved the standing of the GA.5, and when the three additional aircraft were ordered in March 1951, it marked an important stage at which the DH.110 and GA.5 were regarded as equals.

It was in April 1949 that the construction of the first GA.5 began, but a lengthy design programme combined with vacillations from the Air Ministry meant that it was July 1951 when the various sub-assemblies finally began to make their way from Gloster's factory at Bentham to the company's assembly facility and airfield at Moreton Valence. By now the design had been developed still further, with increased fuel capacity, armour protection for the crew, ILS (Instrument Landing System) equipment, and the APQ-43 search and gun-laying radar. As the first aircraft slowly came together it became clear what a huge brute of an aeroplane the GA.5 would be. The delta wing and fuselage were manufactured from all-metal stressed skin construction built around a torsion box created by the main spar, extending into leading edge ribs and the outer skin. Inside each wing five fuel tanks were installed and on the upper and lower surface of each wing an airbrake flap

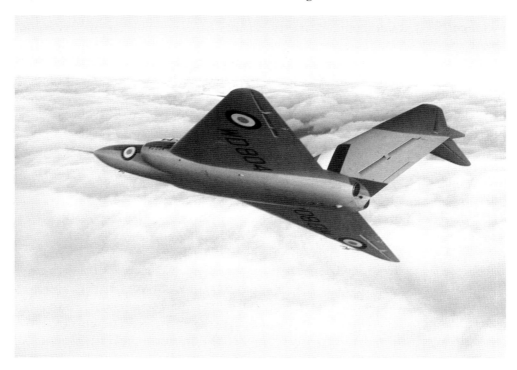

WD804 in flight during early trials. Various engine exhaust fairing shapes were tested in order to cure tail buffeting problems, the interim fit illustrated being just one of many.

A close-up view of WT827 in flight, illustrating the metal canopy hood fitted to early Javelins. This was swiftly replaced by a clear Perspex canopy on production aircraft.

was incorporated. Instead of conventional trailing edge landing flaps, a separate recess was fitted into the lower wings, ahead of the lower airbrake, from which the flaps extended when required. The main landing gear legs retracted inwards into the inner wing, while the nosewheel retracted rearwards into a bay under the cockpit. The fuselage was divided into four main assemblies, the centre section being the largest, with a longitudinal box-beam structure and large frames that formed the engine bays. The crew were seated in a standard tandem arrangement under a single cockpit canopy, the radar operator having only small port holes for external vision, but on later aircraft (after the fourth prototype) this was replaced by separate clear canopies for both crews. Many more weeks of assembly work followed and finally, on 26 November 1951, the GA.5 prototype WD804 made a 34 minute flight from Moreton Valence in the hands of test pilot Bill Waterton. The flight was far from satisfactory, as Waterton subsequently explained:

> I had carried out much high speed taxying and I had few qualms as I lifted her off the runway. But I was no sooner well clear of the ground and picking up a bit of speed when buffeting and banging set in somewhere in the tail end. At 200 mph the whole airframe shook violently – a matter which afforded me considerable concern. As speed was reduced it eased off and I flew around at a very sedate 150 having a quiet look at things. After half an hour I came in for an easy and uneventful landing.

The GA.5 design team inspected the aircraft after landing and established that the cause of the severe buffeting was the interface between the rudder and the jet exhaust, as streaks of oil escaping from the engine through vents below the rudder could be traced across the area and clearly illustrated the instability of airflow in the area. The cure for this problem was an extension of the rear fuselage and a new 'pen nib' fairing around the engine exhausts, although it took some considerable work to find the right modifications to resolve the problem fully.

The prototype continued making flights until 29 June 1952, when the aircraft was again flying in Waterton's hands. During a high-speed run at 3,000 feet, the aircraft's elevators suddenly began to flutter and after only 2 seconds of severe oscillation they broke away, leaving Waterton with the unenviable decision of either ejecting at high speed or attempting to land the aircraft safely. He opted to head for the 10,000 foot runway at Boscombe Down and by carefully controlling the aircraft through judicious use of the variable-incidence tailplane structure (minus elevators) he made a successful landing, but the fast touchdown broke away the undercarriage and the aircraft collapsed onto its belly and caught fire. Waterton escaped with only minor injuries but returned to the burning aircraft to recover the auto-observer boxes – an act that earned him the George Medal.

Flying resumed when a replacement aircraft was completed in the shape of WD808 (which actually became the second prototype) and after making its first flight on 20 August 1952, it was immediately assigned to investigations of the flutter incident. Resonance flight testing was conducted at speeds up to 520 knots.

Javelin prototype WD804 seen nose-on, illustrating the aircraft's capacious circular intakes and air data probe (not fitted on production aircraft).

WD804 at rest in company with a couple of Meteors, at Moreton Valence. Of particular interest is the solid metal canopy hood over the navigator's cockpit.

WD808, the second Javelin prototype, landing at Farnborough after completing a flying display for the assembled spectators.

Second prototype Javelin WD808 gets smartly airborne at Farnborough, turning left to climb over the heads of the assembled spectators.

By May 1953, the aircraft had changed quite significantly, with extended chord wing tips and the sweepback reduced on the outer panels. This slightly kinked leading edge was judged to be preferable to the original straight leading edge, curing a tip-stalling tendency that was unsuitable for high-speed and high-altitude manoeuvring. Other improvements included elevator boost, and a stiffened fin, tailplane and elevator structure, and a redesigned centre spar that would enable the aircraft to be cleared for flights at speeds up to 530 knots. Flight testing continued with this aircraft until 11 June when the aircraft was destroyed after it crashed near Bristol, killing its pilot, Peter Lawrence. Investigations revealed that with a repositioned centre of gravity (further aft) the aircraft had entered a deep stall at a high incidence angle of 50 degrees. It had dropped vertically from 11,000 feet with no forward airspeed recorded on the auto-observer equipment that was installed.

This was a symptom of a problem that Gloster simply had not foreseen, and one that was to affect all aircraft with T-tail designs. If the aircraft flew at a high angle of attack at low speed, the wings blocked airflow over the tail surfaces until they could no longer effect any control, and there was no means of curing this potentially fatal problem other than by avoiding circumstances in which it was likely to occur. This crash also led to the introduction of a power-assisted cockpit canopy, as wind tunnel testing revealed that the original hood was almost impossible to release at more than 40 degrees of incidence. No replacement aircraft was sought, as new production aircraft would be completed before any airframe was available, so the programme was simply delayed until 7 March 1953 when the third prototype (WT827) first flew.

The third aircraft was more representative of an operational aircraft, with installed guns, radar equipment and both a blunt 'bull nose' and a conventional pointed radome, tested to establish which was better suited to the aircraft's performance. This aircraft soon revealed that the original gun barrels located in the wing leading edges were unsuitable for high-speed flight, as vortices formed inside the tubes, heating the cannon shells inside. This problem was easily fixed by simply extending the gun barrels forward. Meanwhile, fuel capacity was improved, not through any manufacturer-led programme or stipulation of the Air Ministry but thanks to the USAF, which sent two officers to Moreton Valence to fly the GA.5. They were largely pleased with the aircraft's performance, but criticised the aircraft's lack of adequate internal fuel. This was an issue that affected most of Britain's early post-war aircraft and one that the Air Staff seemed to be particularly adept at ignoring, even though it was, of course, an important issue. As a result of the USAF visit, Gloster developed a 250 gallon ventral tank, two of which could be snugly attached to the fuselage underside, and these soon became an almost standard fit on production aircraft.

On 14 January 1954, the fourth prototype joined the test programme, having been assembled at Gloster's Hucclecote factory and first flown from this site. WD808 was designated as an aerodynamic test specimen and after initial shakedown flights it was sent to Boscombe Down, where the A&AEE pilots assessed

WT827, the third Javelin prototype, was fitted with a number of radome designs as part of the aircraft's (and radar's) development programme.

WD808 at Gloster's (then) new test airfield at Moreton Valence. Just visible is the fin-top aerodynamic fairing that was subsequently removed.

its handling qualities. Finally, the fifth and (at least technically speaking) final prototype was WT836, and this aircraft made its first flight on 20 July in the hands of Wg Cdr R. F. Martin, who had become Bill Waterton's successor as Gloster's Chief Test Pilot. Although he was tasked with the shake-down flights for WT836, he also devoted a great deal of time to continuing investigation of the GA.5's spin qualities and, in particular, the aircraft's spin recovery techniques. The RAE at Farnborough expressed their own views on the subject (based largely on tests performed with scale models dropped from balloons), although their conclusions often differed from Gloster's. The GA.5 did not behave predictably when it entered a spin and on some occasions the direction of spin reversed as it progressed, so a lot of effort (in excess of 200 spin exercises) was put into the establishment of proper recovery techniques that could be set as standard for service use. Towards the end of 1954, the RAE, A&AEE and Gloster agreed a standard recovery procedure that required full in-spin aileron to be applied when the aircraft's nose dropped, after which the control column was to be moved fully forward. But even with an agreed technique, it was accepted that the aircraft was not going to be approved for intentional spinning in RAF service simply because its behaviour was too unpredictable to be safely handled in such circumstances by anyone other than a test pilot.

A magnificent in-flight view of the prototype Javelin, emphasising its simple design configuration and clean lines which have yet to be interrupted by vortex generators, sensors and probes.

Issues such as spin behaviour were only part of the GA.5's problems. Development had been slow, partly because of unfortunate accidents leading to the loss of both aircraft and pilots but also because of the Air Ministry's position, which often seemed confused. The situation was undoubtedly clouded by the emergence of de Havilland's DH.110, and it took some considerable time for the Air Staff to agree that the GA.5 was the better choice between the two designs. Apart from the eventual acceptance that the GA.5 appeared to have greater developmental potential, it was probably the tragic crash of the DH.110 at Farnborough in September 1952 that ultimately sealed this aircraft's fate, at least as far as the RAF was concerned.

But even as the GA.5 became the favoured aircraft, it still received more than a little criticism, some of which was justified and some which was not. For example, there was a growing rumour within the aviation industry and even the corridors of power in Whitehall that the GA.5 would not be capable of achieving supersonic speed, even though this was a feat that was to become almost routine for the emerging new breed of jet fighters, such as the Hunter, Swift, Sabre and, of course, the DH.110. To add to Gloster's concerns, former Chief Test Pilot Waterton became a correspondent for the *Daily Express* newspaper, and in one of his articles he criticised the GA.5 quite strongly. By way of response, his successor (Martin) got airborne in a GA.5 from Moreton Valence on the night of 4 July 1954 and proceeded to race across South London, placing a sonic boom over the capital as he went. The national media attributed the window-rattling bang to Gloster Aircraft just a couple of days later, but the manufacturer claimed that the sonic booms had been caused by accident, when the pilot's oxygen hose had supposedly become caught in his parachute harness, momentarily distracting him. In reality, it seems clear that Martin had aimed the bangs at Fleet Street, and nobody was left in any doubt that the GA.5 could exceed Mach 1. Even Sir Winston Churchill was woken from his bed in Kent, believing that a meteorite had crashed nearby. But despite misgivings, the Ministry of Supply had placed an order for 200 aircraft on 7 June 1952, and it was at this time that the GA.5 was given the name 'Javelin', together with an initial designation of FAW Mk 1, reflecting the aircraft's role as both a fighter and an all-weather aircraft.

The Javelin captured headlines again in September 1954, when no fewer than five aircraft were sent to Farnborough for the annual SBAC show. Two prototypes were accompanied by XA544 and XA546, the first and third production Javelins, and after being displayed to the public on the ground, they thundered into the air and performed an impressive flypast in a tight V-formation. The Javelin's size and bulk was in itself quite startling to many observers, and the noise of its Sapphire engines was combined with harmonic howls from the wing-mounted gun barrels, producing a spectacle that nobody would ever forget. Air Marshal Sir Richard Atcherley was one of many officials who witness the thrilling event, and after watching test pilot Martin complete an individual aerobatic routine in one of the five aircraft, he exclaimed, 'Good Lord, it's like seeing the Albert Memorial roll over!'

XA546, a Javelin FAW Mk 1 at Farnborough, where the aircraft was assigned to test duties. Sadly, it was lost in the Bristol Channel in 1954 after suffering control failure.

Javelin FAW Mk 1 XA562 was fitted with Avon 210 engines and used as a flying test bed for this engine variant, based at Hucknall.

An RAF publicity image of a quarter of Javelin FAW Mk 1 aircraft from No. 46 Squadron, performing for the cameraman during a sortie from home base at RAF Odiham.

The Javelin FAW Mk 1 was equipped with Sapphire Sa.6 engines, each developing 8,300 lb of thrust. XA544 was the first of forty Mk 1 aircraft assembled and flown from Hucclecote, this particular aircraft making its maiden flight on 22 July 1954. CA Release was issued on 30 November 1955 for this variant, although restrictions on the aircraft were imposed from the very start, with both stalling and looping manoeuvres prohibited and a speed limit of 540 knots (together with a minimum limit of 125 knots). This was hardly ideal for what was to be the RAF's new fighter, but it was expected that as improvements were made, the restrictions would be lifted and the Javelin would be free to fly unfettered. In fact, restrictions were never completely removed and although nobody knew it at the time, the aircraft would continue to be dogged by these issues until its eventual retirement.

Deliveries to Fighter Command finally began in February 1956, with Nos 46 and 87 Squadrons at Odiham being the first recipients. With so many technical issues still outstanding, a considerable number of production Javelins (more than twenty at one stage) were retained by Gloster Aircraft for test flying and trials, encompassing radar development, an all-moving tailplane, Gee navigation equipment, and (dummy) Firestreak missiles. XA552 was assigned to engine development and was fitted with a pair of de Havilland Gyron Junior engines, each rated at 10,000 lb (with reheat), and although some of XA552's work was indirectly connected to the Javelin programme, the engine trials were largely connected with the Bristol 188 aircraft, for which the engines were primarily intended. Painted in a striking Royal Blue paint scheme with white trim, the aircraft was withdrawn and dumped on Spadeadam's ranges just eight years later.

The first reheated Sapphire engines were fitted to XA560 (it first flew on 30 September 1955) but at this stage, the prospect of delivering Javelins to the RAF with reheated Sapphires was still a long way off. The Javelin FAW Mk 2 was a direct development of the Mk 1, the AI Mk 17 radar being replaced in this variant by an American APQ-43 system that had been planned for introduction since 1952. Designated as the AI Mk 22 in RAF service, the radar required a redesigned nose cone that hinged sideways for internal access (rather than being removable as on the Javelin Mk 1). XD158 was used as the Mk 2 prototype and with its new nose it flew for the first time on 31 October 1955. The first production Javelin FAW Mk 2 was XA768, and this aircraft made its maiden flight on 25 April 1956 as the first of thirty such aircraft completed at Hucclecote. Deliveries were made to Nos 46 and 89 Squadrons beginning in May 1957, although as with the Mk 1, a number of aircraft were assigned to testing and trials not always directly connected with the Javelin programme. One well-known example was XA778, which was completed in a dazzling dayglow orange paint scheme as a calibration and 'chase' aircraft for the A&AEE. It flew from Boscombe Down until 1968, when it was replaced by a later-production Javelin Mk 9. Plans were made to increase production of both the Mk 1 and Mk 2 variant to a total of 296 and 123 examples respectively, but these plans were subsequently changed.

The next variant to emerge was the Javelin T Mk 3. The possibility of producing a dual-control trainer version of the proposed fighter designs was first addressed by Gloster in June 1950, during work on the P.319. While Hawker opted to adopt a side-by-side arrangement for its twin-seat trainer version of the Hunter, Gloster concluded that a tandem seating layout would be both aerodynamically and structurally preferable. However, the concept did not generate much interest from the Air Ministry, so it was not until 1951 that the idea re-emerged. One prototype of a dual-control version was eventually ordered and this was ultimately based on the Mk 6 variant, powered by Sapphire Sa.6 engines. Because Gloster was heavily committed to production and continuing design of single-seat Javelins, the trainer project was exported to Air Service Training at Hamble, and it was this company that refined the design and eventually produced WT841, which made its first flight on 20 August 1956 after a protracted development that often saw the aircraft languishing at Hamble with little progress being made.

The T Mk 3 was a minimum-change design that retained the same gun armament (used for conversion and continuation training) but had no radar, resulting in a longer nose (extended by 3.67 feet) designed to retain the same centre of gravity. The absence of radar enabled additional fuel (100 gallons) to be carried, and a revised rear canopy was also introduced, giving the instructor a better view. The

Javelin XA552 (a Mk 1 variant) was used for developmental flying before being converted into a flying test bed for the de Havilland Gyron Junior DGJ.10 engine as part of the Bristol 188 supersonic research programme.

Javelin T Mk 3 XH438 from the Fighter Command Instrument Rating Squadron, pictured at Coltishall in 1961. (*Tony Clarke collection*)

first of twenty-two production aircraft made its first flight on 6 January 1958, the first examples going to No. 228 OCU at Leeming, although eventually each Javelin squadron generally had at least one example of the T Mk 3 on strength, used for continuation training and general duties.

The FAW Mk 4, the next fighter derivative of the Javelin to be produced, was based on the earlier Mk 1 and Mk 2 but introduced a new all-flying tail structure. XA629 was used as the Mk 4 prototype and it first flew in this form on 19 September 1955. Some fifty examples were manufactured, with production split between Gloster and Armstrong Whitworth, easing the burden on the Gloster facilities at Moreton Valence and Chilbolton. Deliveries to the RAF began in February 1957, when the first aircraft joined No. 141 Squadron at Horsham St Faith, and subsequently a further seven RAF squadrons. XA629 was later used for aerodynamic flight trials, and in an effort to improve the Javelin's performance at high subsonic speeds, various modifications were made to the aircraft's wing surfaces. The most obvious were the Küchemann 'carrot' bodies that were mounted on the wing trailing edges inboard of the ailerons, and these were eventually joined by additional fairings on the trailing edges of the wing tips. These modifications were designed to reduce airflow separation and improve the boundary layer of airflow, but although the bodies did create improvements, it was later established that by thickening the wing trailing edge and adding two rows of vortex generators on the wing upper surface, a similar improvement could be achieved more simply (by re-energising the boundary layer flow). The Küchemann fairings were abandoned and all subsequent Javelins incorporated the vortex generators and revised trailing edge thickness. Some Mk 4 aircraft were again assigned to test duties, various examples going to Canada for cold weather trials, while XA630 was used to develop the familiar 'pen nib' engine fairing. XA763 and XA764 were assigned to the CFE for use on tactical evaluation exercises.

The Javelin FAW Mk 5 duly followed, essentially unchanged from the Mk 1 variant but with improved fuel capacity. Even with external tanks, RAF pilots consistently reported that the aircraft was short on range, and although it was not modified externally, provision for an additional 125 gallons of fuel was incorporated into the wing structure. This variant was also designed to carry Firestreak missiles, but with development of the weapon lagging behind that of the aircraft, the Mk 5 never carried the missile in RAF service. Production of the sixty-four aircraft was again divided between Gloster and Armstrong Whitworth, the first example making its maiden flight on 26 July 1956. Deliveries began later that year, the first examples going to the CFE, followed by No. 151 Squadron.

The next development was to repeat the same exercise as had been achieved with the Mk 1 and resulted in the Mk 5. Introducing the improved wing structure (with greater fuel capacity) on the Mk 2 fleet resulted in the Javelin FAW Mk 6, complete with its AI Mk 22 radar. Some thirty-three aircraft were produced at Hucclecote, the first being XA815, which flew for the first time in this form

Javelin FAW Mk 4 XA631 shortly after completion, out in the winter sun at Moreton Valence. Clearly visible is the definitive 'pen nib' jet pipe fairing adopted for this variant.

Delivered to the RAF in 1957, Javelin FAW Mk 5 XA654 was assigned to No. 23 Squadron at Horsham St Faith (now Norwich Airport). It subsequently served with No. 72 Squadron at Leconfield and the Central Fighter Combat School. (*Tony Clarke collection*)

Javelin FAW Mk 5 XA667 performing aerobatics over the North Sea coast. The aircraft served with No. 228 OCU at Leeming, No. 41 Squadron at Coltishall, and No. 5 Squadron at Laarbruch before being sold as scrap in 1965.

on 15 January 1957. No. 89 Squadron received the first production examples in October 1957, followed by Nos 29 and 46 Squadrons. The FAW Mk 7 was a more significant development as this aircraft was fitted with more powerful Sapphire Sa.7 engines, each developing 11,000 lb thrust. With a redesigned exhaust nozzle and an extended rear fuselage, the Mk 7 also introduced the Firestreak missile, two of which could be carried under each wing on weapons pylons. These pylons could also be used to carry up to four 100 gallon drop tanks, although the first 30 examples of the 142 total were completed without the Firestreak weapons fit (having been completed before it was deemed to be ready for introduction) and this batch of aircraft was subsequently retrofitted after completion. The Mk 7 also introduced a yaw stabilizer and a fully powered hydraulic rudder.

The combination of improvements made the Mk 7 a significantly better aircraft than its predecessors and as such it effectively became the 'standard' Javelin variant. The first production aircraft completed its maiden flight on 9 November 1956, but acceptance trials took some considerable time and it was not until the summer of 1958 that deliveries to the RAF began, when aircraft joined No. 33 Squadron. More than a few Mk 7 aircraft were again assigned to trials, including XH706, which was used for general handling research, and XH713, which

An in-flight image of two Javelin FAW Mk 6 aircraft from No. 85 Squadron, both fitted with the huge ventral fuel tanks that became a standard fit for most later-production aircraft.

went to Muharraq (Bahrain) for tropical weather trials in August 1957. XH754 went to Farnborough for rain dispersal investigation, connected with the TSR2 programme (and was deployed to Singapore as part of this project in 1961).

Not surprisingly, Gloster was keen to show its missile-armed fighter to the world. A Javelin Mk 7 was sent to Le Bourget for the Paris Air Show, where it captured a great deal of interest from both the media and public as the only combat aircraft at the event to be armed with what was then a new and exciting weapons fit. The RAF was also naturally eager to begin missile operations, and the Firestreak was officially 'released' for use – on a restricted basis – in August 1959, but it was not until 2 June 1960 that Fighter Command officially fired its first missile, courtesy of a Javelin FAW Mk 7 from No. 25 Squadron.

The final Javelin derivative to be produced as a 'new-build' machine was the FAW Mk 8. Based on the Mk 6 airframe and radar, this variant introduced the Sapphire Sa.7 engine, modified to incorporate a reheat unit to deliver a total thrust of 12,300 lb per engine. Unfortunately, reheat systems were at that time a fairly new concept, and the Sapphire's unit was suitable for use only above 20,000 feet, although it could be used in certain circumstances at lower altitudes. At low level the reheat system was useless; in fact, it reduced overall thrust output, but it did at least give the Javelin a better performance at higher altitudes. The outer wing leading edge was modified to feature a slight droop as part of further efforts to improve aerodynamics, and a pitch stabiliser was incorporated into

A classic publicity photograph of a Javelin crew in front of FAW Mk 7 XH716. This aircraft was converted to Mk 9 standard and served with No. 25 Squadron at Waterbeach and No. 11 Squadron at Geilenkirchen in Germany.

Although completed as a Javelin FAW Mk 7, XH764 was subsequently converted to FAW Mk 9 standard. It served with No. 64 Squadron at Duxford and finally with No. 29 Squadron at Akrotiri. It was grounded after being damaged in a landing accident at Manston in 1967. (*Tony Clarke collection*)

the aileron system, while an auto-stabilisation system was fitted into the rudder function.

Gloster's Hucclecote factory produced forty-seven Mk 8 aircraft, the first of which was XH966, making its maiden flight on 9 May 1958. XJ165 duly became the very last production Javelin to be built (its maiden flight being in August 1960), although the Mk 8 was not the end of the Javelin's development. A further thirteen Mk 8 aircraft were to have been built, but these were cancelled in August 1960 and a batch of existing Mk 7 airframes were brought out of storage for conversion to Mk 8 standard. More than eighty examples of the Mk 7 had been placed directly into storage after manufacture, in anticipation of conversion to a later standard; therefore the final 'new-build' Javelins were no longer required. The first delivery was made early in 1959 to the A&AEE, followed by the re-equipment of No. 41 Squadron at Wattisham, starting in November.

Although the Mk 8 was the last Javelin variant to be built, it was not the final version to be developed. The FAW Mk 9 was the last of the Javelin line, developed as a result of a decision to refit the Mk 7 fleet with Sapphire Sa.7R engines, equipped with reheat. Many Javelin FAW Mk 7 aircraft were therefore flown straight to Maintenance Units for storage after completion before being returned to the manufacturer for conversion, the process also including the modification of outer wing leading edges to improve performance. The conversion process took a long time, so it was not until December 1961 that the last aircraft (XH175) was completed. Deliveries began with No. 25 Squadron on 4 December 1959, and as the final Javelin variant, it was the FAW Mk 9 that earned the distinction of being the last version to remain in active RAF service, officially retiring on 30 April 1968 when No. 60 Squadron disbanded at Tengah, Singapore.

The Javelin is something of a contradiction in terms of its contribution to the RAF's post-war capabilities. It is undoubtedly true that the type suffered from a number of deficiencies that affected it throughout its service life, but at the same time it was also a major improvement over the capabilities of the Meteor that preceded it in the fighter and interceptor roles. It had a true all-weather capability, adequate manoeuvrability and altitude performance, a pretty respectable top speed, and good armament, especially when the Firestreak AAM was introduced on later variants. The very fact that it remained in service for more than a decade indicates that the Javelin was hardly a short-lived embarrassment, even though its eventual withdrawal was probably dictated by the availability of the fighter that succeeded it, rather than the perceived value of the Javelin itself. But the Javelin's crews also liked the aircraft, despite its faults, and many were keen to emphasise that once its limitations were known and accepted, it was relatively easy to operate the aircraft in accordance with restrictions and still perform the all-weather interception task effectively.

Likewise, it is fair to say that none of the RAF's post-war aircraft was without faults, as a great deal of the technology on which these aircraft were based was not exactly 'perfect science' at the time, and it is only with the benefit of hindsight that aircraft such as the Javelin might seem to have been less than

An unusual image of an unpainted Javelin FAW Mk 8 on a test flight prior to being delivered to the RAF.

Javelin FAW Mk 8 XH966 was assigned to the A&AEE at Boscombe Down after making its first flight in May 1958. It subsequently served with No. 41 Squadron at Wattisham before being placed in storage at St Athan late in 1963, prior to being scrapped.

Javelin FAW Mk 8 XJ129 served only with No. 41 Squadron at Wattisham before being placed in storage at St Athan. It was sold as scrap in 1964, just four years after being delivered to the RAF. (*Tony Clarke collection*)

Javelin FAW Mk 9 XH880 in 1960, whilst serving with No. 25 Squadron at Waterbeach, proudly displaying the initials of the squadron's CO on its tail. The aircraft subsequently flew with No. 11 Squadron at Geilenkirchen before being deployed to Singapore. (*Tony Clarke collection*)

XH708 was delivered to the A&AEE as a FAW Mk 7 during 1957. It was converted to FAW Mk 9 standard two years later and assigned to No. 64 Squadron at Duxford, where it was modified still further to FAW Mk 9R standard, complete with a huge refuelling boom.

ideal for the roles they performed. Perhaps more than anything else, the Javelin demonstrated some potentially lethal characteristics if it was flown at low speed. It demonstrated a tendency to self-stall and could enter into a very high rate of descent without any clear indication to the pilot as to what was happening. At low level (particularly on a landing approach) there were obviously many visual cues to alert the Javelin pilot to any major loss of height, but at altitude there were only cockpit instruments. At low level there was no means of recovery from a stall, and it was the introduction of a stall warning device that allowed the Javelin to be operated safely. Conversely, at high speed the Javelin also exhibited some unpleasant behaviour. At Mach 0.88 the aircraft pitched nose-down and at Mach 0.90 a slight buffet would develop, followed by more severe buffeting and then a tendency to yaw at Mach 0.97. Any faster and the aircraft would settle down and accelerate smoothly to Mach 1.05, but if it was held at a speed where the severe buffeting occurred there was every risk that structural damage to the airframe might be caused, and this was not the kind of issue that a regular fighter pilot ought to be expected to deal with. The CFE's evaluation of the Javelin FAW Mk 1 reported that although the aircraft handled well at most speeds, the controls became increasingly heavy as the speed exceeded 450 knots (which was hardly an unreasonable speed for a fighter), and at the maximum permissible speed of 535 knots the rudder was almost out of control, while the elevators were extremely heavy. Manoeuvrability was reported as good, but above 40,000 feet it was less impressive, and the aircraft was restricted to 30 degrees angle of bank. Anything more and it would invariably lose height as the turn progressed. Top speed was Mach 0.93, and this could be achieved at around 40,000 feet, but beyond this altitude the top speed fell away and despite being regarded as a 'supersonic' fighter, the production-standard Javelin was demonstrably incapable of exceeding Mach 1 unless it was in a dive. At 48,000 feet the aircraft was effectively at its operational ceiling and could not accelerate beyond Mach 0.71.

The Javelin Mk 4 was hardly any better, the CFE reporting that its AI Mk 17 radar was less than impressive, so that successful interceptions depended largely upon good GCI (Ground Control Interception) techniques and a ground controller who was adept at directing the Javelin onto its target. It was only above Mach 0.92 that the Mk 4 was judged to be superior to the FAW Mk 1, because of its all-flying tail, but in all other respects the Mk 4 had heavier control feel (which made it tiring to fly) and was actually slower than the Mk 1 at high altitude. The FAW Mk 2, 5 and 6 were regarded as similar in terms of performance and handling, but the FAW Mk 7 was judged to be an improvement, and even though it was heavier, it could attain 50,000 feet relatively easily, although its performance at such a dizzy height was no better. The subsequent introduction of reheated engines might have been a significant boost for the Javelin's capabilities but the rudimentary reheat system fitted to the Sapphire was new and relatively inefficient. The afterburners could be selected at any altitude, but they were fed by a constant output fuel pump and if reheat was selected at altitudes below 10,000 feet, the overall amount of fuel delivered to the engine's combustion chambers was less, and this had the effect of reducing thrust instead of increasing it. At higher altitudes, the engines required less fuel and so the fuel pump was able to deliver the 'spare' fuel to the reheat system, giving the Javelin a useful surge of additional power. But for the Javelin pilots it was undoubtedly frustrating (if not embarrassing) to have a reheat system that could actually slow the aircraft down rather than speed it up. RAF pilots were prohibited from deliberately spinning the aircraft, and even looping manoeuvres were forbidden, although few pilots paid much attention to this restriction.

The rules and regulations that restricted the Javelin's operations were a hindrance, but despite the difficulties, it is fair to say that the Javelin was (at least at the time that it was flown by the RAF) a pretty impressive interceptor. Despite being a big and heavy machine, it could climb well, easily outperforming the Hunter, and even its competitor, the DH.110 (Sea Vixen) in some circumstances. It had a very impressive cannon and missile armament, and a good manoeuvrability (at least at lower altitudes). The Javelin also possessed huge airbrakes that were undoubtedly an asset in air combat scenarios, allowing the pilot to slow his aircraft until his opponent was inevitably forced to fly-through. The airbrakes could deliver a very impressive 1 g of deceleration, and when combined with the Javelin's low wing loading, it created a fighter that was far more capable than its external appearance might have indicated. The Javelin's poor endurance was gradually addressed as the aircraft was developed, and with under-fuselage tanks

A line-up of Javelin FAW Mk 1 aircraft from No. 46 Squadron at a rainy RAF Odiham in July 1957. The last production Javelin Mk 1 is included in the line-up.

Javelin FAW Mk 7 XH892 was converted to FAW Mk 9 standard in 1959, and FAW Mk 9R standard in 1962. After serving with Nos 23, 64 and 29 Squadrons it was withdrawn in 1967. It eventually made its way to Duxford, and finally to the Norfolk and Suffolk Air Museum at Flixton.

and up to four external drop tanks under the wings, the aircraft was no longer short-legged. Ultimately, an in-flight refuelling capability was introduced on the last Javelin variant, and although the monstrous refuelling 'lance' was easily the most grotesque modification to have befallen any RAF fighter, the refuelling system worked well and effectively gave the Javelin almost limitless endurance, if required. This capability became increasingly valuable when the RAF began to lose many of its overseas staging posts in the Middle East and Far East.

The Javelin became a major part of the RAF's Order of Battle during the 1960s, operating from sixteen stations in all. It was deployed to Germany and Cyprus and ultimately to Singapore, participating in the Rhodesia crisis in 1965 and the Indonesian confrontation during the same period. Its eventual withdrawal was by no means an indication of inadequacy but more of an eagerness to introduce the incredibly fast and agile Lightning, although more than a few observers are still eager to point out that disposing of the two-man Javelin with its radar, spacious cockpit, adequate fuel, good range and manoeuvrability for a one-man 'hot rod' might have been done rather differently if the RAF had been given the ability to see into the future, and realise that even the Lightning was by no means a perfect fighter. But, of course, hindsight is always twenty-twenty.

An interesting close-up of the Javelin FAW Mk 9's wing upper surface. It illustrates the array of vortex generators applied to this variant in order to improve the aircraft's tendency to buffet at high speed. The aileron trailing edges were also thickened.

CHAPTER EIGHT
The Fighting Fox

The Royal Navy's early experience with the Vampire jet fighter was sufficient to convince the Fleet Air Arm that jet power was entirely compatible with carrier operations, and that a more capable jet fighter could be produced specifically for naval operations. Discussions between the Admiralty and de Havilland (the designer and manufacturer of the Vampire) began in 1946, and in response to the Navy's projected needs, de Havilland created a direct development of the Vampire that incorporated two engines, and swept wings, based on the company's experience with the DH.108 Swallow, a research project that had yielded a great deal of useful data.

The Swallow was based on a standard Vampire fuselage, to which new swept wings were attached, these having been designed on the basis of data gathered from American research and from the wealth of information that had come from Germany. The DH.108 was created in order to investigate swept-wing behaviour in preparation for what was to become the Comet airliner, and although the project resulted in the loss of all three DH.108 aircraft (and the deaths of three test pilots), the Swallow demonstrated the potential of swept wings – it was the first British aircraft to exceed the speed of sound – even if the design was demonstrably unrefined and potentially lethal. Knowledge gleaned from the project was therefore incorporated into de Havilland's new twin-engine fighter and the result was the DH.110, an aircraft that was clearly based on the Vampire's basic twin tail boom configuration but considerably larger, with two engines and accommodation for two crew, together with all-new swept wings.

The Admiralty issued Naval Staff Requirement NR/A.14 in January 1947, partly based on the design that de Havilland was proposing but also as a project comparable with Specification F.44/46 issued by the Air Ministry. The RAF had a very clear requirement for a new all-weather jet fighter and the Fleet Air Arm wanted one too, but with the necessary capability to operate from an aircraft carrier. Precisely why the two requirements were issued simultaneously remains unclear, and there may well have been some attempt to seek a common design that would be suitable for both the RAF and Royal Navy. On the other hand, it seems equally likely that (in typical inter-service tradition) the Navy simply wanted to ensure that it was not left behind in a race to acquire a new jet fighter that was far more advanced than the first-generation Vampires, Meteors, Attackers and Sea Hawks. The Admiralty's Naval Staff Requirement NR/A.14 outlined a potential night fighter replacement for the Sea Hornet, incorporating two jet engines and capable of attaining at least 500 knots. All-up weight was not to exceed 30,000 lb, and a high degree of manoeuvrability was specified, together with the obvious capacity for carrier operations. De Havilland also paid great attention to the RAF's requirements, as it was hoped that the emerging DH.110 design would be capable of meeting the needs of both potential customers.

The RAF wanted an all-weather fighter capable of reaching more than 40,000 feet, with a speed of 525 knots or more at 25,000 feet. Endurance was stipulated as 2 hours minimum, including a climb to 25,000 feet and 15 minutes of air-to-air combat. Rapid take-off would also be necessary (the aircraft would have to be able to reach its ceiling of 45,000 feet within 10 minutes of engine start), and in addition to having good manoeuvrability it would also have to be tough and capable of withstanding loads of 4 g or more. For both the RAF and Fleet Air Arm aircraft, there would be two crew – the pilot and an observer or navigator – and a stipulation was made that production should be available at a rate of approximately ten aircraft per month.

The Admiralty then decided to order a fleet of Sea Venom fighters to act as interim aircraft until a new twin-engine fighter entered production for the Navy. This was a move that made some sense, but as the Sea Venom was produced by de Havilland, it only served to delay progress of the DH.110. However, in June 1948, the Air Staff opted to order three prototypes of the DH.110, together with four examples of the competing GA.5 design from Gloster Aircraft. By this stage, the design of the DH.110 was essentially the same for both the RAF and Fleet Air Arm machine, although some work had been done on producing a variant more directly suited to naval requirements. In particular, de Havilland considered an unusual forward-swept tailplane and fin structure which promised to be better both aerodynamically and structurally, although it is unclear why the same design could not have been applied to the RAF machine. It was eventually abandoned in favour of a more conventional design.

Missile armament was not specifically mentioned during the project's early days, and armament was specified as four Hispano 20 mm cannon, to be positioned under the cockpit in much the same way as had been applied to the Vampire. The two-man crew was to be seated side by side, although the observer/navigator would be staggered slightly rearwards in the same style as in the later Vampire and Venom designs. Plans for an escape capsule did not proceed far and ejection seats were built into the design.

In January 1949, a more cohesive plan was proposed to create a common design for the RAF and Fleet Air Arm, and six more DH.110s would be ordered for this programme, each aircraft assigned to different aspects of the fighter's design such as aerodynamics, armament, radar and naval features. This would have brought the total of prototypes to thirteen, and both the Ministry of Supply and the Treasury were concerned that this seemed like an excessive number. It was a fairly high figure when related to other aircraft projects, but in reality it was entirely appropriate for a programme of this size and complexity. Three more naval derivative prototypes were ordered just months later (one assigned to the development of a naval strike capability that had also emerged), but by the end of 1949, the proposal for so many aircraft was beginning to change in favour of a more modest fleet, especially when the Admiralty began to look elsewhere for a suitable aircraft and the RAF started to devote more attention to the Gloster GA.5. Eventually, the proposed prototype fleet was reduced to five, and then (as of June 1952) cut still further to just two, and these were completed at Hatfield during the summer of 1951, both intended to pursue the RAF's requirements while the Navy seemingly lost interest in the DH.110 completely, preferring instead a proposed design being offered by Fairey.

The first of the two surviving prototypes was WG236 and this aircraft began taxiing trials at Hatfield during September 1951. Its first flight was completed on 26 September in the capable hands of de Havilland's famous test pilot John Cunningham, who proceeded to take the aircraft through an initial shake-down and evaluation lasting just over 45 minutes. Much to de Havilland's disappointment, the aircraft had been completed and flown just a few weeks too late to take part in the all-important SBAC show at Farnborough, but the design team took some consolation from the initial reports that the machine handled and performed well, exhibiting none of the problems that had dogged the experimental DH.108 Swallow. The only significant problem was a tendency to 'snake' at high speeds, and this was found to be due to the aeroelasticity (flexing) of the two huge tail booms that were considerably bigger than those fitted to the diminutive Vampire. Steel reinforcing strips were fitted and the fin area was increased, and the problem was soon resolved. On 20 February 1952, test pilot John Derry took WG236 past Mach 1 in a shallow dive, earning the DH.110 the distinction of being the first twin-seat and twin-engine aircraft to break the sound barrier. De Havilland then devoted some considerable effort to the improvement of the aircraft's handling, the tailplane being changed to all-moving 'slab' surface, and eventually the manual rudders were also changed to fully powered alternatives.

In the meantime, the second prototype (WG240) was completed, and on 25 July it was flown for the first time. With more powerful Avon engines and a number of airframe modifications, the second aircraft immediately demonstrated an improved performance and so was selected to take part in the 1952 SBAC show with John Derry flying the aircraft and Tony Richards acting as observer/navigator. The DH.110's debut at Farnborough thrilled the spectators, Derry performing a supersonic arrival on each day, during the flying display. However, on the penultimate day of the show (6 September) the aircraft was suffering from engine problems and in order to ensure that the DH.110 participated in that afternoon's flying display, Derry and Richards went back to Hatfield to collect WG236 and arranged to fly the aircraft back to Farnborough and perform a display on arrival. The same supersonic approach was completed, and after the customary sonic bang was firmly planted on the show crowd, the DH.110 zoomed

DH.110 prototype WG236 takes to the air. Its maiden flight took place on 26 September 1951 in the hands of test pilot John Cunningham.

A movie still image, capturing the tragic loss of WG236 over Farnborough during the afternoon of 6 September 1952. Its effect on the Sea Vixen programme was significant, as was its far-reaching influence on air show safety.

De Havilland DH.110 prototype WG236, shortly after completion at Hatfield.

along the crowd line before Derry hauled the aircraft into a wide turn at high speed, to turn back towards the crowd for a high-speed climb. As WG236 began its climb, the aircraft suddenly disintegrated, large portions of the airframe falling near to the runway, while the two Avon engines powered forward and ploughed into the spectators' area, killing twenty-seven people and injuring another sixty-three. Derry and Richards were also killed.

The tragic accident marred the entire SBAC show and made international news, and ultimately had a dramatic effect on the nature of all future air show demonstrations around the world. Investigations of the wreckage and cine film of the crash confirmed that Derry's display routine had begun as normal with a supersonic dive from 40,000 feet, followed by the high-speed pass and a wide left-hand circuit. As the aircraft turned back towards the show crowds and pulled up into a climb, the starboard outer wing had detached, followed by the port wing, at which stage the forces acting on the aircraft caused the fuselage and engines to break free. The combination of a turn and climb had imposed loads on the airframe that were beyond its structural strength, and de Havilland was forced to re-examine the composition of the DH.110 wing design. It was established that although the wing design had been adequate for the Vampire, the same wing structure could not cope with the speeds and stresses imposed by this much bigger and heavier aircraft. WG240 was therefore rebuilt with a new front spar web, thicker wing ribs and reinforced stringers (together with aerodynamic

Photographs of the second DH.110 prototype (WG240) are rare. This is one of the few in-flight pictures taken before the aircraft was repainted in representative Fleet Air Arm colours.

changes to the outer wing leading edge), and the opportunity was also taken to introduce the proposed changes to the fin and tailplane structure. When the aircraft re-emerged from the Hatfield factory in June 1953 it was in effect a very different aircraft and one that was much closer to a production-standard fighter.

It is fair to say that by the end of 1952 the Air Staff had already shifted their interest away from the DH.110 towards the competing Gloster GA.5 design, but the horrific crash at Farnborough was undoubtedly the final straw. The RAF ordered the GA.5 (which became the Javelin), but by this stage the Admiralty's pursuance of an all-weather fighter design had effectively stalled and its attention turned back towards the possibility of creating a new swept-wing version of the Venom (the DH.116), but de Havilland simply did not have the resources to embark upon such an ambitious project. Instead, the company proposed re-visiting the DH.110, suitably modified to naval standards and designed to undertake the carrier fighter and interceptor roles, with a strike/attack capability as a secondary possibility.

The DH.110 had gradually evolved into an aircraft suited to RAF requirements, and a Ministry of Supply study completed in March 1953 concluded that the aircraft would need to be redesigned if it was to meet naval requirements. The proposed AI Mk 18 radar would need to be housed inside a redesigned nose section, and the airframe would have to be strengthened if it was to attain a ground attack capability in addition to its primary role as an interceptor. Air-to-air missiles would also now have to be part of the aircraft's armament fit, but de Havilland believed that the DH.110 could be reconfigured to suit all of these

XF828 was fitted with a bolt-on refuelling probe for the type's initial air-to-air refuelling trials. It retained its instrumentation probe while AAR trials were conducted.

requirements and, on 14 July, the Naval Aircraft Design Committee accepted the aircraft as a suitable way forward.

What emerged was in effect a completely different aircraft, with Rolls-Royce RA.14 Avon engines, folding wings, arrestor gear, stronger undercarriage, larger wing flaps, a redesigned tailplane and a new cockpit layout. Design work was shifted to the company's Christchurch factory (Hatfield having become increasingly involved in the Comet airliner project) and a third prototype was initiated, using some components from one of the original proposed fleet that was subsequently cancelled. The new aircraft would have a top speed of 690 mph at sea level, a ceiling of 48,000 feet and a 14,000 feet per minute rate of climb. Armament would be four Blue Jay (Firestreak) AAMs and two ADEN cannon, or two Firestreaks and four cannon. A batch of 100 aircraft was anticipated but Treasury approval was eventually given for 75 aircraft, later increased to 78. The completed (third) prototype emerged at Christchurch as XF828, which made its first flight, from Christchurch to Hurn, on 20 June 1955 in the hands of test pilot Jock Elliot.

Meanwhile, the surviving WG240 was transferred to Boscombe Down from where it was prepared for initial deck trials. These were conducted on HMS *Albion* in September 1954, although without the benefit of arrestor gear, the aircraft could only perform approaches and 'bolter' launches. Representative missile launch rails were fitted and the aircraft's landing gear was strengthened for the trials, but it seems odd that the most fundamental addition (a tail hook) was not fitted. The all-new XF828 was, of course, more fully modified to naval standards, although the wings could not be folded and radar equipment was not installed (as neither item was needed for initial trials). It

XF828 in flight over Farnborough, the huge ventral air brake extended. This was retained (in modified form) on production aircraft.

DH.110 WG240, resplendent in its short-lived black paint scheme, complete with red cheat line and national insignia.

The third DH.110 prototype was XF828. Fitted with naval equipment, it did not have folding wings. It is seen at Christchurch, about to begin a test flight.

A magnificent in-flight image of XF828, painted in representative Fleet Air Arm colours and fitted with a test instrumentation boom.

was also deployed on deck trials, this time on board HMS *Ark Royal* on 5 April 1956.

The first production aircraft (named Sea Vixen FAW Mk 1 as of 5 March 1957) was XJ474, flown for the first time on 20 March 1957. Although outwardly similar to the original DH.110, it was in fact 80 per cent different. It was the first British fighter not to be armed with guns of any description, as the planned fit of ADEN cannon was abandoned in favour of an all-missile fit as primary armament, although the aircraft was progressively cleared for the carriage of external fuel tanks, bombs and rocket pods. XJ474 performed a series of fifty deck landings and launches from HMS *Ark Royal* and was judged to be well suited to carrier operations; therefore no further major modifications to the aircraft were made. The next successive production aircraft were also assigned to trials including engine performance, missile compatibility, radar development and navigation equipment. XJ482 underwent cold weather trials (in a climatic chamber operated by Vickers), while XJ479 was assigned to tropical trials in North Africa, where it was written off following a bird strike.

XJ488 was the first aircraft to be fitted with an in-flight refuelling probe, and trials with the system were performed without any significant problems, so the entire FAW Mk 1 fleet was therefore equipped with this facility. Unlike the hideous 'lance' fitted to Gloster's Javelin, the Sea Vixen's probe was a straightforward boom attached to the port wing, although it could be removed ahead of an attachment point on the wing leading edge, if not required. The system enabled the Sea Vixen to take on fuel from the RAF's tanker fleet if overseas 'ferry' deployment was needed, but on a more regular basis it would give the Fleet Air Arm the ability to transfer fuel to and from a Sea Vixen, courtesy of a hose and drogue unit housed in a pod that could be attached to its wing pylon.

The Sea Vixen's performance and versatility showed great potential and by the summer of 1957, plans were being made to order more aircraft. The plans translated into an order for forty aircraft, followed by an additional batch of fifteen machines, most of which were completed at Christchurch before that facility closed down in 1962, after which the Sea Vixen programme moved to Hawarden.

The Sea Vixen Intensive Flying Trials Unit was No. 700Y Flight, formed at Yeovilton on 4 November 1958. Tasked with the evaluation of the aircraft and its preparation for operational service, flying began in May 1959 and continued until July when the unit stood down in preparation for recommissioning as No. 892 NAS. From May 1959, No. 766 NAS (also at Yeovilton) became the Fleet Air Arm's all-weather fighter training unit, equipped with Sea Venoms. The first Sea Vixens arrived from October onwards, and the unit divided into two Flights, one retaining Sea Venoms as No. 766B Flight until October 1960, when it became No. 766 NAS. The Flight became the Sea Vixen conversion unit as of 22 October 1959.

Although the Sea Vixen was destined to complete its service career without becoming involved in any significant conflicts, No. 766 NAS did perform a series

Although XJ482 entered Fleet Air Arm service in regular FAA colours, it was subsequently assigned to the A&AEE where it was repainted in a high-visibility black and white paint scheme designed to assist photographic calibration for weapons test recording. It is now preserved in the Fleet Air Arm Museum.

XJ474 was assigned to test duties for most of its service life, operating with the RAE at Farnborough and the A&AEE at Boscombe Down. It was withdrawn in 1970 at RAE Bedford.

Sea Vixen FAW Mk 1 XJ488 was assigned to trials duties and eventually joined the A&AEE, being one of the last Mk 1 Sea Vixens to be withdrawn from use. It was repainted in a striking all-black paint scheme.

Sea Vixen FAW Mk 1 XN649 was converted to Mk 2 standard and remained in Fleet Air Arm service until 1971. It was then transferred to the short-lived Cornwall Aero Park before being broken up. Only the aircraft's nose section now survives.

of operational attack missions for real, albeit on a distinctly non-hostile target. In March 1967, when the oil tanker *Torrey Canyon* went aground off Cornwall, Sea Vixens took part in the subsequent bombing missions, designed to disperse and ignite the fuel oil spilling from the crippled tanker. However, No. 766 NAS earned wider public recognition as the creators of a short-lived but very popular Sea Vixen display team. As 'Fred's Five', a five-aircraft team became the Navy's official aerobatic team for 1962. The Sea Vixen's 'proper' service entry was in fact with No. 892 NAS, during July 1959.

Such was the success of the Sea Vixen FAW Mk 1's entry into Fleet Air Arm service that attention soon shifted towards the possibility of improving the aircraft still further. In February 1960, a design study was completed that examined the possibility of re-equipping the Sea Vixen with two Rolls-Royce RB.163 Spey engines delivering 11,380 lb thrust, or even more with reheat. Firestreak AAMs would be replaced by the more capable Red Top missiles, and endurance improvements were also considered. De Havilland proposed the attachment of wingtip fuel tanks, together with additional fuel capacity located behind the cockpit within a stretched fuselage. Also proposed was an alternative and ingenious design that enabled additional fuel to be housed in extensions of the wing booms, modified to protrude beyond the wing leading edge. After further development, the plans to install the Spey engine and the wingtip fuel tanks were dropped, but the extended wing booms and missile modifications were adopted, resulting in the basis of what became the Sea Vixen FAW Mk 2 as of 26 May 1961.

Two prototypes, XN684 and XN685, converted from existing Mk 1 airframes, were completed at Hatfield, the first machine making its maiden flight on 1 June 1962 in the hands of Chris Capper, followed by XN685 on 17 August, flown by Desmond Penrice. Both aircraft had already been used for trial installations of the Red Top missile, and once the Sea Vixen Mk 2 aerodynamics and handling tests had been completed, they were returned to the Red Top programme. The first new-build Sea Vixen FAW Mk 2 was XP919, and this aircraft took to the air for the first time on 8 March 1963, from Hawarden. A further four aircraft were completed and immediately allocated to trials work and flight testing. Hawarden became the main production factory for Mk 2 Sea Vixens after production of the FAW Mk 1 ended at Christchurch with the 118th aircraft, XN710. A single FAW Mk 1 (XP918) was manufactured at Hawarden, followed by twenty-nine FAW Mk 2 aircraft, the last of these (XS590) making its maiden flight on 3 February 1966. However, a further 65 Sea Vixen FAW Mk 1 aircraft were modified to FAW Mk 2 standard either at Hawarden or at the Royal Naval Aircraft Yard at Sydenham.

This establishment, just outside Belfast, assumed responsibility for all Sea Vixen maintenance, modifications and trials work as of 1960. XP919 was transferred to RAE Bedford for dummy deck landing and launch trials before returning to Hatfield for more flight testing, after which it was assigned to a series of armament trials at Bedford and Boscombe Down, including the release of unguided rockets, the Bullpup air-to-surface missile, and the use of LABS (Low Altitude Bombing

The Sea Vixen was an excellent carrier-borne aircraft, although like any naval aircraft it suffered its fair share of accidents. This hapless Vixen appears to have been brought to a stop by the emergency arrestor barrier of HMS *Victorious*.

A dramatic view of XN684, rocket projectiles blazing. Built as a FAW Mk 1, the aircraft was modified to Mk 2 standard and served with Nos 893 and 899 NAS.

Completed in May 1961, Sea Vixen FAW Mk 2 was initially assigned to weapons trials and fitted with camera recording equipment inside and under its nose cone. It subsequently entered Fleet Air Arm service.

Sea Vixen FAW Mk.1 XJ558 flew with Nos 890 and 766 NAS at Yeovilton. Tragically, it was ditched in the Irish Sea during a test flight in 1967, both crew members being killed.

An unusual image of No. 893 NAS Sea Vixen FAW Mk 1 aircraft, illustrating the Vixen's rather unusual (and less than ideal) windscreen design.

A brace of Sea Vixen FAW Mk 1 fighters prepare to launch from the deck of HMS *Ark Royal*. Both aircraft are from No. 890 NAS, the Sea Vixen Headquarters Squadron based at Yeovilton. *Terry Goulding*

A rare image of a Sea Vixen FAW Mk 1 during early carrier deck trials. The aircraft's extended flaps can be seen, as can the catapult launch strop about to end its useful life in the English Channel.

System) 'toss bombing' manoeuvres for weapons release. It then joined No. 766 NAS at Yeovilton. No. 700Y Flight received the first deliveries of the Mk 2 aircraft and embarked on HMS *Ark Royal* on 3 March to begin carrier trials, shifting to HMS *Victorious* later that year, followed by HMS *Hermes* and finally HMS *Centaur*, sailing to the Far East. No. 899 NAS (as the 'headquarters squadron') assumed the responsibility of introducing the Sea Vixen FAW Mk 2 into regular squadron service.

As mentioned previously, the Sea Vixen was never involved in any major conflicts, the *Torrey Canyon* disaster being the only incident that ever required the type to be used 'in anger'. However, the aircraft did participate in numerous 'show-of-strength' missions during its time with the Fleet Air Arm. More significantly, No. 892 also conducted a handful of attack sorties whilst deployed on board HMS *Centaur* in 1964. The Aden emergency required the support of troops on the ground and, from 18-24 June, No. 892 NAS launched a series of ground attack sorties from HMS *Centaur*. This incident was the only time when the Sea Vixen was employed against hostile targets, although the Aden emergency was not exactly a war. It is perhaps ironic that on the two occasions when the Sea Vixen's abilities were used for real, it was in the ground attack role that it

This unusual view of a Sea Vixen FAW Mk 2 illustrates the design of its aileron, which extends across the wingtip structure. Also visible are the engine access panels, all marked with familiar red safety markings.

An atmospheric image of a Sea Vixen FAW Mk 2 thundering past HMS *Ark Royal* in foul weather.

Sea Vixen FAW Mk 2 XJ582 during a visit to RAF Coltishall's air show in September 1966. (*Tony Clarke collection*)

was employed, even though the aircraft was ostensibly designed as a fighter and interceptor, and the Sea Vixen never saw an opportunity to 'mix it' with hostile fighters throughout its service life.

Ultimately, a variety of equipment fits could be carried operationally, enabling the aircraft to be used in a number of roles. For ground attack missions the Sea Vixen could carry 500 lb and 1,000 lb high-explosive bombs with either contact or proximity fuses, or rocket projectile pods, each containing 32 2 inch high-explosive rockets that could be fired in 2 second 'ripple' launches. Also available was the 3 inch rocket, although this was not used as frequently. For night attacks the Sea Vixen could launch a Lepus high-luminance flare for target illumination, or alternatively Gloworm illuminating flares could be used. The night attack profile was particularly demanding, requiring pilots to perform high-g manoeuvres at low level in almost total darkness. Spatial disorientation was a major problem and the Gloworm projectile often failed to function properly, the combination of these factors (plus others, such as the difficulty of selecting weapons in a dark, cramped cockpit) resulting in many accidents, some fatal.

Less well known is that the Sea Vixen was also nuclear-capable and could carry the Red Beard tactical bomb, although the strike role was almost exclusively assigned to the Navy's Scimitar (and eventually Buccaneer) squadrons. LABS delivery techniques were regularly practised, so that Sea Vixen crews were proficient in the art of 'toss bombing' either conventional or atomic weapons from low level. In the interceptor role, the Sea Vixen was perhaps more suited to its environment, and the combination of Firestreak missiles (ultimately the Red Top) and the reliable AI Mk 18 radar was an excellent mix. The Firestreak introduced on the Sea Vixen FAW Mk 1 was a good first-generation missile, but the faster and all-aspect Red Top carried by the FAW Mk 2 was a much more versatile design. Interception training missions were flown at all altitudes from 500 feet or less, up to 45,000 feet, the intercepts usually being made under the initial direction of a ground controller (either on land or on a carrier) or a controller on board a Gannet AEW (Airborne Early Warning) aircraft.

In 1965, Rhodesia's Unilateral Declaration of Independence prompted Britain to enforce sanctions against the country, and both HMS *Ark Royal* and HMS *Eagle* were sent to the region. Sea Vixens from Nos 899 NAS and 890 NAS were employed on surveillance sorties in the area around the East African port of Beira, but although the patrol missions were vital to the success of sanctions, the Sea Vixen squadrons were never required to do any more than monitor activities in the area. The closest that the aircraft ever got to real air-to-air combat for the first time was in 1967, when Britain's withdrawal from Aden called upon the deployment of forces across the region to ensure that the withdrawal went as smoothly as possible. No. 899 NAS (operating from HMS *Ark Royal*) was assigned to Combat Air Patrol missions, but the exercise was completed without any serious risk of conflict.

This event was in many ways the Sea Vixen's 'swan-song' as by now the Royal Navy was looking forward to the introduction of the McDonnell F-4K Phantom,

HMS *Eagle*'s flight deck, with a Sea Vixen FAW Mk 2 from No. 899 NAS about to take the arrestor cable.

Sea Vixen XJ604 preparing to launch from HMS *Ark Royal*. Sadly, this aircraft ended its days as a weaponry target on the Otterburn ranges in Northumberland. *Terry Goulding*

Sea Vixen FAW Mk 1 captured at the moment of launch from HMS *Ark Royal*. Visible just beneath the Vixen's extended flaps is the catapult launch strop, which was dumped in the sea during each launch. The *Ark Royal* was subsequently modified so this component could be recovered for reuse.

although it was not until January 1972 that the last operational Sea Vixen Squadron (No. 899 NAS) stood down. By this stage, the Phantom had settled into Fleet Air Arm service as the Navy's new fighter, interceptor and ground attack aircraft, but the Sea Vixen soldiered on for two more years in direct support of Fleet Air Arm operations, joining the Air Direction Unit in December 1970. This unit (based at Hurn but eventually moving to Yeovilton) was responsible for the provision of training facilities for Fleet Air Arm squadrons and naval ground controllers, and after replacing its fleet of Sea Venoms with Sea Vixens, the unit – which became the Fleet Requirements and Air Direction Unit (FRADU) – continued to fly the Sea Vixen until February 1974, when the type finally ended its association with the Royal Navy.

A handful of Sea Vixens remained active on trials duties with the A&AEE and RAE, the last example continuing in use at RAE Bedford until the late 1970s. Meanwhile, a number of Sea Vixens remained in use with Flight Refuelling Ltd (now Cobham Plc) at the company's Hurn and Tarrant Rushton facilities. Primarily, the FRU aircraft were used to test target designs produced by the company. Two aircraft (XJ524 and XS587) were used for these trials, and redesignated as Sea Vixen FAW Mk 2(TT) accordingly, and these remained active

A stunning view of a Sea Vixen FAW Mk 2 launching from the deck of HMS *Victorious* over a glistening sea.

until the mid-1980s. Plans were also made to use the Sea Vixen's speed and agility as the basis for a new target drone aircraft, destined to replace the dwindling fleet of Meteor drones operated by the RAE for trials work and for the support of missile firing exercises performed by the RAF and Fleet Air Arm squadrons. A fleet of twenty-five aircraft was to have been produced, using FAW Mk 2 aircraft that had been placed in storage after withdrawal from Fleet Air Arm service. Three D Mk 3 Sea Vixens were duly converted to the unmanned drone configuration, the first of these (XN657) making its maiden flight as a D Mk 3 in 1978.

In 1983, however, the drone programme was abandoned, largely because of costs but also because the Sea Vixen proved to be far from ideal for the role. The Sea Vixen's large tailplane structure served to mask the infra-red image of the aircraft's jet exhaust under certain circumstances, and this would have meant that infra-red missiles might well have been unable to home in successfully. The three completed D Mk 3 aircraft were transferred to Llanbedr and used for various trials, occasionally flying in unmanned configuration, although they were normally used as 'shepherd' aircraft for unmanned Jindivik drones. The last of these machines (and therefore the last active Sea Vixen) was XP924, and when Llanbedr closed down in 1995, the aircraft was sold to a private buyer and flown to Swansea. It remains in civilian hands as an air show performer, based at Hurn.

A brilliant in-flight photograph of 'Simon's Circus', a short-lived Sea Vixen aerobatic team from No. 892 NAS in 1968, under the leadership of Lt-Cdr Simon Idiens.

The Sea Vixen was a successful aircraft, and one that the Royal Navy was undoubtedly satisfied with, even though its original acquisition had been a 'second chance' decision. It handled well, and pilots rarely criticised its performance, although the observers were often less praiseworthy. The Sea Vixen's cockpit layout was certainly unorthodox. Although clearly based on de Havilland's experience with the Vampire and Venom night fighters, it was in some respects even less satisfactory. The observer was buried inside the fuselage, with only a small side window for outside vision (although some aircraft had an additional clear panel in the escape hatch above the ejection seat). De Havilland evidently believed that operating a radar set and navigational equipment could be performed more effectively in complete darkness, but for the observer the Sea Vixen's cockpit created a miserable, confined, darkened 'hole' that inevitably caused even the most hardened aviator to suffer from either claustrophobia or air sickness, or both. The layout was also poorly arranged, although by contrast the radar equipment was regarded as a great improvement over that which had been fitted in the Sea Venom, with improved reliability and a better, stabilised lock-on capability.

For the pilot, the Sea Vixen was a more enjoyable experience, as the aircraft was blessed with good handling, a decent range and a respectable weapons fit. It did suffer from stability problems in landing configuration, particularly on carrier approaches, and the offset cockpit was clearly less than ideal for the demanding nature of carrier landings, particularly when forward vision through the rather

Pictured during a Middle East cruise on board HMS *Centaur*, XJ611 flew with Nos 893, 899 and 766 NAS before being withdrawn in 1968. *Ray Deacon*

Performing a 'bolter', Sea Vixen FAW Mk 1 XP918 roars skywards from the deck of HMS *Victorious*, its arrestor hook still extended.

A nostalgic view from the 1960s, showing a mix of Sea Vixens and Buccaneers from HMS *Hermes* on a visit to RAF Luqa, Malta. A Vulcan can be seen in the background, taxiing to the runway threshold, and a Canberra is just visible in the far distance.

cumbersome windscreen structure was poor. The landing gear could also have been stronger, but in general terms the Sea Vixen was very much a pilot's aeroplane. In combat exercises, it was more than a match for other contemporary designs and could even emerge victorious from engagements with the RAF's Lightnings. With good endurance and (comparatively) good turning performance, naval pilots soon learned how to draw Lightning pilots into a long, turning fight that eventually caused the Lightning pilot to break free, only to fall victim to the Sea Vixen's Red Top missile as he selected his reheat. Some pilots were undoubtedly unhappy that ADEN cannon had not been retained as part of its armament, but even when many aircraft had to be temporarily grounded in order to keep Red Top-equipped aircraft serviceable, the advantages of the sometimes temperamental AAMs were undeniable. There were problems with maintenance, although these were not attributable to the aircraft as such, and issues were also encountered because many aircraft were modified to different standards, some Sea Vixens being new-build Mk 2s, others being new-build Mk 1s, and others were Mk 1s brought (almost) up to Mk 2 standards.

Whether the RAF would have been wiser to have chosen the Vixen in preference to the Javelin is open to question. The Javelin was a good fighter and interceptor, even though it was far from perfect. The Sea Vixen was undoubtedly just as good, and proved to be a capable ground attack aircraft too. Both types had their faults and advantages, and with the benefit of hindsight it would be unfair to describe one aircraft as being better than the other. The Javelin and Sea Vixen were both excellent aircraft, given the technology that was available at that time. They represented an important step from the first generation of jet fighters through to the modern, high-performance interceptors that were to follow.

CHAPTER NINE

Preston's Project

It was during 1943 that the Ministry of Aviation first embarked upon a project to investigate the practical possibilities of supersonic flight, and considering that Sir Frank Whittle's revolutionary jet-powered aircraft (the E.28/39 'Pioneer') had first taken to the skies little more than a year before, it is remarkable that the Air Ministry should have turned its attention to supersonic flight so quickly when so much jet engine development had yet to be undertaken. Seventy years later it is still difficult to establish what factors influenced the Air Ministry's thinking, but there seems to have been little doubt that significant advances in engine (and therefore aircraft) performance would be achieved with relative ease and speed. This was quite an ironic attitude considering that the Air Ministry had been so reluctant to pursue the concept of jet propulsion when it first emerged.

The Ministry of Aircraft Production issued Specification E.24/43, calling for an experimental research aircraft capable of exceeding Mach 1 and a speed of 1,000 mph at 36,000 feet. Miles Aircraft was awarded a contract and the project was initiated under conditions of extreme secrecy. This took advantage of the fact that Miles had its own metal foundry and was creating its own wind tunnel facilities which meant that no unwelcome external attention would be directed towards development of the aircraft, eventually referred to by the company and Air Ministry as the Miles M.52.

The design emerged as a narrow bullet-shaped fuselage combined with small bi-convex unswept wings and an unusual annular air intake surrounding the cockpit section, which was housed inside the intake shock cone. Although the M.52 airframe was certainly unorthodox, the chosen powerplant was rather less exotic and was based on one of Whittle's established designs – a Power Jets W.2/700 that developed a meagre 2,000 lb of static thrust, augmented by a relatively new and unsophisticated reheat system. The very fact that such a relatively low-powered engine had to be chosen for the project illustrates just how imaginative and ambitious the airframe design was, and also highlights how advances in aerodynamic theory were marching ahead of propulsion technology.

Work on the Miles M.52 progressed slowly, but by the end of the Second World War the project was approaching the end of the design phase with the first jigs being prepared for construction of a prototype aircraft. Both the manufacturer and the Air Ministry seemed confident that with further time and development, the M.52 would successfully achieve supersonic flight and that the aircraft at least had the potential to form the basis of further designs which might produce an operational fighter aircraft to enter RAF service during the 1950s, capable of achieving a blistering Mach 1.5 and an altitude of 40,000 feet or more. But just as the aircraft began to show such promise, the project was suddenly cancelled. The official reason given for the cancellation was one of safety concerns. The Ministry of Aircraft Production's Director General of Scientific Research commented:

> ... flying at speeds greater than sound introduces new problems. We do not yet know how serious they are. The impression that supersonic aircraft are just around the corner is quite erroneous, but the difficulties will be tackled using rocket-driven models. We have not the heart to ask pilots to fly the high-speed models so we shall make them radio controlled.

The existence of the Miles M.52 was still secret, so it was not until September 1946 that the absurdity of this statement became clear. The prospect of supersonic flight was indeed just around the corner both in the UK (courtesy of the M.52) and in the USA, where work on a very similar test aircraft was being undertaken by Bell.

The precise reasons why the M.52 was suddenly abandoned have still not been satisfactorily established. The Attlee Government was certainly desperately short of cash (almost to the point of bankruptcy) and this may well have been the main motivation that ultimately led to the project's termination, although it was not a particularly expensive project and was rapidly reaching the stage where it would have yielded a return on the Government's investment. Likewise, the ongoing exchange of technical information between the UK and the USA (especially research data which had been progressively recovered from Germany) may have encouraged some to question the validity of the M.52 design, but when so much work had already been completed and Bell's supersonic X-1 design was remarkably similar in configuration, the argument that there was insufficient confidence in the M.52's design seems very difficult to justify. There was also undoubtedly a great deal of commercial resentment against Miles within Britain's aircraft industry, and it may well be that it was a combination of all these factors which ultimately brought about the cancellation of the project.

However, the seemingly indecent haste with which all design and manufacturing work was abruptly stopped was certainly unusual, and this has led to a variety of stories that have circulated for years, speculating on the reasons why the aircraft was abandoned. Some commentators assert that an order was given to destroy all of the prototype's construction jigs and that research data already created for the M.52 was eventually transferred directly to the US, reportedly in exchange for other research data from the US which (allegedly) subsequently failed to materialise. In fact, there is no evidence to support such claims, and even if information was freely exchanged between the UK and US (which was often the case at this stage in history) there is no reason to assume that it was of any critical value, but history records that it was Bell's X-1 which earned the distinction of being the first aircraft to break the sound barrier in level flight on 14 October 1947.

The only indisputable fact is that the M.52 would have been capable of matching the X-1's performance had development continued. The decision to proceed with rocket-powered model trials was due largely to persistence and pressure from Dr Barnes Wallis (of 'Dambusters' fame), who convinced the Air Ministry that unmanned models would be a much cheaper and safer research tool. It is also notable that Wallis made strenuous efforts to ensure that the trials project should be awarded to his company (Vickers); therefore his motives might not have been entirely altruistic. The resulting RAE/Vickers flight test programme was eventually conducted from St Eval in Cornwall, where the 3/10 scale replica test specimens were carried aloft by a Mosquito bomber prior to launch over the adjacent Atlantic test range. The unmanned flight models (based on the M.52 design) were dogged by technical problems, and a huge amount of money – which could have been spent more wisely on completing the full-scale aircraft – was wasted on continual redesign and modification of the rocket motors that were used to propel the models after air launch. In October 1948, on the second test flight, the model's rocket engine did successfully fire and the aircraft raced towards Mach 1.38, thus confirming the validity of the M.52 project design and the absurdity of abandoning the programme at such a late stage. Perhaps the ultimate irony was the failure of the test specimen to crash land into the sea after the test flight. Radio links with the model were lost and radar continued to provide plots of the tiny aircraft heading out across the Atlantic, tracing the same path which all of the M.52's research data had allegedly taken many months previously.

The story of Britain's most famous jet fighter began in the late 1940s, following the abrupt termination of British attempts to break the sound barrier with the Miles M.52 research aircraft. After the M.52 programme was mysteriously abandoned, supersonic research continued on a low-key basis (mostly by Vickers-Armstrong Ltd in association with the RAE), but exploration of supersonic flight was beginning to capture the interest of other aircraft companies too.

W. E. W. 'Teddy' Petter was Chief Engineer at the English Electric Company in Preston, Lancashire. Responsible for the design of wartime aircraft such as the (Westland) Lysander and Whirlwind, Petter had followed the development of supersonic research with interest and by 1947 had already started work on his own private design studies, and had also embarked upon the design and development of what was to become the Canberra jet bomber. English Electric was still busy manufacturing the almost obsolescent Vampire fighter for export customers on behalf of de Havilland. Petter could not help but notice the distinct and almost comical mismatch in the performance of the new high-altitude, high-speed Canberra bomber and the seemingly obsolescent Vampire fighter, both of which were emerging almost simultaneously from the same factory. However, his recognition of this absurd situation was not shared by the Government and despite constant studying of data and even some high-speed experimental flights from the company's airfield at Warton, near Preston (using a Gloster Meteor), it took some considerable time for the Air Ministry to accept that with a predicted performance of Mach 0.85 at 50,000 feet, the RAF's new jet bomber would clearly outperform both the Meteor and Vampire fighter and it therefore followed that the RAF would be unable to defend UK airspace against any new Soviet bomber which enjoyed a performance similar to the Canberra.

Petter finally succeeded in obtaining a study contract for a research aircraft capable of Mach 1.5 at 30,000 feet under Specification ER.103. In effect, this Specification was little more than a repetition of the now-defunct ER.24/43 which would have led to production of the subsequently-abandoned M.52, but with the knowledge that new high-speed jet fighters and bombers were now becoming a reality in both the US and Soviet Union, there was a greater determination that the specification would deliver results this time. Both English Electric and Fairey Aviation responded to Specification ER.103.

Fairey's programme eventually resulted in the record-breaking FD.2, an aircraft that ably met the requirements of the Specification and ultimately had a direct influence on the design of Concorde (and the French Mirage family). However, the FD.2 was designed from the outset as a pure research vehicle. The English Electric proposal was rather different. Petter tasked his deputy F. W. 'Freddie' (later Sir Freddie) Page with the detailed design of the proposal and the resulting English Electric concept was undoubtedly more ambitious than the Fairey design, and thanks to Petter's eye for practicality, it had the potential to be developed into something much more than a simple research aircraft. The Air Ministry was impressed by English Electric's proposals and a Draft Specification (F.23/49) was issued on 2 September 1949, based on an Air Staff Operational Requirement (OR.268) that had been drawn up some months previously.

Entitled 'Fighter with supersonic performance', the Operational Requirement called for a 'single seat fighter land plane, for day interception duties. Primarily, it is required for operating in Europe, but it is desirable that it is capable of operating in any part of the world.' It also specified that the primary role of the new aircraft would be:

> ... the destruction of high speed, high altitude bombers in daylight, as soon as possible after the bomber is first detected on the early warning system. Great importance therefore is attached to quick take-off, the highest possible acceleration and highest possible rate of climb.

In fact, it stated that a maximum speed of Mach 1.2 would be acceptable, but that an even higher speed would be desirable if it proved to be technically possible. Although the OR seemed ambitious, it clearly reflected the growing confidence in supersonic research and the design plans that had been outlined by English Electric, and it effectively established the basic functions of what eventually became the Lightning. Having established that the most serious potential threat to the integrity of UK airspace would come from new high-speed and high-altitude bombers, the Air Ministry was clear that the new aircraft would not be a 'fighter' aircraft in the conventional sense of the term. Although it would still be designed to destroy enemy aircraft, it would not (at least in its primary role) be designed to conduct direct air-to-air combat with other fighters. Instead, it would be an interceptor, capable of a rapid engine start and a zoom climb to an altitude of 50,000 feet, all within 6 minutes. It is interesting to note that despite the seemingly ambitious nature of the OR, and the clear requirement for a 'pure interceptor' rather than a fighter, it did not make any significant mention of missile armament at this stage, simply stating that the aircraft should carry a minimum of two, with more if possible, of the new high-performance 30 mm ADEN guns. Indeed, the only reference to missiles was a vague note that 'the possibility of having rocket or long range armament should be considered'.

On 3 August 1948, the Ministry of Supply gave a contract to English Electric for a formal design study entitled 'Transonic Research and Fighter Aircraft' which enabled the company to begin the serious business of creating a design which would meet (or exceed) the terms of the Operational Requirement, based on its submission for the earlier ER.103 Specification, but with the emphasis now firmly placed upon operational capability as well as overall performance. Having already made significant progress with development of the basic design, it took only three months for English Electric to complete and submit its formal proposal which received the company designation P.1, a term which some commentators assumed was a reference to the surname of the project's instigator but in reality the prefix had no specific meaning as such and, if anything, merely signified 'Project'.

The English Electric design team considered a variety of aerodynamic solutions to the demands imposed by the OR, but the final layout of the proposed aircraft was surprisingly conventional, due in no small part to the company's belief that all designs should be kept as simple as possible in order to avoid unforeseen developmental problems, costs and delays. This philosophy was already proving to be successful with the Canberra bomber, and it made perfect sense to apply the same rules to the new supersonic fighter. The basic airframe layout was deliberately uncomplicated, consisting of a very simple tubular fuselage combined with swept-back wings – a choice that was based on continuing research in the UK and US, mostly derived from captured German data. There would have been good reason to have adopted a pure delta wing plan form (which Fairey developed for its FD.2), but Page believed that a better solution would be found in effectively removing the inboard trailing portion of the delta shape and that this would offer the most simple and effective means of achieving supersonic flight and acceptable handling over a wide range of altitudes and speeds.

The choice of powerplant was largely dictated by the relatively few options available at that time. Although centrifugal-compressor designs were still under development (both the Meteor and Vampire still taking advantage of gradual improvements to their very basic centrifugal engine designs), it was quickly accepted that the P.1 would be powered by axial-flow turbojets, not only because they appeared to offer the greatest scope for further development (and corresponding increases in thrust) but because they enabled the frontal area of the P.1's aerodynamic shape to be kept relatively small – a vital consideration for an aircraft expected easily to achieve speeds in excess of Mach 1. It was accepted that although a single engine was certainly sufficient to attain supersonic flight (as demonstrated by Fairey's FD.2) the demands of an operational (and therefore heavier) interceptor would require a greater reserve of power and so a pair of engines provided the solution, albeit at the expense of additional weight and (potentially) greater drag. Although twin-engine jet designs were by no means uncommon by this time, the need to achieve supersonic speed demanded a perfectly contoured aircraft that presented a minimal amount of frontal aerodynamic drag, and incorporating two bulky turbojet engines into the simple design was by no means easy. The chosen configuration was another testament to English Electric's ability to combine innovation with practicality. The Armstrong Siddeley Sapphires engines would be incorporated within the aircraft's fuselage, but instead of being fixed in a fairly conventional (and drag-inducing) side-by-side layout, they would be stacked vertically with their combined air supply provided via a central (bifurcated) intake trunk and with one engine staggered rearwards to give space in the nose section for the pilot and other equipment. This would provide the aircraft with double the amount of thrust available to a single-engine aircraft, whilst creating significantly less drag than a side-by-side (or wing-mounted) engine placement. Ingenious though this configuration was, it eventually proved to be a source of constant frustration for the thousands of airmen who would later be charged with the onerous task of servicing and maintaining the aircraft in RAF service.

The proposed configuration of the wing and fuselage structure was quite conventional, but the tail unit was rather more imaginative. Most contemporary high-speed designs favoured the use of swept tailplane surfaces mounted on top of a swept fin. Although this was not an ideal aerodynamic solution, it was generally accepted to be the most practical design compromise possible. English Electric took the view that its new interceptor would need reliable and effective tail control surfaces, particularly at transonic speeds where elevator control inevitably became less effective. Ideally, an all-moving tailplane would be adopted, but this would require a fairly thick (and drag-inducing) fin from which the unit could be fixed and pivoted. Additionally, there was also a distinct possibility that if the pilot jettisoned the cockpit canopy in an emergency, it would strike the tail surfaces leading to a catastrophic loss of control, and should he be forced to abandon the aircraft, he would probably collide with the tailplane after ejecting. The solution to this potential problem was to simply reverse the accepted configuration and mount the fin on the tailplane, so the early English Electric design emerged from the drawing board with a strikingly unusual layout comprising twin fins fixed to tailplane surfaces mounted high on the rear fuselage sides.

This bizarre proposal raised more than a few proverbial eyebrows, particularly within the RAE from where a team of highly specialised aerodynamicists and engineers advised the Air Ministry on aspects of aircraft design. In fact, the RAE had a number of reservations over the proposed configuration of English Electric's design, including the more fundamental question of what the aircraft's wing sweep angle should be. The bewildering (and often conflicting) research data available within the UK and US had encouraged Petter and his team to adopt a wing sweep in the region of 58-60 degrees, but more conservative thinking within the RAE suggested that 45 degrees might offer a more successful (or at least predictable) aerodynamic performance, and this, combined with the question of the aircraft's tail configuration, became the subject of a lengthy dispute between English Electric and the RAE.

On 29 March 1949, the Ministry of Supply instructed English Electric to construct a wind tunnel model, a larger test specimen for Rolls-Royce, another smaller wind tunnel model for high-speed research, and also to begin provisional design work for the prototype aircraft and full-sized mock-up. It was at this stage that the RAE intervened with reservations concerning wing sweep, but Petter remained convinced that his team were making the right decisions, commenting in a letter to the Ministry of Supply, 'we are studying very carefully the question of sweepback, and the pros and cons of 60 degrees compared to 45/50 degrees. I think that there may be good reasons for sticking to the present proposal, subject of course to the wind tunnel tests.' Petter's confidence in his team's design persisted and in October 1949 he wrote to the Principal Director of Scientific Research (Air) at the Ministry of Supply stating, 'It is felt that the stage has now been reached at which it would be possible, usefully, to proceed to an Advisory Design Conference and thereafter to the design and construction of prototype aircraft.'

Despite Petter's encouraging words, his relationship with English Electric's management structure had become increasingly strained and he resigned just four months later, his position as Chief Engineer being taken by his deputy, the former Chief Stress Analyst Freddie Page. Although Petter had, of course, been a vital driving force behind the creation of the P.1 design, his departure did not have any major effect on the project's progress, as Page had effectively been handling the design ever since its inception. By this stage, the fundamentals of the aircraft's design were already in place and the various members of the English Electric team were busy handling their own individual aspects of the overall programme. Indeed, in April 1950, a contract was finally placed with English Electric for the design and manufacture of two prototype aircraft (and a static mock-up) to meet Specification F.23/49 in order to 'investigate the practicality of supersonic speed for military aircraft'.

It is interesting to note that even at this stage, official emphasis was still being placed on the experimental nature of the project. The Ministry of Supply (with its usual tendency to dwell upon seemingly insignificant matters) had previously decided to refer to the aircraft officially as an 'Experimental Fighter' in order to take the emphasis away from the operational nature of the aircraft, even though the Ministry 'hoped to evolve something more than a pure research vehicle'. Indeed, it seems clear that despite the non-committal attitude of the Ministry of

Supply, the English Electric team were already determined to produce a practical and capable warplane.

There was undoubtedly a prevailing attitude at the RAE that its scientists somehow 'knew better' than English Electric. This was illustrated by a letter sent to the Ministry of Supply from the RAE early in 1951, in which an RAE official stated that it would be wrong to regard the English Electric design as 'too much of an operational fighter type', adding that the RAE would 'have to watch it closely from here, help in its progress and bring to bear on it all the best scientific manpower that we can muster'. As wind tunnel tests got under way, the RAE continued to express its concerns over the aircraft's proposed wing sweep and tail configuration, and despite English Electric's confidence that a 60 degree wing sweep would be most suitable, the RAE firmly believed that a 50 degree sweep would be advisable. It also still believed that a more conventional high-mounted tailplane should be adopted, and even though the emergence of wind tunnel data (from both the RAE and EE) tended to confirm the validity of English Electric's approach, the Ministry of Supply eventually decided (in response to the RAE's persistent concerns) to produce a purpose-built research aircraft which could investigate these matters in flight test conditions, and reach a definitive conclusion.

This project was awarded to Short Bros & Harland in Belfast, which constructed the SB.5, an aircraft created purely for research and not officially linked to the English Electric project, although it was in effect a simplified low-speed scale model of the P.1 design with the facility for factory-adjustable wing sweep and

WG768 in flight, with an array of wool tufts attached to the outer portion of the port wing for airflow recording purposes. The aircraft now resides in the RAF Museum collection at Cosford.

tailplane settings so that a variety of configurations could be flight tested. The sole SB.5 (WG768) made its first flight on 2 December 1952, complete with the RAE-inspired 50 degree wing sweep and fin-mounted tailplane. Low-speed handling trials progressed, with the wing sweep eventually being changed to 60 degrees and eventually 69 degrees, while the tailplane was eventually reattached lower on the fuselage.

Meanwhile, as the SB.5 programme plodded along, English Electric had continued development of its design with its favoured 60 degree wing sweep and low-mounted tailplane (albeit with a more conventional centrally positioned fin and rudder) behind wings which were now placed slightly higher against the fuselage sides. Ultimately, after testing all of the wing and tailplane configurations under a wide range of conditions, the SB.5 programme simply served to confirm that the English Electric team had been right all along. This was probably just as well, because by the time that the SB.5 programme had yielded conclusive results, the 'Experimental Fighter' had already progressed way beyond the stage where the wing sweep or tailplane configuration could have been economically altered.

Even though the SB.5 project did produce some useful test data, it can only be regarded as being little more than an unnecessary waste of resources, and the only significant effect it had upon the design of the P.1 was the addition of a small notch cut into the leading edge of each of the P.1's wings. This modification was first incorporated into the SB.5's wings in order to cure a tendency towards uneven control responses and wing drop at very low speeds – a minor problem which had been experienced in the SB.5 on test flights in the 60 degree/low tailplane configuration. The cause was determined to be irregular break-up of airflow over the wings, the incorporation of small notch devices (derived from American research) being sufficient to cure the problem whilst also providing the design team with suitable locations to incorporate the inward vents for the aircraft's wing fuel tanks. Eventually, it was determined that the wing drop had actually been caused by the SB.5's manually controlled ailerons and the notches were filled in, but they reappeared on the P.1 as a cure for further aerodynamic vortex and boundary layer problems that manifested themselves at transonic speeds.

The P.1's wing-mounted ailerons were designed without any major difficulties. Although straight and swept-wing designs had hitherto relied on aileron surfaces being placed on the trailing edges of the wings, experience with a variety of first-generation swept-wing aircraft had revealed that there was a risk of control difficulties arising at high angles of attack, when the wing surface effectively masked airflow from passing over the aileron surface. Consequently, English Electric opted to place the ailerons on the trailing wing tips with the main plane trailing edges (swept at 52 degrees) used for the placement of conventional flaps. Some attention had also been given to the concept of fitting leading edge flaps to the inboard section of the wings in order to improve low-speed handling in take-off and landing configuration, but even though the idea progressed as far as the first prototype, the leading edge flaps were quickly abandoned after it had been established that they were largely ineffective and therefore unnecessary.

The Short SB.5 WG768, illustrating the aircraft's small circular engine air intake and the wings in their final angle of 69 degrees – the largest wing sweep angle flown on any aircraft at that time.

Further attention was devoted to the flight control systems. Early experience of transonic flight had revealed that there was a tendency for the aircraft's controls to lock as speed increased – a potentially lethal situation that had generally been overcome by either slowing the aircraft or abandoning it. It had been established that mechanical assistance was an effective way of overcoming the problem, and new designs were already incorporating various means of boosting aerodynamic control surfaces, and even in Britain, some progress had been made in this area of research. English Electric accepted that a truly supersonic aircraft such as the P.1 would require some very serious engineering in order to overcome the control lock problem, and the flight control surfaces were each fitted with irreversible hydraulic screw jacks, which ensured that control would remain positive at all speeds. Unfortunately, this form of mechanical assistance effectively removed the pilot's direct feel, so a means of artificially replacing feel was devised, consisting of a series of springs, cogs and cams which replicated the usual feel whilst also ensuring that the pilot could not over-stress the airframe by demanding control movements that were beyond the airframe's design limits. This system, fed by a pitot-static intake, enabled mechanical governors and electrical sensors to determine the maximum amount of control movement that was available at any given air speed.

The P1's nose section was also the subject of great debate. From the outset, English Electric had anticipated the use of a single air intake that would pass under the cockpit before splitting into two separate sections, one feeding the lower engine while the other routed upwards behind the cockpit to feed the second powerplant. This was certainly a good way of achieving a small aerodynamic frontal area, but there was little space in which any other equipment could be housed. Plans were drawn up to locate a single 30 mm ADEN cannon in each wing root, but this was not an ideal arrangement, not least because it was thought that a total of four guns (rather than two) would be preferable, and the wing root did not provide any space for housing the associated ammunition or fire-control radar.

Attention turned towards the concept of a more conventional nose layout, comprising a solid nose and cheek-mounted intakes, based on a new design feature being explored by the National Advisory Committee for Aeronautics (NACA) in the US. Their experimental work on flush-mounted air intakes looked promising, but the English Electric team were less than convinced in the validity of the concept, as illustrated by a 1951 letter to the Ministry of Supply in which English Electric forwarded details of the NACA design but asked that until the configuration had been tested in its wind tunnel, the Air Ministry should not be informed about it, on the basis that 'the Service would jump at these suggestions, but of course such things as the air intake efficiency remain to be proved and it would be most unwise to over-sell the project at this stage'.

Official interest in the P.1 was still distinctly lukewarm at this stage and although the design clearly showed great potential, it was still regarded as being an experiment, even though it was accepted that prolonged indecisiveness would inevitably lead to delays in completing design and construction of the aircraft. Although the aircraft would certainly be required to undertake the interceptor role as outlined in the original specification, it was clear that it had plenty of potential to do much more, but that this would require the addition of more equipment and further design changes.

In February 1952, the Vice Chief of the Air Staff (VCAS) produced a paper that went some way towards establishing the role of the new aircraft. Surprisingly, the P.1 was repeatedly compared to the hopelessly outdated de Havilland Venom, and VCAS concluded that despite the P.1's supersonic interception capability, it would lack the Venom's versatility but that it would certainly be needed – and needed soon – if Soviet supersonic bombers were (albeit only figuratively) on the horizon. This remarkably short-sighted view of the P.1's potential is perhaps understandable, given that it might have been difficult to appreciate the quantum leap in capability that the aircraft would provide, but it may also show the first signs of the slightly blinkered official attitude that dogged the aircraft throughout its service life.

However, despite the slow deliberations surrounding the P.1's projected operational role, there was much greater official decisiveness in ensuring that the aircraft's production did not slip too significantly. During 1951, the Ministry of Supply had suggested that at least three pre-production development aircraft should be ordered so that any design changes could be made quickly if early flight testing of the P.1 prototype revealed any major flaws. Indeed, it was also suggested that the proposed redesign of the nose section (with side-mounted intakes) should be test flown on a development aircraft so that the concept could be explored as fully (and quickly) as possible. The paper prepared by VCAS in 1952 also recommended that three additional development aircraft should be ordered, and that they would be designed to incorporate the much-discussed side-mounted intakes, but only after full consideration of the latest brochure being prepared by English Electric at the time. When the brochure was finally issued in July 1952, the cheek intake design had finally been dropped entirely, as the brochure explained:

> The present type of nose intake without centre body was chosen when the design was first undertaken because it was the only type of intake known to operate satisfactorily over the whole speed range. More information is now available on other types of intake. Even so, the simple nose entry is still the one about which most is known and is therefore still the most practicable. The primary objective in modifying the nose fuselage was to make space available for armament and equipment without sacrificing performance unduly. Of course, this space had to be suitable for the equipment to be installed; that is, space for a radar scanner had to be in the nose with an unobstructed view of the forward hemisphere. To achieve this, three different types of intake were considered – chin, side and centre body. The detail design of the intake affects both thrust and drag; the optimum intake is the one which gives the maximum value of thrust minus drag. At first sight, the chin, or side intake placed well aft on the nose fuselage appears to offer the greatest stowage space. However, detailed investigation

shows that to maintain intake efficiency at supersonic speeds, no submerging of the intakes can be tolerated. In fact, either the intakes have to be raised well clear of the surface ahead, or else substantial boundary layer bleeds have to be provided. Thus, an increase in cross-section of the aft fuselage cannot be permitted; the cross-section of the fuselage ahead of the intakes must still be equal to the maximum area less the area of intake, bleeds, etc. This removes most of the apparent advantage of the side or chin intakes as regards stowage space. A considerable amount of data has been accumulated from the USA, and careful analysis of this shows that for the speed range in question, only the centre body intake can compete with the simple nose entry on a thrust minus drag basis without the need for excessive and elaborate transonic wind tunnel testing and special provisions such as boundary layer bleeds. Transonic tunnel facilities in this country are unfortunately very limited. Detailed investigation of the centre body air intake shows that the centre body provides a very suitable space for radar equipment of increased size and that, owing to the associated changed in the forebody lines, more space actually becomes available. The forebody shape is also improved, giving reduced drag, which offsets the effect of the raised canopy. A wind tunnel model of this intake has been constructed and the EE transonic wind tunnel provided with a large pumping plant so that measurements of intake efficiency and drag may be made across the speed of sound. Preliminary results are very encouraging, and we believe that these are the only tests of this type so far attempted in Europe.

It was agreed that the three additional prototype aircraft would incorporate a circular intake featuring a fixed bullet-shaped centre body that would provide space for the necessary radar equipment. This would free up space for ADEN cannon in the lower fuselage and would also enable the nose landing gear leg to be simplified. In the first two prototypes, the nose gear leg had to be designed to pivot and lie flat under the lip of the ovoid intake, but with a centre body shock cone, its central supporting structure would provide just enough space for the nose gear leg to retract into it.

Significantly, it was also decided that all three of the new prototypes would be able to carry de Havilland's new Blue Jay AAM, linked to a Ferranti Airpass (Airborne Interception Radar and Pilot Attack Sight System) in the new nose section, and in order to differentiate between these aircraft (which represented a step between the first prototypes and the eventual production-standard aircraft), the three aircraft were designated as P.1Bs, and the earlier aircraft redesignated as P.1As. As Freddie Page later stated, unlike the P.1A, 'the P.1B was envisaged from the start as an integrated weapon system' and this required what was in effect a new airframe, complete with different (more powerful) engines, a new navigation system and instrument display, plus an autopilot and stabiliser system that was linked to the throttles and ILS.

In many respects, the P.1B was effectively a completely new aircraft based on the design of the P.1A, rather than being merely a development of it. Most significantly, the P.1B incorporated the newly developed Ferranti Airpass fit and the ability to carry two AAMs (both slaved to the radar system), and this would form the basis of the operational aircraft's weapons system. Although outdated by modern standards, Airpass was remarkably sophisticated when first developed over fifty years ago, and even featured a rudimentary HUD (Head Up Display) that transferred the radar image onto a reflector screen, enabling the pilot to vector the aircraft onto target without the need to constantly bury his head inside the cockpit. Miniature high-intensity CRTs (Cathode Ray Tubes) were not available during the early 1950s, so the system relied upon miniature high-intensity incandescent light bulbs, which reduced the effectiveness of the display but would have been sufficient to enable pilots to use the radar, weapons system and aircraft in much greater harmony. Unfortunately, the Air Ministry lost interest in the revolutionary HUD facility and turned its attention to an American development using CRTs, eventually abandoning the HUD concept in favour of a more conventional radar screen mounted atop the aircraft's main instrument panel. It was just one of many potentially exciting advances that could have been embraced but were simply abandoned.

Although the P.1As had been equipped with Armstrong Siddeley Sapphire Sa.5 engines, these powerplants were soon regarded as stopgap equipment, pending the development of Rolls-Royce engines that offered the promise of significant increases in available thrust. The Sapphire's 8,100 lb of thrust was sufficient to enable the P.1A programme to proceed without delay, but even with the combined thrust of two engines the P.1A was unlikely to achieve sustained supersonic flight, not least because the severely limited fuel load of the first P.1A meant that the aircraft would be more likely to run out of fuel before acceleration to Mach 1 or more was achieved. The second P.1A had the advantage of a rudimentary reheat system that provided some additional thrust, but it became clear that the Sapphire was unlikely to be developed to a stage where any major improvements in thrust would be available.

Freddie Page turned his attention to Rolls-Royce and entered into discussions based on the possibility of creating a completely new engine for the P.1 that would be ideally suited to supersonic flight. Unfortunately, Rolls-Royce was less than enthusiastic at the prospect of embarking on a completely new engine and after further discussions with Bristol (based largely on the concept of using just one Olympus engine) it was accepted that the best compromise would be to opt for a development of the Rolls-Royce Avon engine, fitted with reheat.

Early EE/RR proposals explored the possibility of a fixed nozzle reheat system that would enable a relatively small, light and uncomplicated jet fighter to be designed and manufactured. However, RAE research suggested that this system would reduce the P.1's cruising height by as much as 10,000 feet or create an endurance reduction of some 15 per cent if reheat was used to restore the cruising height. This was too high a price to pay, so as an alternative, EE proposed a very odd concept consisting of a jettisonable baffle that governed the size of the reheat nozzle, maintaining a small diameter (for dry thrust) until detached, at which stage full reheat could be selected. Although the idea had some merit (enabling full reheat to be employed without any loss in height or endurance), the prospect of continually replacing part of the reheat unit after every sortie was not quite so appealing, and both Freddie Page and Rolls-Royce continued to discuss the possibility of creating a completely new convergent-divergent reheat nozzle specifically for the P.1B programme. Eventually, English Electric opted for the RA.24R Avon engine, but only after completion of a Ministry of Supply/EE-funded design study in order to establish that the engine could be successfully mated with the airframe. The study revealed that the engine would be suitable but only after extensive redesign of the centre and rear fuselage. Even with this redesign, any observer could have been forgiven for thinking that the P.1A fuselage had literally been built around the engines, such was the snugness of the installation, and the extremely tight fit was to become a permanent engineering nightmare throughout the aircraft's service life, with many areas of cabling and ducting being accessible only through the complete removal of one (or even both) engines.

The main company airfield at Warton was the obvious choice for the P.1A flight trials, but with an anticipated landing speed in excess of 160 knots, it was accepted that Warton's 1,900 yard runway would be too short to accommodate the aircraft safely. Work began on a runway extension to 2,500 yards, but in order to expedite progress the first P.1A (WG760) was dismantled after ground tests were completed at Warton and the aircraft headed south by road to the A&AEE at Boscombe Down in June 1954. The first flight was completed on 4 August, as reported by English Electric's Chief Test Pilot Roland Beamont:

P.1A WG760, streaking past the assembled crowds at the 1954 SBAC show at Farnborough.

F.23/49 WG760 Flight No. 1

Weather conditions: Dry runway. Light variable wind at 90 degrees to the runway, backing; 6/8 high cloud; small amount scattered low cloud; visibility 4-5 miles in slight haze. Runway 24.

A full cockpit check was carried out which revealed no defective items except for the leg straps on the Mk 3 ejection seat. The individual leg harnesses had been checked previously but the lacing had not been completed during the previous checks. On coupling the lacing in accordance with the maker's instructions it was found that the lacings were required to inter-connect between the left and right leg. With feet on the rudder pedals this resulted immediately in a severe restriction of backward control movement. After re-checking this case it was decided that flight could be accepted without the leg harnesses owing to the existing speed limitation and the circumstances of the flight. Radio checks with the tower and flight test van were satisfactory. Stopwatch failure soon after initial tripping prevented a time record being taken of the flight. Instrumentation was switched on after start up. Take-off was made with flaps down and without attempting to lift off at the lowest possible speed. After lifting the nosewheel at approximately 120 knots the aircraft became airborne easily with slightly under full elevator at approximately 145 knots. The attitude was checked immediately on becoming airborne with a small amount of forward stick, and as the aircraft gained speed it became progressively nose-up in out-of-trim.

The undercarriage was selected up at approximately 160 knots and power was reduced to maintain approximately 200 knots in a shallow climb. The undercarriage retracted rapidly with slight asymmetry which caused a small lateral displacement. This was over-corrected with aileron control which under these conditions was very sensitive, but the resultant oscillation was damped immediately by centring and momentarily relaxing stick hold. The undercarriage locked home before 200 knots and as speed was gradually increased above this point buffet was noticeable from the flaps. As Indicated Air Speed exceeded 250 knots the flap blow-back valve operated and the flaps returned to neutral with the selector down. This resulted in further nose-up out-of-trim and full nose-down trim on the indicator was not sufficient to return to in-trim flight. Speed was reduced to 200 knots, the flap selector moved to 'up' and then at 190 knots selected to 'down'. Flap operation was normal and it was noted that there was little buffet from flaps below 200 knots. Flaps were retracted at 210 knots. At this speed nose flap only was selected and apart from a very slight nose-down trim change no other effects were noted (lessening of the existing nose-up condition).

With flaps retracted power was increased and altitude increased to 8,000-9,000 feet. IAS was increased progressively up to 400 knots and at this point there was no buffeting or roughness. The ailerons, which were noticeably sensitive, became progressively more so with increase in IAS with the result that lateral damping seemed to be rather lower than desirable. Releasing the stick in all cases damped out the lateral oscillation immediately however, and it was thought that much of this oversensitivity in lateral control resulted from the fact that the pilot had at all times to hold a small but noticeable nose-up out-of-trim force. Height was increased to 13,000-14,000 feet and speed increased to 400 knots IAS/Mach 0.75. Under these conditions the lateral control remained very sensitive but adequate. During a course alteration to avoid a cloud layer the nose was depressed slightly and speed inadvertently increased at idling power to approximately 440-450 knots. This was reduced as soon as level flight could be resumed. Dive brakes were checked at 300-400 knots at 13,000 feet over approximately 2-4 degrees of movement. In each case after the initial slight nose-up trim change, very heavy buffet began. This was associated with an erratic directional characteristic which immediately resulted in an erratic rolling displacement due to yaw. These circumstances were not regarded as satisfactory and the tests were discontinued subject to further progressive investigation at low speeds. During the climb it had not been easy to control the air conditioning with the cold air unit, as with this there was a tendency either to be too hot or too cold. The cabin air ram valve was opened and found to produce a pleasantly distributed flow of cooling air. This was kept open at all times during the flight except for a short period at 14,000 feet where it was closed to test pressurisation, which was found to be satisfactory at this height. During the descent the inner surface of the centre armoured glass panel became misted with the NESA switched at 'half.' Switching the NESA system to 'full' cleared this condition in a few minutes. During descent with power reduced to idling considerable difficulty was experienced in obtaining a reasonable rate of descent while keeping IAS below 400 knots. This may tend to be a minor limiting factor in the flight test operation if the present dive brakes prove to be unsatisfactory. With the fuel state at 1,000/1,000 lb it was decided to return to base and during this some difficulty was experienced at a critical point in obtaining homing facilities from Boscombe. Once the circuit had been regained, circuit manoeuvrability at 350-250 knots proved excellent with vision forward and sideways rather better than on the Hunter. Turns at and up to 2.5 g were comfortably executed with nose flap up and with nose flap down turns up to 2 g at 250-300 knots again were positively stable. In a proving flight of this description a detailed appraisal of feel is not possible, but the increase in Q-feel forces on the tailplane control with increase in airspeed seemed to be precisely suitable. The undercarriage was selected down at 230 knots and locked rapidly with green indicator lights at 210 knots. There was asymmetry in this operation which resulted in the expected lateral displacement and correspondingly momentary over-correction with aileron. This case is similar to that experienced on the Hunter. Flaps were lowered at 200 knots and in doing so returned the aircraft to in-trim longitudinally, still with full nose-down trim. A final turn was carried out at 200-190 knots and speed reduced to 160 knots at short finals and the throttles returned to idling. A normal hold-off was made crossing the boundary and a final check comfortably and easily executed at 150 knots. The touchdown was smooth at a reasonable attitude with excellent vision of the runway, at approximately 140 knots. The parachute was streamed at approximately 135 knots and this operated with a delay of the order of two seconds. There was an immediate nose-up pitch and weathercock yaw to starboard requiring approximately full port rudder to hold. This condition was easily controlled and once the nosewheel had returned to the runway light wheel brake was applied to bring the aircraft to a standstill. The parachute jettisoning operation was satisfactory. At standstill the port wheel thermocouples indicated 160 degrees C. During the flight a pitot position-error check was carried out with the pacing Canberra WH775 and this gave 195/195 knots at 8,000 feet.

Summary

From this short flight the following main points were clear:

1/ The main services functioned satisfactorily with the exception of the dive brake which gave heavy buffet, even at the small angles employed.

2/ The trim actuators were satisfactory on rudder and aileron, but that on the tailplane control provided inadequate nose-down trim.

3/ Longitudinal and directional static stability was positive in all flight conditions experienced so far. The aircraft was neutrally stable laterally with adequate damping, stick free.

4/ Tailplane feel and response was entirely satisfactory under all conditions and there was no sign of over-sensitivity leading to pilot-induced oscillation. Aileron response and spring feel was very sensitive and powerful, and required a light touch to prevent fairly continuous over- correction. It was not easy to apply this light touch owing to the necessity of holding nose-up out-of-trim force throughout the whole flight with engines above half power. This condition may be less noticeable when the longitudinal trim range has been adjusted accordingly.

5/ The power control circuits were remarkably free from noticeable friction or backlash.

WG760 at Boscombe Down. This view emphasises the simple design of the P.1A's fuselage, with the two engine exhausts emerging at the extremity of the long fuselage 'tube'.

6/ The engines were used as required and no detailed attention was paid to engine conditions beyond observing the limitations. They responded normally and entirely satisfactorily to all requirements.

In this short flight the aircraft proved to be pleasant and straightforward to fly, with the take-off and landing operations lacking in complication. The oversensitivity in lateral control will require careful observation during subsequent tests.

WG760 was towed back into the flight test hangar for an overnight inspection and was declared ready to fly again the next day. This time, Beaumont took the aircraft up to an altitude of 30,000 feet where he recorded a speed of Mach 0.98. The English Electric flight test crew were encouraged to learn that at this speed and altitude, the aircraft had performed well with no handling or stability problems being evident. Following the second flight the aircraft's instrumentation was fully corrected and it was discovered that the true speed of the aircraft had actually been Mach 1 – the speed of sound. Although Beamont did not know it at the time, just a few more seconds of full power would have comfortably pushed WG760 cleanly through the sonic shock wave and his instruments would have jumped over to the magic figure. Some non-critical problems required rectification by this stage, but the flight test team were keen to forge ahead and so the next (third) flight was scheduled for 11 August. Basking in warm summer sunshine, Beamont immediately took the aircraft to 40,000 feet and headed east over Swanage before commencing a full-power, high-speed run along the path of the Solent towards Selsey Bill. As experienced on the previous flight, the aircraft instruments recorded a speed of Mach 0.98 and appeared to stick at this figure. With the aircraft handling well in all axes, Beamont noted that just 4 minutes had passed since departing from Boscombe Down and now the P.1A was at 40,000 feet on the edge of supersonic flight. Still accelerating, and without any noticeable changes in handling or even any vibration, the Mach needle suddenly jumped and settled at a new figure – Mach 1.01. Almost effortlessly, WG760 was supersonic. Acceleration continued and briefly reached Mach 1.08, but with the P.1A's fuel load beginning to dwindle, Beamont brought the aircraft round through a 30 degree bank over West Sussex, as the speed dropped back through Mach 1, producing a slight tremor and nose-up trim change as the aerodynamic shock wave retreated ahead of the aircraft again. Once within view of Boscombe Down, Beamont entered into a shallow dive at 36,000 feet, allowing the aircraft briefly to accelerate back to Mach 1.01 in order to produce a loud – and very gratifying – sonic boom over the airfield for the benefit of the assembled test flight team.

The second P.1A (WG763) made its first flight at Warton on 18 July 1955. Although externally similar to the first aircraft, the second P1.A incorporated some noticeable changes. Externally, the most obvious difference was the addition of an external fuel tank designed to conform to the aircraft's lower fuselage, giving the impression that it was part of the fuselage structure whereas it was in fact detachable (as were all external tanks subsequently fitted to Lightnings). The almost desperate need for additional fuel had been recognised at an early stage in the development process and with an external tank containing 250 gallons of fuel, WG763 was a much more flexible aircraft in terms of attainable range and endurance. The aircraft was also fitted with conventional hinged wing flaps (unlike the split flaps fitted to the previous aircraft) and these were also to become a standard fit on later production aircraft, eventually accommodating additional fuel cells. In the nose section, two ADEN 30 mm cannon were fitted ahead of the cockpit and at the other end of the fuselage, the Sapphire engines were standard un-reheated examples, contrasting with the afterburner modifications being made concurrently to WG760. The wing's leading edge nose flaps were deleted and internally the rudder pedals were modified to incorporate toe brakes, in preference to the control column-mounted brakes in WG760.

With the first P.1A assigned to aerodynamic testing, the second P.1A was allocated mostly to development of operational equipment such as the 30 mm cannon. WG760 was fitted with reheat in the form of a fixed nozzle system which proved to be another technical headache for both the engine and aircraft manufacturer, requiring significant (and time-consuming) testing before being declared flight-worthy. While the system was being developed, the P.1A was assigned to other aspects of the aerodynamics programme, including minimum speed landings and the performance with the elimination of the wing-mounted nose flaps. When the reheat system was finally fitted and flown on WG760, Beamont reported that the aircraft performed well, although the additional thrust and modifications to the engines provided new problems that had to be handled during the test flights.

With the new reheat system, WG760 had insufficient thrust for a safe take-off on dry power alone; therefore every take-off relied upon successful engagement of reheat, and dry thrust was only marginally sufficient for low-speed handling in the airfield circuit. Likewise, the additional thrust came at the expense of fuel consumption – particularly frustrating when the second P.1A had the advantage of an external fuel tank. However, the disadvantages of the fixed nozzle system were understood and simply overlooked in order to concentrate on the exploration of the aircraft's handling characteristics in advance of the P.1B aircraft, which would have more representative reheated engines. Speeds of up to Mach 1.4 in level flight were easily achieved, and sustained flight at such speeds was maintained for up to 5 minutes at a time with no adverse handling characteristics being encountered. Such was the aircraft's phenomenal performance, Beamont reported that its altimeter rotated so rapidly after take-off that it was easy to develop a phase-lag of around 10,000 feet in reading it, and that the vertical speed indicator was simply 'off the scale' for most of the time. Clearly, the P.1's instruments needed to be improved to match the performance of the aircraft they were fitted to.

Additional test pilots had now started to join the programme, and one of them – Desmond de Villiers – had the misfortune to encounter one of WG760's less desirable characteristics: the sudden self-jettisoning of the aircraft's canopy. This happened on three occasions (once with Beamont and twice with de Villiers) thanks to an inadequate locking system that was eventually re-engineered and strengthened. On one occasion the canopy (still intact) was found by a member of the public in Southport and although it was unfit for further flight operations, it was subsequently refitted to WG760.

With the testing of the fixed nozzle reheat system complete, the aircraft was temporarily grounded for further modifications, this time centred on the aircraft's wings. Having finally abandoned the leading edge nose flaps, the featureless leading edge could be redesigned to provide better stability and drag reduction (and a corresponding improvement in endurance), and English Electric produced a new cambered leading edge (together with slightly reduced-span trailing edge ailerons) that was 'cranked' chord-wise on the outboard surfaces, eventually tapering to a squared-off wing tip which would then hold the potential of becoming a mounting point for missiles at a later stage.

The first flight in this configuration took place on 15 February 1957, and a series of fifty-four test flights was conducted during which the aircraft appeared to handle similarly to the non-modified configuration at supersonic speeds, but handled more precisely and responsively at subsonic speeds with a better buffet threshold, improved aileron control feel and better pitch response in the landing configuration. The test pilots certainly believed that the redesigned leading edge

XG308 was one of English Electric's P.1B Development Batch aircraft. After completing handling trials with EE, it was assigned to the A&AEE before being fitted with a larger F.3-type tail fin. It was withdrawn from use (at RAE Bedford) during 1968.

would be a useful improvement that should be incorporated into production aircraft and English Electric's test data convinced them that the revised wing would be worth adopting. However, the Air Staff eventually declined to accept the modification – an odd decision when compared to their evident desire (at that time) to see the aircraft developed as fully as possible. The decision not to proceed was probably due to a report from the A&AEE in which they had been less than convinced that the modification was entirely necessary, reporting that handling with the unmodified leading edge was adequate for the skills of service pilots and that any small performance shortfalls at high speed and high altitude could probably be compensated-for by a slight dive or the adoption of a rocket motor pack (a further modification which was being planned at the time). The less than enthusiastic view of the A&AEE may have been enough to eventually rule out adoption of the modification, although like so many potential improvements to the aircraft, the cost may have been the deciding factor. However, the result was that the modified wing was abandoned and did not reappear in the design process until the Lightning's final production variants emerged many years later – much to the frustration of English Electric and countless RAF pilots who felt that the modification should have been incorporated right from the start.

P.1B XA847, the prototype P.1B, was used for a wide variety of trials work as part of the Lightning's development. It was fitted with an enlarged fin structure for aerodynamic testing, and was on display for some time in the RAF Museum at Hendon.

On 4 April 1957, the first of the P.1B development aircraft (XA847) made its inaugural flight, marking the start of the next significant stage in the P.1 programme and effectively beginning the transition period between what were essentially research aircraft and true prototype aircraft. Although similar in outline to the two P.1A airframes, the P.1B incorporated many design changes. The most obvious differences included the appearance of the now-familiar shock cone, which was positioned ahead of a new circular air intake trunk, housing the Ferranti AI 23 Airpass equipment. Although the wings remained virtually identical to those fitted to the P.1A (prior to the leading edge modification), the fuselage was noticeably different, having been expanded to accommodate the slightly larger Rolls-Royce Avon engines (and incorporating repositioned and improved airbrakes), while the pilot's canopy was raised and bulged in order to improve visibility. The new canopy's aerodynamic profile necessitated the creation of a raised spine that ran along from the rear of the canopy to the base of the spine. This created a suitable space to house the engine starting system that relied on the use of ignited Avpin to provide sufficient pressure to wind up the Avon's turbine blades.

The concept of the starter system made sense in that it enabled the aircraft to self-start without the aid of ground equipment, and the 3 gallons of Avpin stored in the spine would provide enough power for up to six starts. This meant that the aircraft would theoretically be able to operate independently of ground starter support anywhere around the world, although – with some irony – the starter system actually created mobility problems in later years, when widespread airfield supplies of Avpin gradually dwindled. Unfortunately, the realities of the Avpin system were less attractive than on the drawing board. Isopropyl nitrate is a notoriously toxic, corrosive and volatile substance that had already demonstrated considerable dangers. Many horror stories of fires, explosions and significant damage had convinced English Electric that the system would be better replaced by a simple cartridge starter, but official support remained in favour of Avpin – a decision that both pilots and ground crew would ponder with some frustration for the next four decades.

Equipped with two ADEN cannon, provision for a pair of de Havilland Blue Jay (later to become Firestreak) AAMs and new RA.24 Mk 210 Avon engines (each rated at 11,250 lb dry thrust), the P.1B was a major advance over the relatively unsophisticated P.1A. However, despite the various modifications, XA847 retained the same tail fin design that had been applied to the prototypes, although this too was soon to be redesigned, largely as a result of the revised fuselage shape of the P.1B, which significantly affected the aircraft's directional stability characteristics. The first flight of XA847 was certainly a great success. Equipped with a pair of engines delivering a combined thrust of 30,000 lb in reheat, the aircraft's all-up weight at take-off was less than 30,000 lb, giving it a positive thrust-to-weight ratio that, at least in theory, meant that the aircraft could climb without any aerodynamic lift at all. However, for the first test flight, the new variable-nozzle system was not used, but Beamont reported that take-off acceleration (in cold power) felt similar to take-off in the P.1A with reheat. At 25,500 feet the aircraft was pushed to maximum cold thrust acceleration, reaching an impressive Mach 1.13/495 knots IAS.

Although 4 April 1957 should have been regarded as a memorably good day in the Lightning's history, it was probably one of the worst. While Beamont was successfully taking XA847 through the sound barrier, the now infamous Government White Paper produced by Defence Minister Duncan Sandys was being read in the House of Commons. Sandys announced a radical shake-up of Britain's armed forces, with particular emphasis on the future shape of the RAF. Having concluded that the fundamental basis of future defence should lie with nuclear deterrence, Sandys announced that a whole range of promising aerospace projects would simply be abandoned, on the basis that they were either simply too expensive to pursue or incompatible with the new era of nuclear terror and the corresponding reduction in worldwide commitments. With hindsight, many commentators have concluded that Sandys was little more than a 'butcher' who had no real understanding of Britain's defence needs, but he probably made the best decisions he could, based on the information he was given. Relatively rapid developments in Surface-to-Air Guided Weapon (SAGW) technology was showing great potential, and it gave defence chiefs the tantalising promise of an all-missile system capable of destroying incoming enemy bombers without reliance upon expensive (and vulnerable) manned interceptors.

Despite the concept being barely off the drawing board in 1957, confidence in the concept was high and it was anticipated that an effective SAGW system could be operational in five or six years. Consequently, the idea of pouring significant amounts of money into development of fighter aircraft seemed pointless and wasteful, and although the very idea of entirely replacing manned fighters with missiles might now seem absurd, it was clearly a plausible proposition in 1957, so aircraft such as the rocket-powered SR.53 and Gloster's 'thin wing' Javelin were abandoned. Miraculously, English Electric's P.1 survived and although many commentators have concluded that this was simply because the project had proceeded too far to be cancelled economically, the reality of the situation was rather more complex.

The Air Staff had already accepted that there was no guarantee that SAGW defences would be entirely effective or that they would become available within the predicted timescale. Likewise, it was also accepted that the only effective means of defending the UK (particularly the nuclear bomber bases) against attack from Soviet bombers until a SAGW was fully operational would be a supersonic interceptor. Freddie Page believed that the P.1 survived cancellation because it had already become a much more capable aircraft than the one which had originally been proposed. Having started out as a simple gun-armed day interceptor, it had been developed into the basis of an all-weather, day and night fighter equipped with an advanced radar, guns and AAMs, and with further potential for rocket armament. Although the P.1B and subsequent production aircraft could justifiably have been officially designated as a completely separate design project (indeed, the original Specification was revised effectively to keep up with the projected capabilities of the aircraft), Page was careful to ensure that the project was still regarded as being only a natural development of the P.1A. He believed that it was this decision that encouraged the Government to continue with it, whereas the presentation of a completely new Specification and design (which would probably have been the P.5), together with all the necessary procedures that would have had to be started from scratch, would probably have been too much for both the Air Ministry and the Government to contemplate.

Page's adherence to the original P.1 project may well have been the act of genius that ultimately saved it from abandonment, although in many respects this survival was only a partial victory. The 1957 White Paper had far-reaching effects, not least the creation of the notion that all manned fighters – including the P.1B – should be regarded as mere stopgaps, pending the arrival of technically superior missiles that would render fighter aircraft obsolete. It was the White Paper that fostered the fundamental (and hopelessly misguided) belief that the P.1B was little more than a temporary solution to a long-term requirement – a belief that persisted throughout the Lightning's service life.

Even though it would seem that a variety of circumstances contributed to the P.1 programme's survival of the savage cuts, it is fair to say that by early 1947 the project had certainly gathered a great deal of momentum, and the promise of an operational aircraft being available to the RAF undoubtedly made the prospect of continuing to fund the project rather more acceptable to the Treasury. By this stage, some three years had already passed since the Treasury had sanctioned the purchase of an initial batch of twenty pre-production aircraft that would be more representative of the final operational design, and would ultimately enter service – if ordered. Although the three P.1Bs were outwardly similar to the final production Lightning F.1 (and the two P.1As are usually regarded as being the prototypes), they were in effect the true prototypes, while the earlier P.1As were something of an interim step between the drawing board and the prototype stage. The batch of twenty pre-production aircraft were intended to act as an extended 'prototype fleet', spreading the trials and development programme across a substantial number of aircraft in order to avoid the difficulties (especially delays) which a small number of prototypes would have created. (This had been a particular problem with the Hunter.) The idea had been picked up from American experience, but in practice it was flawed, chiefly because of the amount of time and resources that were required to keep the whole fleet (plus the three earlier P.1B aircraft) to a similar state of modification. Time was wasted on duplication, spreading continual modifications across no fewer than twenty-three aircraft. The batch of twenty pre-production aircraft (which were, in effect, developed P.1B airframes) never received any official designation, although the Ministry of Supply insisted that they be referred to as Development Batch (DB) aircraft in order to avoid the use of the term 'pre-production' which implied a follow-on order. This would suggest that even by 1955, there was still no great confidence that a production batch would be financed.

In fact, an order was finally placed in November 1956 for fifty Mk 1 aircraft to Specification F.23/49, just a few months ahead of the Defence White Paper. Meanwhile, the P.1B flight trials began to increase in intensity during 1957, the second P.1B (XA853) joining the test programme in June that year. Both aircraft were flown as frequently as possible in order to work through the test schedule, and this often meant heavy workloads for the engineering crews who regularly worked long night shifts in order to prepare the aircraft for flying the next day.

Serviceability was the main difficulty. It came as no surprise that a relatively sophisticated high-performance jet would be difficult to maintain, especially in prototype form, but continual problems with fuel, hot gas and hydraulic leaks combined with relatively minor electrical problems ensured that the flight test team were constantly struggling to keep up with their schedule. To compound their problems still further, the reheat system proved to be temperamental and regularly failed to ignite – a particularly embarrassing situation for the test pilots when a variety of VIP demonstrations were required. These difficulties 'backed up' through the DB aircraft fleet as each aircraft reached completion and flight status, making matters still worse. For example, at one stage, when seven aircraft were available for test flying, only one was serviceable for some weeks, and the concept of maintaining such a large fleet of test aircraft began to look increasingly like a counter-productive move.

Despite these problems, good progress was made as more DB aircraft finally became available, exploring different aspects of the aircraft's performance envelope together with the weapons systems and associated equipment. One of the most notable highlights of the test programme took place in 1958 when XA847 was assigned to exploration of engine and systems handling. Some of the flights had been quite eventful, particularly low-level trials over the Irish Sea when Beamont occasionally experienced intake duct surges, producing a great deal of noise which he compared to cannon fire, causing him literally to duck in his seat, while the condensation emerging from intake shock waves (illuminated by sunlight) looked like flashes of flame – something that Beamont became accustomed to after the alarm of his first experience of the phenomenon.

Having attained speeds of Mach 1.8 or more on some of the more recent flights, the English Electric team were confident that with plenty of available engine thrust in reserve the aircraft could go still further, and a flight was planned that would take the P.1B up to Mach 2. Surprisingly, there was little official interest in the proposal, largely because the service requirement of Mach 1.7 had already been comfortably exceeded, but on 25 November the flight went ahead. Having climbed to 44,000 feet, Beamont selected full reheat and the aircraft accelerated to Mach 1.9, at which stage power was briefly reduced to check speed control. With full reheat reapplied, XA847 immediately surged back through Mach 1.9, and at Mach 1.98 Beamont reduced power to one-quarter reheat, which was sufficient to push the aircraft gently to Mach 2 at 42,500 feet. Almost effortlessly, the P.1B had reached twice the speed of sound.

Earlier in 1958, a team of pilots from the RAF's CFE arrived at Warton to make their own preview test flight appraisals of the P.1B, and although they were undoubtedly greatly impressed by the aircraft's performance, they also highlighted a number of deficiencies which would need to be addressed before production aircraft were completed. For example, they were unimpressed by the temperamental Avpin starter system that consistently failed to function adequately and rarely produced a successful engine start on the first attempt. Even before getting airborne, they had identified the heavy braking pressure required on the foot pedals, and it was agreed that this would probably be tiring (and therefore potentially hazardous) whilst taxiing around long perimeter tracks. On arrival at the runway, the aircraft had to be lined up carefully on the centreline otherwise differential braking was needed to keep it on the runway at the beginning of the take-off run until a speed was reached where the rudder became effective. Once airborne, the aircraft had to be immediately climbed in order to keep the acceleration under control, until the landing gear had successfully retracted. The undercarriage limiting speed (250 knots) occurred just seconds after take-off, and the landing gear (particularly the forward-retracting nose leg) was unable to function above this speed. However, the team also felt that the undercarriage retraction cycle was too slow. Maintaining the initial climbing speed of 450 knots IAS was easy, but after passing 18,000 feet and switching to Indicated Mach Number (IMN) 0.90, effective control was much more difficult because of the relatively large fore-aft control column movements required and the poor design of the Machmeter instrument which was difficult to read, especially at subsonic speeds. After reaching the top of the climb, the pilots reported that the fairly large control column movement required to push the aircraft over into level flight obscured the pilot's view of the attitude indicator – hardly an ideal situation. Likewise, some force on the control column had to be maintained until the tailplane trimmer caught up, otherwise the aircraft would continue to climb.

General handling qualities were felt to be good, with exceptionally good rate of roll, except at low speed when coarse application of the ailerons could induce adverse yaw that needed to be corrected by a rudder input. Similarly, control below 220 knots was regarded as being rather poor. The reheat system was impressive, but only when it actually worked, and at speeds beyond Mach 1 or heights above 30,000 feet reheat light-up was particularly unreliable, so accelerations up to Mach 1 were made in cold power at 28,000 feet before reheat was selected. Once in full reheat, the acceleration was reported as being very rapid and great attention was needed to avoid climbing or exceeding the aircraft's limiting speed. The reheat controls (selected by pushing the throttles through the full cold power detent, and cancelled by lifting a small catch to allow the throttles to be pulled back) were thought to be rather clumsy, resulting in jerky movements that often caused the pilot to overshoot his desired setting. Supersonic handling was reported as good, although concentration was required in monitoring flight instruments during turns as there was a lack of harmony between the light control inputs required and the relatively heavy control column movements needed for the tailplane, and it was felt that this was an unsatisfactory situation when a pilot would be busy operating the radar at the same time. However, it was understood that production aircraft would have an auto-stabilisation and autopilot system, which would rectify this problem. One rather interesting quirk of the aircraft's supersonic performance was the difficulty in attaining Mach 1.3, a speed that was too high to maintain in cold power but immediately exceeded with the use of reheat. Although airbrake application would be appropriate in such a situation, it was felt that the redesigned brakes were still inadequate and that their variable positioning was unnecessary, as they inevitably had to be fully extended when required. At lower subsonic speeds, forward visibility was found to be acceptable at circuit speeds, but at slightly higher recovery speeds visibility was sometimes almost zero in heavy rain. The nose-down attitude maintained during descent caused the fuel gauges to consistently under-read, sometimes by more than 200 lb per gauge.

This list of deficiencies was significant, but most of the problems reported were not considered serious, especially when compared to the many outstanding attributes that the aircraft exhibited. The CFE pilots agreed that the aircraft would probably be capable of achieving a speed of Mach 2 in RAF service and an operational ceiling of at least 55,000 feet. This would give the aircraft a comfortable performance advantage over potential adversaries such as the Soviet Tu-16 Badger bomber, and with this level of capability the RAF was clearly going to get the aircraft that it needed.

Away from Boscombe Down, the P.1B fleet was assigned to a wide variety of trials, exploring every aspect of the aircraft's aerodynamic properties and equipment performance, with improvements and modifications being incorporated into the aircraft when necessary. One of the most noticeable developments during the P.1B programme was the appearance of a new tail fin design, larger in area (with greater chord and a squared-off tip) than those fitted to the first P.1Bs and the two P.1A aircraft. XA847 had demonstrated that the aircraft's directional stability was slightly degraded at very high speeds, and as a short-term fix the aircraft was modified to incorporate a small dorsal extension to the existing fin. This proved to be a partial solution, but a test flight limit of Mach 1.53 was imposed on the fleet, pending more permanent fin design modifications, as faster speeds had already been successfully investigated and could be explored in more detail when the stability problem had been overcome. In May 1958, XA847 first flew with a completely new tail fin, this being the Stage Two design that became standard on the first production-standard aircraft and proved to be sufficient to counter stability problems on aircraft fitted with the small ventral tank and Firestreak missiles.

Following modification, XA847 was assigned to air-to-air refuelling (AAR) trials – an important aspect of the test programme, considering the aircraft's extremely critical endurance. Various designs for the aircraft's refuelling probe had been proposed, English Electric favouring the installation of a retractable probe in the port upper gun position, but by the time that flight testing began in 1959,

XA847 had adopted a rather more basic design, comprising a simple removable probe attached to the underside of the port wing. Inevitably, cost considerations had forced EE to adopt a less ambitious design, but it is important to bear in mind that at this stage in the P.1 programme, official interest in aerial refuelling was only connected with potential future overseas deployments; therefore the idea of incorporating a permanent, retractable probe system probably seemed unnecessary when a temporary bolt-on probe would be sufficient for the RAF's needs.

With hindsight, it seems incredible that an aircraft with such limited endurance, tasked with the interception of high-speed bombers, was not equipped with AAR equipment as standard from the outset, but, as ever, the Air Ministry appears to have assumed that the P.1 would simply be required to climb rapidly to altitude and destroy incoming bombers. Little thought seems to have been given to the obvious attractiveness of intercepting such aircraft as far away from the British mainland as possible. Flight trials took place with Canberra and Valiant tanker aircraft and were fairly uneventful, although Beamont did break off the refuelling probe's tip nozzle on one early flight. XA849 received a coat of white fuel-sensitive paint across port nose and wing surfaces, in order to trace the dispersal of waste fuel when connecting and disconnecting from the tanker basket.

Subsequent to the refuelling trials, XA847 was assigned to development of the cockpit centralised warning panel (CWP), an important part of the aircraft's internal equipment designed to monitor the integrity of the on-board systems. Because of the way in which so much equipment was effectively crammed into the P.1 airframe, English Electric were well aware from the outset that the risk of fire would always be a possibility. The CWP would enable the pilot to become immediately aware of any problems, but the early CWP system was prone to malfunctions and erroneous alarms, which eventually encouraged the test pilots almost to ignore it. However, on 8 May 1958, the CWP in P.1B XA853 proved its potential when it illuminated a fire warning during a test flight from Warton. On touchdown, the aircraft's elevator controls immediately seized and by the time that the machine came to a halt, smoke was pouring from the rear. The cause of the fire was a hot air leak, which had ignited pools of oil and fuel trapped within various recesses in the fuselage structure. The fire had caused so much destruction that the entire rear fuselage had to be replaced, and more than a year was spent on the exploration of ways to ensure that the near-catastrophe was not repeated. The fire detection system was redesigned and a limit of 20,000 feet placed on reheat relights. But the risk of fire could not be eliminated completely, and with two reheated engines squeezed so closely together within a cramped fuselage, the potential for problems was clear. In fact, the risk of fire was something that continued to plague the aircraft until the every end of its service life.

The P.1B fleet continued to provide valuable test data, aircraft being temporarily assigned to Boscombe Down (on cannon firing trials), Rolls-Royce at Hucknall (on engine and reheat development work), de Havilland at Hatfield (for missile test flying), Ferranti at Turnhouse (for radar development) and elsewhere as required. The majority of test flying remained at Warton, however, and in September 1958, two aircraft were dispatched to Farnborough to participate in the SBAC show. It was on 23 October, whilst at Farnborough, that the P.1 was finally given a name. Choosing a name had been the subject of debate since 1954, and with an established policy of assigning names suggestive of aggression or speed to fighter aircraft, a variety of potential names were suggested, such as Defender, Arrow, Scorpion, Challenger, Flash, Astra, Eagle, and even Scimitar and Harrier. The Deputy Chief of the Air Staff recommended that 'Lightning' be chosen, but official adoption of the name was held off because the aircraft was then barely at prototype stage. Further names were put forward such as Avenger, Destroyer, Excalibur, Lancer and Thunderblast, but the Air Council concluded that 'Lightning' would be the most appropriate name for the RAF's Mach 2 interceptor, and an official champagne 'christening' was conducted at Farnborough, with the Chief of the Air Staff (Sir Dermot Boyle) performing the ceremony. At last, the Lightning was born.

CHAPTER TEN
The Lightning Years

The first production contract for the Lightning was placed in November 1956, covering a batch of fifty aircraft, one of these being destined to become a static test airframe. Subsequently, the precise nature of the order shifted slightly, becoming divided into an early batch of nineteen interim F Mk 1 aircraft followed by twenty-eight improved F Mk 1A aircraft, whilst two aircraft were cancelled completely. The reason for this mixed order was the Air Staff's eagerness to get the aircraft into operational service. Although the P.1 programme had suffered from many delays (often caused by official confusion as to precisely how the aircraft should be equipped, combined with a general reluctance to pursue the project), there was a noticeable shift in attitude from around 1956, prompted largely by advances in Soviet offensive capability and the recognition that the RAF's existing fighter force (comprising Hunters and Javelins) was less than capable of countering the growing threat. It also seems quite likely that as the nature of the 1957 Defence Review became more clear, the Air Staff may well have been more willing to accept that the P.1 was going to become the only game in town and that it would be sensible to make the best of it if there was likely to be little chance of anything better coming along. Despite Defence Minister Sandys being convinced that the way forward lay with surface-to-air missiles, the Air Staff consistently took a more realistic view, accepting that there was never any guarantee that SAGW defences would prove to be adequate to defend UK airspace.

The first production Lightning F Mk 1 was XM134, which made its maiden flight (from Samlesbury to Warton) on 3 October 1959. Following a series of fourteen test flights, the aircraft was ready for delivery by March 1960, and test pilot Jimmy Dell flew it to Boscombe Down on the last day of the month. The A&AEE flew a series of acceptance flights with the aircraft, although the long and detailed P.1B test programme had already established virtually every aspect of the Lightning's handling and performance. The A&AEE trials were therefore comparatively short, and by the end of June the aircraft was ready to be delivered to the Air Fighting Development School (AFDS) based at RAF Coltishall, although the unit was temporarily located at Leconfield while Coltishall's runways were being resurfaced. The AFDS pilots eagerly flew the aircraft on a variety of trials flights, joining the DB aircraft, which had been with the AFDS from the end

Probably the most famous Lightning photograph ever taken, this memorable image is of P.1B XG332 about to crash at Hatfield on 13 September 1962, following an engine fire. Test pilot George Aird can be seen ejecting from the aircraft.

of the previous year, examining its operational capabilities and establishing the techniques and tactics required to use the aircraft in its intended role. The aircraft quickly returned to Warton, however, so that the type could gain a full CA Release.

It was not until 11 July that the RAF's first operational Lightning squadron (No. 74) got a chance to acquaint itself with its new aircraft, when XM134 returned to Coltishall leading a flypast to mark the return of the AFDS from Leconfield. No. 74 Squadron's CO flew the aircraft for the first time on 14 July, and over the next few days the squadron's pilots eagerly took turns to get airborne. Deliveries of new Lightnings began to trickle through from Samlesbury and Warton, and eventually the entire production batch of F Mk 1 aircraft (apart from XM168, which was the static test airframe) entered service with the squadron.

From the perspective of the lucky pilots, the Lightning immediately lived up to expectations, demonstrating a breathtaking performance when compared to the Hunter, which most of the pilots had previously flown. All of the new Lightning pilots were experienced (with at least 1,000 flying hours to their credit), but less able pilots would have had no difficulty converting onto the type. At the time there was no dual-control trainer variant, which effectively meant that any new pilot assigned to the Lightning made his very first flight and his first solo simultaneously. These first flights often proved to be 'interesting', but they rarely resulted in any catastrophes. The aircraft's radar system worked well and proved to be surprisingly reliable (in stark contrast to the problems associated with the Tornado F2 interceptor that came along more than twenty years later) and the Firestreak missiles also functioned well, much to the surprise of many who were less than convinced that the growing reliance on AAMs was necessarily a good thing.

The Lightning's entry into RAF service, from a flying and capability point of view, was a great success. However, from the perspective of the ground crew who were responsible for maintaining the fleet, it was a dark period of frustration and hard work. It was already accepted that it would be challenging to keep the aircraft serviceable, but this assumption was soon proved to be an underestimation. The RAF's problems were compounded by the fact that ground crews often consisted of national servicemen who lacked sufficient specialised training, but even with the best training possible, the Lightning's many complex systems would have represented a technical nightmare for those tasked with its maintenance, especially when gaining easy access to so many of the internal components was almost impossibly difficult and time-consuming. This is not to suggest that the Lightning was significantly different from other aircraft of the same era, but with hindsight it is clear that the RAF was not prepared for the realities of maintaining a growing fleet of supersonic interceptors. Most importantly, the Air Force's logistic system was poor, and a great deal of aircraft unserviceability was caused by the RAF's inability to get sufficient spare parts to the right base at the right time, and this situation was very slow to improve. Initially, most Lightnings could achieve no more than 20 flying hours per month even though English Electric insisted that 40

Lightning F Mk 1A XM171 served with No. 56 Squadron and No. 226 OCU before being withdrawn from use. It was scrapped early in 1974.

Lightning F Mk 1 XM139 was one of the first of the type to enter RAF service. After flying with No. 74 Squadron the aircraft was assigned to the OCU and finally to target facilities duties before being used as a decoy airframe at Wattisham.

No. 226 OCU was the RAF's first Lightning training unit and for a short period during the early 1960s, it was based at Middleton St George, where the unit's aircraft were painted in eye-catching red and white colours. After moving south to Coltishall, the flamboyant markings were abandoned.

hours ought to be possible. The company was right, but many years passed before the RAF achieved this figure.

The Lightning F Mk 1 fleet, small in numbers, was regarded only as a short-term measure pending delivery of the more capable Lightning F Mk 1A, which featured a series of improvements that were not developed in time to incorporate into the early aircraft delivered to No. 74 Squadron. The F.1A had the advantage of a UHF radio and improved windscreen rain dispersal, making it more suitable for all-weather operations. Additionally, the aircraft was also 26 lb lighter than the F.1, weighing in at 25,737 lb. Most importantly, the Avon 210R engine had a four-position reheat system that was more flexible and reliable, and the aircraft was also equipped to carry the bolt-on refuelling probe now cleared for service. In essence, the F.1A was the true first-generation Lightning with which Fighter Command could begin to re-equip. No. 56 Squadron was the first to take delivery of the aircraft, with the first (XM172) arriving at Wattisham on 14 December 1960. The squadron's Lightnings were joined by yet more Lightning F.1As when No. 111 Squadron re-formed at the base, having finally relinquished the famous all-black Hunters. XM184 and XM186 were the first to arrive, on 13 April 1961, with re-equipment completed by the end of August.

Following the introduction into service of the F Mk 1 and F Mk 1A, the next Lightning variant made its service debut. Although on first impressions any observer might conclude that the Lightning F Mk 2 was merely a refined version of the F.1A (being identical in appearance save for a small intake duct on the

The Lightning F Mk 1 cockpit. Later versions of the aircraft featured a redesigned instrument panel that incorporated strip reader indicators, replacing some of the more traditional 'clock face' instruments seen here. The interception radar screen is clearly visible to the upper right-hand side.

A magnificent formation of Lighting F Mk 1A aircraft flown by pilots of No. 56 Squadron at Wattisham. The 'Firebirds' team was short-lived but thrilled spectators across the country from 1963 until the following year.

XM144 was one of the last Lightning F Mk 1A aircraft to remain in flying condition, operated by the Leuchars Target Facilities Flight. It also spent some time with the Wattisham TFF as illustrated, with the unit's distinctive markings carried on the nose and tail.

spine), the F Mk 2 was in fact a substantially better aircraft that represented an interim stage between the early-production aircraft and the later second-generation machines. The F Mk 2 was the first variant to be equipped with a CRT attack display, part of the planned instrument suite outlined in OR.946, and this effectively made the F Mk 2 the first all-weather Lightning variant with improved instruments, better radar, four 30 mm cannon, a liquid oxygen system (replacing the earlier gaseous system with its associated cumbersome and accident-prone pipe work), a standby DC generator and the Avon 210 engine which featured a fully variable reheat system, delivering a maximum thrust of 14,140 lb. It was also initially planned to equip the F.2 with the modified wing leading edge first explored on the P.1A, but although this became an accepted part of the various modifications to be incorporated into the F.2 (and an agreement that the revised wing would then be capable of carrying wing tip external fuel tanks), the idea was subsequently dropped and the order for fifty aircraft, received in December 1959, reduced to forty-four.

It was at this stage that plans were first made to equip the Lightning with larger external fuel tanks carried on the wing upper surfaces (the lower surface being occupied by the main landing gear wells), but English Electric estimated that suitably modified wings (equipped to transfer fuel from external tanks) could only be incorporated into the production line at the forty-first aircraft. Given that only four aircraft would therefore be available for modification, it was agreed that the modification would be held over until production of the Mk 3 aircraft began, although, of course, this decision was also subsequently postponed still further. However, even without the wing modifications, the F Mk 2 was certainly a major improvement over previous Lightnings. The new instruments (effectively only a partial OR.946 suite but significantly better than the F.1/1A's austere fit) were capable of processing inputs from the master reference gyro and the air data controller, providing a navigation display that could give compass, ILS, UHF homer or Tacan readout. There was also the provision for a data link facility but this was never fitted. The radar B-scope could present a course for the pilot to steer manually and could also present programmed climb, altitude and heading hold, plus ILS track and glide information, and a course could be flown automatically by the autopilot system. This, combined with a much less temperamental engine, made the F.2 a very popular aircraft with every pilot who was fortunate to fly it, and in subsequent years it has become regarded as the 'best of breed' in terms of capability and handling qualities.

Unfortunately, it was slow to reach operational service thanks largely to the continued delays in completion of the OR.946 instrument system. Designed and developed under the control of the Ministry of Supply and RAE, the system was to have been supplied to English Electric as being fully approved and functional, but EE quickly found that the various components did not work together satisfactorily and the programme had clearly been supervised and co-ordinated very badly. Consequently, EE engineers had to retest and renew the tolerances of each component as a total system, taking into account likely

P.1B XG311 was assigned to the A&AEE and spent some time at Khormaksar in Aden for tropical trials. It was abandoned near Warton in July 1963 after suffering undercarriage failure.

service deterioration, and this process held up the F.2's delivery schedule by many months.

The first F.2 to fly was XN723, which took to the air on 11 July 1961, but the delays with OR.946 meant that the airframes were completed ahead of the intended instrument fit, so they emerged from the factory at Samlesbury only to be ferried over to nearby Warton, where they were stored prior to being stripped-down again and refitted to production standard. Consequently, it was 14 November 1962 before the first aircraft (XN771) entered service with the AFDS (now located at Binbrook), the first aircraft joining No. 19 squadron at Leconfield on 17 December. By this stage, plans were already in hand to introduce the next Lightning variant and despite the F.2's significant place in the story of the Lightning's development, its introduction into service was somewhat overshadowed by the delays in actually getting the aircraft into service, combined with the prospect of a more capable variant being just months away.

Although the first F.2 had reached No. 19 Squadron during mid-December, the next delivery did not take place for many weeks, the scheduled second aircraft failing to arrive on 9 January when XN778's flight was curtailed by technical problems and the aircraft diverted to Finningley where it remained pending repairs. It was not until April 1963 that the squadron received its final delivery

Completed in July 1961, XN723 was a Lightning F Mk 2. It is seen in flight without its ventral fuel tank – a rare event normally reserved for post-servicing test flights. The aircraft crashed in March 1964, following an engine fire.

A nostalgic glimpse into one of RAF Leconfield's hangars during the early 1960s, with a Lightning F Mk 2 from No. 19 Squadron undergoing maintenance in the foreground, with an F Mk 1 from No. 92 Squadron in the background. The same hangar is now full of Army trucks and the Lightnings are long gone.

from Warton, completing its full complement. No. 92 squadron was then the next unit to receive the Lightning, its first aircraft (XN727) having arrived at Leconfield on 23 January and the final aircraft being delivered in August.

By 1964, both Leconfield squadrons were operational on the Lightning and No. 92 Squadron was afforded the honour of becoming that year's Fighter Command display team, making the now customary show-stealing appearance at the annual SBAC Farnborough show. Their stay at Leconfield was rather short, however, as the Air Staff had decided to deploy two Lightning squadrons to Germany. With a requirement for twelve operational Lightning squadrons, Treasury pressure eventually reduced this figure to just ten. Of these, one would be assigned to the Far East (Singapore) and another to the Near East (Akrotiri), while a further five squadrons would be based in the UK. All of these units would ultimately be equipped with Mk 3 aircraft (although the Mk 3 was in effect what eventually became the F.6, as explained later) and in most cases these would be capable of rapid overseas deployment should reinforcement be required. However, with East-West tensions still high, there was an ever-present need to have two fighter squadrons assigned to the defence of German airspace, particularly the Berlin corridors. As the Lightning F.2 did not have sufficiently 'long legs' to deploy rapidly from the UK when compared to proposed later variants, it was decided that the two Leconfield squadrons would be the most appropriate units for permanent relocation in Germany. No. 19 Squadron began its transfer to Gütersloh on 23 September 1965, followed by No. 92 Squadron (after a brief stay at Geilenkirchen) from 29 December.

Because of the rapid advances in the Lightning's design, work on the later Mk 3 variant was proceeding almost in parallel with the earlier F Mk 2, and some consideration was given to the concept of modifying the F.2 fleet to F.3 standards. However, the prospect of saving more than £10 million was enough to convince the Air Staff that the programme was unnecessary, and it was (albeit for the time being) abandoned. It could be argued therefore that the RAF over-ordered the F.2, and records do show that many F.2s spent a significant amount of time in storage with No. 33 MU at Lyneham.

Approval to begin design work on the Lightning Mk 3 was given in 1959, the production contract for forty-seven aircraft being placed in June 1960, although, as ever, there was an almost grudging acceptance that an order needed to be placed. The Secretary of State for Air wrote to the Chief of the Air Staff:

> … it is now necessary to place follow-on orders for the Lightning and that your department, in consultation with the MoA, are seeking authority from the Treasury to convert an existing order for materials into a full production order for 47 aircraft. I have been reluctant to see further orders for Lightnings placed in advance of general decisions on provision for air defence; nevertheless, I am prepared to support the ordering for these aircraft and to see both the Mks 2 and 3 brought up to the full operational requirement for the Mk 3 in due course. This will, I understand, suffice to maintain a front-line strength of 60/72 aircraft of Mk 3 standard. I must make

it plain, however, that on the information now available to me, I am not prepared, either to see any further orders placed for Lightnings, or for the Lightning to be developed beyond Mk 3 standard.

The Chancellor of the Exchequer was even more forthright in his views, stating:

> ... on the basis of existing plans, annual expenditure on air defence, at current prices, seems likely to be up by about twenty per cent by 1964/5. This is to me an entirely unacceptable prospect. On the contrary, a substantial and progressive reduction from the current level seems an absolute necessity.

Given this prevailing attitude, it is little wonder that the Lightning programme faced an uphill struggle to secure funding for even the most basic level of improvements when the Government was still deluding itself into believing that SAGW defences might somehow render the manned fighter obsolete, or that effective air defences could somehow be acquired 'on the cheap'. However, despite the Secretary of State's comments, a further order for an additional forty-five Mk 3 Lightnings was eventually placed in January 1962, after further (presumably rather heated) discussions had taken place towards the end of 1960.

The Mk 3 was the second-generation Lightning, built around the carriage of two Red Top AAMs. Ironically, although the P.1 had started life as a purely cannon-armed interceptor (with no initial interest in AAMs being expressed by either the Air Ministry or the manufacturer), the rapid development and undeniable success of the de Havilland Firestreak (as fitted to the earlier Lightning variants) eventually shifted official interest towards the perceived potential of the missile, at the expense of the tried and trusted ADEN cannon. This process culminated in the decision to completely remove all cannon armament from the proposed Lightning F Mk 3, in order to provide facilities for two Red Top missiles (originally referred to as Firestreak Mk IV).

Although the Firestreak had proved to be both effective and reliable, it was undoubtedly hampered by its inability to usefully engage a target from anything other than a stern approach. Naturally, this limited the Lightning pilot's options, and the much-improved Red Top promised the ability to attack from any angle, even head-on if necessary. The Red Top had a new seeker head fairing (a single dome in place of the earlier faceted design) and revised control surfaces, together with a more powerful 68 lb warhead. The improved seeker head, which provided the all-aspect capability, was matched to an improved rocket motor that gave the missile a range of more than 7 miles. The earlier redesign of the DB aircraft's tail fins had resulted in the Stage Two fin, which was fitted to all subsequent aircraft as well as being retrofitted to the majority of the DB fleet. This larger-area fin improved the Lightning's directional control and stability, but English Electric quickly concluded that an even larger-area fin would be desirable, and as the Mk 3's Red Top missile promised to slightly degrade directional stability, it was decided to design and manufacture the Stage Three fin which incorporated another 15 per cent increase in area, effectively broadening the chord of the upper surfaces which were cropped off, creating a square-cut fin tip.

In order to expedite progress on the F.3 programme, one of the DB fleet (XG310) was selected to act as an aerodynamic test bed for the new variant and was dispatched to Boulton Paul's airfield at Seighford, where it was refitted with a new Stage Three fin together with the necessary internal frame strengthening. The aircraft subsequently appeared at the 1963 SBAC show, billed as being the prototype Mk 3, although, technically speaking, the true prototype was in fact XP693, which emerged from the production line almost a full year ahead of the remaining F.3 production, having been rushed through the factory in order that it could be delivered to Boscombe Down to undertake CA Release trials as rapidly as possible. Three further DB aircraft were subsequently modified by Boulton Paul to carry Stage Three fins, and after being fitted with uprated engines, instrumentation and Red Top systems, they were all assigned to the F.3 development programme.

Although future developments created a different outcome, at the time of development, the F Mk 3 was expected to be the ultimate variant of the Lightning. The Red Top all-aspect missile was at the very heart of the design, so much so that the once-obligatory cannon was deleted completely (a decision which was clearly a mistake). Externally, the aircraft was similar to the F.2, with the exception of the new larger 'square fin' and slightly longer cable ducting along the fuselage sides. Internally, a great deal was different, particularly in the cockpit where the new Red Top-configured AI 23B radar was linked to a new display, consisting of Search and Attack CRT, 'S' Band homer and a Light Fighter Sight system together with AI/autopilot coupling and 'S' Band homer/autopilot coupling. The traditional dial instruments were partially replaced by a new strip display, going some way to addressing the deficiencies of the older instruments (which often caused the pilot's awareness to lag behind the aircraft's true speed and altitude) but causing some pilots to conclude that the unusual presentation system created more problems than it solved. Within the airframe, a new fueldraulic system was fitted with wing-to-wing transfer facility, larger main undercarriage jacks and a cross-linked flap hydraulic system that reduced the risk of asymmetric flap occurrence. The Avon engine was the new Mk 301 design featuring fully variable reheat, delivering a maximum reheated thrust of 15,980 lb, giving the aircraft a much improved rate of climb, manoeuvrability and maximum speed, and enabling service clearance for routine operations in excess of Mach 2.

Two aircraft were also taken from the F.2 production line to assist with F.3 trials, both being upgraded to F.3 standard and fitted with the much-discussed overwing fuel tanks (which would have been fitted to the entire F.2 fleet had the decision to adopt them been taken in good time). Again, the tanks were subsequently abandoned as the Air Ministry saw no good reason for equipping the fleet with (subsonic) tanks that would have to be jettisoned prior to attaining supersonic flight, even though with the benefit of hindsight it now seems obvious that any opportunity to increase the Lightning's range – even if only for ferry flights – ought to have been eagerly accepted. But as was always the case with the Lightning programme, cost considerations and short-termism triumphed over logic.

The first F Mk 3 production-standard deliveries were made to the CFE at Binbrook, where they were immediately assigned to evaluation and trials flights, enabling the RAF to establish the necessary tactics and operational procedures. It was No. 74 Squadron that took delivery of the first operational-standard aircraft, with the first (XP700) arriving at Leuchars (the squadron's new base) on 14 April 1964. Three months later, the squadron relinquished its last first-generation Lightning F.1A. On 19 August, the first two Lightning F Mk 3s for No. 23 Squadron (XP707 and XP708) arrived, enabling the squadron to bid a less than fond farewell to the Javelin, an aircraft which had performed well in the all-weather fighter role but was completely outclassed by the Lightning's speed and manoeuvrability.

Being located in Scotland, the Leuchars-based Lightnings naturally took more than their fair share of QRA (Quick Reaction Alert) 'trade', and Lightning pilots were regularly scrambled to intercept Soviet Bears and Badgers that were skirting the UK's airspace with gradually increasing frequency. The time (and fuel) necessary to get the aircraft from the airfield's main apron was obviously wasteful, and although Hunters had traditionally been positioned on concrete pads situated next to the runway thresholds (often rendering aircraft unserviceable after having stood in the open for long periods), the rather more complex and temperamental Lightnings clearly needed a rather more benign environment in which to wait for their call to scramble, and the creation of shelters was the solution.

QRA shelters (colloquially referred to as 'Q-Sheds') were constructed at Leuchars, Binbrook and Wattisham (together with a similar shelter at Gütersloh for the German-based units), each designed to house two Lightnings and positioned next to the runway threshold. The Lightning pilots and ground crew were provided with their own accommodation next to the shelter, this enabling the crews to race rapidly to their prepared aircraft, start up and roll straight out onto the runway, getting airborne in a matter of seconds, once the order to scramble was given. Not surprisingly, every Lightning scramble also required a Victor to be scrambled from Marham (or diverted from a sortie already in progress) in order to support the short-legged interceptors on their distinctly long-legged missions.

Wattisham was the next station to receive the Lightning F Mk 3, the first aircraft for No. 111 Squadron (XP741) arriving in December 1964. Two months later, the first F.3s for No. 56 Squadron began to arrive, and almost immediately the squadron's personnel turned their attention to the possibility of decorating their new aircraft even more colourfully than their existing F.1A fleet. The result was a bright red spine, a futuristic arrowhead design on the nose and an almost jaw-dropping red/white chequerboard design emblazoned across the entirety of the tail fin. The Lightning squadrons had enthusiastically embraced the notion of revising the colourful pre-war markings that had traditionally been applied to fighter aircraft, and No. 56 Squadron's efforts were certainly the most eye-catching. Sadly, they also proved to be the last, as some less imaginative senior

RAF officers took the view that combat aircraft should be decorated more conservatively, so the delightful markings which adorned so many Lightnings were gone by 1966, save for the aircraft of No. 92 Squadron, which by virtue of their location in Germany fell outside of the new ruling. Air and ground crews were saddened to lose their opportunity to foster their squadron's *esprit de corps* on such a grand scale, but, as ever, official short-sightedness had again got in the way of plain common sense.

When No. 56 Squadron was fully operational on the Lightning F Mk 3, it was announced (in February 1967) that the unit would be transferred to Cyprus, replacing the Javelins of No. 29 Squadron as the primary defenders of Near East Air Force airspace. After ferrying the Lightnings to Akrotiri in two waves, the squadron officially took over on 11 May. Aircraft were assigned to Cyprus Sovereign Base Area (SBA) defence, and were held at various states of readiness. During the 1967 Arab-Israeli war, the alert state was increased and the squadron's F Mk 3 were rearmed with Firestreaks (the F.3 being capable of carrying both generations of AAM), which suggests that the Firestreak was regarded as being rather more reliable than the Red Top, despite its limited aspect deficiencies. Back in the UK, No. 29 Squadron said farewell to its Javelins and re-formed at Wattisham as the final all-F.3 squadron, being declared operation on 16 August, effectively completing Fighter Command's re-equipment with the Lightning after some seven years.

Despite the fact that the F Mk 3 had long been regarded as the 'definitive' Lightning that would represent the end of the type's development, circumstances continually changed throughout the procurement process and the Air Staff's requirements shifted with regular (and frustrating) frequency. By the end of 1960, it had been decided that the fundamental role of Fighter Command should be redefined and now referred to the investigation of unidentified aircraft, the prevention of enemy aerial reconnaissance flights, the blocking of attempts to jam radar systems and – perhaps most significantly for the Lightning – the supply of reinforcements for overseas bases and commitments. This translated into a distinct shift from its original role as a 'point defender' to a more flexible aircraft that could intercept a target and stay with it for a considerable amount of time. It also meant that the aircraft needed to be capable of reaching overseas bases efficiently and swiftly, without necessarily relying upon the support of expensive and logistically challenging tanker support.

Ironically, it had been specified during the infamous 1957 Defence Review that the Lightning would be confined exclusively to the defence of UK airspace and would not be required to deploy overseas (and that even in the UK it would represent no more than a back-up to the proposed SAGW defences), and yet just a couple of years later, the aircraft was essentially at the very heart of the RAF's defensive structure, destined for Germany, the Near East and Middle East, and regarded as the primary means of defending airspace, rather than being merely secondary to missiles. Having so far shown little interest in the Lightning's limited endurance, attention was finally directed to ways in which the aircraft's range could be extended – something that would have been addressed from the very beginning of the P.1 programme had the Air Staff been wise enough to recognise the necessity.

It was quickly accepted that the early Mk 1 Lightnings would not be worth improving. Some consideration was given to the possibility of equipping them with bolt-on refuelling probes (as carried by the F Mk 1A) but the idea was dropped. More serious consideration was given to the possibility of equipping both the F Mk 1A and F Mk 2 with overwing fuel tanks, but the idea was too costly to adopt as this would effectively mean the construction of new-build wings, although English Electric did offer the possibility of designing smaller 100 gallon drop tanks that could have been carried under the existing wings (but this idea was also abandoned). Ultimately, no attempt was made to improve the range of the F.1 or F.1A aircraft, although the F.2 was eventually modified, as described later.

Attention was concentrated on the Mk 3 Lightning, which was in effect the standard variant and would remain in active service in significant numbers. The most obvious means of improving the Mk 3's endurance (in addition to the now standard bolt-on refuelling probe) was to redesign the proportions of the relatively small ventral tank that was identical to that carried by the earlier variants. English Electric had already looked at the concept, an enlarged fairing having been flown on XA847, although this new fuselage attachment (manufactured by Boulton Paul) was primarily designed to house the 'RP3' store – the American nuclear-armed Genie rocket, which had been a potential weapon for the Lightning until (as usual) official interest in the project waned. The extended fairing not only provided accommodation for the missile (in a recessed launcher) but also created space for additional fuel. The Air Staff now wanted the aircraft to possess a 2,000 mile ferry range (with one in-flight refuelling) and this indicated that the existing ventral tank should clearly be redesigned and enlarged, and that overwing tanks should also be available. English Electric produced a variety of designs in order to meet this requirement, all with various capacities but all having an effect on the aircraft's performance depending on the tank's proportions.

It was also accepted that the wing leading edge could be modified in order to improve the aircraft's subsonic cruising efficiency, and having previously abandoned any interest in the CLE (Cambered Leading Edge), the idea was resurrected. The absurd abandoning of proposals and their subsequently revival was a common occurrence during the Lightning programme, but in the case of the CLE the reasoning was simple: the modification certainly improved handling and range at subsonic speeds, but it had a detrimental effect on supersonic performance. This was sufficient to discourage interest in modifying first-generation Lightnings with Avon 210 series engines, but the F Mk 3's Avon 301 engines would provide sufficient thrust to overcome the supersonic penalties of the CLE wing.

By the end of 1961, it had been agreed that the F Mk 3's range would be increased by replacing the small 250 gallon ventral tank with a much larger 560 gallon pack (eventually rising to 600). This, combined with overwing tanks providing a further 540 gallons, would give the aircraft a much more respectable fuel capacity. It was also agreed that the CLE modification would be introduced, particularly because emphasis was now shifting towards the aircraft's combat-fuel (rather than ferry-fuel) capacity. The CLE design was similar to that which had already been test flown on P.1A WG760, although the precise dimensions of the design were primarily dictated by the need to avoid the redesign the leading edge fuel tank, and the new cambered edge began at the outboard edge of this tank. It was test flown on F Mk 2 XN725, which had already been assigned to carriage trials of the overwing tanks.

Additionally, XP697 was taken from the production line and refitted, at Filton, with the CLE wing (incorporating slightly reduced-span ailerons) and the new ventral tank (with stabilising fins), prior to returning to Warton for a series of fifty test flights. It then went to Boscombe Down where the A&AEE performed an evaluation, concluding that although longitudinal control had deteriorated slightly at high speeds, overall handling was satisfactory. XN725 and XN734 were assigned to testing the overwing fuel tanks that were now to be adopted. Original interest in the tanks had disappeared when the Air Staff decided that the Lightning needed a longer supersonic flight time capability, which would have meant that the subsonic tanks would simply have to be jettisoned before accelerating to supersonic speed. However, now that the aircraft would have a much larger internal fuel capacity (thanks to the bigger ventral tank) the overwing tanks would provide potential for a useful additional ferry flight capacity. In order to meet the 2,000 nm ferry range requirement, the only other option would have been to develop an even larger 860 gallon ventral tank, but as this would be only subsonic it would require the smaller supersonic tanks to be either transported overseas separately or pre-stocked wherever required. Consequently, the overwing tanks appeared to offer the best solution to the RAF's needs, but when flight testing of the tanks began, it quickly became clear that they would only extend the aircraft's range by around 100 nm rather than the 300 nm which had been envisaged. This was because the tanks were fitted with cumbersome vertical and horizontal fins, necessary in order to separate the tanks cleanly from the wing when jettisoned. However, now that it had been established that the tanks would be used only for ferry purposes, the tanks would be either partially or completely emptied if jettisoning was ever necessary (fuel dumping being used if an emergency re-landing was required); therefore the fins were no longer necessary and they were subsequently removed, thereby restoring their range improvement to 300 nm.

English Electric was keen to offer a variety of other improvements based on the larger ventral tank, including the possibility of fitting two ADEN cannon to the forward portion (an option which was later revived), a reconnaissance pack, and even a drop-down rocket pack. Likewise, it would have been possible to fit additional weaponry to new underwing stores points or attached to the overwing tanks and even the wing tips, but official interest never materialised. As ever, there was still an all-pervasive view that the Lightning was an 'interim' design and that only the most necessary and basic modifications should be incorporated. Consequently, although noticeably different in external appearance, the redesigned aircraft were not significantly changed in terms of equipment or systems when compared to the basic F Mk 3 model, and initially the modified aircraft were simply referred to as the Extended Range Lightning Mk 3, before being redesignated as the Lightning F Mk 6 (Interim) and finally the standard production Lightning Mk 6.

The first production examples (XR752-XR767) were taken from the F Mk 3 production line and modified to Interim standard, although they were not equipped to carry the overwing tanks (but subsequently brought up to full F.6 standard in 1967-68). The first aircraft took to the air on 16 June 1965, prior to being delivered to the AFDS. In addition to this first batch of sixteen aircraft, a further seven aircraft were completed to F Mk 3 standard but placed in temporary storage before being converted to full F Mk 6 standard prior to delivery. An order for a further thirty-three Mk 3 Lightnings (subsequently built as F Mk 6 models) was placed in January 1964.

As a former Javelin squadron, it was No. 5 Squadron which took delivery of the first F Mk 6s, XR755 and XR766 arriving at Binbrook in December 1965, with the rest of the squadron's aircraft being delivered over the next three months, joining the handful of F.6s already routinely operating from the base with the AFDS. Further deliveries of the F.6 enabled No. 74 Squadron to exchange the new

Pictured close to 'home' at Warton, Lightning F Mk 6 XR754 poses for the cameraman off Blackpool's famous beach. More than forty years later, only the aircraft's nose section survives, as part of a private collection in Suffolk.

An excellent photograph of two Lightnings from No. 5 Squadron scrambling from RAF Luqa, Malta, during an air defence exercise. Two aircraft are at rest on the ramp in the foreground, while two others line up on runway 24 in the distance.

variant for its existing fleet of F.3s, which were ferried south to Wattisham in order
to re-equip No. 29 Squadron. The first F.6 reached Leuchars on 1 August 1966,
but it was December before the last F.3 was withdrawn. Intensive flying covered
all aspects of the now almost standard training syllabus, but particular emphasis
was placed on aerial refuelling, combined with routine carriage of the new
overwing tanks. This was in anticipation of the squadron's move to Singapore, the
Lightnings making their long ferry flights overseas in three waves in June 1967,
supported by Victor tankers and Britannia transports. Once settled into their new
base at Tengah, the aircraft became responsible for air defence of the region as
part of the Far East Air Force, replacing the last examples of the Javelin, which
could now take a well-deserved (and welcome) retirement.

Meanwhile, back in the UK, the next deliveries of F.6 airframes were made to
Binbrook, allowing No. 11 Squadron (another former Javelin unit) to re-equip
with the type, the first aircraft (XS928) arriving on 4 April and the remainder
being delivered over the next couple of months. This brought Binbrook up to
full strength and began what was to be a long and happy association with the
Lightning until the type's retirement from RAF service more than twenty years
later. It also marked the peak of the RAF's Lightning strength, with two squadrons
at Binbrook, two at Wattisham, two at Leuchars, two more at Gütersloh, plus
the Akrotiri and Tengah units. The F Mk 6 progressively replaced a substantial
number of F Mk 3s with each squadron (with the exception of No. 29 which
operated only the F.3), although the reverse situation also applied, with some
F.3s eventually going to Nos 5 and 11 Squadrons, as the mix of aircraft variants
between units slowly evened out.

Although the F Mk 6 was essentially only an extended-range derivative of the
F Mk 3, it was undoubtedly the most versatile and useful variant. It was 1,100
lb heavier than the Mk 3, but it could carry 3,100 lb more internal fuel and had
the facility to carry overwing tanks. Performance was very similar to the F.3, but
with the advantages of more internal and external fuel supply plus the redesigned
wing, it possessed an endurance that albeit sometimes uncomfortably short was
markedly superior to the limitations of earlier models.

Endurance aside, however, the F.6 offered few improvements over the preceding
F.3. In fact, the only other significant improvement to be made shortly after the
F.6 entered service was the incorporation of an airfield arrestor hook, enabling
the aircraft to engage RHAG (Rotary Hydraulic Arrestor Gear) if a brake failure
occurred, rather than relying on the more traditional runway-end barriers which
tended to straddle the Lightning's fuselage and cause significant damage to the
spine and tail. Although only a 'one shot' system (which had to be repositioned
on the ground), the hook was trial-fitted during 1967 and subsequently fitted as
standard to all of the second-generation Lightning variants. It was not until 1970
that a more fundamental improvement to the F.6 fleet was instigated, when most
were retrofitted with a pair of 30 mm ADEN cannon in the forward section of
the ventral tank. With hindsight, it is clear that this modification should have been
part of the original build (as proposed by English Electric), but, as ever, official

Five from Five: Lightning F Mk 6 aircraft from No. 5 Squadron formating line abreast over Spurn Point for the RAF's cameraman in 1972. In the foreground is XR761, an aircraft that was to crash less than 7 miles away from this point in November 1984 after an engine reheat fire broke out.

wisdom had dictated that there was no need for gun armament on the F Mk 3, and this nonsensical belief was carried over onto the F Mk 6. Clearly, the addition of cannon came at the expense of some fuel capacity (ultimately this resulted in a reduction in range of only around 50 nm), but with the option of two Firestreaks or two Red Tops, and the addition of two 30 mm cannon, the F.6 pilot had a much more versatile fighter at his disposal, enabling him to pursue an attack after firing missiles if necessary, and also providing him with the capability to return fire on an aircraft if attacked, without having first to fall back (by more than a mile) to set up a missile attack, by which stage any enemy pilot would be well aware of the Lightning pilot's intentions and would have evaded interception accordingly.

It is also important to consider that even though the Lightning was by now regarded as an all-weather fighter, its missile armament was unable to function in bad weather, the infra-red seeker being incapable of acquiring a target in cloud or heavy rain. Initial plans for a four-cannon fit were dropped in favour of just two (this being a weight compromise in order to preserve the aircraft's radius of action). Precisely why the Lightning's cannon armament was ever removed is still unclear, although it seems quite likely that as with so many other aspects of the Lightning's history, there was an almost blind faith in the capabilities of missiles, and once refitted with cannon the Lightning earned a reputation as being a very effective and stable gun platform, contrasting with the less than accurate capabilities of the Phantom (and its pod-mounted gun) which replaced the Lightning in RAF service.

But even with the addition of cannon, the Lightning was still short of armament, especially when compared with some other contemporary fighter designs that were being developed. Although a twin-missile carrier, in most combat scenarios the two missiles would be launched simultaneously in order to maximise the chances of a kill, and this meant that prior to the cannon refit the Lightning was essentially only a one-shot interceptor. As the aircraft grew older, the meagre range of weapon options became increasingly embarrassing, but when one considers that the Lightning was perpetually regarded as being on the verge of withdrawal (for a quarter of a century), the lack of will to invest in any armament improvements does not seem quite so ludicrous and the logic of the many short-term austere improvements is easier to understand. What is much harder to comprehend is why the Government and Air Staff were continually incapable of accepting just how valuable the Lightning's potential was, and why they continually believed that 'something better' was just around the proverbial corner.

While the production of F Mk 3 and F Mk 6 aircraft was under way, consideration was also being given to the possibility of improving the capabilities of the earlier F Mk 2, which went into regular squadron service in Germany. From the outset, it had been accepted that these aircraft should eventually be modified to bring them up to a standard more compatible with the later F.3 and F.6 force, although it was ultimately agreed that they would still be incapable of carrying the overwing tanks available to the F.6 squadrons. The reasoning for this was because the commitments in Germany were regarded as being separate to the aircraft's

A close-up of the Red Top AAM that was fitted to the Lightning F Mk 3 and F Mk 6 (and T Mk 5 trainer). The infra-red seeker head is clearly visible, and also illustrated is the Lightning's well-known 'thin' main wheel, designed to fit comfortably inside the equally thin wing structure.

other UK and overseas operations; therefore the Lightnings assigned to Germany would not be available for any other overseas deployments – which required the longer-range ferry fuel capacity.

However, the area of the ADIZ (Air Defence Identification Zone) in Germany was relatively substantial, so it was felt necessary that the new 560 gallon ventral tank should be fitted to the F.2 fleet. Initially, it was also intended to equip the F.2 with Red Top capability, although this plan was later dropped and the aircraft was to remain compatible with only the Firestreak, but having already been equipped with two ADEN 30 mm cannon (and the option of carrying a further two in the lower nose section, albeit at the expense of missile carriage capability) the improved F.2 (designated F Mk 2A) would still be a suitably flexible fighter. In 1962, it was agreed that thirty-one aircraft should be modified to F.2A standard, this being based on the assumption that both squadrons would each operate a complement of twelve aircraft, rather than the current sixteen which reflected their additional commitment to the defence of the Berlin corridors. This left ten unconverted aircraft, their fate to be decided at a later date, although by 1963, the Air Staff expressed the opinion that these aircraft might be best held in storage pending their possible use in extending the life of the existing Lightning fleet post-1972, as no replacement aircraft had yet been identified. This was the first of few acknowledgements that the Lightning would probably be around for much longer than had originally been anticipated.

Although the F.2A would incorporate the larger ventral tank and larger F.3-style fin, there was no immediate plan to fit the CLE wing, as flight tests (performed with XN975) revealed that although overall performance and handling was inferior to that of the Extended Range F.3 (the F.6), it was felt to be adequate for service use. However, and perhaps rather unusually, the Air Staff decided that the CLE should be fitted, in order to achieve a great degree of commonality with the rest of the Lightning fleet and to give the aircraft the additional performance that the CLE provided. This decision may well have been influenced by the fact that the F.2A's engines would remain unchanged (albeit with some minor modifications) and would therefore be less powerful than those fitted to the later second-generation Lightnings. Other improvements included a strengthened shock cone (enabling the aircraft to operate routinely at speeds in excess of Mach 2), an arrestor hook and improved brakes.

The first completed conversion to re-enter service was XN789, which arrived at Gütersloh on 15 January 1968, and by February 1970 both Gütersloh squadrons had re-equipped with the F.2A, although a small number of unmodified F.2s remained in use for some considerable time even after the last F.2A conversion (XN774) arrived at Gütersloh in September 1970. Of the thirty-one aircraft on order, XN975 was never fully completed to F.2A standard, while three other F.2s (XN725, XN734 and XN795) were all effectively partially converted aircraft that had been completed to different standards as part of the variant's test programme. Even though the F.2A was undoubtedly inferior to the later F.6 in terms of overall performance, it was a particularly popular aircraft with pilots, who appreciated its cannon-carrying capability and its surprisingly good range – the F.2A's Avon 211R engines required fewer drag-creating vents and intakes along the fuselage, and pilots claimed un-refuelled endurance at high level of up to 2 hours.

Of course, the Lightning was also developed into a twin-seat trainer variant, designed to incorporate side-by-side seating and dual controls. The T Mk 4 was in effect a direct trainer derivative of the F Mk 2, while the T Mk 5 was a development of the later F Mk 3. The trainer versions retained the same AAM capability and, as such, they could have been used as part of the RAF's combat fleet had they been required, but in service use they were exclusively assigned to training and should not be regarded as part of the fighter's design process as such.

The whole story of the Lightning's illustrious service career is essentially a separate story in itself. Suffice it to say that the aircraft remained in RAF service long after it had been due for retirement. It had many deficiencies, not least a potential for engine fires that caused numerous aircraft losses. It was woefully short on range, but this was rarely an issue when the RAF's refuelling tanker force was on hand to keep it topped up. The aircraft was also under-armed, with only two AAMs (or the addition of cannon on some variants), and no development programme was put into place despite the obvious need for better armament, chiefly because the RAF continually regarded the Lightning as an 'interim' aircraft, even though it defiantly remained in service much longer than any other of the RAF's post-Cold War fighters. Even with limited range, poor armament, barely adequate radar and many serviceability issues, the Lightning was extraordinarily fast, surprisingly agile, easy to fly and, above all, remarkably effective as a short-range interceptor. It remained active in RAF hands because there was not (at least for a long time) anything that could better it. It was not until 1988 that the last two RAF Lightning squadrons disposed of their aircraft, and even then the story was not completely over, as British Aerospace retained a small fleet of Lightnings to act as high-speed target and chase aircraft for the continuing Tornado radar development programme.

The irony of the way in which the Lightning was forced to remain flying (until December 1992) in order to enable its successor to reach an acceptable status was not wasted on the many pilots who cherished every minute at the controls of what was undoubtedly only a partially developed machine, but one that was undoubtedly the fastest and most advanced all-British fighter ever produced. The RAF had consistently regarded the Lightning as a short-term solution to Britain's air defence requirements, and even before it entered service it had suffered at the hands of defence officials and politicians who never quite knew what Britain needed, or when.

It was probably a case of sheer good luck that the Lightning was already so advanced at the time of the 1957 Defence Review, otherwise it seems likely that the aircraft would never have been built at all. But even though it did survive (when many other projects did not), it certainly never realised its true potential. There was never any will (or money) to improve the Lightning's endurance, nor was there any effort to equip the aircraft with better armament. It never seemed worthwhile, because it was always on the verge of retirement – even though the retirement never seemed to arrive. The introduction of the Phantom might have been the logical stage at which the Lightning could have been withdrawn, but with the Phantom being assigned to ground attack and strike duties (at least in the short term), the Lightning stayed in business, and when the Phantom did finally switch to the fighter role, the RAF was still far from eager to dispense with the Lightning entirely. It was only when the Tornado ADV began to reach operational status that the Lightning was finally redundant, even though by this stage the aircraft was undoubtedly obsolete. But even an obsolescent aircraft has to be regarded with more than a little respect when it can easily achieve Mach 2.

CHAPTER ELEVEN

Phantoms and More

During the mid-1960s, Britain's defence capabilities underwent drastic changes that were not directly attributable to the scale or nature of the Soviet threat facing the country. Instead, it was the cost of procurement that became a paramount factor, simply because the UK was facing a growing economic crisis. Britain was almost bankrupt. The realisation that the country could no longer afford the luxury of procuring the most effective defence solutions possible regardless of cost was a proverbially bitter pill that politicians and industrial chiefs were reluctant to swallow, but the infamous TSR2 programme was enough to convince even the most optimistic observers that Britain could no longer indulge in such ambitious programmes when they inevitably ran out of control and consumed almost limitless amounts of money.

Concurrent with the ill-fated TSR2 programme, plans were being made to re-equip the Fleet Air Arm with a new fighter aircraft, intended as a direct replacement for both the Sea Vixen fighter and also the Scimitar strike aircraft. Hawker's P.1154 was an ambitious design, capable of taking off and landing vertically and achieving speeds in excess of Mach 1. The Navy embraced the project with great enthusiasm and Britain's politicians also regarded the aircraft as an exciting venture, particularly because the RAF could also adopt it as a replacement for the Hunter in the ground attack role. The prospect of producing a single aircraft design that met the requirements of both the RAF and RN was too good to resist, and even though the P.1154's performance seemed almost too good to be true (and in some respects it was), it promised to deliver a very capable warplane.

However, far away across the Atlantic in St Louis, McDonnell had produced its outstanding F-4 Phantom and having secured huge orders for its home market, it was inevitable that the company would turn its attention towards potential export customers. Canada and France were approached (unsuccessfully), but Britain's Fleet Air Arm was quickly identified as a very important target customer. McDonnell approached the Royal Navy and the British Government, but although the Phantom did look like an attractive project, it generated no serious interest because the P.1154 was already being developed. McDonnell persisted with its sales efforts, investing a great deal of effort in producing design studies for

Above and below: Models of the ill-fated Hawker P.1154. As can be seen, the proposed naval version was a twin-seat fighter (with a secondary attack capability), while the RAF version was a single-seat attack aircraft, destined to replace the Hunter. After abandonment, the Royal Navy (and eventually the RAF) acquired the Phantom.

a derivative of the F-4B that was suited to the Royal Navy's aircraft carriers. The Navy ostensibly continued to claim that the P.1154 was its preferred choice, but behind the scenes there was a growing interest in the Phantom and over the course of many months the Royal Navy and McDonnell continued to examine ways in which the Phantom might be manufactured for Fleet Air Arm operations.

It might seem odd to note that the Royal Navy was therefore pursuing two projects destined to meet just one requirement, but there was a very clear reason why this situation developed. The advantages of an all-British aircraft were obvious in terms of job creation, but the Admiralty also had the Fleet Air Arm's long-term future firmly in mind. Adopting the P.1154 would result in an aircraft that demonstrably did not require huge aircraft carriers such as the *Ark Royal* or *Eagle*. It seemed quite likely that the country's growing economic difficulties would eventually encourage Whitehall to conclude that without any need for huge aircraft carriers, the Navy's surface fleet could be reduced in size and the P.1154 could be operated from more modest ships. Naturally, the Admiralty did not relish the idea of losing its mighty carriers, and the McDonnell Phantom was an obvious means of ensuring that the Navy would have to keep its existing carrier fleet. In public, the Navy slowly began to express a growing lack of confidence in the P.1154, with issues such as combat effectiveness and the practicality of its PCB (Plenum Chamber Burning) engine being raised. (It was feared that the engine exhaust would destroy the carrier's deck.) However, it was the Navy's preference for the Phantom, rather than the P.1154's alleged unsuitability, that was behind its gradual dismissal of the project.

McDonnell had sent its new F-4B to the Paris Air Show in 1961, and as it was technically necessary to refuel en route in the UK, it was no surprise that RNAS Yeovilton was chosen as the stop-over location, and McDonnell seized the opportunity to show the Navy the outstanding machine that it could obtain. This was probably the point at which the Navy's interest in the Phantom began, but it was not until July 1964 that the Navy finally got its way, and an order for two prototype aircraft was placed. By this stage, the Navy's hostility towards the P.1154 was clear and the continual attempts to pursue a design that met the needs of both the Fleet Air Arm and the RAF were becoming a pointless, time-consuming and expensive exercise. The Government finally accepted that there was no longer any prospect of meeting the Navy's expressed needs with the P.1154 and so the Phantom was adopted, leaving the RAF to pursue the P.1154 in isolation.

By the time of the decision to order the Phantom, McDonnell had already done a great deal of work on modifying the aircraft for British requirements. The F-4J was adopted as the basis for a new version, fitted with Rolls-Royce Spey turbofans, so that the aircraft was better suited to the Fleet Air Arm's relatively small carrier decks. The Spey promised to deliver a 25 per cent increase in thrust, and this would give the aircraft a much better take-off performance whilst also reducing overall fuel consumption. (It would also provide a healthy supply of bleed air for a boundary layer control system.) However, there is no doubt that the primary reason for adopting the Spey was so that the aircraft would be more

A publicity image of what the best-dressed Phantom pilot was wearing during the 1980s. Posing in front of a Phantom from No. 92 Squadron at Wildenrath, the pilot is wearing a NBC (Nuclear, Biological and Chemical) mask attached to a respirator, enabling him to access his aircraft in even the most brutal wartime conditions.

politically acceptable. British engines and many other British components would enable the Government to portray the aircraft as a partially British aircraft, even if it was an American design.

But fitting Speys to the Phantom was far from simple, and the Spey's proportions (and increased intake airflow) required the Phantom's entire centre fuselage to be redesigned. The result was a fuselage that was wider by some 6 inches, intakes that were 20 per cent larger and a deeper, lower fuselage that extended downwards towards the jet exhausts. In effect, it was a new fuselage attached to the Phantom's existing wings, tail and nose, and it was probably inevitable (although nobody seemed to have predicted it) that the modified aircraft would therefore create more drag and negate most of the advantages offered by the Spey. Another important modification was the creation of a new nosewheel gear assembly that had a double-extension facility, raising the aircraft's nose to an alarmingly high angle so that the Phantom could be launched at an increased angle of attack. McDonnell wisely designed this modification in 1963 and tested it on an F-4J, so that the concept was proved well in advance of the British order. It is believed that the US Navy also had some interest in the possibility of adopting a Spey-powered F-4 for use on its smaller Essex-class carriers, although nothing ever came of this idea.

Initially, Britain was offered a very generous 50 per cent work share on the Phantom, so that many components could be built under licence in the UK, as well as the Rolls-Royce engines. This share eventually fell to 40 per cent, and BAC Preston agreed to construct the entire aft section of the aircraft, while Short Bros in Belfast was assigned the manufacture of the outer wing sections. Ferranti was awarded a contract to manufacture the AN/AWG-10 radar, and another thirty primary components were contracted to British companies.

When a new Labour Government assumed power in October 1964, the Phantom programme was under way and the new Defence Minister, Denis Healey, was encouraged to see that the Navy was pursuing what seemed to be a practical off-the-shelf purchase, while the RAF was still awaiting the development of the troubled P.1154. The monstrous TSR2 programme was well advanced by this stage, and although it became Healey's primary cause for concern (it was finally abandoned just six months later), the P.1154 was also another serious issue. The project was already delayed and was becoming increasingly expensive, with no reliable evidence to suggest that it would ever translate into a practical warplane. Healey's instinct was to find a way of cancelling it at the earliest opportunity if a suitable alternative could be found, and the obvious solution was to order a fleet of Phantoms for the RAF as well. Much to Healey's relief, the Air Staff were equally unsure of the P.1154's future and readily accepted that the Phantom would be a good aircraft with which to replace the Hunter in the ground attack role, with the additional possibility that the aircraft could also be re-roled as an air defence fighter at some stage in the future if necessary. The P.1154 was therefore cancelled in February 1965, although Healey fought hard to keep the VTOL concept alive, and pushed Hawker's less-ambitious P.1127 towards fruition in the shape of the legendary Harrier. An order was duly placed for a second version of the Phantom for RAF operations, on 1 July 1965.

However, despite the Air Staff's willingness to abandon the P.1154 in favour of the Phantom, the RAF was far from happy with the aircraft that was ordered. The RAF had proposed a standard F-4C aircraft (albeit with British equipment where possible), powered by General Electric J79 engines. The adoption of Spey engines was regarded as unnecessary for land-based operations, and there was an obvious advantage in buying an aircraft that was already proven to have good performance and good reliability. But the prospect of purchasing a machine almost identical to the Navy's aircraft was too hard to resist, as it would enable an entire fleet to be powered by the same engine and would also reduce the amount of foreign expenditure that the Government would have to make. The RAF reluctantly agreed to accept the F-4M, a direct Spey-engine derivative of the F-4C, while the Navy would receive the F-4K, which was in effect a Spey-powered F-4J.

The first aircraft to be completed, YF-4K XT595, made its first flight from McDonnell's factory site on 27 June 1966 in the hands of test pilot Joe Dobronski. Although most of the Phantom's flight testing had already been completed, the YF-4K had to be tested again in order that the performance of the new engine installation could be examined, together with the aerodynamic properties of the redesigned fuselage. It soon became clear that the Spey 201 did indeed offer much better fuel consumption and a very satisfactory improvement in acceleration at low level. At higher altitudes, however, performance was not so good, being inferior to the F-4J. Throttle response was poor at altitude and the engine exhibited flame pattern fluctuations and unpredictable reheat light-up. Rolls-Royce at Hucknall worked hard to improve the Spey (resulting in the Mk 202) but, of course, there was nothing that could be done to change the aircraft's proportions, not least the destruction of the original F-4J's area-ruled fuselage. The proposed service entry date slipped by two years while the engine problems were resolved, and eventually it was accepted that the F-4K would achieve only Mach 1.9 as an upper altitude limit, compared to the F-4J's Mach 2.1 figure. But the top speed shortfall had to be compared with the advantages that the Spey offered at lower altitudes. For the Royal Navy it meant that the Phantom would be able to operate comfortably from British carrier decks, and for the RAF it meant an aircraft that was undoubtedly superior to the F-4C at lower levels, where the RAF would inevitably operate.

Testing of the first aircraft continued both at Edwards AFB and at Patuxent River NAS, the first aircraft being joined by YF-4K XT596. The third aircraft (XT597) was assigned to carrier trials on board the USS *Saratoga*, and this aircraft became the first 'British' Phantom to arrive in the UK, joining the A&AEE Test Squadron at Boscombe Down during 1977. (It remained in use by the A&AEE until its retirement in 1994, and its engines were subsequently used in the Thrust 2 world land speed record vehicle.) Deck launches and landing trials were conducted at RAE Bedford and subsequently on board HMS *Eagle*, one of two carriers scheduled to be equipped with Phantoms (the other being the *Ark Royal*). Two Phantoms were assigned to trials on board the *Eagle*, and modifications to the carrier had to be made in anticipation of their arrival. Experience on board the USS *Saratoga* had shown how the F-4K's huge downwards-canted engines could cause considerable damage to the carrier deck, with buckling and holes often becoming visible after launches. *Eagle*'s jet blast deflectors were deemed inadequate, so huge steel plates were chained to the carrier's deck behind the catapult launcher in order to minimise the Spey's powerful effects. The deck had to be cooled with fire hoses after each launch.

Initial plans had proposed an order for 143 F-4K Phantoms for the Royal Navy (including prototypes), but the situation changed rapidly as the sheer cost of procurement became clear. With the UK's economic situation deteriorating (and the Dollar exchange rate becoming increasingly poor), the gradual increases in developmental costs were hard to bear and the original order was cut to 137, then to 110, and finally a more drastic cut to just fifty, together with options on a further seven.

In wider terms, the future of the Navy's carrier fleet also became the subject of great scrutiny, particularly when HMS *Victorious* was badly damaged by fire in 1967. Much to the Admiralty's horror, the Government eventually concluded that with much-reduced international commitments (particularly in the Middle East and Far East) the carrier force was unsustainable and that it would be reduced to just one, HMS *Ark Royal*. The much-anticipated all-new CVA-01 aircraft carrier was cancelled and plans to equip HMS *Eagle* for Phantom operations were abandoned in 1968, on the basis that it would have cost some £5 million to modify the carrier for routine Phantom operations. Oddly, the cost of improving the *Ark Royal* was estimated at £32 million, as it was judged to be in poorer condition, but once the decision had been made it was also necessary to reappraise the proposed Phantom order. Consequently, the order for fifty aircraft was readjusted so that fourteen aircraft from the order would go directly to the RAF, even though the F-4K was not fully equipped for the ground attack role or the overland strike role that also arose after the cancellation of the F-111K programme (originally instigated as a replacement for TSR2).

Without the F-4M's Inertial Navigation and Attack System and the capability to carry the SUU-23/A 20 mm cannon pod, the F-4K was effectively only suitable for the air defence role, so a plan was drawn up to form a land-based RAF air defence squadron, specifically to operate the F-4K. For the Navy this was a bitter blow, as not only had the carrier fleet been almost written off (even the *Ark Royal* was slated for withdrawal by the mid-1970s) but the plans for a huge fleet of fleet defence fighters had resulted in enough aircraft to equip just one operational squadron. It seems likely that many Admiralty figures must have questioned the wisdom of pursuing the Phantom programme so enthusiastically in the first place.

The first Phantom deliveries were accepted by No. 700P NAS from June 1968, and by September the unit was proudly displaying the Phantom's agility, its almost brutal proportions and its considerable noise to appreciative crowds at the annual Farnborough SBAC show. With acceptance trials completed, No. 767 NAS became the Phantom training squadron from January 1969, tasked with the training of crews for both the Navy's operational squadron (No. 892 NAS) and the RAF's No. 43 Squadron. In order to complete this task, a handful of aircraft assigned to the RAF were temporarily transferred to Yeovilton, and despite wearing standard RAF grey/green camouflage, they received Fleet Air Arm unit markings on their tails and were used as part of a 'pooled' fleet for training, while No. 43 Squadron formed at Leuchars, where the aircraft would be well placed to perform long-range interception duties far out to the eastern and northern extremities of the United Kingdom Air Defence Region (UKADR).

However, the costs and logistics of conducting training at Yeovilton made little sense when the Navy required crews for only one operational squadron but the RAF would have a larger and longer-term requirement. In 1972, training was therefore transferred to Leuchars and the RAF assumed control, training crews for the Fleet Air Arm as required. No. 892 NAS formed on 31 March 1969, although the refurbishment of HMS *Ark Royal* was not completed until February 1970, so initial carrier qualification training was completed on the USS *Saratoga*. The USN carrier's deck was duly subjected to repeated scorching from the engines of the four Phantoms deployed from the UK, but the co-operation between USN and Fleet Air Arm crews was undoubtedly a good move which fostered good relations that continued for many years. Indeed, the Fleet Air Arm Phantom crews joined their USN counterparts on a series of air defence missions during the Lebanon crisis, and many exchange visits were made between USN carriers and HMS *Ark Royal* until the *Ark*'s sad demise and the disbandment of No. 892 NAS on 15 December 1978.

The RAF's first YF-4M (XT852) completed its maiden flight on 17 February 1967. Naturally, a great deal of the flight testing and systems development was common to both the F-4K and F-4M, but additional attention had to be devoted to the RAF variant's specialised equipment such as the Ferranti INAS and AN/AWG-12 radar. However, most of the trials work was conducted in the UK while the aircraft was being introduced into service, with XV410 assigned to development of the HF radio and XV106 assigned to development of the monstrous reconnaissance pod that was being designed by EMI for the aircraft.

The first UK delivery was XT891 and this aircraft arrived at Aldergrove on 20 July 1968. After final preparation it was subsequently transferred to Coningsby on 23 August as the first aircraft for No. 228 OCU. As the first production Phantom FGR Mk 2 it was (like all of the first twenty-four aircraft built) a 'twin stick' aircraft with duplicated flight controls in the rear cockpit, although the second control column could be removed if necessary, rendering the aircraft virtually identical to its 'one-man' counterparts. Having been designated as the RAF's TSR2 training base, Coningsby had lain dormant for some years after TSR2's cancellation. It was an ideal choice for the new OCU, and became the RAF's main Phantom base for almost another twenty years.

While the RAF began the introduction of the Phantom into service at Coningsby, the Fleet Air Arm seized a golden opportunity to demonstrate the

At Coningsby shortly after delivery to the RAF, Phantom FGR Mk 2 XV465 went on to fly with UK- and Germany-based squadrons before being withdrawn from use at RAF Leeming in 1981. (*Tony Clarke collection*)

aircraft's capabilities to the British public on a grand scale. The 1969 Daily Mail Transatlantic Air Race was arranged to commemorate the fiftieth anniversary of the first non-stop crossing of the Atlantic by Alcock and Brown, and both the RAF and Royal Navy were invited to participate in the event, which called for crews to race from the top of the Empire State Building in New York to the top of the Post Office Tower in London. The RAF decided to use Harriers for the race, realising that the aircraft's unique VTOL ability would enable its crew member to land in the very heart of London and New York, while the competing Navy team would have to rely on a helicopter for parts of the race. The Navy did not really have any alternative to the Phantom, but with its supersonic speed it looked more than a match for the subsonic Harrier.

Beginning on 4 May 1969, the Fleet Air Arm allocated three Phantoms to the race (XT860, XT861 and XT858), its transatlantic dashes starting at Floyd Bennett NAS in New York and ending at BAC's Wisley airfield to the south-west of London. The three Phantom runs achieved a best time of 4 hours and 46 minutes from runway to runway, although service regulations on the continuous use of reheat had to be exceeded in order to make good time. The Navy's point-to-point best time was 5 hours and 11 minutes, some 20 minutes better than the Harrier's best, even with the distinct advantage of being able to land in downtown Manhattan and in a yard adjacent to St Pancras station. The winning Phantom (XT858) achieved an average true air speed of 1,100 mph.

The Royal Navy's Phantoms then began a short but successful service life with No. 892 NAS on board HMS *Ark Royal*, returning to RAF Leuchars as their shore base between cruises. The aircraft were hugely popular with the Fleet Air Arm crews who were lucky to fly them and despite being used intensively for a decade, few serious accidents occurred. The first loss was XV566, which crashed into Lyme Bay in May 1970 whilst being operated as a target aircraft for interception practice as part of the Phantom's initial intensive flying trials. Two Phantoms were lost off the Cornish coast near Newquay on two separate occasions, XT862 being the first (May 1971), followed by XT876 in January 1972. XV565 crashed off Florida in June 1971, and XT871 was destroyed on 25 July 1973 when the aircraft launched from HMS *Ark Royal* to recover to nearby Leuchars. Engine failure at the critical moment of launch resulted in the aircraft ditching off the carrier's bow into the Firth of Forth, the crew completing their journey in a rescue Wessex helicopter. XT869 crashed on approach to Leuchars in October 1971, and XV588 was abandoned near Leuchars after an engine fire developed shortly after take-off. The last Fleet Air Arm Phantom loss was XT868, this aircraft being destroyed during a practice air display at Abingdon, the aircraft's wing clipping the ground during a low manoeuvre on 12 May 1978. The list of losses makes grim reading, but for an aircraft that was flown hard and flown regularly for ten years in some very harsh environments, it was a record that the Navy was satisfied with.

By 1977, the end was in sight for the Navy's Phantoms, but in typical naval fashion there was no prospect of retiring with a whimper. For the Silver Jubilee Royal Review of the Royal Navy at Spithead, most of No. 892 NAS's Phantoms were suitably decorated with stylish red and white flashes across their radomes, and despite foul weather the aircraft took to the skies for what was in effect their last major public appearance. Just a year later, HMS *Ark Royal* had reached the end of its useful life, and on 27 November No. 892 NAS delivered its first aircraft (XT864) to RAF St Athan, ready for hand-over to the RAF. Proudly wearing 'Fly Navy' titles on its fuselage, it was the first of a series of deliveries, and on 15 December the unit disbanded, ending the Navy's happy association with the Phantom. It was somewhat ironic that the Royal Navy eventually had to transfer its much-loved Phantoms to the RAF, when the RAF had been quite ambivalent when it was first offered the aircraft. There was certainly no reason why the Navy's Phantoms could not have continued in service for at least another decade, but without a carrier to fly them from, their future was decided. It was, of course, a real tragedy that in 1982 the Fleet Air Arm went to war and had to rely on Sea Harriers to provide air superiority over the Falklands, when a truly magnificent fleet defender had literally been given away just four years previously.

For the RAF, the story of the Phantom was a far longer one, and was undoubtedly a good one too. No. 228 OCU at Coningsby, swiftly built up during 1969, was tasked with the training of all future Phantom crews, although training on the FG Mk 1 was performed by the Phantom Training Flight at Leuchars. At this stage, the aircraft was assigned to the ground attack role, although it was also slated to assume the overland nuclear strike role in Germany too, while two specialised units would operate the aircraft in the reconnaissance role. However, many miles to the north at Leuchars, the RAF also received 'surplus' naval Phantom FG Mk 1 aircraft that had originally been ordered for carriers that the Navy would not now have. These aircraft were not entirely suitable for the attack role, so were used to form an air defence unit, No. 43 Squadron becoming established on 1 September 1969.

With two Lightning air defence squadrons already operating from Leuchars, the Phantoms were also assigned to the northern regions of the UKADR, and it soon became clear that despite the Lightning's outstanding performance, the Phantom was a far more suitable aircraft for the air defence task. Although it could not quite match the Lightning's top speed or altitude, the Phantom was no slouch by any means, but with a two-man crew, a much more effective radar, a vastly superior fuel capacity and a blistering array of eight Sidewinder and Sparrow missiles plus a 20 mm cannon at its disposal, the mighty Phantom completely outclassed the Lightning in terms of its fighting ability. The aircraft were soon integrated into the RAF's air defence network, and No. 43 Squadron's aircraft regularly intercepted Soviet Bears, Coots and Badgers far out over the North Sea and in the Faroes-Iceland gap.

The RAF's early experience of the Phantom in the air defence role certainly augured well for the future, when it was anticipated that the Phantom FGR Mk 2 fleet would also be reassigned to air defence when the Lightning force reached its retirement date. The process began late in 1974, when No. 111 Squadron acquired Phantoms from No. 54 Squadron, which disbanded earlier in the year, in preparation for re-equipment with Jaguars. The Phantoms moved north from Coningsby to Leuchars and formed the second RAF air defence Phantom unit, enabling the resident No. 23 Squadron to relinquish its Lightnings and re-form on Phantoms at Coningsby. This complicated 'shuffle' was a welcome move, as the RAF was keen to get more Phantoms into the air defence role. Even with eighteen aircraft at its disposal, No. 43 Squadron was hard-pressed to maintain all of its commitments in an air defence region that was (at that time) continually busy with Soviet incursions. No. 111 Squadron's Phantoms were, of course, FGR Mk 2 models, but they were easily adapted for fighter operations. They remained with the squadron until 1980, by which stage the Fleet Air Arm's Phantoms had been refurbished and issued to No. 111 Squadron so that both of the Leuchars units could standardise on the same variant. The station was still extremely busy even by this stage, and during one week in 1980, No. 111 Squadron performed 100 interceptions.

The two Leuchars Phantom FG Mk 1 squadrons remained in business for many years, and throughout their time in Scotland they were inevitably very busy, although time was made for a crew to practise an annual air display routine seen by countless spectators across the UK and beyond. The sight and sound of No. 43 Squadron's Phantom, complete with black and white chequerboard markings and 'fighting cock' on its tail became a highlight for many air shows, and for those who were lucky enough to see the mighty beast performing aerobatics at low level, the display was something that was not easily forgotten.

Having operated its FG1s as intensively as the Navy, it was no surprise that by the late 1980s some of the aircraft were beginning to show signs of fatigue. In December 1987, XV575 was found to be suffering from a series of structural faults, rendering the aircraft unfit for further use. Just months later, many of the FG1s were withdrawn and replaced by FGR Mk 2s drawn from other units, but this was essentially a short-term measure, as the end of Phantom operations was by now in sight, the Tornado F Mk 2 and F Mk 3 having entered RAF service. No. 43 Squadron completed its last Phantom flight on 31 July 1989, and No. 111 Squadron flew its last aircraft (the all-black XV582) for the very last time on 22 September 1990. By this stage, the surviving Leuchars Phantoms had made their way to Wattisham, where they were unceremoniously reduced to a crumpled heap of scrap metal.

The first Phantom FGR Mk 2 squadron formed at Coningsby in May 1969, No. 6 Squadron taking crews from the first OCU course. No. 54 Squadron followed in September and both units were assigned to No. 38 Group, tasked with ground attack duties in direct support of Army units as part of the UK Mobile Force. For this role the Phantom was equipped with a variety of weapons including 1,000 lb conventional HE bombs, SNEB rocket pods and Hunting BL755 cluster bombs, together with the monstrous 20 mm SUU-23/A cannon pod carried under the aircraft's belly. Of course, the Phantom could also carry four Sparrow missiles in the purpose-designed recesses under the fuselage, and this endowed the aircraft with a very useful self-defence capability that could be enhanced by the carriage of Sidewinder missiles if necessary.

Declared to NATO's SACEUR (Supreme Allied Commander Europe), the two Phantom squadrons were also committed to UK operations and so the units spent a great deal of time deployed away from Coningsby, either on exercises in Europe or further afield in Singapore, Malta or Cyprus. In August 1974, No. 6 Squadron's Phantoms flew to Akrotiri just 10 hours after notification, as part of Britain's response to the Turkish invasion of Cyprus. No. 54 Squadron duly followed, demonstrating the RAF's impressive rapid reinforcement capability. The two Coningsby squadrons were then followed by Nos 14, 17 and 31 Squadrons, which were based in Germany, assigned to the nuclear strike role. In addition to similar ground attack duties performed by the UK squadrons, the RAF Germany Phantoms assumed the strike role that had hitherto been performed by Canberras, and as the Canberra fleet was withdrawn, the role was shifted to Phantoms based at Brüggen, armed with the same American tactical nuclear weapons that had been supplied (under a 'dual key' arrangement) for the Canberra units, these being the B28, B43, B57 and B61 bombs. Buccaneers were also assigned to this role, but the Phantoms were primarily tasked with the destruction of advancing Warsaw Pact forces within shorter range, the deep strike task being assigned to the Buccaneers. No. 14 Squadron stood up in June 1970, followed by Nos 17 and 31 Squadrons, and all three squadrons remained active in this vitally important role until Jaguar aircraft began to reach RAF Germany from 1974 onwards.

Although the Phantoms could carry up to three nuclear bombs at any time, only one was normally carried for QRA duties, and a 28 lb training store was usually carried for peacetime training, this store being capable of mimicking the ballistics of the full-size nuclear weapon. A fourth RAFG squadron also formed, but this unit was tasked primarily with reconnaissance, using a purpose-built centreline pod developed by EMI. With an array of four F135 cameras, an infra-red linescan system and a flash unit, the pod gave No. 2 Squadron's Phantoms an outstanding capability, and a second unit (No. 41 Squadron) was duly formed at Coningsby in April 1972, assigned to the same reconnaissance role. Nos 54 and 31 Squadrons were also given reconnaissance as a secondary capability, although only a few aircraft were modified to carry the reconnaissance equipment.

The arrival of the first Jaguar aircraft in 1974 enabled the process of withdrawing the Phantom from the attack roles to begin. Coningsby's Nos 54 and 6 Squadrons re-formed on Jaguars, followed by the RAFG squadrons and finally No. 41 Squadron in March 1977. The OCU's training system switched to air defence operations and No. 29 Squadron re-formed at Coningsby in the air defence role. Nos 23 and 56 squadrons followed, before moving south to Wattisham. Having become part of No. 11 Group, Coningsby joined Leuchars and Wattisham as part of an overall air defence chain, together with Binbrook, where the last Lightning

One of No. 29 Squadron's fleet for some considerable time, Phantom FGR Mk 2 XV399 was withdrawn from use during the early 1990s and sold as scrap, although its nose section survived with a private owner in Norway.

squadrons remained in business. All four bases maintained aircraft on QRA alert, although the majority of 'live' scrambles were inevitably performed by the two Leuchars units, these being significantly closer to the region where incursions usually occurred.

Meanwhile, two squadrons of Phantoms were reassigned to Germany, this time dedicated to air defence rather than ground attack. Nos 19 and 92 Squadrons (both based at Wildenrath) were former Lightning units from Gütersloh. Assigned to 2 ATAF, they were given responsibility for the defence of airspace reaching from West Germany out to the boundary of the UKADR over the North Sea. Their role was slightly different to that of the UK units in that most missions (including training) were conducted at low level, at an altitude that would be beneath the Nike missile belt that extended across the region. Sorties were also shorter-ranged, as the expected threat was not from Soviet long-range bombers but from Warsaw Pact aircraft approaching from East Germany.

The Phantom performed well in its new role in Germany, although its suitability for operations in that region is arguable. Some crews regarded the aircraft as less than ideal for low-level air defence, as the aircraft was obviously not designed for flight at heights of 500 feet or less. On the other hand, the Spey engines gave it an excellent performance at low level, and its good fuel capacity enabled the fighter force to be moved away from the border region where the aircraft would have been at a much greater risk from surprise attack. Wildenrath's Phantoms maintained continual QRA, and most commentators believed that if an East-West conflict had occurred, these aircraft would have been the first to engage the enemy.

However, the closest that the RAF's Phantom force ever came to a real conflict was as a result of the 1982 Falklands crisis, when No. 29 Squadron was tasked with supplying a three-aircraft detachment to Ascension Island during April, relieving Harriers that had been temporarily assigned to the task. The three aircraft maintained air defence cover for the region and during their stay on the island were scrambled on numerous occasions to investigate both surface targets and unidentified aircraft in the area. Their most notable intercept occurred on 11 July, when two Soviet Tu-142 aircraft were found monitoring the return of Task Force elements from the South Atlantic. The Phantom detachment ended on 20 July, but by September the Phantoms of No. 29 Squadron were again back at Ascension, this time en route to the Falklands, now that the landing strip at Stanley had been extended to enable Phantoms to operate from the site. Nine aircraft arrived in October and remained at Stanley until July 1992, by which stage No. 29 Squadron had given way to No. 23 Squadron, and finally the smaller No. 1435 Flight. Rather than return the aircraft to the UK for retirement, they stayed at their second Falklands home at the newly built RAF Mount Pleasant and were eventually cut up as scrap (apart from one example that was retained as a static display).

Phantom flying over the Falklands was particularly challenging, as although there were few opportunities to intercept targets other than other RAF aircraft, the weather conditions were often appalling. Until RAF Mount Pleasant was completed, recoveries to Stanley also required the use of arrestor gear, as the runway was too short to comfortably accommodate a Phantom, even with its brake parachute applied. Despite these challenges, RAF crews relished the opportunity to fly it over the South Atlantic, especially when there were plenty of opportunities to operate the aircraft to its limits, far away from the restrictions of European airspace.

The need for Phantoms in the South Atlantic had a direct effect upon the capabilities of the UK air defence force, and in order to redress the sudden shortage of fighters, the RAF looked at the possibility of acquiring 'second-hand' Phantoms from the US. Of course, there were no other Spey-powered derivatives in existence, but surplus examples of American examples were certainly available, with countless examples resting in open storage at Davis-Monthan AFB in Arizona. From a political perspective, the concept of purchasing standard F-4 models powered by J79 engines was not difficult, as few people outside of RAF Strike Command understood the fundamental differences between the British Phantom and its American counterparts. A Phantom was a Phantom after all. But in practical terms, the standard F-4 was in effect a completely different machine – with different performance, different equipment and different handling qualities – and an off-the-shelf purchase of any available fighter type would have been equally practical. However, it transpired that the F-4 was the swiftest and cheapest solution, and after the RAF's Vice Chief of Staff visited the US, a batch of fifteen F-4J aircraft was purchased at a cost of £125 million, including all support for a projected service life of five years.

The aircraft were transported out of Davis-Monthan AFB to North Island NAS, where they were refurbished and modified for RAF operations. Modifications effectively brought the aircraft up to F-4S standard, although the provision for wing leading edge slats was not taken up in order to keep costs low. Compatibility with the Skyflash missile was introduced (this missile replaced the Sparrow on the Phantom FG Mk1 and FGR Mk 2) and new zero-houred J79-GE-10B engines were fitted. The aircraft's ejection seats were also subsequently replaced by later models compatible with the existing RAF fleet. After all of the necessary modifications were made, the aircraft were essentially as new, although they were, of course, old airframes, some even having served in Vietnam. However, they were deemed suitable for at least five years of operations, by which stage the Tornado F Mk 3 was expected to be in regular RAF service and the F-4J could be withdrawn.

RAF crews were trained with VMAT 101 at Yuma Marine Corps Air Station, and the first completed F-4J(UK) was rolled out on 10 August 1984. By January 1985, all fifteen aircraft had made their long transatlantic flights via Goose Bay and supported by VC10 tankers. No. 74 Squadron re-formed at Wattisham to operate the aircraft and within a matter of months the F-4J had become an integral part of the UK's air defence system.

Naturally, the F-4J was a very different plane to the F-4K and F-4M, although its differences were mostly positive. The F-4J's starting system was an issue that

No. 74 Squadron was the last RAF unit to operate the mighty Phantom, although at least two aircraft carried the markings of both Nos 74 and 56 Squadrons (as illustrated) during the type's last year on the UK air display circuit.

caused logistical problems and some components were specific to the variant, most notably those connected to the engines but also other items such as the main wheels, which did not have an anti-skid system (obviously unnecessary on a carrier). This meant that on wet runways, many landings had to be completed courtesy of an arrestor barrier. Less obvious differences were smaller items, not least the aircrew's flying clothing and helmets, and the instrument layout in the navigator's cockpit, which was completely different. However, navigators in the F-4J had a much better outside view, with fewer pieces of equipment stuffed into every available recess. For the pilots, the F-4J was a delight. Despite being old, the aircraft performed exceptionally well, being capable of reaching 60,000 feet, while the RAF's F-4M struggled to maintain 45,000 feet. The AWG-10B radar was also highly regarded, and even though it did not match the F-4M's AGW-12 performance at very close range, it was judged to be superior. Likewise, the FGR Mk 2 and FG Mk 1 fleet had eventually been restricted to a 3 g stress limit with external stores carried. By comparison, the F-4J was usually flown 'clean' or with a single centreline tank, enabling the aircraft to withstand 6 g manoeuvres. Even though the INAS, ILS and other useful British equipment were not fitted, the F-4Js were regarded as 'hot rods' by the lucky pilots who were able to fly them. They remained active with No. 74 Squadron until late in 1990, when it was accepted that the growing scarcity of spares and the greater availability of FGR Mk 2 airframes (which were now being retired) made the operation of a non-standard variant unnecessary, and No. 74 Squadron duly re-equipped with Phantom FGR Mk 2 aircraft, the much-loved F-4Js being removed for disposal, despite having many hours of flying left in their airframes. Their withdrawal made financial sense, but for the pilots it was a sad loss.

The existing fleet of Phantom FG Mk 1 and FGR Mk 2 aircraft continued to serve in the air defence role for many years, and when the Tornado F Mk 2 began to suffer seemingly endless problems with radar development, it looked as if the Phantom fleet would be required to continue in service for much longer than had been envisaged. Some seventy-five aircraft were re-winged from 1987 onwards in order to provide them with additional airframe life, but the gradual withdrawal process began on 1 December 1986, with No. 29 Squadron standing down in preparation for re-equipment with the Tornado. The Phantom OCU moved north to Leuchars so that Coningsby could be prepared to become the RAF's main Tornado F Mk 2/3 base, and Nos 43 and 111 Squadron then exchanged their Phantom FG Mk 1s for Tornado F Mk 3s, and by January 1990, the F-4K had finally been completely withdrawn apart from XT579, which remained in use with the A&AEE. The two RAF Germany Phantom units (Nos 19 and 92 Squadrons) disbanded late in 1991, but they did not re-equip with Tornado F.3s, as the situation in Europe had changed drastically; with the Cold War effectively at an end, there was no longer any obvious need for the RAF's interceptors in that region. The last two units to say goodbye to the Phantom were Nos 56 and 74 Squadrons at Wattisham, the former disbanding in June 1992, followed by No. 74 Squadron at the end of September.

Plans were made to place some examples in storage as a 'combat reserve', but with a much-reduced need for fighter aircraft in the post-Cold War era, and the new Tornado F.3 settling into service, the idea was dropped and the Phantoms were sent off to various locations to end their days as gate guardians, museum exhibits, or as piles of scrap metal. The A&AEE's XT597, which had been the first British Phantom to make a carrier deck landing (during the initial trials in 1968), earned the distinction of becoming the very last active British Phantom, making its last flight on 28 January 1994, ending the type's distinguished service career that had been longer and far more successful than anyone could have predicted.

The Phantom proved itself as an excellent fighter and interceptor and had also given the RAF an excellent attack platform that bridged an important gap between the outdated Canberra and Hunter and the all-new Jaguar. The RAF's association with the Phantom had been an entirely satisfactory story, although it was perhaps a less than joyous tale for the Royal Navy – the service that fought so hard to get the Phantom and then had almost its entire fleet snatched away, left with only one squadron of aircraft with which to operate for only a decade. The Air Staff chiefs must have raised a smile if they ever considered how the aircraft which the Navy effectively forced upon them by proxy became such a versatile, valuable and capable warplane.

Of course, the Phantom was not the end of the Royal Navy's association with fixed-wing warfare. Before the Phantom, naval interest had concentrated on the abortive P.1154 – a machine that had the potential to become a formidable multi-role aircraft. But with a fixated interest in conventional aircraft (which fostered the notion that large aircraft carriers remained essential), the Royal Navy had embraced the Phantom and the prospect of a new-build carrier to augment the four that were already in service. Any project which contradicted the notion of a strong fleet of carriers was doomed from the outset, and it was only when Britain's costs and political considerations changed that the Harrier's maritime fortunes shifted. The Government, desperate to make cost savings, finally abandoned Britain's planned new carrier and announced that the other existing carriers would also be progressively withdrawn, and with them all of the Navy's fixed-wing air power too. This was a massive blow to the Royal Navy, from which it took many years to recover, and it was only through the adoption of the Harrier that the Navy succeeded in its ambition to remain in the fixed-wing combat aircraft business.

In some respects, it was surprising that the Navy had taken so little interest in the P.1127 when it first emerged, but in fairness it must also be accepted that the P.1127 was first regarded as a 'proof of concept' design and then as a potential ground support aircraft, and neither was of any direct relevance to the Navy's perceived future. The Navy required much more than a simple military support aircraft and would inevitably need a fleet defence fighter too; therefore it was only when the P.1154 emerged that there seemed any realistic prospect of developing a multi-role aircraft that could meet all of the Navy's requirements. But as has been said, the prospect of buying Phantoms proved to be irresistible. However, when the carriers were suddenly abandoned (together with the Phantoms and Buccaneers that would have operated from them) the Navy had to drastically reappraise its situation.

It was assumed that the RAF would undertake future maritime missions and that its Harriers might also somehow go to sea. Precisely how, on what vessels, and for what precise purpose was never properly established, nor did anyone question how the relatively small Harrier force could be expected to undertake its assigned roles in support of NATO and in Germany, and also take on a maritime commitment at the same time. But despite this, No. 1 Squadron was cleared for ship deployment early in 1971, even though it did not take too long to realise that sustained operations at sea would not be possible. No. 1 Squadron was assigned to wartime deployment in Norway and it could hardly be in two places at once. Likewise, the squadron had no capability to operate in the air defence role even if it had been able to handle two operational tasks at the same time. It was obvious that a dedicated maritime Harrier force was the only practical solution to Britain's needs.

It took until 1971 before the Navy finally embraced what was first referred to as the Maritime Support Harrier (this was subsequently abbreviated to Maritime

The Navy's Sea Harriers were delivered directly from Dunsfold in a smart grey and white paint scheme (and full-colour national insignia), and within days they were adorned with flamboyant unit markings. The beginning of the 1982 Falklands Conflict suddenly saw the Sea Harriers reappear in dark camouflage with toned down insignia.

Harrier and then Sea Harrier). Exploration of precisely what this aircraft would be took place over many months and included a variety of potentially exciting options, including the use of a new 25,000 lb Pegasus engine being developed by Rolls-Royce at Bristol, and the employment of various weapons systems. However, it was also obvious to the Navy that there was very little money available, and whatever the Sea Harrier was to be, it would have to be something relatively modest if it was ever to be financed, not least because there was also the fundamental issue of which ships the Harrier would operate from – and the considerable cost that these would incur. In fact, the ships appear to have been openly considered before the Harriers, and it was in 1969 that the concept of a through-deck cruiser was first proposed by the RN Ship Department at Bath. This vessel was to be assigned to three main tasks: the deployment of anti-submarine helicopters, the command and control of naval and maritime air forces, and a 'contribution to air defence'. This latter category was vague, but it seems likely that this was the first indirect reference to the notion of reintroducing fixed-wing air power into the Navy, even if nobody had the will to specify overtly such a capability.

There was clearly not the slightest chance of restoring the conventional carrier force, but the prospect of creating a 'mini carrier' with a fleet of maritime Harriers evidently seemed far preferable to the prospect of having nothing at all, and the Royal Navy believed that it stood a good chance of persuading the Government to finance such a proposal – especially if every opportunity was taken to portray the idea as being completely different from (or at least far less ambitious than) the accepted concept of carrier power. The RAF, however, smelled a proverbial rat, and disputed the Navy's claims that any new aircraft carriers were needed or that an aircraft was needed for defence of the fleet. Indeed, it asked (with tongue firmly in cheek) what fleet was to be protected, and precisely how much defence could be attained by maybe a dozen Harriers that would be facing maybe hundreds of supersonic, missile-armed Soviet bombers. More to the point (as far as the RAF was concerned), the introduction of Sea Harriers might convince politicians (who probably would not know any better) that the Navy was somehow capable of defending itself, and this might lead to the abandonment of orders for an air defence variant of the Tornado – a project regarded as far more important. But the Sea Harrier concept persisted and it was agreed that the Royal Navy could pursue a Naval Staff Target for a minimum-change version of the existing Harrier, redesigned to achieve air defence ability over a range of up to 400 nm at altitude, reconnaissance ability over an area of 20,000 square miles within one hour at low level, and a strike and ground attack capability with a radius of action extending to 250 nm. In effect, this specification outlined a truly multi-role aircraft albeit with a fairly modest capability, but one that could be successfully operated from a through-deck cruiser.

The changes to the Harrier airframe were divided between those necessary to meet these specified demands and those required for operation to and from a carrier. For the former category, the weapons system was revised to incorporate a Smiths HUD driven by digital computer, combining air-to-air and air-to-surface weapon aiming capacity. Also included was a self-aligning attitude-reference platform, and a radar in the shape of Ferranti's Blue Fox which was developed from the Seaspray system used in the Lynx helicopter. Modified for the air-to-air and air-to-surface requirements of the Harrier, it was also suitable for the hostile ECM environment in which the aircraft was expected to operate. Good though the new radar was, a plan to incorporate radar information into the HUD was dropped due to cost considerations, and the radar's display became a head-down TV screen inside the cockpit. Most of the new equipment was designed to be self-checking, and most fault diagnosis could be achieved without external equipment and easily fixed by replacement of the appropriate module. The five weapons pylons were similar to those fitted to the RAF's Harrier GR3 but with stronger release units. Compatibility with a wide range of weapons was incorporated from the start, including Sidewinder (outboard pylons), Martel and Harpoon. Perhaps most significantly, the Sea Harrier was afforded a strike function and was cleared to carry the WE.177 nuclear store, giving the aircraft a destructive capability far beyond its more typical ground attack capacity. For carrier operations, other changes were incorporated, such as the removal of many magnesium components that would suffer from salt corrosion and the incorporation of deck tie-downs (later fitted to RAF Harriers for operations in the Falklands). The other (and most obvious) change to the Harrier airframe was the redesign of the forward fuselage necessitated by the new radar. The larger nose profile provided an opportunity to raise the cockpit and canopy so that it emerged beyond the height of the upper fuselage, thereby affording the pilot greatly improved all-round vision, which enhanced the Sea Harrier's potential as a fighter. This became a feature common to all subsequent Harrier developments.

In 1975, the Admiralty formally redesignated its new through-deck cruisers as 'command cruisers' in the shape of HMS *Ark Royal*, HMS *Illustrious* and HMS *Invincible*, each of which would ultimately accommodate six Sea Harriers. It was envisaged that two of these carriers might be deployed simultaneously, so with this in mind and a requirement for shore-based training, an order for thirty-one aircraft was issued (the total order eventually rose to fifty-seven aircraft) together with three development aircraft, designated Sea Harrier FRS Mk 1. Such was the Government's indecisiveness, it was not until May 1975 that this order was finally placed. The initial contract for design study had been issued in 1972, but with issues such as a fuel crisis, the 'three-day week' and high inflation, progress slowed until both customer and manufacturer began to accept that the order might never be placed at all. It was therefore something of a surprise to both Hawker Siddeley and the Navy when Defence Minister Roy Mason finally gave the go-ahead.

The first development aircraft to be completed (XZ439) took to the air, still unpainted in yellow primer, on 20 August 1978 in the hands of John Farley. Used primarily for handling trials, it was subsequently assigned to stores clearance work that largely revolved around the release of unguided bombs and rocket pods, although the Sea Eagle missile had also been envisaged as part of Sea Harrier's inventory for some time. Even before the Sea Harrier was manufactured (and before Sea Eagle became available), trials with a Harrier GR3 were flown using a Martel round (precursor to the Sea Eagle, using the same missile body) with a balancing store on the other wing. It was demonstrated that the Harrier could hover and land vertically in this configuration (a fairly heavy store for the diminutive Harrier) and test pilot Farley successfully fired a Martel round to demonstrate that the missile's exhaust plume did not affect the performance of the Pegasus engine.

On 26 March 1979, HMS *Invincible* commenced sea trials, and the first Sea Harrier unit – No. 700A NAS – was commissioned on 18 September at RNAS Yeovilton in Somerset, having taken delivery of Sea Harrier XZ451. This unit eventually operated the first five production Sea Harriers and after completing its role as the Intensive Flying Trials Unit it became No. 899 NAS – the Navy's shore-based training unit. The three operational squadrons (Nos 800, 801 and 802) followed on as production of more Sea Harriers was completed. Oddly, no twin-seat derivative of the Sea Harrier was ordered, the Navy having concluded that specialist training for STOVL deck operations was not necessary. Conversion training onto the Harrier was undertaken by the RAF's OCU at Wittering and one of this unit's Harrier T4As (XZ455) was funded by the Navy as part of this arrangement. However, a handful of former RAF Harrier T4s were eventually transferred to No. 899 NAS at Yeovilton and redesignated as the Harrier T4N, with three new-build aircraft subsequently delivered directly to the Navy, enabling No. 899 NAS eventually to assume all naval conversion training on the type.

Having barely settled into service, the Navy's Sea Harriers were soon in action. Initial Operational Capability had just been achieved by early 1982, but as the crisis in the South Atlantic unfolded, the creation of a Task Force with which to recapture the Falkland Islands quickly emerged. It was obvious that the very core of this force would be carrier power, and therefore the Sea Harrier, as this was the only combat aircraft that Britain could deploy in the South Atlantic. The RAF's Vulcan bombers could be (and were) operated as a strategic asset, flying attack missions to and from Ascension Island, but this required a complicated and hugely expensive (and risky) journey over thousands of miles for each sortie. More to the point, the Vulcans could not operate in theatre and could not directly support ground troops. Likewise, they could not provide any air defence capability.

The RAF's Phantoms, Tornados, Buccaneers and Jaguars all required an airfield from which to operate, and until the islands could be retaken no such facility existed. Carrier aircraft were the only solution, and the Sea Harrier (supported by RAF Harriers) was the only option that Britain had. Of course, the Sea Harrier was never intended to be operated in the South Atlantic. Designed to operate primarily as part of NATO, it was expected to counter Soviet bombers or carrier-borne Yak-38s. Nobody imagined that the Sea Harrier would ever be expected to

An interesting scene on the deck of HMS *Hermes* during the Falklands Conflict, with two Sea Harriers on view, one painted in dark grey 'low-level' camouflage, while the other wears 'air defence' light grey. In the foreground is a RAF Harrier GR Mk 3.

fight Mirages. Even more alarming was the disturbing fact that the Navy did not even have any AEW cover, its ageing (but adequate) Gannets having been retired some years previously when the last conventional carrier (the *Ark Royal*) had been withdrawn.

It was a perilous prospect, but with no other option available the assembled Task Force set sail with every available Sea Harrier (twenty-four aircraft) embarked on board HMS *Hermes* and HMS *Invincible*. History records that both the RAF's Harrier GR3s and the Navy's Sea Harriers achieved great success in the weeks that followed. It is true that the Argentine pilots were obliged to operate their aircraft at the very limits of their fuel endurance, which prevented them from engaging in any significant air combat over the Falklands, but it is equally true that the skill and professionalism of the British pilots was a deciding factor in what seemed (at least to Britain) like an inevitable victory. In fact, it was a close-run affair and it was a combination of ingenuity, hard work, planning, skill and sheer good luck that enabled the British forces to prevail, but the Harrier was, of course, the key asset.

Various last-minute upgrades were made to the aircraft. For example, the all-important AIM-9L Sidewinder was not even cleared for Sea Harrier use at the beginning of April 1982; an emergency programme provided clearance in just a matter of days. Likewise, the aircraft's chaff and flare dispensers were not fitted at the start of the deployment south and had to be dropped by parachute for fitment en route. But despite so many shortcomings and disadvantages, the Sea Harriers enabled crews to achieve the downing of twenty-two enemy aircraft (plus a helicopter) at the expense of only two losses, both of which were due to ground fire. Only four more aircraft were lost due to other accidents. The Falklands crisis demonstrated clearly the value of carrier power and the versatility of the diminutive, unsophisticated but disproportionately potent Sea Harrier.

Naturally, the Falklands experience enabled the Navy to re-evaluate the Sea Harrier's effectiveness, and plans for future improvements were revised accordingly. It had been envisaged that a radical re-winged Sea Harrier design would eventually be procured, but when a similar plan being pursued by the RAF was dropped in 1980, it seemed clear that the Sea Harrier's development would have to be more modest. Most importantly, the sinking of HMS *Sheffield* and the *Atlantic Conveyor* had demonstrated that a look-down radar capability was essential and that both aircraft and sea-skimming missile detection would be a priority. It was also evident that the AIM-9L missile (and the 30 mm cannon) required Sea Harrier pilots to manoeuvre at close range if they were to successfully acquire a target, and the aircraft was not designed to be a dogfighter.

Despite a great deal of ill-informed media hype (which often portrayed the Sea Harrier as a latter-day Spitfire) the combat pilots had a more realistic picture of the aircraft's capabilities, with its relatively poor thrust (compared to modern purpose-built fighters) and a high wing loading that restricted the aircraft's turning ability. The Harrier's unique viffing ability was certainly an asset, but vectoring the aircraft's thrust inevitably resulted in a significant loss of energy and although it gave pilots a formidable self-defence capability, it was of only limited use in terms of pressing home an attack. Thankfully for Britain, the Argentine pilots had been equipped with aircraft that were relatively old and without the advantage of a good BVR (Beyond Visual Range) radar and missile capacity, and which they were obliged to operate at distances that used every drop of available fuel. Clearly, this balance of capabilities could not be relied upon for every conceivable conflict.

A Mid Life Update programme was therefore embarked upon, and in the meantime a more immediate Phase One update was initiated, for completion in 1987. This gave the Sea Harrier some important improvements, most notably the incorporation of twin Sidewinder launch rails, thereby doubling the aircraft's missile capacity. A new 'nozzle inching' facility was introduced to enable the pilot to trim the engine nozzle position by a further 10 degrees to provide additional deceleration, and a new MADGE (Microwave Aircraft Digital Guidance Equipment) system was installed, roughly equivalent to the more common ILS fitted to many combat aircraft, enabling the Sea Harrier to recover in poor weather without a talk-down facility.

Development of the Sea Eagle missile continued and it entered service in 1987, providing the Sea Harrier with an outstanding fire-and-forget system that could be employed against surface targets at long range. More Sea Harrier FRS Mk 1 aircraft were ordered, largely to replace those that had been lost (a total of seventeen by this stage) and, at long last, an AEW system was reacquired for the fleet, courtesy of the Sea King AEW.2. Of course, after the cessation of hostilities, the British Government constructed a new purpose-built airfield on the Falklands that eventually enabled the RAF's Phantoms (subsequently replaced by Tornado F3s and finally by Typhoons) to operate directly from the islands, so the Navy's increased capabilities were arguably unnecessary – at least for deployment in the South Atlantic.

The Sea Harrier's MLU Phase Two was intentionally more ambitious. In February 1985, British Aerospace (into which Hawker Siddeley was absorbed) and Marconi received a project definition contract for the upgrade of thirty aircraft as part of a Sea Harrier Improvement Programme (SHIP). At the core of this project was new radar – the Ferranti Blue Vixen, and the Hughes (subsequently Raytheon) AIM-120 AMRAAM (Advanced Medium-Range Air-to-Air Missile). The new Pulse-Doppler radar was regarded as ideal for the much-needed look-down capability and work on a production system was advanced by the time that an order was placed in December 1988 for the conversion of twenty-nine FRS Mk 1 aircraft to the new FRS Mk 2 standard. (Four more conversions were ordered in 1995, together with a batch of eighteen new-build aircraft.)

With the new radar (designed with a high degree of automation) and the fire-and-forget AIM-20, the new Sea Harrier also incorporated a longer fuselage, courtesy of a 35 cm plug that provided extra space to house the radar's processor and other avionics equipment. The radar also required the aircraft's nose profile to be revised again, and this time a more bulbous nose cone was simply grafted onto the existing forward fuselage. (Some commentators suggested that it must have mysteriously evaded the attention of the aerodynamicists.) Even with this modified fuselage, the Sea Harrier FRS Mk 2 was still no slouch and could theoretically maintain the top speed of Mach 1.2 attainable in the FRS Mk 1, although the later aircraft's stores were never cleared to such speeds. The design of its wing leading edge was changed in order to improve handling, with a new kinked shape, deletion of one of the vortex generators and an additional wing fence. Other improvements were also proposed (such as leading edge wing root extensions and additional missile capability) but, as ever, the projected costs prevented these from proceeding. The only other significant change made to the FRS Mk 2 was the incorporation of a slightly more powerful Pegasus Mk 106 engine with improved thrust at lower operating temperatures.

The first completed FRS Mk 2 (ZA195) made its maiden flight from Dunsfold on 19 September 1988 in the hands of test pilot Heinz Frick. The second prototype (XZ439) was shipped to the US on board a new *Atlantic Conveyor* in January 1993, after which it was used to carry out live firings of the AIM-20 missile against target drones at Eglin AFB in Florida. The Sea Harrier FRS Mk 2 completed evaluation at Boscombe Down and after an official handing over ceremony at Dunsfold (on 2 April 1993) the first aircraft was delivered to No. 899 NAS at Yeovilton in the shape of ZA176 in September 1993.

Taking the Sea Harrier FRS Mk 1 aircraft out of service for this MLU conversion created significant headaches for the Fleet Air Arm (the already modest fleet was effectively cut still further while the aircraft were out of service) and it was the arrival of the new-build aircraft which finally eased the problems. With Kingston now gone, these aircraft were manufactured at BAe's Brough factory, before being dismantled and transported to Dunsfold for final assembly and test flying. Quite why the aircraft could not have been flown out of Brough remains a mystery. Although new-build, the aircraft were fitted with what were actually rather older Pegasus engines, in the shape of used Mk 103s taken from redundant RAF Harrier GR3s before being refurbished and modified to Mk 106 standard.

In May 1994, the FRS Mk 2 designation was changed to Sea Harrier FA Mk 2, reflecting the fact that the new aircraft no longer had a reconnaissance role, and because the strike capability had been abandoned. The WE.177 was withdrawn from naval service in June 1992 (as, indeed, were all of Britain's air-launched nuclear weapons, during the 1990s). No. 801 NAS became the first operational unit to take delivery of the FA2 (in October 1994), and the FRS Mk 1 was withdrawn from use over a period of months until the last example (ZD581) left No. 800 NAS on 17 March 1995. Deliveries of FA2 aircraft were protracted, and it was not until 24 December 1998 that the last (ZH813) was handed over to the Fleet Air Arm. This was in fact the very last of the first-generation Harriers to be completed and it also therefore earned itself the distinction of being the very last all-British fighter to be manufactured – if the Sea Harrier could truly be described as a fighter in the traditional sense.

Of course, the Falklands Conflict was not the last time that the Navy's Harriers went into action. In subsequent years, the Gulf Wars, Balkans operations and

Sierra Leone all called upon the Navy's participation, and the Harrier (either in the form of the FA2 or the later GR7/9) continued to play a significant part in the Navy's Order of Battle until 2010. It was originally intended to retain the original Sea Harrier fleet in service until at least 2012, when the Navy was to acquire the all-new Lockheed Martin F-35 strike fighter, but as the projected delivery date for this complicated and expensive design slipped further and further away (and the likely cost grew ever higher), the Government's thinking began to change. In 2002 – and without any serious hint of such a radical move – the Ministry of Defence announced that the Sea Harrier was to be withdrawn from 2006. The decision was taken ostensibly on capability grounds, on the basis that there would be difficulties in upgrading the Sea Harrier still further (until F-35 was available) and that 'other capabilities' were now available (referring to the Type 45 anti-air warfare destroyer rather than any other aircraft type).

It seems obvious, however, that despite protestations to the contrary, the decision to abandon the Sea Harrier was made purely on the basis of cost savings, as it was accepted that its early withdrawal would save £135 million, and that a further £230 million could be saved by not implementing another engine upgrade for the fleet. The move was greeted with astonishment (particularly within the Fleet Air Arm) and an understandable amount of resentment, but the plan was indeed implemented. On 28 March 2008, No. 801 NAS performed a five-aircraft flypast over Yeovilton to mark the rather premature retirement of the Sea Harrier from British service. On the following day, the remaining Sea Harriers were ferried to RAF Shawbury and placed in storage, pending disposal.

CHAPTER TWELVE
The Winds of Change

The very last of Britain's true Cold War era fighters was in fact a bomber. The Tornado came into being because of TSR2, a long and monstrously expensive and often bitter saga that came to an end in 1965, when a new Labour Government finally axed the aircraft, and the RAF tried to forget the painful years of mismanagement, confusion and clouded thinking that had left it without any kind of credible tactical bombing capability.

By this stage, the Canberra had progressively moved out of the medium- and high-altitude bombing business in order to make way for Vulcans and Victors that had given the UK a powerful strategic nuclear and conventional attack capability. Good though the Canberra undoubtedly was, it had never been expected to remain assigned to its primary role for long, and from the very outset of its introduction the aircraft had been regarded as not just a figurative leap into the post-war era but also as a useful step towards the establishment of what was in effect a strategic bombing force, even though it was rarely described as such. By 1965, the Canberra could still function as a very effective shorter-range tactical bomber, but it was undoubtedly a creation of the 1950s and as new Soviet defensive systems emerged, it gradually looked increasingly obsolescent.

TSR2 had been the solution to the Canberra's inevitable decline, but even the RAF, which had fought so hard to get the aircraft into service, finally accepted that TSR2 was a machine that the country simply could not afford. More importantly, it was also a machine that the RAF no longer really needed. Luckily for the RAF, the American F-111 had come along at just the right time. Designed for virtually the same role, it matched TSR2's predicted performance but promised to deliver it at a much lower price and, much to the delight of the British Government, could be purchased on very reasonable payment terms that avoided making a huge one-off cost for the Treasury. Defence Minister Denis Healey succeeded in getting TSR2 replaced by this more affordable alternative, and the longer-term future for Bomber Command's structure looked secure.

However, defence procurement is inextricably linked to politics and as the Government's appetite for withdrawal from its East of Suez commitments grew stronger and stronger, the very idea of buying any sort of long-range strike aircraft suddenly seemed open to question. This growing political unease about F-111 was moderated by the Government's decision to join France on a programme to design and build AFVG – the Anglo-French Variable Geometry aircraft, which promised to give both the UK and France a smaller strike aircraft than the F-111 with a nominal range of around 600 miles. A force of around 175 AFVGs for the RAF was anticipated, combined with perhaps only fifty of the longer-range F-111 aircraft. Together, the two aircraft would create an effective and affordable strike/attack force that would satisfy the Government's appetite for international (particularly European) collaboration, and also enable far fewer of the expensive F-111 aircraft to be purchased.

AFVG came into being as part of an ongoing dialogue between Britain (particularly Healey) and France, concerning a future requirement for both an advanced trainer and a light attack aircraft. The RAF had been looking for a potential replacement for the Gnat and Hunter trainers for some time, while France had been looking for something similar, albeit with a combat capability too. France's primary interest in the aircraft's combat capabilities conflicted with the RAF's preoccupation with the trainer specification, but when TSR2 was finally dumped, the RAF began to show more interest in the concept of creating not only an advanced trainer but perhaps a more combat-capable machine along the lines required by France.

Ultimately, the RAF clearly needed something rather more sophisticated than France was envisaging, but a solution was found after a great deal of negotiation and it was agreed that two different designs would be pursued. One would be the advanced trainer based on Breguet's existing Br.121 studies, and the other would be an advanced combat aircraft based on BAC's P.45 studies. France would take leadership of the trainer programme, while BAC would have authority over the design of the combat aircraft. This agreement made perfect sense, especially when BAC had so much relevant experience from the years of TSR2 development. BAC also knew a lot about variable-geometry (swing wings), but even though Vickers-Armstrong had done a great deal of research into the concept there was insufficient confidence to justify introducing it into a project as important as TSR2. However, by 1965, the situation was very different and continuing research had now confirmed the practicality of the swing wing concept; BAC believed that variable geometry was the way forward, and France (influenced by research being conducted by Dassault) agreed.

Just a few weeks before TSR2 was cancelled, Healey had agreed to purchase a fleet of F-4M Phantoms for the RAF in order to compensate for the cancellation of the P.1154. The new Phantoms would be assigned to the ground attack role as a replacement for the Hunter fleet and in Germany would also be equipped for the nuclear strike role so that the Canberra could be withdrawn. But when the new advanced trainer (which became Jaguar) and AFVG were ready for introduction into service, the Phantom would be reassigned to the air defence role, allowing the Lightning interceptor fleet to be retired. AFVG would therefore be designed to perform well as both a fighter and bomber and although no detailed plans emerged, it was expected that the same basic AFVG airframe would be used for both roles, with new avionics fitted to the aircraft when it eventually switched from being a bomber to a fighter. This was probably a slightly naïve supposition, but at the time it all seemed to make perfect sense, even though in practical terms AFVG never made much sense at all. The basic idea was sound but it was also obvious that meeting the conflicting demands of two countries would never be easy, even with two very different designs.

Early in 1967, the Editor of *Flight International* commented:

> The French now say that the agreed design will not meet their interceptor requirements. This has come rather tiresomely late in the day, making it even more difficult to produce one basic aeroplane that will be all things to all men – from a 36,000 lb French naval interceptor to a British Canberra replacement. There has always been a certain technical improbability about a 36,000 lb aeroplane performing the heavy-strike task of a 60,000 lb Canberra, even with variable geometry. Desirable though such a common aeroplane is politically, the new French requirements appear to make it impossible – even if funds and the ability of designers to perform miracles were unlimited, which they are not.

Perhaps it is fortunate that the project was soon killed-off by France, leaving only the Jaguar programme to continue. With typical French national interest firmly in mind, AFVG had soon become a far less attractive proposition to the French Government when Dassault announced its intention to create a remarkably similar aircraft itself. Having studied the concept of variable geometry wings for some time, and having now learned even more from Britain, Dassault became confident that it could produce an aircraft better suited to France's requirements than AFVG ever would be. Consequently the French Government immediately recognised the national value of pursuing an indigenous project and resolved to dump AFVG as swiftly as possible. This they did, ostensibly on the grounds of cost. Technically speaking at least, they were not lying. Defence Minister Healey was clearly wounded by the news of France's withdrawal, but was equally satisfied that the F-111 was still on the way, so he believed that the RAF would still be getting the aircraft that it had really wanted, regardless of the abandonment of AFVG. But Britain's economic state was deteriorating badly and it was therefore inevitable that the increasingly expensive F-111 would be subject to even closer scrutiny. After just a few more months it became clear that, like TSR2, it too could not survive. In January 1968, Prime Minister Wilson announced:

> We have decided to cancel the order for fifty F-111 aircraft. Further study is being given to the consequences of this decision on the future equipment of the Royal Air Force. Leaving out of account the results of this study, the cancellation of the F-111 is estimated to yield total savings on the Defence Budget of about £400 million between now and 1977-78. This figure allows for likely cancellation charges. The saving in dollar expenditure over the period, again allowing for likely cancellation charges, will be well over $700 million. Because of the credit arrangements, these

savings will mature over a period of years. We are discussing with the United States Government future arrangements for offset orders and credit for the Phantom and Hercules aircraft. The reduction in our overseas commitments will make it possible to cut down the RAF transport force.

Remarkably, despite the huge resources, time and money that had been poured into TSR2, the F-111 and (to some extent) AFVG, the RAF was now approaching the 1970s with still no sign of the elusive Canberra replacement that had been sought for so long.

The complicated saga continued, some six months passing before the Government agreed to purchase a batch of Buccaneers for the RAF as direct replacements for the cancelled F-111 and AFVG. Having battled against the Buccaneer for so many years during the TSR2 programme, the RAF was, to say the least, reluctant to accept the Buccaneer, but it was now clear that it was the only suitable aircraft on offer. With the need for an East of Suez long-range bomber having almost gone, the Government inevitably reverted to its long-held belief that the Buccaneer was perfectly capable of undertaking the RAF's strike/attack role, especially if the Air Force's projected theatre of operations were within Europe.

However, the RAF's lack of faith in the Buccaneer's suitability meant that even before the aircraft had entered service, the RAF's chiefs were already looking for an aircraft to replace it. Across the Channel, France elected to leave NATO in pursuit of an even more independent military posture. Having destroyed any hopes of developing the AFVG project into a viable warplane, the RAF had virtually been forced to accept an aircraft that it had bitterly opposed for years. Likewise, it is arguable whether the Jaguar was an aircraft that the RAF really wanted, especially when it ostensibly was not the advanced trainer that had been sought in the first place. As a light attack aircraft it was hardly better than the Phantom that it would swiftly replace, and for the RAF it was yet another less than ideal solution. Indeed, had the British Government known just how eagerly the French would abandon AFVG when it no longer suited them, it is quite likely that the Jaguar would also never have been produced, especially if it had been known how France would eventually dissuade potential export customers from buying Jaguar so that its own indigenous aircraft could be sold instead.

International co-operation seemed like a poisonous recipe, and in the wake of the AFVG cancellation, BAC's Preston Division continued to work on the projected design as a purely private venture, albeit with the tentative and discrete support of the RAF. The British Variable Geometry (BVG) aircraft and British Advanced Combat Aircraft (BACA) were both direct derivatives of the stillborn AFVG, but with the Buccaneer now on order for the RAF, the Treasury simply did not want to hear about anything that was perceived as an attempt to resurrect the AFVG, F-111 or TSR2 saga. It was obvious to BAC and the RAF that the only way forward, despite its evident risks, was international co-operation. The same conclusion had been reached in Europe where NATO members were already looking at potential designs that might eventually replace the ubiquitous F-104G Starfighter.

In January 1968, the Air Force Chiefs of Germany, Belgium, Italy and the Netherlands agreed to establish a working group to develop a joint requirement for a new strike/attack aircraft that could replace the Starfighter. Initially referred to as the Multi-Role Aircraft (MRA), it was soon known as the MRCA, the Multi-Role Combat Aircraft. By July, the British Air Staff had joined the working group, as had Canada. Basic design proposals were duly submitted by BAC, MBB (Messerschmitt-Bölkow-Blohm), and also from Canada, as the basis for further study. Canada and Belgium quickly decided to pull out of the project, claiming that changes to their national defence strategies meant that the MRCA would not be suitable for their needs. In fact, it was more likely that when the complex and advanced nature of MRCA was laid before them, the anticipated cost probably persuaded both countries to abandon interest in it and pursue closer ties with the USA from where off-the-shelf purchases could be made far more cheaply.

By the end of 1969, the group had agreed that the BAC and MBB proposals were suitable for the requirements of all four nations and work began on combining the assets of both designs to create one coherent project. In effect, it was the British (BAC) design that formed the core of the MRCA design (it was essentially a refinement of the earlier AFVG aircraft) and with this process at a satisfactory stage, the four countries came together to establish a joint company to share the management, design and production of the MRCA. Panavia Aircraft GmbH was the result, but the Netherlands decided to leave the project in July 1969, having become influenced by the same thinking that had persuaded Canada and Belgium to leave previously. Germany opted to purchase a huge fleet of some 700 aircraft, while the British Government finally agreed that some 385 aircraft should be ordered, on the basis that by the time the MRCA was translated into an operational warplane it would meet the right timescale to begin replacement of both the Vulcan bombers (assigned to a tactical role from 1970) and also the Buccaneer, which was committed to the overland strike role in Germany. Germany also appreciated the likelihood of a long development programme. Rather than soldier on with its fleet of Starfighters for any longer than necessary, the Luftwaffe opted to purchase the F-4E and F-4F Phantom as a short-term partial replacement and reduced its order to 324 MRCAs as a result.

However, while the Tornado IDS (Interdictor Strike) programme began to develop into solid machinery, the RAF was also considering the longer-term future of its fighter-interceptor force. The RAF's fleet of Phantom fighters had illustrated how an aircraft with sufficient performance could successfully undertake a variety of roles, ranging from nuclear strike through to close-in air combat, and by the time the Phantoms began to approach retirement, they had assumed two fairly distinct fighter roles. In Germany, they were assigned largely to the defence of relatively local areas of airspace, where Warsaw Pact fighter-bombers were expected to appear in force, should any land battle begin. Wildenrath's Phantoms had to react quickly, and the RAF's crews fully expected to engage the enemy in close air combat dogfights. Meanwhile, back in the UK, the Phantom's role was slightly different, as the anticipated threat was expected to come from long-range

Soviet bombers, most of which would probably be armed with cruise missiles. This threat could not be countered by a dogfight (it was quite likely that the enemy would be seen only on a radar screen) and required an interceptor that could reach out far across the North Sea and into the Faroes-Iceland gap to launch stand-off missiles that could destroy the enemy bombers before they could get within range of the UK mainland.

These differing roles were very much in the minds of Air Staff chiefs when a replacement for the Phantom was first considered. The success of the Phantom undoubtedly influenced the Air Staff's initial thinking, and all of America's existing fighter types were examined as potential off-the-shelf purchases. The F-14 Tomcat was a promising candidate but was expensive, and its dedicated Phoenix missiles were some three times more expensive than the Skyflash that equipped the RAF's Phantoms during their latter years. The F-16 was less suitable, as its all-weather capability was not as good and it simply did not have the range to conduct the kind of missions that the RAF performed. The F-15 Eagle was somewhere between the other two candidates, with a good all-round performance and an affordable price, although it was in essence a single-seat fighter (the later Strike Eagle had yet to emerge) and the RAF firmly believed in the two-man crew concept.

In fact, the most promising design was one that the RAF was already preparing to accept in the shape of the Panavia Tornado. From the very beginnings of the Tornado programme it had been accepted that the aircraft would have a true multi-role capability, and although it was ostensibly designed as a strike and ground attack platform, it was also more than capable of being modified to operate as an interceptor. It would not possess the agility of a true 'fighter' aircraft, but in all other respects it promised to be just as effective as any of the existing American fighters that were on offer. Of course, there was also a very important political and financial issue to consider too, and if a derivative of the Tornado was chosen for the air defence role it would enable a great deal of support infrastructure to be shared between a larger single-type fleet and would provide more employment for British companies. Eventually, the Air Staff concluded that despite the plethora of fighter designs that were potentially on offer, an Air Defence Variant (ADV) of the Tornado would be the most logical choice. Other NATO forces could provide the close-in fighter cover needed in Germany, and the RAF could concentrate on engaging the enemy at far greater ranges, with a new fleet of long-legged Tornado interceptors that could reach out towards approaching bombers and engage them by radar, before destroying them with long-range stand-off missiles.

Official agreement to pursue a specialised version of the Tornado can be traced back to March 1977 when an Instruction to Proceed was issued to British Aerospace at Warton for three prototypes of what was referred to as the Tornado ADV. The aircraft would primarily be designed to counter the Soviet Backfire and Fencer at altitudes from sea level up to 50,000 feet. Missile armament would be as comprehensive as possible, and radar equipment was specified as having a look-down and shoot-down capability and track-while-scan. The aircraft's electronics would have to be capable of withstanding a heavy ECM environment, and ideally the aircraft would also have a good short-field runway performance. Unusually for a fighter, no great emphasis on top speed, climb or even ceiling was specified, provided that stand-off missiles were employed that enabled the aircraft to destroy its projected targets successfully.

The basic Tornado IDS airframe was a good basis from which the ADV could be developed, but some significant changes had to be made in order to equip the aircraft for the interceptor role. Provision for Skyflash missiles was perhaps the most important modification, and in addition to new systems and electronics, recesses were built into the lower forward fuselage to accommodate two missiles, while two more would be attached semi-recessed between the landing gear doors. Provision for Sidewinder missiles was incorporated into the inner wing pylons, with a missile rail built into each side of the wing pylon. As part of the new design, the IDS variant's radar was also replaced by new interception radar. The most obvious external change to the existing Tornado design was the incorporation of a fuselage 'plug' behind the cockpit, designed to incorporate more internal fuel, and also partly designed to provide additional keel space for the forward missile installation. This fuselage extension and the new radome designed for the interception radar gave the ADV an overall fuselage length some 4 feet 5.5 inches greater than the IDS equivalent. The wing glove leading edges were also redesigned so that they extended further forwards and (when the wings were fully swept) produce a concave leading edge kink – as opposed to the convex kink

Tornado F Mk 2 prototype ZA254 just after take-off as the undercarriage units retract. Visible on the fin leading edge is a camera fairing fitted for weapons release trials.

created on the Tornado IDS. This brought the centre-of-lift further forward to reflect the forward shift in the aircraft's centre of gravity.

The first ADV prototype was rolled out at Warton on 9 August 1978 to begin engine runs and taxi trials. Its first flight was completed on 27 October in the hands of David Eagles, with navigator Roy Kenward in the rear seat. The first flight lasted for 92 minutes (a long first flight by any standards) and Eagles took the aircraft (ZA254) up to Mach 1.2. He reported that the redesigned fuselage enabled the aircraft to achieve better acceleration with lower drag at transonic speed. Initial flight testing was hugely successful, and any doubts that the aircraft might suffer from developmental delays soon evaporated. The RAF dropped a proposal to lease a fleet of F-15 Eagles that were intended to act as stopgap fighters, although there was never any obvious reason why the existing Phantom fleet could not have continued to operate. In fact, the RAF requested that the ADV's in-service date of 1984 should be brought forward to 1983 on the basis that the programme was progressing very well, but BAe felt unable to hurry the aircraft's progression so drastically, and with the benefit of hindsight, it is clear that the company was wise to exercise caution.

On 18 July 1980, ZA267 joined the test programme and incorporated more of the aircraft's planned systems, including CRT displays and Sidewinder missiles, although it was not equipped to carry Skyflash and did not have the new radar. It was a third aircraft (ZA283) that took on the first radar trials, after flying for the first time on 18 November 1980. Development of the aircraft's systems was satisfactory, although somewhat slower than its aerodynamics, as the Tornado ADV demonstrated a much better performance than its bomber counterpart. During 1980, ZA254 achieved a speed of 800 knots at 2,000 feet, this being as much as 100 knots beyond the normal low-level limiting speed of most contemporary aircraft. Structural limitations normally restrict aircraft to these lower speeds, but the Tornado ADV's rugged fin and tailplane structure, and swept main wings, proved to be more than capable of achieving 800 knots. This would be an asset that the aircraft would exploit to its advantage.

The decision to create a long-range interceptor certainly made sense at the time of the Tornado ADV's inception, but as the development programme continued it became increasingly obvious that the aircraft would have to do much more than simply launch missiles at long range. It had been expected that Soviet long-range bombers would be the primary threat facing Britain if a war occurred. There was little prospect of the Tornado being required to fight any adversary, but the appearance of the Sukhoi Su-27 changed everything. This huge, powerful and manoeuvrable fighter demonstrated an ability to engage in aerial combat with an astonishing degree of agility, but more importantly it also possessed the ability to escort Soviet bombers at great distances, and this meant that the new Tornado ADV might well have to resort to old-fashioned dogfighting.

But, of course, the Tornado was not designed for aerial combat, and a great deal of effort was increasingly put into the ADV programme to try and make the aircraft as flexible and effective as possible. The RAF ordered a twin-dome computerised combat simulator with which to train its new Tornado pilots, while BAe developed new column-mounted controls that would enable the pilot to fly and fight more effectively. More importantly, the variable wing sweep system was redesigned so that the wings could sweep automatically, responding to the flight conditions at any given time. Perhaps less importantly, the IDS variant's bolt-on refuelling probe was replaced by a fully integral unit designed to retract into the fuselage structure.

The aircraft's potential slowly became apparent as the ADV trials programme continued, and although it was obvious that it could not be turned into a dogfighter, it was clear that the ADV would fly far and fly fast. By the end of 1980, the aircraft had exceeded Mach 2, and in January 1982, test crew Paul Millett and Leslie Hurt took ZA254 on a very impressive long-range sortie lasting 4 hours. The aircraft was flown out over the North Sea, carrying four Skyflash and two Sidewinder missiles, together with two 330 gallon underwing fuel tanks. After leaving Warton, the aircraft flew some 374 miles before a racetrack CAP (Combat Air Patrol) pattern was flown for 2 hours. When ZA254 returned to Warton, Millett remained in the airfield circuit for 15 minutes before landing with more than 5 per cent of the aircraft's fuel still remaining. The sortie demonstrated that there was no limitation on the ADV's range, and with in-flight refuelling, its endurance would be limited only by the amount of liquid oxygen carried on board for the crew, although this would last for more than 24 hours.

Official roll-out of the Tornado F Mk 2 took place on 28 March 1984, when the first two production aircraft (ZD899 and ZD900) were placed on show at Warton for invited guests and the media. ZD900 had already completed its maiden flight on 5 March, ZD899 having been delayed by the installation of additional equipment in preparation for deployment to the A&AEE at Boscombe Down. A further sixteen aircraft were duly manufactured as part of Batch 4 of the RAF's entire Tornado programme, this fleet of eighteen aircraft being designated as the Tornado F Mk 2. Subsequent ADV aircraft would be designated as the F Mk 3, signifying the installation of the RB.199 Mk 104 engine that delivered approximately 10 per cent more thrust. This later engine derivative featured a modified reheat system, requiring the Tornado fuselage to be extended rearwards by some 14 inches, the F2's 'notch' at the base of the rudder being replaced by a new and rather less elegant fairing.

The type's entry into RAF service took place on 5 November 1984, when ZD901 and ZD903 were delivered to No. 229 OCU at Coningsby. The RAF proudly invited the media to see its sleek new interceptors, but nobody pointed out that despite their impressive outward appearance, they did not have any radar system with which to perform their intended mission. Their radomes contained only concrete ballast.

Development of the GEC Avionics (Marconi) AI Mk 24 Foxhunter radar was a long and frustrating saga, dogged by frequent delays. The radar system consistently failed to live up to expectations, although the RAF compounded problems by changing its specified requirements after development of the radar had begun. The radar's capability to track multiple targets was regarded as below standard, and there were also issues with the system's ability to distinguish between low-level targets and ground clutter. The radar was subjected to a series of improvements, but by the time of the Tornado F2's entry into service, radar of acceptable operational standard was still more than a year away. Ultimately, it was not until the early 1990s that the Tornado F Mk 3 finally acquired a fully functional radar system that did all that had been promised. But when Foxhunter did finally achieve its potential, it worked very well indeed and the RAF was more than satisfied with the Tornado F.3's radar by the mid-1990s.

However, No. 229 OCU's acceptance of the first aircraft enabled the task of training crews for the new type to begin early in 1985, but despite the RAF's original plans to get the Tornado ADV into operational service in 1984, it was not until 1987 that the F Mk 3 joined No. 29 Squadron at Coningsby, to begin the RAF's gradual transition from the Phantom and Lightning onto an all-Tornado interceptor fleet. No. 5 Squadron was the next unit to form (also at Coningsby), after which attention shifted to RAF Leeming in North Yorkshire. This former training base had been extensively modified in anticipation of the Tornado ADV (in effect, returning to its much earlier status as a fighter base), and new HAS

This underside view of the Tornado F Mk 3 illustrates the launchers for the Skyflash AAMs (two of which are fitted) and the Vinten flare dispensers fitted to most Tornado interceptors during their service lives.

(Hardened Aircraft Shelter) complexes were constructed for the three Tornado F3 units that were eventually assigned to the base, these being Nos 11, 23 and 25 Squadrons. Finally, RAF Leuchars relinquished its Phantoms and Nos 43 and 111 Squadrons re-equipped with the Tornado F Mk 3, and by the end of 1990 the last of the RAF's new Tornado F3 squadrons (No. 111) was operational on the type.

The Cold War was over, of course, and although the Tornado IDS and ADV had been developed in response to the threat of possible Warsaw Pact and Soviet aggression, this threat had diminished rapidly to a point where it hardly existed any longer. The Tornado IDS had already been in service through the uncertain latter years of the Cold War, but the Tornado F Mk 3 had reached an operational capability at precisely the time when the threat it had been designed to counter had suddenly gone. The very idea of Soviet bombers approaching the UKADR with their deadly cruise missiles suddenly seemed unlikely at best, and the RAF found itself facing a very uncertain future. The Falklands crisis in 1982 had demonstrated that conflicts beyond the European theatre were by no means impossible, but few people imagined that the RAF might be called upon to participate in any more significant operations outside of Europe. The primary threat was still the Warsaw Pact – or what was left of it – but it had already become obvious to many observers that the RAF's next generation fighter after Tornado would have to be just that – a fighter, and not an interceptor.

The concept of creating an aircraft to counter the threat posed by Soviet long-range bombers had made perfect sense at the time of its inception, but by the time that the requirement was translated into hardware the threat had effectively disappeared. The RAF was therefore equipped with an aircraft supremely capable of performing a role that no longer existed. More importantly, the aircraft was ill-equipped to perform any other role, particularly that of a fighter. It is true, however, that the RAF's Tornado crews quickly learned to maximise the assets that the F3 did have, and use them to advantage. Despite the Foxhunter radar's troubled gestation, it did eventually become an outstanding piece of equipment and the Tornado F3 was ultimately blessed with radar that was second to none. Likewise, even though the aircraft could not match the agility of a Su-27 or MiG-29, it did possess a very impressive top speed well in excess of Mach 2. A combination of powerful engines and a redesigned sleek fuselage enabled the Tornado F3 to boast a high-speed 'dash' capability that could beat any other contemporary fighter. This might seem like a seemingly modest advantage, but the ability to launch missiles in a combat scenario and then head for home at a blistering speed would enable the Tornado crew to survive to fight another day. The early-production F Mk 2 was rather less capable, and as the F3 came into service (the type's first flight took place on 20 November 1985) it had been proposed that the F2 fleet would be withdrawn for installation of Mk 104 engines and more developed radar. The F2 fleet was duly withdrawn, but after having been placed in storage the aircraft were never modified for further use and by 2001 most had been scrapped.

Of course, the Tornado F3 did go to war. In 1991, as part of Operation Desert Storm, F3s were deployed to Dhahran in Saudi Arabia with improved

An excellent image of a Tornado F Mk 3 from No. 56 Squadron, with the unit's famous 'Firebird' marking just visible on the tail. A full complement of Skyflash and Sidewinder inert training rounds is being carried.

weapons options and better defensive equipment (plus improved engines). Although the aircraft performed a vital role, they were deliberately operated away from Iraqi airspace, where encounters with enemy aircraft were more likely. Without the latest IFF (Identification Friend or Foe) and secure communications equipment, the Allied Forces concluded that if any aerial combat engagements were likely (which they rarely were), they should be left to the more capable American assets. But despite being assigned to less hostile airspace, the RAF flew more than 2,000 CAP (Combat Air Patrol) sorties during the war. After the conclusion of Desert Storm, Tornado F3s stayed in Saudi Arabia in order to maintain routine air defence of the region, but throughout the type's stay at Dhahran, the RAF crews did not have the opportunity to engage with any hostile aircraft.

The RAF's Tornado F3 force also participated in Operation Deny Flight (Bosnia) and Operation Allied Force (Yugoslavia), but once again the Tornado was denied any opportunity to demonstrate its capabilities. Shortly before the 2003 Gulf War, the RAF opted to convert a small number of F3s into SEAD (Suppression of Enemy Air Defences) aircraft. Experience had shown that there was a growing need for aircraft that were equipped for this role, able to destroy or at least incapacitate enemy radars and associated defence assets. The Tornado F3 was a good choice for the role, having already been modified to carry the necessary AMRAAM and ASRAAM missiles, albeit after a rather protracted and troublesome development programme. It seems logical that the aircraft could also be further modified to carry ALARM (Air Launched Anti Radar Missile), and with suitably 'tweaked' radar warning receivers the aircraft could have a basic Emission Location System. The Tornado F3's impressive low level speed and excellent range suggested that it would be ideal for the role, and although a number of aircraft were eventually modified (and unofficially designated as the Tornado EF Mk 3), the RAF did not deploy them in the Middle East. A more ambitious programme to develop a full fleet of modified SEAD Tornado aircraft was never started, simply because there were no funds to support it.

In July 2004, plans were announced to begin the gradual rundown of the Tornado F3 fleet, in anticipation of the arrival of Typhoon. The RAF had an exciting multi-role, fast and agile fighter in its sights and although the F3 had become a much-admired interceptor, there is no doubt that the RAF was more than happy to dispose of it at the earliest opportunity. By the end of 2009, the Tornado F3 force had been reduced to just one operational squadron, and the F3 was retired from RAF service in March 2011 when No. 111 Squadron stood down in order to transition onto Typhoons. Four aircraft survived with QinetiQ at Boscombe Down, assigned to trials of the Meteor missile, but when this trials programme ended they were flown to Leeming on 9 July 2012 and the Tornado F Mk 3 was finally gone, with no ceremony and no farewell.

It is undoubtedly sad that the aircraft was withdrawn with virtually no recognition of its many years of service, but almost from the very beginning of its service life the Tornado F3 had been a victim of circumstances. Dogged by the laborious development programme of a troublesome radar system, the aircraft arrived late and with a reputation that it did not deserve. Worse still, it entered RAF service to counter a threat that had almost disappeared, and by the time that it was declared operational it was in effect redundant. The RAF needed a fighter but had got an interceptor. This was, of course, no reflection on the capabilities of the Tornado, nor was it an issue that could be attributed to jumbled defence planning. It was the end of the Cold War that destroyed Tornado ADV's *raison d'être* and there was nothing that the RAF could do about it, except patiently wait for a more suitable aircraft to come along. Of course, that aircraft did finally arrive in the shape of Typhoon, but even though the RAF embraced the new Typhoon fighter with almost indecent eagerness, there was no criticism that could be aimed at Tornado ADV itself. It was, in simple terms, a great interceptor. Unfortunately, it was the wrong aircraft at the wrong time.

With the departure of the Tornado ADV, the RAF standardised on the new Eurofighter Typhoon, an aircraft that represents the beginnings of a new generation of post-Cold War fighter designs that will inevitably emerge. The Typhoon was conceived during the Cold War, but has been designed to operate in a post-Cold War environment and, as such, is something of a 'transitional' design that appeared during a period when defence thinking changed drastically. The Cold War era that had lasted for approximately 40 years ended, and with it, the established assumptions of what kind of threat Britain's defences faced. Despite having been conceived at a time when Britain's most serious (indeed its only) threat was the Soviet Union, the Typhoon eventually entered service with an air force that faced a far more uncertain future, with seemingly countless potential areas of conflict around the world. It is therefore understandable that the Typhoon is a true multi-role machine and, unlike the aircraft that preceded it, is demonstrably capable of undertaking virtually any type of combat role.

A rare (possibly unique) image of three Tornado F Mk 3s demonstrating the type's variable wing sweep, at fully forward, fully swept, and an intermediate position.

A fascinating line-up of RAF fighter types captured during the early 1960s. The immortal Hurricane and Spitfire are led by a Meteor, Hunter, Javelin and Lightning.

The Tornado began life as the MRCA, but in effect it was an attack platform. Even the British development of the aircraft into a long-range interceptor did not change its basic performance or capability, whereas the Typhoon was designed as a true multi-role aircraft from the outset, even though the consortium that created it (Eurofighter) inevitably gives the impression that the aircraft is ostensibly a fighter. It would be wrong to portray the Typhoon as some kind of mirror image of the Tornado, as the Typhoon was not created as a fighter but with a ground attack capability. It was in fact designed as an all-embracing, versatile and capable warplane that could undertake both the fighter and attack roles with equal effectiveness, and it seems entirely likely that although the RAF will operate the Typhoon as both a fighter and bomber, it will almost inevitably be assigned largely to the offensive role, simply because there are few potential scenarios that would require the RAF to engage enemy aircraft.

The Typhoon will be joined by the new F-35 in due course, and this aircraft has also been designed as a true multi-role aircraft that the RAF will use as both an attack platform and fighter. The F-35 will also enable the Fleet Air Arm to return to the world of fixed-wing combat flying, and with its new aircraft carrier and a fleet of F-35s the Royal Navy will once again be able to engage in worldwide commitments with a substantial strike force at its disposal, one that also possesses a formidable self-defence capability. In some respects, this will take Britain's air forces through a proverbial full circle, back to a similar (although much smaller) capability that the RAF and Fleet Air Arm embraced in the years before the Cold War began. The Cold War is undoubtedly over, but Britain's future security remains as uncertain as ever.

Striking nose-on view of Lightning BF-2 hovering just inches above the deck of the USS *Wasp* during the F-35s initial sea trials in 2011. (*Lockheed Martin*)

A gaggle of Typhoons from No. 6 Squadron (together with RAAF F/A-18 Hornets), pictured en route to Malaysia for Exercise Bersama Lima 11 in 2011. The factory-fresh Typhoons contrast with the "forty-something" VC10 tanker, supporting the fighters on their long-distance deployment. (*Geoff Lee, Eurofighter*)

Typhoon FGR.Mk.4 ZJ932 served with No. 11 Squadron before returning the BAE Systems for upgrading as part of the Block 5 Upgrade Programme. It returned to Coningsby complete with a new PIRATE sensor ahead of the cockpit windscreen. (*Tim McLelland*)

The first British F-35 (BH-1) ZM135 pictured during its maiden flight in the hands of test pilot Bill Gigliotti on 13th April 2012. (*Lockheed Martin*)

F-35B Lightning BF-2 pictured en route to the USS *Wasp* (LHD-1) for the commencement of the F-35B's sea trials, on 3 October 2011. Lt. Col. Fred Schenk is at the controls. (*Lockheed Martin*)

BF-04, piloted by Major Richard Rusnok, arrives on board the USS *Wasp* on 6 October 2011. The RAF and Fleet Air Arm F-35s will operate from the new HMS *Queen Elizabeth* aircraft carrier, which is scheduled to begin sea trials in 2017. HMS *Prince of Wales* (the second new carrier) is expected to be held in reserve. (*Lockheed Martin*)

Lt. Col. Matthew Kelly takes BF-02 back to NAS Patuxent River after completing sea trials on board the USS *Wasp*, 11 October 2011. RAF and Fleet Air Arm F-35s will operate from one of two new aircraft carriers that are being built, with shore bases likely to be at RAF Marham and Lossiemouth. (*Lockheed Martin*)